INTERNATIONAL
PROPAGANDA
AND
COMMUNICATIONS

INTERNATIONAL PROPAGANDA AND COMMUNICATIONS

General Editor:

DR. CHRISTOPHER H. STERLING
Temple University

Editorial Advisory Board:

DR. MORRIS JANOWITZ
University of Chicago
DR. JOHN M. KITTROSS
Temple University
DR. BRUCE LANNES SMITH
Michigan State University

COMES
THE RECKONING

R. H. BRUCE LOCKHART

ARNO PRESS
A New York Times Company
New York • 1972

Reprint Edition 1972 by Arno Press Inc.

Reprinted by permission of Robin Bruce Lockhart

International Propaganda and Communications
ISBN for complete set: 0-405-04740-1
See last pages of this volume for titles.

Manufactured in the United States of America

Library of Congress Cataloging in Publication Data

Lockhart, Sir Robert Hamilton Bruce, 1887-1970.
  Comes the reckoning.

  (International propaganda and communications)
  Reprint of the 1947 ed.
  1. World War, 1939-1945--Propaganda. 2. World War,
1939-1945--Diplomatic history. 3. World War, 1939-
1945--Personal narratives, English. I. Title.
  (Series.)
D810.P7G758 1972   940.54'81'42   72-4672
ISBN 0-405-04756-8

COMES THE RECKONING

R. H. BRUCE LOCKHART

COMES
THE RECKONING

PUTNAM

42 GREAT RUSSELL STREET
LONDON

First published, October 1947

PRINTED IN GREAT BRITAIN BY ROBERT MACLEHOSE AND CO, LTD
THE UNIVERSITY PRESS GLASGOW

CONTENTS

"THE PRIVILEGE OF free action belongs to no mortal—we are tied down by the fetters of duty—and our most indifferent actions are but meshes in the web of destiny by which we are all surrounded."   SIR WALTER SCOTT

BOOK I

PRELUDE TO PERIL

"ANY COUNTRY WHICH thinks more of its ease and comfort than of its freedom will lose its freedom, and the ironical thing about it is that it will lose its ease and its comfort too."   CARL L. BECKER

CHAPTER ONE

ALTHOUGH THE SHADOW of coming disaster had hung heavily over Britain for many months, most of us, who are not politicians or generals, memorise the advent of the actual tragedy by the moment when war or the threat of war altered the settled course of our daily existence. In my own case the date is clearly fixed. It was August 29, 1938.

After many years spent abroad in the service of the Foreign Office, in banking, and in journalism I had retired from Fleet Street and was living quietly in Tomintoul, the tiny Highland village which nestles at the foot of the Cairngorms and from which my mother's family had gone out into the larger world. No surroundings could be more peaceful or more sheltered from the intrusion of war. Yet throughout that summer of 1938 I had been unable to find peace within myself. The Czechoslovak crisis was slow in developing, but its menace was always present. I took a special interest in the Czechoslovaks who had projected themselves into my life in 1918 when I was head of our Mission in Moscow. At that time there were 80,000 Czechs in Russia, all eager to fight for their country on the Western Front. I was bombarded with telegrams to secure their exit. Since then I had spent seven years in their country, had learnt their language, and knew their leaders intimately. By August the crisis was already approaching its Munich climax, and the Runciman Mission was then in Prague in a desperate effort to cajole the Czechoslovaks into a surrender which we know today from German evidence was tantamount to self-destruction. Even in Tomintoul the villagers, much better informed about world affairs than the population of our industrial cities, had begun to show anxiety. The village had always been a recruiting centre for the Gordons. The young men listened to the radio. They came to me for advice. All their sympathies were with the Czechoslovaks.

I felt unsettled, discontented with my inactivity, eager to help and yet not knowing how.

Then on that Monday of August 29 I was summoned to the telephone. The call was from Mike Wardell, the general manager of the *Evening Standard*. He had been in touch with Sir Robert Vansittart, then Chief Diplomatic Adviser to the Foreign Office. The European situation was very serious, and the next ten days would be critical.

War and peace were in the balance; no one knew which way the scales would tip. Would I go to Prague for the *Evening Standard* at once? There would be no difficulty about money; an aeroplane would be at my disposal. His voice was insistent. For a moment I was tempted. But I had long ago determined that nothing should ever induce me to return to Fleet Street. So I gave a non-committal answer and said that I was coming to London at once.

As soon as I arrived, I went to the Foreign Office to see Rex Leeper, the Head of the News Department. We had met first in 1917 when I came home from Russia for consultation before being sent back to establish unofficial relations with the new Bolshevik Government. Leeper had known Litvinov who during his years of exile in London had supplemented his wages as an assistant in Williams and Norgate's foreign bookshop by giving Russian lessons. In 1917 Litvinov had been appointed Bolshevik Commissar in London, and it had been arranged that he should have unofficial diplomatic privileges in return for similar privileges to me in Russia. Leeper had been one of his pupils, and, when I set out on my mission to Moscow, he was appointed by the Foreign Office to maintain a liaison with his former teacher.

Both he and his brilliant brother, Allen, were then temporary civil servants. In 1920 both were given permanent appointments in the Foreign Office. Born and brought up in Australia, the two brothers differed in many respects from the traditional Foreign Office clerk. The sons of a distinguished Greek scholar, they shone equally in argument with dons or diplomats and they brought into the Foreign Office an experimental zeal which was responsible for several useful innovations. It is by Rex Leeper's initiative that the Foreign Office has today a News Department and that, just in time, the British Broadcasting Corporation introduced the foreign broadcasts which during the second world war contributed so greatly to the maintenance of morale among the occupied peoples of Europe.

When I saw Leeper on that August morning in 1938, he looked tired and harassed. He told me that he was working fourteen hours a day, but he took time to give me all the news he properly could. Mr. Chamberlain was going to Balmoral that night to see the King. Sir Nevile Henderson, who had been in London for consultation, had just returned to Berlin. It was impossible to foresee how the crisis would end. According to Henderson the Germans did not want war, but, as in England, so in Germany, no one knew what was going to happen: everything depended on the strange little man at Berchtesgaden who communed with the mountain-tops before making any decision. The information, Leeper admitted, was vague and unsatisfactory, but it was difficult to be optimistic. Very sinister indeed was the organised campaign of slander by the German Press against Czechoslovakia.

He also gave me a piece of personal news. He had tried hard to persuade the Government to appoint me as assistant to the Runciman Mission to Czechoslovakia. He had failed. I was regarded as too pro-Czech. Today, he said, the Foreign Office had no power. Mr. Chamberlain, who thought that foreign affairs were simple and that the Foreign Office made them too complicated, ran his own foreign policy and relied more on Sir Horace Wilson than on his Foreign Office advisers. Sir Robert Vansittart, who had predicted the course of events with uncanny accuracy, was without influence. He was an adviser whose advice was not sought and, when given, was never taken, and many of his closest friends and admirers felt that he would have done more good as a free lance than as a member of the Foreign Office.

Leeper also hinted that, if there were war, the Foreign Office would require my services. I left him with mixed feelings. The prospect of peace was black; at the best it could only be a peace of surrender. At the same time I was relieved that I had not been asked to join the Runciman Mission. A refusal would have been difficult. To have gone to Czechoslovakia would have been disastrous, for my eyes might have been blinded by the same sand which the Nazis threw in the eyes of the Mission. I might have accompanied Lord Runciman on his week-end visits to Nazi-infected noblemen. I might even have had to listen to the Nazi-staged demonstration at Petrovice when organised Nazi demonstrators sang outside the house: "Dear Lord, deliver us. Free us from Czechoslovakia." And, let it be said, the Lord in this impudent performance was not the Almighty, but a comparatively new and susceptible English earl.

It was indeed a lucky escape, for my presence would have availed nothing, and I should have lost my good name with the Czechs.

Throughout September I remained in London with occasional week-end visits to my father's house at Crowthorne. On the whole the weather was fine with glorious sunny days and clear nights already fresh and cool with the approach of autumn. Intermittently there were damp, muggy days, which jangled the nerves and deepened the prevailing depression.

Meanwhile, the crisis swirled and surged nearer. There were, it is true, moments when it seemed to ebb, when the optimists clutched at every hope and when rumour, gaining strength as it travelled, promised the impossible: an amicable solution which would satisfy both the victim and the aggressor. One day the Stock Exchange would recover on a report that the Czechoslovaks had accepted nearly all the demands of the German Bohemians and that agreement had been reached or was now certain to be reached. Incredulous and suspicious, yet willing to believe, I would go back to my club and listen to the wireless. Then I would hear the full violence of the Nazi speeches from the Party Congress at Nuremberg: the raucous voice of Herr Wagner reading the truculent proclamation of Hitler; the sneering tones of Goering as he referred to the Czech "pygmies who hailed from goodness knows where"; and, finally and conclusively, the flaming speech of Hitler himself which left no doubt that nothing but complete surrender would divert him from war.

Hope could not survive in this atmosphere, and in the heart of the man in the street, who did not want war but who realised instinctively not only the evil but also the futility of capitulation, hope was almost dead. Yet in the clubs of London there were optimists who resented fiercely any criticism of Mr. Chamberlain and who became violent if anyone suggested that we should fight for the Czechoslovaks. To justify their attitude they used two arguments: Czechoslovakia was a misconception and was not worth fighting for; if there was war, all Europe would go Bolshevik.

It was the second argument which carried more weight. But as the relentless days passed, even the cocksure optimism of ignorance began to dwindle. Before the tape-machines and news boards in the clubs there were long faces, and men whom I knew only by sight came up to me and asked: "What do you think will happen? You know Europe."

I knew no more than anyone else. Throughout Britain families were divided into pro-Chamberlainites and anti-Chamberlainites. In my own home my youngest brother, who loathed war, insisted that we had no choice but to fight. My soldier brother, just home on leave and now ordered back to India, gave me most depressing figures about our lack of preparations. The fighting services were not to blame. From their rearmament budget for that year the Chancellor of the Exchequer, Sir John Simon, had made a cut of £200,000,000 on the ground that the sum was more than the country could stand.

Obviously the practical problems of defence were for the experts, but the moral issue of right and wrong was for each of us to judge for himself. Perhaps many people faced it hesitatingly. I know that I myself stilled my conscience with the hope of postponement. But I had then and have today the firm conviction that, given a proper lead, the vast majority of the British people would have given full support to a resolute stand against German aggression, and would have accepted whatever consequences ensued with the consolatory knowledge that they had acted according to their conscience. Indeed, it is a fallacy to believe that public opinion is always on the side of peace. In my lifetime Britain has waged two wars for her own existence. Both were forced on the Government by the moral strength of public opinion.

Unfortunately in 1938 the public was not given adequate information or guidance. For in foreign affairs the Government announces events and actions in the manner in which it wishes them to be understood. Unfortunately, too, Mr. Chamberlain was certain that he could settle all difficulties if only he could meet Hitler face to face. There were moments when his convictions were shaken, not by reports from the Foreign Office which he mistrusted, but by some chance reading of his own. There was one occasion when he was much upset by the perusal of a book called *The House That Hitler Built*. It was a sound book, but it contained nothing that had not appeared in official reports. Pointing out that, if the facts were as the book stated, we should have to alter our whole policy, Mr. Chamberlain asked for a Foreign Office opinion. Before the answer was supplied, Mr. Chamberlain had regained his self-confidence, and down in his diary went the entry: "These things are not true; I must go forward with faith and hope in my policy."

When a crisis is prolonged, it is impossible for anyone to maintain high tension for every hour of the day. When it lasts for a whole month, the prevailing uncertainty induces in many of us a nervous recklessness. We spend more money; unsettled in mind, we yield easily to temptation; we are ripe for the more expensive forms of relaxation. St. Petersburg was never gayer than during the month before the revolution. In that fateful September of 1938 the spirit of London was affected by a more restrained, but not dissimilar gaiety. The public houses, the night-clubs, and the restaurants were crowded. At Mayfair parties politicians with inside information were in great request.

For myself I had nothing to do but wait. I had just finished a book. No one but the most phlegmatic Englishman would have had the courage to start another at that moment. I therefore lived nervously and riotously. The Australian cricket team, having ended its Test matches, was still in London, and I saw much of those sterling cricketers Stanley McCabe and Bill O'Reilly. A rich Australian friend and I made merry with them. Both were of Irish extraction and highly intelligent; both, more particularly McCabe, had a strong streak of Celtic imagination. I remember very vividly an evening we spent in a club run by two daughters of the night-club queen of the period between the two wars. Bored with dancing, McCabe suddenly became serious and began to discuss war and peace. He was sure that war was inevitable. His conviction was based solely on superstition. "When we left Australia last March to come to England, Hitler invaded Austria. We were held up for a few days, but there was no war. Now we are going back to Australia in a few days, and you will see that Hitler will march into Czechoslovakia. These things don't happen twice. This time there will be war."

When the Australians had left, I went to see Leeper again. I wanted to know where I stood. I could not continue indefinitely to waste my substance in London. A crowd of journalists was waiting outside his room. He looked more tired than ever; there were dark lines under his eyes and all the colour had gone from his cheeks. He told me that I was certain to be given some official job "if and when war started."

I asked him what he meant by "if". He informed me that there would be no war—at least, not at present.

"Have you become an optimist?" I said.

"No," he replied, "I am a fatalist."

"Then the Czechoslovaks are to be sacrificed," I said and, knowing that he was a stout opponent of appeasement, I pressed him for more information.

He smiled bitterly: "I am not at liberty to tell you now, but you'll learn later; very soon, in fact."

That evening I went to the Grosvenor Hotel to say goodbye to my brother who was returning to India the next morning. As I came into the hall, I saw a knot of people surging round the tape-machine. Unable to see over the forest of heads, I asked the man in front of me what had caused the excitement. He turned round with a jubilant gleam in his face. "It's all right," he said, "Chamberlain is flying to Berchtesgaden to open direct negotiations with Hitler."

All was far from right. The British public and the unfortunate Czechs had still to endure sixteen more days of uncertainty during which the tension became almost unbearable, and Mr. Chamberlain was more in the air than on the ground. No sane man will ever doubt the sincerity or the honesty of his purpose, but unfortunately as much harm can be done in public affairs by an obstinate man as by a weak man, and, above all, Mr. Chamberlain was obstinate. Moreover, the Press propaganda, which accompanied all his movements, was nauseating. His own speeches, too, lacked force, and nothing could have been more pathetic than his quotation of: "If at first you don't succeed, try, try, try again."

Our Foreign Office, certain that it would be blamed for events over which it had no control, parodied it cynically as:

"If at first you can't concede,
Fly, fly, fly again."

It was a period of gnawing anxiety such as Great Britain had never known before, and infinitely more poignant than the tension of July and August, 1914. Scientific invention and the increased speed of modern life had affected the traditional phlegm of the English people, and a stream of words, carried on the air, swept the homes of the people like a hail of machine-gun bullets. During these critical days nearly every adult in Britain must have listened in to a wireless set. Assailed by a battery of conflicting opinions and advice and too dazed to think for themselves, they waited for the answer to one question only: Was it war or was it peace? The humiliation was to come later. But events were now moving fast to one end. For the British and French politicians the issue had become simply: war with Germany or a peace at Czechoslovakia's expense. And yet the movement was far from smooth. Daily, almost hourly, with irritating irregularity, it was retarded by eternal hope, only to surge again onward. The blackest moment came when Mr. Chamberlain returned from Godesberg and could give no more than a feeble assurance that all hope was not destroyed.

The next day Hitler's intentions were revealed. He delivered a speech at 8 p.m. on September 26 to a frenzied mob in the Sportpalast in Berlin. It was a violent speech delivered in the Fuehrer's most raucous, ranting manner, and his denunciation of Beneš was the raving of a maniac. There was no trace of conciliation in his speech. He gave the Czechoslovaks until October 1 to hand over the German-Bohemian areas.

The next morning in a muggy drizzle I went to the Westminster City Hall to get my gas mask. There was almost no one there, and I received my mask without delay, tried it on clumsily and then, in order to dispel an unpleasant feeling of confinement, went to Hyde Park. In the rain workmen were digging trenches, pitiful muddy ditches which were to provide shelter for the millions of London when the bombs came. On the way back I stopped at the St. James' Club. The news was grave. France and Britain had not accepted Hitler's ultimatum. The anti-aircraft detachments of the Territorials had been called up. Like two meteors travelling through space, the rival forces in Europe were moving in a collision line.

As I went out, the hall-porter handed me a letter from my school-master brother, and a telephone message.

The letter informed me that private schools were being moved from the East and from London. One school had booked an hotel in Perth. Did I know of any suitable buildings in Scotland which would house a school of sixty boys?

The telephone message was from Leeper. Would I see him at the earliest possible moment? I telephoned at once. He was out but had left a message for me to ring him early next morning at his house.

I went back to my flat where I found a letter from Rex Hoare, our Minister to Roumania, who had been dangerously ill with pneumonia. He had asked me to stay with him for a week at his brother's lovely house in Hampshire. I had put him off because of the crisis, and now he had written again to beg me to come if only for one night. He felt helpless and isolated and wanted news. I decided to go for one day only.

Early next morning I telephoned to Leeper. The Foreign Office was reviving the Political Intelligence Department which had functioned during the first world war. Leeper was to be head of it. He wanted me to take over the Russian section. He was asking Harold Nicolson to do Central and South-Eastern Europe. I gave my answer at once. If I were wanted, I was ready. Then I drove to Waterloo to catch the 9.30 train to Winchester.

With only three more days to the first of October the crisis was now at its peak, and its gravity was reflected in the solemn faces of my fellow-passengers. At Winchester I was met by Rex Hoare, who looked frail and worn after his illness. We had met for the first time in Russia in 1917 when he was second secretary in our Embassy. Even in those days he was entirely free from prejudices of class and tradition, and fearless, not always to his own advantage, in expressing his views to the Foreign Office. What I admired most in him was his self-control. No crisis, however violent, could ruffle the even surface of his temperament and he could think as clearly in an earthquake as in the most peaceful security.

As we drove to Ovington with its attractive stretch of the Itchen running through the grounds, we talked of Czechoslovakia. Was I sorry for the Czechs? He himself thought that morally we ought to fight, but like millions of other British people he confessed that his feelings were dominated "by a craven reluctance to see the end of the world". He felt that war was inevitable, because the wheels of mobilisation had moved so fast and so far that they could not be reversed.

As much as he ever permits himself to show his feelings, he was pessimistic, but he refused to allow his preoccupation to interfere with what he thought were his duties as a host. He insisted on my casting a fly over the Ovington water. He lent me a rod and waders, and before luncheon I had two hours of most pleasant angling.

At luncheon I had a warm argument with his wife Joan, a sister of Bill Cavendish-Bentinck, later our Ambassador to Poland. A sentimental pacifist, she was firmly opposed to any idea of war on behalf of Czechoslovakia. I pointed out that any compromise with Germany at the expense of a small nation could only hasten the day when we ourselves, without friends, would have to face a Germany with whom no compromise was possible. She protested that twenty million people would have to die in order to keep three million Germans, against their will, under Czech rule and professed her faith in God and in a last-minute miracle. Her argument was only a tiny part of an ugly truth, but at that time it was widely used by many people.

I caught the 4.5 p.m. train back to London and in the carriage tried to crystallise my thoughts. Like Rex Hoare I thought that we ought to fight. The big problem was not Goering's idiotic question where the Czechs came from, but where France and Britain were going to. We did not know, but I feared that if we did not make a firm stand now we should have to fight later in worse conditions. I felt sorry for Chamberlain and Daladier and thought of Proteus's remark in Shaw's *Apple Cart*: "One man that has a mind and knows it can always beat ten men who haven't and don't."

My instinct told me that we would not fight now, and the more I reasoned that there would be no war, the more the feeling of relief strengthened my conviction that we ought to fight.

As I mused, my train stopped at Basingstoke, and heads were thrust out of every carriage in search of newspapers. Fortunately, a boy was near my window, and I bought an *Evening News.* Fudged in the Stop Press was the bald statement: "Premier announced in House he will fly to Munich tomorrow." Joan Hoare had been given her miracle.

When I reached London the whole face of the capital had changed. Gone were the looks of anxious strain. The long weeks of tension had been broken by an optimism as sudden as it was instinctively correct. As I drove up Lower Regent Street, I passed a small procession carrying banners with the slogan: "Stand up for Czechoslovakia." The demonstrators were mostly poorly dressed men and women. They looked tired and dejected and they passed almost unnoticed between the smiling faces on the pavements. None of us knew yet what the price was, but every man and woman in Britain realised that it was peace. A British Prime Minister could not fly three times to Germany and then make war.

Two days later I learnt the terms and witnessed the hysterical scenes which followed the announcement of Mr. Chamberlain's false triumph. They were Hitler's terms, and, brutal as they were, I felt that they were not the end. I had seen his march into Austria; I had heard his shouted declaration in Vienna: "The bases of my programme are blood, fire and personality." Now he was marching into Czechoslovakia. I was sure that, whatever agreement he signed, he would not stop until he had entered Prague. Already the irreparable damage to our prestige was manifest from one plain fact. While we were making some show of firmness, Poland was rallying to our side. As soon as she realised that we were bent on capitulation, she sent a brutal ultimatum to the Czechoslovak Government, demanding the transfer to Poland of the Teschen territory and the district of Tristadt within twenty-four hours. Otherwise, Polish troops would immediately "enter into action". A French protest, warning Poland of the grave risks of her step, because one day she herself might have to suffer a similar humiliation, was disregarded.

Like others I felt ashamed, but for the moment I yielded to the general relief which flooded the whole country and submerged all other emotions. As Sheridan said of Amiens, Munich was a peace of which everyone was glad and nobody proud. But the joy came before the shame. Curiously, too, the desire for peace at any price was accompanied by a perverted respect for violence. By violence Stalin had succeeded. By violence Mussolini had made himself master of Italy. By violence Hitler had triumphed. Violence might be loathsome, but it seemed the quickest road to success, and all over

Europe including England there were men who had a sneaking regard for the super-men of violence. It was the respect of fear. It was like the mesmerising fascination which the python exercises over the mouse-deer of the Malayan jungle.

For myself I spent two riotous days of relaxation and made a round of the night-clubs, finishing with a visit to the Regal Cinema on the Sunday evening of October 2. When pictures of the Munich Conference were shown on the screen, there was some boo-ing when Hitler and Mussolini appeared. There was also some counter-cheering. When Mr. Chamberlain was shown, there was a storm of applause, which, however, did not entirely drown the shouts of: "What is your peace worth?" and "For how long?"

The cheers for Hitler and Mussolini knocked the party spirit out of me, and I went home to take stock of my position. If and when war came, I was pledged to go back to the Foreign Office. There was now no sense in returning to Tomintoul to try to write books. During the respite which the Chamberlain peace had given us I must earn my living by other means. The next day I went down to the offices of the *Evening Standard* and agreed with Wardell to come back to the newspaper for a limited period of three months.

On October 10 my new book, *Guns or Butter*, was published. At the end of the opening chapter I had written: "I left Fleet Street—I hope for ever—in 1937." On the day on which my book appeared I was back.

CHAPTER TWO

IF THE FIRST reaction to Munich was one of thankfulness for temporary mercies, hostile criticism soon followed. From the moment of Hitler's advent to power, the Liberals, although opposed to any form of conscription at home, had denounced every form of appeasement of Nazi Germany. They were now in full cry after Mr. Chamberlain.

The Labour Party, too, who had wanted collective security without rearmament, and whose attitude at the time of the crisis had vacillated with a heavy lean towards peace, provided that it was at Mr. Chamberlain's expense, began at once to attack the Government. Even more opportunist was the attitude of Lloyd George who, after accusing Beneš in July of having created the German-Bohemian problem by his greed and intolerance, in October denounced Mr. Chamberlain for having betrayed a model democracy.

Among the Conservatives there was a small, but strong element which, realising the irreparable damage done to the Tory cause by the moral weakness of the Baldwin-Chamberlain régimes, raised its voice against the surrender and began to look to Mr. Churchill to restore the country's lost prestige and the fallen fortunes of the Party. In the Munich debate in the House of Commons on October 3 Mr. Chamberlain made a bad best of his worst job by declaring his belief that there was "sincerity and goodwill on both sides" in the declaration signed by Hitler and himself; and in the Upper Chamber Lord Halifax poured the salt of hypocrisy into the wounds of the agonised Czechoslovaks by thanking President Beneš for having *chosen* the path of peace and for having helped us to avoid a European war. Speaking two days later in the House of Commons, Mr. Churchill expressed his views in one of his finest orations:

"I venture to think," he said, "that in future the Czechoslovak State cannot be maintained as an independent entity. I think you will find that in a period of time which may be measured only by months, Czechoslovakia will be engulfed in the Nazi régime. . . . It is the most grievous consequence of what we have done and of what we have left undone in the last five years—five years of futile good intentions, five years of eager search for the line of least resistance, five years of uninterrupted retreat of British power, five years of neglect of our air defences. Those are the features which I stand here to expose and which marked an improvident stewardship for which Great Britain and France have dearly to pay. . . ."

The most pungent comment on Munich came from M. Molotov who declared bluntly that "the second imperialist war has already begun"; the most curious and quixotic action was taken by Mr. H. G. Wells, a good friend of Czechoslovakia and an ardent admirer of the late President Masaryk. Indignant over what he called the cowardice of the politicians, he began busily to collect signatures to a petition recommending President Beneš for the Nobel Peace Prize.

Apart from a few notable exceptions like Mr. Churchill, Mr. Eden and Lord Cranborne, British statesmen cut a poor figure after Munich. For, in spite of the respite, the European situation could not and did not improve. Munich, in fact, killed appeasement, and now it was useless for ministers to make smooth speeches about their respect for the German people and about our readiness to establish a new order under which all grievances would be removed. To such advances the Nazis had one reply with which nearly every German agreed: "You had fourteen years in which to establish a new order of international justice. During these fourteen years you did nothing."

We had done worse than nothing; we had allowed the Germans to rearm. Now they were fighting-drunk with success. In German eyes Hitler was infallible.

Fortunately, even if not more than ten per cent. of the British people realised the full consequences of Munich, the public had an instinct that all was not well, and in the country ministerial stock fell heavily.

The England of 1938 differed greatly from the England of 1914. Apart from other changes there had been a bloodless revolution: a revolution of speed, a change from the cart-wheel to the motor-tyre, an invasion of the stolid countryside by the cities. Life moved incredibly faster; nerves were subjected to a greater strain. Yet the average Englishman retained many of his old virtues. He was still not easily rattled, because the Englishman, as distinct from the Scot, the Irishman and the Welshman, is seldom rattled. His greatest asset and his greatest handicap is his reluctance to think ahead. In times of peace this makes him blind to an approaching crisis but in the hour of danger brings out the doggedness, the determination and the refusal to admit defeat which are the enduring qualities of his race. Munich made him uncomfortable. He was humiliated and irritated to find his country's defences so weak. Moreover, the revolution of speed with its quicker dissemination of news, had given him a new quality. He had become more political-minded and with this new consciousness more suspicious of the professional politicians. After

Munich he was ripe for a lead. But, above all, he was on guard.

The lead, however, was not forthcoming and, as most men have to work for their daily bread, there was little outward change in the life of Britain. The pleasure-lovers continued to play; the bread-winners went on toiling.

As for myself, Munich had altered the course of my life, and after two years of freedom I found the return to journalism both irksome and difficult. There was, however, a welcome compensation for the loss of liberty in the many interesting people with whom my newspaper work put me in touch.

My first impulse immediately after Munich was to write to Jan Masaryk, the Czechoslovak Minister in London. During the thirteen years of his mission in Britain he had established himself as the most popular of the foreign diplomatists. Everyone who knew him liked this tall, cheerful-looking Slovak with the twinkling eyes and high-domed forehead, whose every phrase was an epigram, who could tell rollicking stories in half a dozen languages and vary his wit according to his audience and who at parties was always in great demand because he could improvise so brilliantly on the piano. "Jan" to great and small, he seemed to many people a man without a care in the world. Nevertheless, I found my letter difficult to write. Because I had known him intimately since the end of the first world war and had seen him in all moods, I knew that there were two Masaryks. There was Masaryk the successful diplomatist who by his personal charm and irresistible humour could cajole concessions from British statesmen where a technically more skilful negotiator would have failed. There was the other Masaryk, the real Jan whose carefree exterior concealed a sensitiveness the depths of which only his most intimate friends could fathom; Jan the Slovak with the wistful melancholy of the Slav; Jan who disliked politics and who longed for a quiet retreat in his native mountains and for the plaintive music of the Slovak reed-pipe; Jan the devoted son and hero-worshipper of a philosopher father; Jan the ideal companion who could cook a risotto or a goulash with all the skill and loving care of a Perigord chef; Jan the democrat whose sympathies had always been with the under-dog; above all, Jan the humane idealist who loathed cruelty and injustice, who never did an unkind action in his life, and whose heart was now bleeding for the sufferings of his countrymen.

I tore up several sheets of paper and then wrote two lines to say that I was sorry and that if he wanted to see anyone, I was close at hand. The next day his secretary telephoned. Would I come to the

Legation that afternoon? As I drove to Grosvenor Place, a violent gale was blowing, strewing Bird Cage Walk with leaves and stripping the trees of half their foliage. Jan was not in his study, but was upstairs in the small room next to his main office. When I was shown up, he was sitting on a sofa with Gillie, his Aberdeen terrier, beside him. I was shocked by his appearance. His eyes had sunk. His face was a pasty white. In a month he seemed to have aged ten years.

He rose with difficulty, held my hand and said quietly: "I haven't seen anyone yet. I'm worn out. But I wanted you to come." He was, indeed, shattered. Making a great effort to control himself, he talked slowly. But he had only one complaint: "Why did you not tell us at the beginning? Your Government advised us to mobilise. Then you told us to abandon our defences. Now we are finished."

There was no answer that I could give.

Then he took me by the arm and we went round the Legation offices. In the main office there were portraits of his father and Beneš. Jan pointed to them. "These will have to come down," he said. "Thank God that my father did not live to see this day." Then he added: "Beneš is resigning tomorrow. He will have to flee the country. I expect that he will come here."

We continued our tour of inspection, finishing with the big L-shaped drawing-room where I had often been present at Jan's musical parties and, after the guests had gone, had listened to him playing and singing Slovak songs. He waved a weary arm: "I shall have to sell these houses to get money for my staff. This is too big a Legation for a truncated state. We shall need £250,000,000 to restore it."

We came back to the first room. He pointed to a vast pile of letters, and his heart-strings loosened. The letters were from English sympathisers. They had moved him profoundly and he admitted it. There were messages from Mr. Churchill, Mr. Eden and Lord Cranborne whose support he said he would never forget.

Then the sadness returned, and he said: "Unfortunately, disaster and ruin cannot now be altered by words." Wearily he told me that he would stay on until the new Czech Government appointed someone to take his place. And with that I left him.

Two other episodes of those days I shall remember always: first the distress of Roland de Margerie, the First Secretary of the French Embassy with whom I had worked closely for several years and who told me in deep anguish of soul that, if Britain was humiliated, France was disgraced; and, secondly, an appeal by Harold Nicolson who was then a comparatively new member of Parliament and who alone had the courage to remain seated in the Commons when the House rose to welcome Mr. Chamberlain on his return from Munich. Three days later Harold went to Manchester where he made a brilliant speech in which he was alleged to have attacked Mr. Chamberlain for having ignored the warnings of Sir Robert Vansittart "who had been consistently right" and listening to Sir Horace Wilson "whose advice was never inconvenient". The speech was given great prominence in *The Times* with special emphasis on the references to Vansittart and Wilson. Harold told me that he had never made the remark. He had included it in his written speech and had given a copy to his secretary. On his way to Manchester he decided to omit the reference on the ground that, as Vansittart was then a high official, it might do him harm. While Harold was in the train, his secretary gave her copy to the London newspapers. As he had had a previous misunderstanding with Vansittart, he begged me to smooth things over.

I went at once to see Vansittart who was not only not displeased with Harold but full of admiration of his conduct during the crisis. He said that he had been surprised when he read the article in *The Times,* but, as for any damage to himself, the very idea was preposterous. "Nothing", he said, "could make my position worse than it is." He was profoundly pessimistic, prophesied war within a year in far worse conditions for us, and said that he was advocating a trebled rearmament and aid for the Balkans. He had little hope of much being done. "I have been right too long about the Nazis," he added, "and that is fatal."

If the Government were unwilling to accept British advice, there were Germans in London who could have given it even more serious warnings. One was Count Albrecht Bernstorff, the former Counsellor of the German Embassy. Like Jan Masaryk he had spent many years in England. Like Jan, too, he knew his London, mixed with all kinds and conditions of men, and had friends in every political party. Certainly there was no German who had so thorough a knowledge of every side of British life. With his huge bulky figure, his massive bald head, chubby red face and pale blue eyes, he was almost a London landmark. Sociable, fond of good food, a connoisseur of wine, a generous host and a brilliant conversationalist, he went everywhere and was liked by those who knew him best. Of all the German critics of the Nazis he was the most fearless and the most outspoken. When he saw the way events were moving, he resigned from the German diplomatic service and took a post in Wasserman's Bank in Berlin. But he came often to London and always brought valuable information and serious warnings. So violent was he in his criticism of the Nazi régime that many members of our Foreign Office mistrusted him and suspected that he must be a Nazi stool-pigeon.

I believed in him. The last time I saw him was on December 13, 1938. Soon after Munich I had arranged almost at the eleventh hour to undertake a lecture tour in the United States. I told Albrecht that I was sailing for New York at the end of the year. He begged me to cancel my visit. The European situation was too dangerous. Hitler, he said, was bent on using the military machine which he had created. He would not wait. He was angry because of the Munich delay and furious with Chamberlain for checking his Czechoslovak joy-ride. He was determined to make Prague a German city, and no power on earth, no hazard of fortune except his death, would stop him. It was the most direct warning of Germany's intentions that Bernstorff had ever given me, and his information had been culled from many reliable sources. He volunteered one piece of practical advice: "Tell your Government to increase your broadcasts in German. During the Munich crisis nearly all Germans, including the leading generals, listened in to the B.B.C. German bulletins."

I never saw Albrecht Bernstorff again. Admittedly he did not look the hero type. But his courage was cast-iron. I received two letters from him during the war and several messages through Switzerland. All showed that neither his opinions nor his attitude had changed. One message, which came through a direct contact, stated that, as the result of a mean family intrigue, he had spent several months in a concentration camp. After the attempt on Hitler's life on July 20, 1944, he was arrested again. Shortly before the end of the war the Nazis took him out and executed him.

There were other Germans whose presence in London should have been proof positive of what the Nazi slogan of "Blut and Boden" (blood and soil) meant in Europe. These were the German and German-Jewish refugees who had escaped in time or who had bought their exit visas by the sacrifice of all their possessions. They came not only from the Reich but also from Austria and Czechoslovakia and were now to be numbered in tens of thousands. Inevitably they concentrated in London, had their own favourite restaurants, and like most people in despair continued to live desperately until they had spent their last penny. I knew many of them.

One or two fell by the way and made their peace with the Nazis. Some perhaps were Nazi agents who had come to England disguised as refugees and who in order to establish their bona fides had submitted to a Nazi flogging. But the vast majority had nothing to hope from Germany, were bitterly anti-Nazi, and waited only for the day when the retribution of war would overtake the Nazi devil. Pathetic in their despair, they revealed all the political weakness of German democracy, for they quickly separated into a series of water-tight sections and in London re-formed the multiplicity of small political parties which had destroyed the Weimar and Austrian Republics. Much as I sympathised with them, I could not help feeling that they would not be of great value to us when war came.

During the late autumn of 1938 I went several times to Kempinski's, the once famous Berlin restaurant, which had now been transferred to London. In the tavern downstairs there was a replica of a Berlin or Viennese cabaret with an excellent Viennese pianist and an attractive young London girl called Margaret Dale who sang in both English and German. The atmosphere was Viennese; the songs were mainly Viennese, and the audience was two-thirds German and Jewish and one-third English sympathisers or lovers of continental night-life. The effect on the foreign audience and, indeed, on myself was one of nostalgia for the Europe that was dead. In her rendering of "Wien, Wien," Margaret Dale changed the tense of the verb in the last line from the present to the past and instead of singing, "dort wo ich glücklich und selig bin," sang "dort wo ich glücklich und selig war." Some of the audience sang mournfully with her. She also sang in English a boastful anti-Nazi song of which the refrain ran: "Today a lot of people try to rule by bluff and bluster, but let them try; we'll black their eye." This jarred horribly on me, but the refugees, who lived on wishful thinking, cheered enthusiastically.

One night I took my son of eighteen. He was not impressed. At the time I was greatly concerned about his attitude. He had been at Dartmouth and had been a member of the Alpha class which was supposed to contain the best brains and entitled its members to six months' seniority on passing out. Then I had been forced to withdraw him from the Navy on account of defective eyesight. Before sending him to Cambridge, I had arranged for him to go to a family in Germany in order to learn the language. He had been so disgusted by the attempts of the family to convert him to Nazism that he had sent me a telegram informing me that he had left and was on his way home. He was violently anti-Nazi. But he was quite as violently opposed to war which he said settled nothing. My generation had fought one war, and the result today did not seem to have been very successful. I was sad, but made no attempt to coerce him. Having lectured several times to university audiences, I knew that there were many young men who felt as he did. My restraint was one of the few wise things that I have done. When war came a year later, he rejoined the Navy at once. Today he has moved far from his early political ideas which were a confused mixture of pacifism and neo-Communism.

Taken all in all, my three months in England after Munich were an unhappy period, and I longed for the day when I could leave for my lecture tour in the United States. It was merely one form of the escapist feeling which was wide-spread among the British at that time.

On December 23 I went to say goodbye to Jan Masaryk who had resigned his post as Minister and like me was sailing for the United States. He still looked tired and sad, but the strained look had gone from his eyes. All the bitterness had left him, and he was his usual gentle self. He had been hurt, he said, by some of our politicians who, to justify their pro-Germanism, had made unfair criticisms of his countrymen, but he begged me not to mention their names. He was magnanimous about the supporters of appeasement. If they could save the world from the tragedy of a general catastrophe, he would forgive and bless them. He was pleased, too, with *The Times* which, one of the worst appeasers, had made amends in a farewell note on Jan himself. He showed me the cutting: "Diplomats are known in society as Excellencies; the Czechoslovak Minister is known to the whole public as Jan Masaryk."

"You see," said Jan, "it pays to be kind."

"You are kind," he continued, "and what's more you've been a good friend to my country. We shan't forget it."

In my career I have seen much of diplomatic life both from the inside and from without. No professional ambassador of great lineage and years of training could have behaved with greater dignity, greater nobleness of mind, and greater generosity of heart than Jan Masaryk throughout the long and unhappy calvary of Munich.

I went home to Crowthorne to spend Christmas with my father and to prepare for my American tour. All the happiness of a family reunion was shattered for me when on Boxing Day I received the news of the death of Karel Čapek. I went out of the house at once in order to be alone. The ground was deep in snow and the skies were leaden-grey. As I thought of Čapek, I bitterly regretted my wasted years in Prague after the last war. Of all my Czech friends, he was the one who attracted me most. I could and should have seen much more of him than I did, for I think we were drawn naturally to each other from the start. Rather stockily built, clean-shaven, and with mobile features and deep-set eyes which reflected instantaneously the changes of his moods, he had a rich fund of humour which relieved and added attraction to the intense serious-ness of the real man. His wife, the beautiful Czech actress and poet, used to tease me about my likeness to him. He stood for nearly everything for which I stood. He was the disciple and the literary interpreter of the great Masaryk. He believed in the small nations and felt and preached that, in order to survive, they must be more efficient than the Great Powers. He hated and loathed war. The last two plays which he wrote—*The White Sickness* and *Mother*—not only dealt with the evils of dictatorship, war, brute force and ruthless invasion; they also gave a remarkably accurate picture of what was to come. He was the one really big literary figure which Central Europe produced during the barren period between the two wars.

Two years before he had given a gay party for me in his Prague villa. We had talked late into the night over a bottle of real Scotch whisky produced specially in my honour. He had autographed a copy of his latest play with a clever drawing of himself and me. We had planned a tour of Scotland for the next summer. It was and remains a happy memory of the true Čapek.

The last time I saw him was in Prague a few days after Hitler's entry into Vienna. He knew at once what it meant and was over-whelmed by the impending tragedy to his country, a tragedy which he foresaw only too clearly. This time there was no light of humour in his eyes. He asked me plainly as man to man what I thought Britain and France would do, and I told him. One day we should have to fight, but he must not pitch his hopes too high. He under-stood. He was a democrat and an internationalist. But, above all, he was a humanitarian who believed in the new order of justice, decency and reason which his country had gone further than any other to establish.

The message which I received said that he had died of pneumonia, but I guessed at once—and guessed rightly—that he had ceased to live because everything for which he had previously lived had now been outraged and strangled.

On January 13, 1939, my three months with the *Evening Standard* were up, and I sailed for the United States.

CHAPTER THREE

MY VISITS TO the United States have been few in number and have been spread over a period of nearly thirty years. I have learnt just enough to realise that I know nothing of the country and the people and that every visit has forced me to alter my previous impressions and to start afresh. In the life-chart of nations we British are in advanced middle age or perhaps beyond it; the United States is still in the prime of youth.

My 1939 trip, however, was stimulating because of the melodramatic and almost hysterical attitude of the Americans towards Britain. Before leaving London, I went to see Mr. Eden who had just come back from New York. Over cups of the palest green China tea—typical of the Oriental scholar who at Oxford took the only First in his year in Persian and Arabic—he warned me of the pitfalls that I should encounter. He told me that, while most people in New York were very anti-Nazi, they were critical and almost contemptuous of Britain and France for their betrayal of the Czechoslovak democracy. Mistrust of Mr. Chamberlain was widespread, and with other members of his Government he was suspected of Fascist sympathies. Moreover, many Americans regarded all British information as tainted, and even the best-informed seemed obsessed with the belief that a severe censorship was imposed on British news and that the British public was not allowed to know the truth.

During a tour of three months extending over large areas of the United States, I received ample confirmation of the accuracy of Mr. Eden's conclusions. Nearly everywhere I went, anti-Nazi sentiment was strong. But criticism of the British Government was even more bitter, and those British lecturers who chose to attack its policy reaped a rich benefit. Most of the popular wisecracks, too, were directed, not against the Nazis, but against British ministers. The most pungent was Dorothy Parker's epigram on Mr. Chamberlain. In referring to his various air-journeys to Germany, she described him as "the first Prime Minister in history to crawl at 250 miles an hour". A curious symptom of the prevailing sentiment was the appearance of a miniature Chamberlain umbrella in white piqué which was put on sale by an enterprising store and sold well at a dollar. It was worn as a lapel pin by those women who thought that Britain should have fought at the time of Munich.

23

One fact impressed itself on my mind very quickly. Criticism of Britain was strongest and most violent among those Americans who favoured a stand by the democracies against the dictators. Their bitterness was aggravated by a conviction that British democracy, as represented by the Chamberlain Government, bore little resemblance to what the Americans understood by democracy. Since 1929 nearly every writer in the United States had extended his sympathies downwards, as the lean years following the slump emphasised the inequalities of American social life; and these writers, whose influence was considerable, regarded Britain as the land of privilege in which the social barriers were stronger than in any other country in the world.

Their attitude found its most emphatic expression in a pamphlet called *England: A Dying Oligarchy*. The author, Mr. Louis Bromfield, knows England well and likes the English people, but he did not spare the English upper class or, for that matter, the unfortunate Mr. Chamberlain. On the cover of the pamphlet the publishers stated, "Mr. Bromfield's sense of outrage that a British Prime Minister, anxious to wear a halo, should have sold out democracy to the gangsters has inspired this effective commentary on perhaps the most significant event of our time."

At the end of thirty pages of mordant invective Mr. Bromfield listed "in good Birmingham style an account book of the record of the National Government". I quote the items from the debit side because they represent what many Americans said and seemed to feel at that moment:

1. Immense loss of prestige throughout Europe, Asia and America.
2. Immense damage to the cause of Anglo-American friendship and American respect for England.
3. Immense losses to British investors, as well as foreign investors, both in revenue and capital.
4. Immense comfort and stimulus to the dictators and lawless elements of the world.
5. The loss of British leadership of the democracies.
6. Foreign domination of the Mediterranean, so vital to the life of the British Empire.

The pamphlet, which had a large sale, finished with the words: "What Great Britain needs is a great man, a great leader! What it has is a clique of second-rate nineteenth century politicians trying, weary and bewildered, to cope with twentieth century problems."

So much for the critics and for Mr. Bromfield's accurate forecast of Britain's need of Churchill!

I found everywhere an almost general belief that Americans were much better informed about Europe than the Europeans themselves. To the extent that they saw the wood where we Europeans were only too inclined to see the trees, I think the belief was justified. It had one natural and slightly dangerous reaction. The Americans preferred an American's views on Europe to those of any Englishman, even if the American had spent only a few days in Germany and the Englishman had lived there half his life. But we British had no cause for complaint, for ninety-nine per cent. of the American correspondents were on the side of the democracies and against the dictators and performed a noble and notable task in awakening their own countrymen to the German danger.

Although many Americans would have liked to see us fight in September, 1938, I found no one who was in favour of active American intervention. The average American was ready to defend his house, but not to fight in Europe. This sentiment was particularly strong among the university students. There were also many rich men whose attitude was determined by their hatred of the New Deal and by their almost fanatical dislike of Mr. Roosevelt whom they regarded as a traitor to his own class.

The anti-Roosevelt business men condoned and sometimes even praised Mr. Chamberlain; at the same time they were severely isolationist. Isolationism, however, was not confined to one Party or even to one class, but was actuated by reactions to the Versailles Treaty, against which the German *émigrés*, strongly represented in the American universities, had conducted a steady and subtle propaganda for nearly twenty years. One form of criticism which I encountered frequently can be summarised as follows: "We Americans went into the last war to save democracy. We pulled you out of a hole and we received very grudging thanks. At Versailles and after Versailles you trampled on democratic ideals. Now, largely through your own fault, you are in trouble again and you want our help. Well, we've learnt our lesson."

This opinion was wide-spread until Hitler marched into Prague. Indeed, Mr. Eden told me that the biggest applause he received from his huge audience in New York at the end of 1938 was when he said: "I am not here to ask you to pull our chestnuts out of the fire."

After Hitler's entry into Prague there was a slight change of sentiment and, as the shadow of war loomed starker on the horizon, American criticism of Britain became more restrained.

There was a sentiment deeply rooted in America that the English were now decadent and that the British Empire was in the last stages of disruption. In the anti-British Americans this idea had its roots in a malevolent wish to see us weak; in other Americans it was provoked by a fierce desire to see us strong. There was one type of question which was flung at me at nearly all my lectures:

Questioner: "Surely, Mr. Lockhart, the British are very badly informed?"

Lockhart: "On the contrary, I think that we have been and are well informed; the British Government know all the facts."

Questioner: "If that is so, will you explain why for six years your country did nothing to avert a danger which from 1932 onwards was obvious to the rest of the world?"

And to this question only Mr. Baldwin and Mr. Chamberlain could supply the answer.

My lectures were, therefore, beset with difficulties and were, in fact, a failure, mainly because I took an unpopular line in defending Britain and in not attacking, even if I did not support, the policy of the British Government. The Americans were impressed by the strength of Germany, and the American papers vied with one another in publishing sensational articles about the marvels of German rearmament. Colonel Lindbergh, who had been our guest during the distressful period of the murder of his child, did not help us. He had recently returned to the United States after a visit to Germany and Russia. He had been shown everything in Germany and little or nothing in Russia. Not unnaturally he had formed a high opinion of the German Luftwaffe and had underestimated Russia's new capacity of resistance. Still a great national hero, he expressed his views frequently and forcibly, stating that if he were an Englishman he would feel very uncomfortable, and advocating American abstention from a European quarrel which would end badly for the British.

His compatriots accepted his opinions as those of a great military expert. Their feelings were a little incoherent and perhaps were inspired by the realisation that for the first time in history the American continent, including South America, was no longer free from the risk of invasion. The slackness of which they accused the British was, therefore, a danger to themselves, and for the first time in my experience I heard Americans say publicly and rather heatedly: "Why, we have always looked on the British Navy as our first line of defence!"

My opening lecture, which was much too reassuring about Britain to satisfy an American audience, was a dismal fiasco, and in despair I sought the advice of Alex Gumberg who had emigrated to the United States from Odessa as a penniless young boy. I had met him first in Petrograd in 1918, when he was assistant and interpreter to Colonel Robins, the head of the American Red Cross Mission to Russia, and had formed a high opinion of his ability. He not only knew all the Bolshevik leaders but, having studied Marxism, was able to hold his own in Marxist dialectics. Had he chosen, he could have been a Commissar, but he preferred the freedom of American life which gave ample opportunities to his financial genius. By 1939 he had established himself as America's best-informed expert on Russia, was consulted on financial matters by the leading American bankers, and had turned his knowledge to profitable financial account. He would, I think, have been a dangerous enemy, but as a friend I can ask for none better. His death in the summer of 1939 was a great shock to me and a loss to the cause of Anglo-American co-operation against Germany.

Early in 1939 he had made up his mind that war was inevitable and that both Russia and the United States would be involved. He was therefore working behind the scenes for American intervention at the earliest possible moment. I told him that I was not prepared to attack the British Government in a foreign country. He understood my attitude, but begged me to refrain from any justification of a policy of surrender. The safest line was to confine myself to a general analysis of British foreign policy and of the British character and to point out Anglo-American similarities and differences.

It was wise counsel, and I did my best to follow it. I pointed out that the fundamental characteristic of British foreign policy was never to make commitments in advance, and that in this respect American foreign policy differed little from our own. With Gumberg's aid I elaborated an answer to a stock question first asked me by Dorothy Thompson and repeated at all my lectures in more or less the same form: "We cannot understand why you did not fight when reason and moral principle so clearly pointed your course." My reply was: "If by reason you mean self-interest, I agree that nations fight for self-interest, but if we have to do the fighting, then, rightly or wrongly, it is our privilege to determine where our self-interest lies. If it is a question of morality, you are affected as much as we are, for surely moral principles have nothing to do with geographical distance." This argument was not popular.

I was a little more successful perhaps on the subject of British character and British decadence. I was quite frank. I admitted that the history of all empires was the same. They had their birth, their youth, their manhood, their middle age, and their decline. I said that no one could state exactly where England stood on this age-ladder of nations. I could only tell my audience that for more than two hundred years especially before and after every war, foreigners had predicted that the British were on their last legs. I illustrated my argument with numerous quotations from the past, including Chateaubriand's final condemnation of the English in 1822 when his mission as French Ambassador in London had ended. The frivolity of the upper classes, the discontent of the masses, he said, left him with a sentiment of decadence. He no longer believed in the solidity of England.

I ended each lecture with a eulogy of British youth and refuted the American argument that the British were great as long as the horse was the fastest means of locomotion, but were no good in a mechanical age, by reminding them that we held nearly all the speed records in aviation. This went a little better, partly because in most places a majority of the audience wished to be reassured that the British were not down and out.

But the effect of my lectures, like that of most British lecturers, was insignificant, if not indeed harmful, and the only benefit of my tour was one of self-education. At the end my mind was a tangle of doubts. I had covered most of the Eastern seaboard. I had been as far south as Florida. But the major portion of my time had been spent in the Middle-West. I had received much kindness and almost too much hospitality. I felt confident that, if war came, the sympathies of many Americans, perhaps a majority, would be on our side. But beyond this I was not prepared to hazard even a guess.

Indeed, it is difficult for any foreigner to prophesy what the attitude of the American people will be towards any particular problem. The defects of the American Constitution, admitted privately by many politicians, but challenged publicly by none, nullifies the President's last year of office as far as any active interest in foreign affairs is concerned. The attention of the whole country is rivetted on purely domestic issues, and, if the President's party has committed itself to any form of intervention in foreign affairs, it is certain that in normal times the opposing Party will be isolationist, at any rate for the duration of the campaign. In his attitude towards the United States the fundamental error of the average British visitor is his conviction that he knows and understands Americans. The truth is that they are a more difficult people for us to understand than even the most obscure European race. In particular, the English will never understand Americans until they realise that throughout the United States there is a strong prejudice against the English ruling class. Among the rich Americans there are plenty of snobs who will loosen their money-bags in order to entertain a title, but the country, as a whole, is opposed to privilege. In the past, failure to recognise these facts has caused us to make many mistakes.

Fortunately, in 1939 the errors of our enemies were far greater than our own. The best British ambassador we have ever had in the United States was Adolf Hitler, and the crass stupidity of the Nazi propaganda, which reached the height of insolent absurdity in a pamphlet entitled *George Washington, the First Nazi*, did more than any British statement could have done to counteract the subtle efforts of the German democratic circles who, while denouncing Nazism, blamed the Versailles Treaty for all that had happened in Europe and in Germany itself.

My American visit was a confusing, yet stimulating experience, and I left the United States with one firm conviction: the immense and terrifying influence of radio on the American public. Radio was breaking down geographical barriers; for the first time it was beginning to create a national public opinion in a country which is too vast for newspapers to have a national circulation. In those early months of 1939 the craze for listening-in had swept the whole country like a new and virulent epidemic. The special announcers, who were given a far freer licence than any European broadcaster and who, during any crisis, slept by their microphones, had developed to a high pitch the art of playing on the emotions of the public. The result was startling and produced in many listeners an hysterical reaction akin to the ecstasy of a Negro under the influence of "hot" jazz. Yet the effect was not wholly detrimental. During my 1934 visit the Middle-West showed no interest in Europe. By 1939 it had become acutely Europe-conscious.

I came home in the Aquitania in the second week of April. On board we received by radio the news of Mussolini's Good Friday rape of Albania. I wondered what I was coming back to, and the foreigners on board paced the deck feverishly and, with gesticulating arms or gloomy immobility, as their moods changed, discussed this new outrage and the consequences it might have on their own lives.

But the English passengers seemed and, I think, were indifferent. They drank their cocktails at the usual hours, played patience or read their books during the day, and in the evening danced and taught the foreign passengers the Lambeth Walk. Certainly, if they felt any emotion, they never showed it. As a temperamental Scot, I admired their phlegm. But once again it was brought home to me forcibly that no one can make the English appreciate a crisis until it hits them between the eyes.

CHAPTER FOUR

BACK IN LONDON on April 10, I found London basking in warm sunshine and much less emotional than New York. Not knowing what to do, I spent a few weeks at my club and wrote a confidential memorandum for the Foreign Office on my impressions of the United States. In Whitehall there was much talk of war and of Russo-Franco-British negotiations. Hitler, having finished his brutal job in Czechoslovakia, was now turning his attention towards Poland. Most of my Foreign Office acquaintances thought that war was merely a question of time, but in home political circles there were still sharp divisions. Appeasement was not dead, but the anti-Chamberlain element was stronger than at the time of my departure for the United States, and in the clubs men who had cheered Munich now even refused to drink German wines and German beer. My clearest and most comforting impression was of the calm of the general public. The hesitation of the previous September had disappeared. The attitude of the average man could be summed up in one sentence: "If we have to fight, let's do it now and get it over."

Within a week after my return Rex Leeper asked me to come to see him at the Foreign Office. He wanted to know my movements and to have my address in the event of war. There was to be a change in my work. Harold Nicolson as a member of Parliament was not eligible for a post in a government department and would, therefore, be unable to deal with Central Europe and the Balkans for the Political Intelligence Department when it came into being. Leeper could find no suitable substitute, but had found another Russian expert. Would I be willing to switch from Russia, which had originally been allotted to me at the time of Munich, to take over Central Europe and the Balkans? I agreed and tried to find out more about the job and when it was likely to start. But Leeper had no information. The tension, he said, might last for months. Unless and until there was war, the new department, which had been sanctioned by the Treasury as a temporary war department, could not begin to function.

It was not a very satisfactory position, but doubtless thousands of other people were in the same predicament as myself. Patience was the proper medicine, but I found it hard to tear myself away from London. On the first of May I went to the opening of the season at

Covent Garden. The opera given was Smetana's *Bartered Bride*. At once I felt my choler rise and I was glad that I was not with Jan Masaryk. To put on Czechoslovakia's national opera as a compliment to a crucified and tortured nation was an insult; to sing it in German was a crime.

Three days later I read with astonishment the news of Litvinov's resignation. Bolshevik Commissars do not resign: they are dismissed. Litvinov had been the chief Russian advocate of collective security and indivisible peace; in other words, of an Anglo-Franco-Russian alliance against aggression. Now he was being replaced by the cold and enigmatic Mr. Molotov. The change of Commissars must mean some change of policy. Seeking information, I was told that Litvinov's resignation had come as a complete surprise to the Foreign Office, but that the Poles were pleased and believed that his removal would assist Polish-Russian relations. Only half reassured, I was considerably more perturbed when some weeks later I received a letter from the late Samuel Harper, who was then in Moscow. Harper was the leading American expert on Russia. I had known him for many years, had met him first in St. Petersburg, and had seen him quite recently in Chicago when he was planning his last trip to Moscow. His letter was brief and to the point. We should, he said, "stop fooling with the Russians and make our pact with them at once"; otherwise there would be big trouble. He had, he told me, written a report in this sense and had sent copies to Sir Bernard Pares and to the American State Department.

A few days later I happened to meet Mr. Eden who was spending the week-end in the same house. He told me that he was doing his military training as a Territorial three nights a week. His battalion shared a shop-store in Oxford Street with the London Scottish. They had no hall and no equipment. The War Office had offered £1,500 for the best hall in the district, but the owner had demanded £3,000. So the two battalions had to drill in the store after the shop-girls had left. He was afraid of the Government's policy because he was sure that the Germans were convinced that we would never fight for anything east of the Rhine. I asked him whether we could do anything now to persuade them that they were wrong. "Of course," he replied. "If Chamberlain would only say that we would fight and put Winston in the Cabinet, the Germans would believe him quickly enough." But, unfortunately, Mr. Chamberlain still thought that his policy had given us peace in our time and that the Germans were "cooing doves".

Mr. Eden was very unhappy about the resignation of Litvinov whom he knew well. He was also critical of the slowness and inadequacy of our rearmament. As I understood it, his quarrel with Mr. Chamberlain was that, whereas both men were agreed that on account of our unpreparedness our policy must be defensive, Mr. Eden wished to *fight* a rear-guard action, while Mr. Chamberlain was opposed to any show of resistance. Spain was obviously the tool and the testing-board of Germany, and Mr. Eden wished to bring Russia, France, Britain and the United States together and to bomb or sink Spanish ships every time that Franco bombed a British ship. In his view such measures afforded the best means of preventing war; in Mr. Chamberlain's opinion they were certain to provoke war.

It was not a reassuring week-end.

From the Labour side I saw Walter Citrine whom I have known for many years. Tall and clean-shaven with a fine head of silver-grey hair and a lean athletic figure, Citrine is hard-working and austere, but can unbend at parties. He began life as a trombone player in a Liverpool band. By sheer ability and painstaking attention to detail he became General Secretary of the Trades Union Congress before he was forty and held this key post for nearly twenty years. The position gave him great power and the ear of every British Prime Minister. Sensible, shrewd and reliable, he has been entrusted with many official secrets. His forte and his pride is his shorthand which he writes with great speed and with such exemplary neatness that months afterwards his secretary can decipher it without difficulty. He always carries a shorthand note-book in his pocket and keeps a record of every conversation. This gift and this habit enable him to produce his various books on Russia, Finland and other countries more or less as he travels. His files would fill several volumes of the Encyclopaedia Britannica and should be a rich mine of information to future historians of the social-economic life of Britain.

I found him anxious but still hopeful that we might avoid war which, he said, was always unpopular with the working-class. But in order to do so, we must be strong. He was concerned about the slowness of our rearmament and complained of Mr. Chamberlain's dilatoriness. But of his own accord he admitted that all the political Parties, including his own, and, indeed, the general apathy of the public were also greatly to blame for the disastrous state of our defences. He was, he said, now advocating conscription and urging an acceleration of rearmament. This was strong meat from Citrine who had always opposed conscription and loathed militarism and who, like most Labour men, welcomed secretly, if he did not openly bless, the Munich respite.

Another sound, but even more disturbing informant was Sir Horace Rumbold, our Ambassador in Berlin from 1928 to 1933. To the world he presented a stiff and almost wooden exterior, but of our modern diplomatists he was the kindest and the wisest. No man knew better the value of an impassive silence. Foreigners who mistook his reserve for stupidity made a fatal error. When he spoke, what he said was always to the point, and on Germany, which he understood profoundly, he was rarely, if ever, wrong. His views on the situation were straightforward. Every surrender to German aggression was in German eyes a sign of weakness and therefore a direct incentive to further aggression.

He was, too, the most accurate of political prophets. On March 15, 1939, the day on which Hitler entered Prague, there was a dinner at the Grillions Club, a famous political centre where ministers and politicians meet and exchange views in privacy. That night there was a long and lively discussion on foreign affairs with Mr. Churchill in his most trenchant and eloquent form. At the end he turned to Sir Horace Rumbold. "Horace," he said, "you ought to know about these matters and you haven't opened your mouth yet. Where do you think the Axis will make its next coup?" Sir Horace put up his eyeglass, muttered, "Memel, Albania," and relapsed into silence. Within a month the Axis had taken both.

Although outwardly life in London had changed but little, I found it difficult to concentrate in the atmosphere of crisis in which I had enveloped myself. I felt restless, wanted action, and longed to go abroad again to see things for myself. Unless and until there was a war, there was no official job for me. After an expensive month in London I decided that I was doing no good and was merely wasting busy people's time and my own substance. Taking a sudden decision, I made up my mind to go back to Tomintoul.

On my way North I went to the Royal Air College at Cranwell to give a talk to the cadets. It was a most inspiring experience. I have seen many military colleges in many countries. My father's home is close to Sandhurst. But none that I have ever visited was up to the Cranwell standard. Nowhere had I found a finer or more alert type of cadet, and the keenness, the healthy outlook, the quick intelligence, the complete absence of "side", and, above all, the remarkable esprit de corps of these young men who were afterwards to win imperishable fame and to save their country, made a profound impression on me. Obviously the Commandant, Air Vice-Marshal Baldwin, had done a wonderful job. He told me that the youth of Britain had become air-minded and that he now received the pick of the public schools. But he was far from satisfied and complained bitterly about the lack of interest shown in the College by the Air Ministry.

From Cranwell I went to Sedbergh to stay with my headmaster brother and gave a similar talk to the senior boys of this hardy Yorkshire school. There, too, I formed a high opinion of the modern English schoolboy who was so much better educated, more serious, and more interested in world affairs than the happy-go-lucky, unsophisticated boys of my own generation. When during my lecture-tour I used to tell the Americans that there was nothing wrong with British youth, I believed and hoped that what I said was true. Now I was quite certain.

Back in the clean, bracing air of Tomintoul I was happier than in London. But I was still restless, and even fishing failed to distract me. The Germans were increasing their pressure on Poland. Hitler now wanted Danzig. I found it impossible to work. The longing for action remained.

In the middle of July fulfilment came suddenly and unexpectedly in the form of a letter from Jack Wheeler-Bennett, the author of an excellent life of Hindenburg called *The Wooden Titan,* and a great authority on Germany. He was now writing a life of the Kaiser. Could I take him to Doorn?

Although thirteen years younger than myself, Jack was one of my oldest friends. He had had an extraordinary career. Educated at Malvern, he won a history scholarship at Oxford, but before going up with a view to entering the diplomatic service he was blown twenty-five yards by the blast of a German bomb. He lost his power of speech for a time and was subsequently afflicted with a bad stammer. With great courage he gradually conquered his infirmity, but his hopes of a diplomatic career were shattered. Having money of his own, he set out to make himself an expert in foreign affairs, travelled extensively, and acquired a vast and intimate knowledge not only of world affairs but also of the principals who conducted them. His main study was Germany which he had visited many times. At one period a strong financial supporter of the Royal Institute of International Affairs, he had produced a series of valuable historical works on such subjects as disarmament, reparations, and the Brest-Litovsk Treaty. He knew nearly all the leading German politicians and soldiers. He had never met the Kaiser.

His proposal attracted me. For the last ten years I had been in more or less regular relations with the Kaiser, and had visited Doorn several times. I therefore wrote direct to him, and suggested that I should bring Wheeler-Bennett, with a strong recommendation that in his own interest the Kaiser should receive him. I was confident of a favourable reply. Ten days passed without any answer to my letter. I was surprised, not without reason. Then by a lucky chance Jack met Prince Friedrich, the Kaiser's grandson, in London, just as the Prince was leaving for Doorn. Jack told him what had happened. The Prince took action, and within two days I received an invitation to bring Jack to Doorn on August 16 and to stay the night. The Kaiser had never received my letter. The Nazi agents in his entourage had withheld it.

We left Croydon by air on August 15 in the finest weather of the whole summer.

After spending the night at Utrecht, we set out by car the next morning for Doorn. On our way we passed a funeral, and a mile or two farther on we were held up for a few moments by an accident. Two cars had collided, and a dead body, covered by a white dust-coat, lay by the roadside. The Danzig boil, latent, but not inactive since June, was now coming to a head, and Jack, always superstitious, predicted the worst. We should be caught in Holland by the war.

On arrival at Doorn we were met by General von Dommes, the Hofmarschall, and taken to our quarters in the Torgebaude or Gate House, a picturesque and typically German two-storied lodge with red-and-white shuttered windows, which had been specially built for the Kaiser in 1924. Both of us were given suites. Mine was ultra-Victorian. Above my bed was a Biblical text from Corinthians: "Watch ye, stand fast in the faith." Looking down on me from the opposite wall was a gold-framed monstrosity with mounted photographs of all the Coburgs including Queen Victoria and the Prince Consort. The other pictures—and they occupied almost every inch of space on the walls—were seascapes, mostly of the German fleet and of the Kaiser's yacht. In the passage between our suites hung two alleged Rubens, one of Samson and Delilah and the other of Joseph being sold by his brethren. The second title reminded me that Czechoslovakia was the Joseph of the European nations.

Shortly after mid-day Freiherr von Sell, the Kaiser's aide and the most trustworthy of his servants, came to take us to Huis Doorn, the former Bishop's Palace which was the Kaiser's home in exile. In the warmth of the clear summer sky it looked wonderfully peaceful

with its English park, its well-kept garden and its clean placid little
lily-pond which, alive with roach and perch, guarded the front of
the house like a moat. We were taken at once to the Kaiser's study
in the Tower room. Every preparation had been made for his
English visitors. In a tray on his desk lay English newspapers with a
copy of the *Evening Standard* prominently displayed for my benefit.
There were photographs of the Duke of Windsor and other members
of the British Royal Family. Lying on a table, too, were signed portraits of the Kaiser. They were obviously destined for us. Moreover,
our host himself had made special sartorial arrangements for this
English occasion. He was dressed in a blue-grey English tweed suit
with white waistcoat and lavender-topped boots, and as a tie-pin he
wore a huge cameo of Queen Victoria.

We spent a most strenuous day. We had three long talks alone
with the Kaiser: before luncheon; from 5.30 p.m. to 7; and again
from 8.45 p.m. till ten o'clock. Although the heat was trying and
although the Kaiser had celebrated his eightieth birthday that year,
he talked incessantly and always with the greatest animation. For
Jack's benefit the talk was chiefly about the historical past. The
Kaiser's two main themes, developed at great length, were the
wickedness of official historians, all of whom were guilty of suppres-
sing the truth and suggesting the false, and the miscarriage of historical justice with regard to himself. With a great show of documentary
evidence he explained how he—and he alone—had prevented
France, Russia and Germany attacking Britain during the Boer war.
"For that," he said, "I got 1918." More than once, too, he punctuated
his historical references with a shrug of the shoulders and a plaintive
ejaculation: "After all, I am the most misused man in the world."
Another favourite interjection was "one of the greatest scoundrels
unhung." During the day it was applied to several people including
Stalin, Mola, the Spanish Republican general, and Sir Sydney Lee,
who in his life of King Edward had, the Kaiser alleged, suppressed
certain relevant material in the Kaiser's letters.

Yet if he felt bitterness, the Kaiser made a brave effort to conceal
it. Probably he was too interested in his own conversation, for he
talked not only with his tongue, but with all the physical force that
was left in him. His eyes danced and sparkled; his good arm was
freely moved to point a warning finger or to make a broad sweep to
far distant menaces like Russia and Japan. And when he made a sly
hit at the English, a foxy smile lit up his whole face. He talked much,
too, of the imperialist greed which had been the downfall of all great

nations and told us that in his years of trial he had evolved a new
theory. No nation should occupy more land than Providence intended for it. Providence in its own good time would punish those
who sinned against this law.

I asked him if his reference to punishment was meant to apply to
the British Empire or to the Third Reich of Hitler. He paused for a
moment and then replied firmly: "to all empires and, therefore, to
both."

In his talk he did no more than touch on the crisis of the moment.
He did not like or trust the Poles and said so, but, mindful of his
pact with Providence, added that he had no wish to see them incor-
porated in Germany. He was careful, too, not to say much about the
Nazis, although he made it quite clear that he was opposed to them.
Indeed, at one moment he burst into anger. "I am a prisoner in my
own house," he said. "They (the Nazis) treat me far worse than the
Socialists ever treated me."

I learnt from his grandsons and also from Sell that the Kaiser
received all his money from Germany from which he had not been
allowed to remove his capital. The Weimar Republic sent him his
remittances without any hampering conditions; the Third Reich
used this money lever not only to ensure satisfactory behaviour but
also to establish their own control.

The Kaiser was anti-Russian, and, as a man who in exile had found
great consolation in his religion, he delivered a five-minute blast
against the Bolsheviks for their persecution of the Church. Then he
added cryptically: "But don't go away with the idea that Russia and
Germany will go to war; the relations between the German army
and the Red army are far too close for that." The Molotov-Ribben-
trop Pact had not then been signed. I have often wondered since how
much, if anything, the Kaiser knew of the Russo-German negotiations which must have been going on at that very moment.

At luncheon he was gay. His English was very good and fluent,
but not quite so accurate as when I made my first visit to Doorn in
1929. This, however, was the only sign of the increase of the years.
He engaged in a long duel with Jack on the merits of various
historians. He asked me where my kilt was, supposed that I was now
too fat to wear it, and announced with great glee: "I did not know
that writing books ever made anyone fat." He had a word for each
member of his suite all of whom, I noticed, had been changed since
my previous visits. The loyal and aged supporters, like Count
Hamilton and Count Finckelstein, had departed or had been removed.

The men who had taken their place were younger, stiffer, and less forthcoming.

In the afternoon we had tea alone with the Empress who, eager to impress Jack, promised him all help for his book and urged him to finish it quickly because it would give great joy to the Kaiser, who in his exile had so few pleasures. She begged Jack never to write to Berlin but always through Sell who could be trusted and who had been with the Kaiser a long time. The Nazis opened all the Kaiser's correspondence. Then, asking us to draw nearer and lowering her voice, she warned us solemnly to beware of the Umgebung, the Kaiser's entourage at Doorn, and to reveal no confidences to them. "They are here," she said, "as spies. They report everything to the Nazis. I do not say that the Nazis have not done some good things. But they are evil, and great harm will come from them." I had the impression that I was taking part in a conspiracy.

After tea the Empress showed us the room in which the Kaiser's first wife died. I had never seen it before. It had been left exactly as it was in the Kaiserin's time. On the bed lay a sheaf of bronze palm leaves and on the pillow a bronze chaplet. The dressing table, also left as if still in use, was decked with photographs of all the Kaiser's children. I thought of Queen Victoria and the Prince Consort. Here in Doorn the departed were commemorated in the same way as at Windsor. The Kaiser, I reflected, not only worshipped Queen Victoria; he was a Victorian.

In the evening we dined with the Umgebung in the small staff dining-room. There were three of them: General von Dommes, the Master of the Household; Herr von Marschall, a German Colonial official; and a German naval captain whose name I never caught. They were big stern-looking men, and Jack and I were sandwiched between them like two soft roes between layers of hard toast. Conversation was difficult. True to instructions, we avoided all controversial subjects. The Germans were civil, but the atmosphere was heavy with hostility. I felt that they hated us and that they knew war was coming.

At 8.43 precisely we were summoned to the Kaiser for the last time. On my way upstairs I noticed a superb set of tin soldiers deployed for action in a great glass case. Did he still play with and think of soldiers? I remembered noticing that the large map of China in the hall was carefully marked with little flags showing the Japanese advances. But in the study there was little mention of war; only more talk about historians with special praise for Karl Nowak, the Jewish historian who wrote with some frankness a life of the Kaiser and became his literary counsellor and executor. The Kaiser told us naively how astonished he was that Nowak, an Austrian, should have come to consult him about history, since, as he said, "German historians never come to me." He told Nowak so at their first meeting. Whatever reputation Nowak may have as a historian, he was a natural diplomatist, for his answer was a gem of tact and won him instant and lasting favour. "Majestät," he said, "there is a difference. I come to seek knowledge. German historians always know everything."

We had a friendly and slightly emotional farewell. As we shook hands, the Kaiser reminded us that he was eighty and that next year Providence might call him. Then with the gesture of an actor taking his last curtain, he handed us the signed photographs of himself and a copy of a sermon preached in the Berlin Dom which justified the Kaiser's attitude in 1914!

The next morning we left for the Hague. The gentle and friendly Sell accompanied us for part of our journey. His life-long loyalty to the Kaiser had imposed on him the unpleasant task of travelling between Doorn and Berlin in order to arrange his master's financial and business matters. He hated it, fully expecting each journey to be his last. He told us that every time he crossed the frontier he was searched by the Gestapo who examined every scrap that he carried and cross-examined him at great length. Then he gave us the most direct and solemn of warnings. The Nazis would go to all extremes. Today it was too late for them to draw back. They meant and expected war; they needed and must have continuous successes abroad in order to remain in power at home.

Sell was murdered by the Nazis after the attempt on Hitler's life in July, 1944.

CHAPTER FIVE

THE HAGUE IS almost my favourite capital, being what Pepys called "a very neat place in all respects". When we arrived an hour before noon, the weather did its best for us with a sky of cloudless blue and a sun so radiant that the asphalt melted under our feet. We spent a pleasant afternoon looking at the pictures in the Mauritshuis and inspecting the bookshops. Then towards evening we set out by car for Leyden, sentimentally dear to me because of its Scottish connexion and because it was the scene of David Balfour's romance with Catriona. The university, which among its distinguished alumni includes Goldsmith and Fielding, was closed for the summer vacation. The atmosphere was sleepy, and in the poorer quarters stolid old men sat on stools before their house-doors and smoked and gazed vacantly into space as though too tired and hot to move.

From Leyden we went on to Scheveningen and dined at the Oranje where Krassin and Chicherin stayed for the Hague Conference of 1929. From the verandah we saw trenches mounted with sandbags. The scare of war had invaded Holland, and she was preparing to guard her neutrality. Her precautions showed clearly where she thought the danger of aggression lay. At Scheveningen and at the Hook she had posted a handful of sentries; the rest of her troops were on the German frontier.

We went early to bed to prepare for the morrow which was to be my last day—and my last night—in the old Europe in which I had spent the best years of my life. It was to be a performance which seemed likely to tax even my robust constitution. It began at noon with a visit to Edgar Mihiels, a colleague of my Prague days and now the Dutch Ambassador in London. He had been ill and still looked a sick man. But he was reasonably confident that there would be no war. Then we walked down the Lange Voorhout to lunch with Colijn at the Vieux Doelen.

Freed from the cares of office and with a government of officials in power pending the elections which everyone assured me would bring him back as Prime Minister, Colijn was in his best form. I had known him for some years, and luncheon with him at the Vieux Doelen was always the highlight of my various visits to the Hague. I admired him greatly. Tall, powerfully built with immensely strong hands and a great head of closely-cropped hair which stood straight up like the bristles of a hair-brush, he was a giant both of intellect and of physical strength. By far the greatest Dutchman of his time, he had the same energy, the same courage, and the same powers of endurance as Mr. Churchill. He was, too, a great trencherman and, as an inveterate cigar-smoker, he left Mr. Churchill far behind. Although he had recently celebrated his seventieth birthday, he had lost none of his capacity for food and drink. Luncheon was a heavy meal dominated by Colijn who ate everything, drank everything, smoked three cigars, and enlivened every course with brilliant conversation which ranged from stories of his adventurous youth in the Dutch East Indies to trenchant comment on the European crisis. He was very confident that there would be no war; he was certain that the Nazis would not fight, if Britain meant business. His arguments were based on two assumptions: first, that there was much unrest in Germany and that the Nazis were aware of it and, secondly, that the Dutch were much better informed about Germany's intentions than we were. We had only to show a stiff front and put Mr. Churchill in the Cabinet, and the Nazis would climb down. If the worst happened, he did not think that the Germans would violate Dutch territory. He knew that we should not. He was prepared for all events. If war came, Holland would be able to hold up large forces. On her Eastern frontier, he had built 1700 new casements, of which 1200 were of steel.

Colijn added substance to his confidence by a long account of his political plans. At the end of September he was going to visit the United States, China and Japan. He was convinced that the Japanese would never seek to violate the Dutch East Indies. It suited them well to have the Dutch there rather than the Americans or British. On his return from his tour he had arranged to deliver a hundred speeches in the election campaign. He had no intention of abandoning his political career. He still felt full of vigour. If he came back as Prime Minister, he would modify the Dutch Parliamentary system. Parliament, of course, must remain. But when it had approved and accepted the government's programme, it must give the government a reasonable chance of carrying it out. His last words to me were: "My dear Lockhart, if ever your country tries to adopt proportional representation, fight it like the devil."

Our talk had lasted more than two hours, and, dazed, a little comforted, but far from reassured, I walked out into the blazing sunshine. Robert Gordon, the American Minister, who had also been at our luncheon, urged us to come to his house. Much against Jack

Wheeler-Bennett's wishes, I yielded to further temptation. Gordon produced champagne, and I drank most of it.

To escape from the heat of the city Jack and I drove out to Warmond, a summer restaurant situated in the heart of the countryside. The scenery was typically Dutch. There was a slow-running river lined with poplars. Frisian cattle were feeding in the meadows. The atmosphere of complete tranquillity had a pleasant and soothing effect, and for some time we sat by the edge of the river listening to the Viennese music of the restaurant orchestra. Jack, pleased with his visit, gave me an excellent dinner, and I let myself go. Discovering that the band could play Russian gipsy music, I plied them liberally with Jack's brandy. They responded with a zest which was not wholly alcoholic and which astonished and, in the end, amused the stolid Dutch. It must have been an expensive evening for Jack, but, glad to forget the present, I enjoyed this descent into a nostalgic past.

The next morning we flew back to London and at once reported to Vansittart who was not interested in our news of the Kaiser and bitterly sceptical of Colijn's optimism. He was, in fact, in his most pessimistic mood, thought that the war would break out before the end of the month, and advised Jack with all solemnity to return at once to the United States, where, if the clash came, he had a job to do. He told us that he had warned the Government for years and that, compared with the period before the first world war the warnings had been more serious and more frequent. He likened the Cabinet to a football team in which all the members were running in different directions.

I was deeply impressed by his sincerity which speedily dissolved the dregs of my gaiety of the night before. His position was tragic. He was like an honest blunt doctor. His diagnosis was always right. But his bedside manner was said to be unfortunate and his remedies were regarded as dangerous. It was true that he did not handle Mr. Chamberlain successfully. But Mr. Chamberlain was not the only British patient. That same evening I met a high official of the Air Ministry. He was brimming over with confidence in the Prime Minister and was quite certain that there would be no war. He made a savage attack on the Foreign Office which, he said, was always tainted with excessive pessimism.

Two days later Jack took me to see Dr. Bruening whom I had never met. He was gentle, quiet in manner and soft in speech. Dressed in black and spare in figure, he reminded me of a lean crow. He was anti-Nazi and pro-British, but to some extent he held us responsible for Hitler's triumph and blamed Ramsay MacDonald and Lord Simon for their failure to support the Weimar Republic during their periods of office as Foreign Secretary. He spoke without bitterness, and his talk covered a wide range of subjects—including the food that we were eating. He reminded us that he had made a comparative study of the wages and living standards of the British and German textile-workers. The British, he found, were better paid, but the Germans were better nourished, because British women could not and would not cook—and the British working men did not seem to mind. He talked with the same restrained detachment about the European crisis and expressed a cold optimism. The Nazis, he felt, would not press their demands to the point of war. But he told us that he himself was leaving for the United States the next day.

I drew my own conclusions. There was now only one wish in my heart: to see my Highland home again before the floodgates burst. After saying goodbye to Jack, I left that night for Scotland. While I was in the train, Ribbentrop was arriving in Moscow with a mission of thirty-two officials to sign the treaty with Russia which, known as the Russo-German Pact of Non-aggression, was to give Hitler the freedom which he needed for more aggression.

The memory of my last peace journey to Scotland will remain with me always. Even now I can relive with the deepest vividness every minute of the long drive from Aviemore to Tomintoul through the finest and loveliest stretch of Strathspey. The air was warm and balmy, and the interplay of cloud and sunshine gave an added glory to the mystic majesty of the mountains. I stopped several times on my way: at Loch Pityoulish, a natural gem in a mountain setting of pine and rowan-tree and birch, and again at the highest point on the cross roads with its immense view of pleasant wooded strath and of the Spey running through it like a silver thread against the vast background of the Cairngorms. I was wise to have come, for never again shall I see so fair a sight. I shall tell later of re-visiting the same scene during the war.

It was market-day in Tomintoul when I arrived, and the village square was full of farmers. The first person that I ran into was Major Sir Murdoch Mackenzie Wood, the former Liberal member of Parliament for Banffshire. He was indignant. After the war of 1914-18, in which he fought most gallantly and was severely wounded, he had been one of the first men to raise his voice in favour of a just peace for Germany. For this he had been defeated at Ayr

Burghs in the "khaki" election of 1918, mainly by the efforts of a group of Tory M.P's who sent a letter to Lloyd George warning him not to make a soft peace. Now, he said, the survivors of the men who had signed this letter were urging Mr. Chamberlain to placate the much viler and unappeasable Nazi Germans.

Mackenzie Wood's Highland face glowed red against the green of the square. Only three weeks ago, I had stood on almost the same spot listening to Mr. Mair, the prospective Labour candidate for Banffshire, making a bid for the votes of Tomintoul. Apart from a pledge to raise agricultural wages to the same standard as those of New Zealand, he promised a return to a golden age of peace and international brotherhood as soon as Labour was in power. It was a long, drivelling speech punctuated by frequent references to the horrors of war which a Tory Government had brought to our door-steps through its programme of rearmament! We British are a curious race. Our instinct is sound enough, but we have a dangerous and apparently ineradicable tendency to do the wrong things first. Fortunately the man in the street and especially in the village is not always taken in, and the attitude of the Tomintoul folk towards this speech was healthily cynical. They looked on politics as a racket in which one Party was no better than another. As I turned away from the group round the earnest and, doubtless, sincere speaker, Mitchell, the village policeman, came up to me, cocked an eye at the impro-vised platform and, with a comprehensive sweep of his arm which was meant to include the whole tribe of politicians, said bluntly: "They're a' the same; when they want your vote, they promise you the moon, and when they're in they dae nothing."

That summer of 1939 was a record year for visitors, and Tomin-toul's two hotels were full. As the European crisis advanced rapidly towards its climax, the hotel guests hung on the words of the radio. Convinced that war and my recall were now merely a question of days or even hours, I greedily sought every opportunity to fish. But I could not resist the urge to listen to the unseen speakers whose voices penetrated every corner of this remote Highland village. On August 24, the day of my arrival, I had sought refuge in the private room of Duncan McNiven, the proprietor of the hotel where I always stayed. At 3 p.m. the B.B.C. announcer said, "In a few min-utes we shall give you the first report of the speech which Mr. Chamberlain is now making in the House of Commons. It will be ready very soon. Meanwhile the B.B.C. orchestra will play *The Serenade to an Ass.*" McNiven, who was a sniper in the first world war and who blamed Mr. Chamberlain for everything, laughed and sneered.

I listened in to both Mr. Chamberlain and Lord Halifax. Even now I can hear the sepulchral voice of the then Foreign Secretary intoning the same old arguments: "There is no question, no dispute which cannot be settled at the council table." The hour for meetings was long past. I felt no violent bitterness against Mr. Chamberlain or against the City magnates who supported and gave strength to his policy of appeasement. I had no doubt that they acted honestly for their best.

There was, in fact, nothing immoral in the word appeasement which to many had now become a term of abuse. Appeasement is the proper function of diplomacy, and if Munich had given fifty years of peace to Europe it would have won general approval. Where Mr. Chamberlain erred grievously was in pursuing a policy which in the opinion of his proper advisers was bound to fail. That was immoral. But few of us, I felt, were guiltless. Too many of us had pursued a tortuous course of zigzags which prescribed aggressiveness when war seemed remote and cooed appeasement when Mars was on the doorstep.

After the first world war hate lasted too long. We did little or nothing to support the Weimar Republic. At the best our efforts were but half-measures. Then after allowing Germany to rearm, we had fallen over backwards to appease. Now the Germans were saying: "When we were weak you spat on us; all that we have gained has been won by the strength of our strong German right arm."

During the last few days of August rumour in Tomintoul ran riot, and the visitors were in constant conference. One morning a former high Colonial administrator packed his bags, ordered his car and drove away. The rest followed like sheep. By the end of August the hotels were almost empty.

The village, however, was full. The Army, Navy and Air Force reserves had been called up. The children were being evacuated from Glasgow and Edinburgh, and Tomintoul was expecting a large contingent. The farmers from the outlying districts were flocking in to seek news, and the village square was full of sturdy silent men who, when they had anything to say, spoke gravely and slowly in their soft Highland speech. McNiven and the local policeman were busy arranging the distribution of gas-masks and of black-out material.

For myself I had no special problem to solve. I had received several telephone messages from the Foreign Office. They were unimportant. Could I recommend a suitable press attaché for Sofia? All that mattered was that I was to remain where I was until I received my instructions. They might not come for several days after the declaration of war. I felt resigned and relieved that my course of life would now be determined for me.

On Friday September 1, we received the news of Germany's attack on Poland, and I expected our declaration of war at any moment. The Saturday was my birthday and the anniversary of my arrest by the Bolshevik Government in 1918. Altogether it was a date of bloody anniversaries: of Napoleon's entry into Moscow, of Sedan, of Omdurman. It ought to have been the date of the beginning of the second world war, but our declaration was delayed by the last-minute hesitations of the French Government. At noon Colonel Oliver Haig, a nephew of the Field Marshal and the owner of the great deer-forest of Inchrory nine miles up the river Avon from Tomintoul, came into the hotel. He seemed dazed and looked suddenly very old. He asked McNiven and me if we would like to fish his stretch of the Avon.

I looked at McNiven. He had much to do. There was a shortage of black-out material in the village; yet the orders were that no lights were to be showing after 9 p.m. The refugee children had begun to arrive. "Mac" hesitated for a minute which seemed like an hour to me. Finally he said with Highland gravity and Highland imprecision: "It may be for the last time."

We set out at once. When we reached the river, we separated, and I went far above him up the lonely glen. A hundred years ago some four hundred people, including forty of my Macgregor ancestors, inhabited these nine miles of valley. Now the only residents were Colonel Haig and his keepers. More than the ravages of war, emigration, taking the best sons of successive generations, had drained the Highland glens of their life-blood.

The river-side was lined with silver birches and rowan-trees already heavy with their blood-red berries, the accepted Celtic presage of a hard winter. The day, however, was suffocatingly hot, the atmosphere as still as death, the sky overcast and the air surcharged with electricity. As I walked, I could hear the tramp of my heavy, nailed boots echo against the granite rocks of the river. Conditions for fishing were hopeless, for the water was low and crystal-clear and the few salmon to be seen lay listlessly at the bottom of the river-bed.

I lit a pipe, sat down on a grassy bank and let my fancy wander. I thought of Romilly Fedden, a sensitive painter, who, hating militarism, enlisted at forty and fought in France all through the first world war. In the trenches he wrote what I think is the greatest o fall fishing books. It was called *Golden Days*. The prologue, I remembered, began with the words: "B.E.F., France, 1918. Today I have fished again in France." I thought of my own fishing adventures in Europe. After the war of 1914–1918 I was the first British subject to fish the Bavarian Semt. But during that war Roger Casement, who was then conspiring with the Germans and organising an Irish battalion to fight against us, stole a day from his sinister activities to spend a few hours by its quiet waters and landed a four-pound trout. I reflected on the waywardness of human nature. Was what Fedden said true: that no man who likes fishing could be wholly bad? I wondered if I should ever fish in Europe again.

In the enveloping solitude of the glen I found peace of mind. My own selfish ambitions and desires were now of no importance. Middle age had only duties to perform. The sacrifices would be made by youth. I thought of my only son who was not yet twenty, of my brothers' sons who were well-known athletes, of the splendid young cadets that I had seen at Cranwell. As I sat, I heard the whirr of an aeroplane engine through the clouds. It was, of course, one of ours, but it brought with it the stark realisation that even these Highland glens were no longer safe from the range of civilised man's capacity to destroy himself.

The sky now looked menacing with great banks of black closing in from the hidden mountains. Fearing a cloud-burst, I went off to look for McNiven. I found him playing a twenty-pound salmon. When he had landed it, we sat down by the water's edge to watch the storm which passed without breaking. Hoping for better conditions we stayed late until the moon, big and full, came out in a clear star-lit sky. Then "Mac" abandoned hope. "No good in this light," he said gloomily, and we turned for home. All the way down the tor-tuous road the moonbeams cast their incandescent light on the giant granite boulders, on the trees and steep banks, and on the swiftly running water, turning the whole valley into a fairy-like grotto peopled with strange fantastic shapes and spirits. It was a satisfying farewell.

On the Sunday the rain came down pitilessly from a leaden Scot-tish sky. At ten in the morning I went into McNiven's room to wait for the news from the B.B.C. I had no doubt what it would be. But there were irksome delays during which a saraband was played. Then came an irritating peal of bells, clamant and joyful as though celebrating victory. I kept my eyes fixed on a painting on the wall opposite me. It was a pleasant water-colour of a deserted croft with the cone-pointed peak of Ben Rinnes in the background. Twice a mournful voice interrupted the music to bid us: "Stand by for an important announcement." Then more clanging of bells, and finally the news which everyone expected. At 11 a.m. we should be at war with Germany. It was the end—and the beginning.

Before luncheon the village recruits came in to say goodbye. Their new uniforms were dank with rain. I ordered drinks, and we drank soberly and gravely. The young men were more interested in what they were fighting for than in whisky. They wanted to know if they had what they called "got it right". A young bank clerk was their spokesman. Fiddling with his wet cap, he explained in halting jerks how the village lads saw the future. The war would be no joy-ride. There was no one who would not sooner be at home. If it was to be a war for the landed proprietors and big financiers, it would be better to stay at home. Perhaps it would end that way. They could not tell. But one thing was clear; there could be no hope of peace for anyone so long as the Germans kept on interfering with other people's lives. So there was a job that had to be done. Did I see it that way too?

I agreed with them. For a long time my faith in the new youth had been strong. I felt, too, that their instinct was sounder than the floundering calculations of the professional politicians. We should win this war, with God's grace, with the help of good government and, if necessary, in spite of bad government. It would be a different war from that of 1914; there would be different motives of personal conduct and a more sober realisation of ultimate responsibilities. But the war would be fought by the same British people who change their characteristics more slowly than other races. Scotland would again do her part. These village lads were the living symbol of the continuity of a race which had never shrunk from hardship.

We shook hands, and they went out into the friendless rain.

Three days later I received my own instructions and left at once for the South.

BOOK II
CZECHOSLOVAKIAN ODYSSEY

"INDIVIDUALS NEVER RISE to greater heights or sink to lower depths than in a violated and calumniated nation. However wretched life may be in an atmosphere of threats, violence and reprisals, it bears within it a strain of nobleness and grandeur which is not attained by a prosperous life or a life of brute force." JOSEF ČAPEK

*(written in a concentration camp
shortly before his death)*

CHAPTER ONE

I REPORTED TO the Foreign Office four days after the outbreak of war and was informed that I should not be wanted until the tenth of September. Glad of the respite which I believed, foolishly of course, would enable me to put my private affairs in order, I went out into the streets to study London at war. The weather was hot and sultry; there was some decline in the traffic; many people were carrying gas-masks. But there was less outward change than I had imagined; far less, in fact, than in Tomintoul. I strolled up to Piccadilly Circus and had my shoes brushed by the shoe-black whose stand is outside the Pavilion and whom I have known now for close on twenty years. We exchanged impressions. I told him that London seemed much the same; that there were as many people and much the same kind of people as in peace time. He corrected me: "There is more change than you think. Three out of every four persons in the Circus today are foreigners—mostly Germans." My mind flashed back to the spy mania of 1914. Doubtless, this would revive.

Mechanically I noted the faces of the passers-by. They seemed list-less and apathetic. Going to my club, I found it fuller than usual. The bar was crowded; drink flowed more freely than ever. But there was a graver tone and more reserve in the general conversation, and many men made no secret of their view that the war would be the end of their world. Neither in the streets nor in the clubs was there any enthusiasm. This was the big difference from August, 1914. The soberness of the general attitude impressed me; it seemed to my temperamental Celtic nature to denote that unquestioning deter-mination which in times of crisis brings out the best qualities of the English race. Yet, although it did not so strike me then, what I took for fixity of purpose may perhaps have been only the mental torpor of uncertainty and the presage of the period of "phoneyness". A people hating war and divided by a policy of appeasement could not be brought to the full force of their united strength in one short week. The English had to be hit hard before they could be roused.

In my club I found a mass of letters waiting for me. Among them was a letter in circular form from the new Ministry of Information. It was addressed to Captain (!) R. H. Bruce Lockhart. It said that I was one of those authors whose services might be useful in war-time. It *ordered* me not to undertake other war-work without con-

53

sulting the Ministry; it requested me to forward a list of my qualifications. The new bureaucracy was at work. Having been "signed on" by the Foreign Office in September, 1938, I felt suitably humbled.

The next day *The Times* published a list of the Advisory Council and senior staff of the new Ministry. It gave me a rude shock. The personnel, with the exception of Sir Eric Drummond, now Lord Perth, contained almost no one who knew anything about Europe. It was easy to foresee trouble and chaos. The truth is that the Ministry had been organised by the men of Munich. Those who should have done the job and who, indeed, began it—men like Lord Lloyd and Rex Leeper—had been ousted.

That afternoon I went to see Lady Rosslyn. While we were having tea, a telegram arrived. It announced briefly that her grandson, Peter Erskine, had been killed while trying out a Spitfire at Northolt. He had just left Eton.

On Sunday, September 10, I received my instructions about my war job in the revived Political Intelligence Department of the Foreign Office. I learnt with relief and apprehension that we were to be quartered in the country: with relief because everyone expected London to be bombed, with some apprehension because I could not understand how an intelligence department could function efficiently fifty miles away from the centre of all intelligence. I took the afternoon train to Dunstable where I was met by my new chief, Rex Leeper. We drove off in a car, and on the way he explained to me our destination and the nature of my work. We were going to a small house on the Duke of Bedford's estate at Woburn. We ourselves were not a secret department, but we had to be near Woburn because Leeper had been appointed Foreign Office adviser to a secret propaganda organisation which was lodged in the ducal abbey. The Political Intelligence Department, known afterwards as the "Pids" or P.I.D., was beginning to assemble.

Leeper had collected experts for each country or group of countries. I was to deal with Central Europe and the Balkans with the exception of Germany and Austria. My countries were therefore Czechoslovakia, Hungary, Yugoslavia, Bulgaria, Rumania, Greece and Turkey. My main tasks would be to prepare special memoranda for the Foreign Office and to write a weekly review of my countries for a secret Political Summary which would bear the Foreign Office cachet. The Summary, Leeper hoped, would serve as official guidance to other departments and would thus prevent a repetition of the multiplicity of contradictory political reports which caused so much muddle and confusion during the first world war. In order to carry out my task I should have to work very closely with the Southern and Central Departments of the Foreign Office and to maintain regular relations with the embassies and legations of the countries which had been allotted to me.

After half an hour we arrived at Foxgrove, a small red-brick villa situated close to one of the gates of Woburn Park. Here I found E. L. Woodward, the Oxford historian, George Martelli, and Christopher Warner of the Foreign Office. Woodward was to be our German expert and Martelli, who had written a book on the Mediterranean, was in charge of Italy. Warner, whom I had known before, was to be Leeper's Foreign Office assistant and to act for him in his absence. Later, we were to have quite a formidable array of talent including Sir Kinahan Cornwallis, the famous Oxford quarter-miler and half-miler and a well-known expert on the Middle East. At present, however, we had no accommodation for more than a tiny nucleus, and when I was shown my room my face fell. It was an attic at the top of the house and had not even a chest of drawers.

At Foxgrove the atmosphere was very different from that of London. Rex Leeper had been a resolute opponent of Munich, and our department contained no "guilty men". We all felt frustrated by our lack of preparation and irritated by our inability to help the unfortunate Poles. Telegrams were pouring in from our ambassador in Warsaw requesting to know how he was to explain our inactivity to the Polish Government. We were dropping leaflets instead of bombs. The propaganda organisation next door to us was already in action, but I think that even the most rabid pamphleteer felt the futility of leaflets at this stage of the war. The propaganda organisation was protected by the iron curtain of secrecy, but the Ministry of Information, over-staffed and inexperienced, was already under a fire of criticism, and stories of its incompetence were rife. Doubtless, many were invented by the journalists, but there was truth enough to illustrate the initial chaos.

In these early days an enterprising American correspondent went to the Ministry and sought permission to translate and publish the leaflets which we were dropping over Germany. The Ministry official, unwilling to offend an American, hesitated. He was afraid, he said, that there might be difficulties. Finally, being pressed to give a reason for his refusal, he murmured blandly: "Well, you see, they might fall into German hands."

Requests and refusals to publish leaflets were to continue until the end of the war. I had an open mind on the subject, but the Cabinet maintained the ban on the ground that publication would provoke acute controversy in the House of Commons and that Goebbels would make propaganda capital out of the criticisms and suggestions. There was some force in the argument. The whole country was divided on the question of a "hard line" or a "soft line" to the Germans in our propaganda, and, wisely in the beginning, if perhaps not so wisely towards the end, Mr. Churchill never allowed the subject to be debated. The propagandists themselves had little say in the matter. In war-time, propaganda is the handmaid of strategy and foreign policy and has to conform to official rulings.

My impressions of the first day at Woburn are clearly imprinted on my memory. They formed a gradual declension to pessimism ending in a night of gloom. Towards evening Leeper took me for a stroll in the ducal park. It was like the paradise parks described in Xenophon's *Anabasis*: pleasantly undulating, with smooth grass rides between the great oaks, lakes on which every variety of water-bird were swimming, partridges and pheasants in such profusion that one almost stumbled over them, and hares, so fat and sleek from the rich, lush grass that they were scarcely able to move. Hundreds of deer swarmed at large. They had been carefully selected and contained several rare types including the only European specimens of the Père Davids. There were also rheas—small South American ostriches which looked peaceful enough but which, if approached too closely, were capable of giving a powerful backward kick, while in the shrubberies little Javanese muntjaks nibbled the rhododendrons and exposed their ridiculous behinds to the passers-by.

In a special field were kept the pride of Woburn, the almost extinct aurochs of which until the war the only existing herd was in White Russia. When I went later to visit Whipsnade, Mr. Julian Huxley told me that the aurochs were long extinct and that the animals at Woburn were the rare European bison. But I liked to think of them as aurochs and to recall the great scene in Sienkiewicz's *Quo Vadis* in which Ursus, the slave, saves the lives of himself and his Christian friends by wrestling with an aurochs in the gladiatorial arena and breaking its neck. As an outdoor game reserve Woburn was far more attractive than Whipsnade because the animals had no confinements and virtually no keepers. Later, the wags of the Foreign Office were to christen us "the tenants of Whipsnade".

Assuredly no surroundings could have been more pleasant. But when I went to bed, gloom descended on me. I could not sleep. In the first world war the Political Intelligence Department had been housed in the Foreign Office building. It had been under the direct control of Lord Tyrrell, whose counsels carried weight not only with the Foreign Secretary but also in the Cabinet. In this new war we were on the circumference instead of in the centre of events, and plain Scottish reason told me that distance from London meant divorce from the Foreign Office. Nor could I see how I was to fit into this circle of intellectuals. All my official life had been spent out of England, and any contribution that I could make to the war was as an observer of the foreign scene. Of all people it seemed to me that I was the least fitted to be a cog in a bureaucratic machine. It overwhelmed me by the chaos of its swollen vastness. Thousands of other temporary civil servants and come-backs must have felt as I felt. I resolved to take the first suitable opportunity of applying to be sent abroad.

Presently, however, order began to emerge. Within a week our department moved from Foxgrove to Marylands, a modern house on the other side of Woburn Park. It had been built by the Duchess of Bedford as a nursing-home, was well-equipped and comfortable, and stood alone close to the road from which it was guarded by an Alpine rock-garden. Otherwise its charms were as cold as its corridors, but behind the house there were fields and woods with pleasant walks. I had a bedroom to myself which also served as my study. Very soon I organised my life into two separate and contradictory sections. At Marylands I lived a communal existence, rose early, made my own tea, and did most of my written work before breakfast. The rest of the day was spent in meetings, in planning, and in endless discussions of the war situation. I lived frugally, took daily exercise, and kept myself reasonably fit. As I had so many countries to deal with, I had to spend more time in London than my colleagues. I therefore took a permanent room at my club and divided my week into three and a half days in London and three and a half at Marylands. The contrast was considerable but not unsatisfactory. In London I made my weekly round of the Balkan ministers, called at the Foreign Office to exchange information, and lunched and dined out every day. At Marylands I repaired the ravages of late hours and gastronomic irregularity by a régime of ascetic simplicity.

I enjoyed my visits to the Balkan Ministers who, eager for scraps of inside information, gave freely of their own. M. Tilea, the Rumanian Minister, entertained sumptuously, had one of the best chefs in London, and was an entertainment in himself, being intelli-

c

gent, quick-witted, extremely frank and emotionally temperamental. He was and, in spite of a cruel fate, remains very pro-British. King Carol—and it was to be a disadvantage to M. Tilea—had no more devoted friend. M. Simopoulos, the Greek, was a courteous and cautious diplomatist of the old school but was already a tired and sick man when the war started. Even more canny was M. Subotić, the Yugoslav, who had, I felt, little faith in Britain's ability to win through or, to be strictly fair, in our power to help his country. The cleverest was M. Aras, the Turkish Ambassador, who even then regarded Russia as the key to the final solution and was on the best of terms with M. Maisky, the Russian Ambassador. The steadiest and the soundest was M. Momtchilov, the Bulgarian Minister. Of the five he was, I think, the only one who never had the slightest doubt of our ultimate victory. From the beginning of the war he was frankly and openly on our side and, when Bulgaria threw in her lot with the Germans, he resigned his post and remained in this country.

Establishing good relations with the Foreign Office was a much more difficult matter. The superintending under-secretaries of the two departments, the Southern and the Central, which controlled my work, were Sir Orme Sargent and Sir (then Mr.) William Strang. My previous knowledge of both men was slight, but very soon I realised that they took a cold view of a Foreign Office department which was situated in the heart, not of Whitehall, but of Bedfordshire. Sargent, indeed, was almost brutally frank. If we came back to London, we could do an increasingly important job. If we stayed where we were, we must expect to be out of touch. I felt, too, that I myself was on trial. With my past Russian record I was regarded as a dangerous person. The Foreign Office is masonic in the secrecy of its mysteries. It has the advantages and the defects of every close corporation. Towards the uninitiated it maintains a polite reserve. When it has tested and accepted the neophyte, it opens its arms—and its secret files. Its security is the strictest and best in Whitehall.

Perturbed by Sargent's advice which seemed to me the plainest common sense, I went to consult Harold Nicolson who in the years between the two wars had abandoned his official career for the pleasanter but more uncertain pottage of freedom. He gave me wise counsel. In war, he said, temporary departments like the P.I.D. must begin slowly and must expect rebuffs and frustration. We should take a long-term view. There was much work which the permanent departments, fully engaged in day to day activities, could never undertake. There was our chance. With patience we could become a centre of usefulness long before the end of the war. We should not worry, but should go slow.

It was, I realise today, sound advice. But Harold himself was perturbed by the state of the war, which was going as badly as possible, with Poland being over-run both by the Germans and the Russians and with little or no effective counter-activity by France and Britain. He saw no hope of victory under the Chamberlain Government. He was, he told me, a member of a small but important political group which met regularly and whose ultimate object was to replace Mr. Chamberlain by Mr. Churchill. The country, he said, was becoming increasingly incensed by the lack of thrust in our conduct of the war. Leaflets were no substitute for bombs, and all our propaganda organisations, including the Ministry of Information, were under a heavy fire of criticism. The truth of this last statement was speedily confirmed. On leaving Harold, I bought a copy of the *Evening Standard*. It contained a cartoon by Low showing a very efficient Goebbels in a broadcasting studio and a Colonel Blimp with a toy balloon. The explanatory text was:

"The Worst Cause in the World and the Best Propaganda!
The Best Cause in the World and the Worst Propaganda!"

I make no defence of our propaganda at this stage. But the plain truth is that propaganda is, or should be, always easy for the winning side and always difficult for the losing side. Low's point, therefore, was scarcely fair. That it reflected the feeling of the public at that moment is beyond doubt.

I pondered over Harold's advice, decided to take it, and went back to Marylands. Then I had a great stroke of luck. On my arrival Leeper met me with a smiling face and informed me that on his recommendation the Foreign Office had agreed to my being their liaison officer with Dr. Beneš and the Czechoslovaks in Great Britain. This new job, Leeper explained, was to be in addition to my existing functions as a member of the Political Intelligence Department. I could do all that was necessary for the Czechs during my three and a half days in London. Progress was bound to be slow, he said, because the Czechoslovaks were not in favour and were not regarded as very important.

Although the prospects did not sound encouraging, I accepted the offer with gratitude. Now, at any rate, I had an active political job as well as my academic intelligence work.

CHAPTER TWO

IT WAS FORTUNATE for me that, whatever my faults, lack of enthusiasm is not one of them. I like difficulties, they rarely fail to stir my erratic energies. My job with the Czechoslovaks was to be perhaps the most difficult of my career and was to put a severe strain on my reserves of patience, obstinacy, and restraint. For, strange as it may appear, the position of the Czechoslovaks at the outbreak of the war was a tragic illustration of the dislike that men feel for those whom they have wronged. The attitude of the British Government was cold and careful; that of the French Government almost sinister. The men of Munich had to find a scapegoat, and Dr. Beneš was the obvious choice. There was no proper central Czechoslovak organisation. The French Government was backing M. Osusky, the Czechoslovak Minister in Paris, against Dr. Beneš. The British Government was bent on placating the French Government which itself included appeasers of Germany. The British Foreign Office never obtrudes its internal differences on the public, but it is no secret that on the subject of Munich it was divided. In the autumn of 1939 it was not geared to action, it carried caution to excess and it was preoccupied with the post-war consequences of a war which not only had not been won but was not even being fought. The Central Department which dealt with Czechoslovakia had not a single Slav expert among its personnel. The Poles, who a year before had been stigmatised for their rape of Teschen, were now the heroes of the hour. The Czechoslovaks were severely cold-shouldered, and both in France and in Britain the same politicians who at the time of Munich had ordered them not to fight now blamed them for pusillanimity and subservience.

The shock to the unfortunate Czechoslovaks was shattering. Wittingly or unwittingly, France, with the British Government lagging behind, seemed to be doing what was best calculated to spread dissension and despair among potential allies. Fortunately, the Czechoslovaks possessed leaders who were proof against despair.

My first act in my indefinite position of liaison officer was to go to Westminster Gardens to see Jan Masaryk and to arrange with him for my first official visit to Dr. Beneš. I had to wait for a quarter of an hour. Jan was at our Foreign Office with Dr. Beneš who was seeing Lord Halifax. It was the first time that the Czechoslovak President, who was still called President by his supporters, but not by the French and us, had been received by a member of the British Cabinet since Munich. There were to be singularly few similar contacts until Mr. Churchill became Prime Minister.

While I waited, I noticed two things in Jan's flat that I had not seen before. On the wall to the right of the door was a scroll conferring on him the honorary degree of Doctor of Civil Law from the University of California. Above his desk was another scroll with a red border and the following letter-press printed in bold characters:

"In resigning your post keep *early* in mind. When you are no longer fit to hold a position, do not be tempted by avarice or pride to continue in it, but rather retire while your energies are still active. When meritorious services have led to fame, it is time to follow the heavenly rule and retire into obscurity. If you do not resign in time, you will not only lose your fame, but being unable longer to perform your duties adequately, you will also betray your trust."

LAO-TSE, 604 B.C.

A weakness of our modern state is that this sound advice is rarely followed either by the politicians or the bureaucrats. Resignation was very much in Jan's mind at this time, but with his country under the heel of the German oppressor he would and could never quit his post. When he arrived, he told me that he had just cancelled a most lucrative contract for a lecture and broadcasting tour in the United States. Our business was quickly despatched. Dr. Beneš would receive me the next afternoon. Then Jan gave me a photograph of himself and his Aberdeen terrier, Gillie, as a memento of Munich.

With the gift came the story of Gillie's contribution to history. When Henlein, the leader of Hitler's Fifth Column in Czechoslovakia, came to England in 1938, he was received and entertained by several prominent Englishmen. He also asked for an appointment with Jan Masaryk. At the agreed hour he arrived at the Czechoslovak Legation together with a bruiser who was an obvious Gestapo agent. Both men were shown into Jan's study, and Henlein introduced his companion who, he said, was always present at his interviews. Jan smiled and, arranging four chairs round a table, said in his pleasantest manner: "If you are to be two to one, you won't object, I take it, if I bring in my representative." Henlein agreed. Jan opened the door and whistled. In trotted Gillie and took his place on the chair beside Jan.

Later in the war Henlein was to boast how he had fooled the

English, and in the last days of Germany's collapse he was to take his own life. But to do him justice, he had a sense of humour and accepted Gillie's presence with good grace. Doubtless, he made the mistake of thinking Jan a buffoon.

The next afternoon, in warm, sultry weather, I drove out to Putney to visit Dr. Beneš. He was living in one of a long row of stereotyped red-brick suburban villas in Gwendolen Avenue. The name of the street seemed incongruous in connexion with a man who has nothing feminine in his character, whose habits are those of an ascetic and whose only holiday is a change of work. I noticed, however, that there was a Disraeli Street just round the corner. The little villa was simply but pleasantly furnished, and into it Madame Beneš had brought some of the atmosphere of Prague. In the tiny drawing-room downstairs there were some modern Czech pictures and an attractive water-colour portraying the Hrad and St. Vitus's cathedral. Neatly arranged on a small table were leather-bound pocket editions of Czech poets and of the works of Comenius and Hus. On the top of a writing bureau there was a fine oblong cigarette box with the hammer and sickle embossed on it. The box had been presented to Madame Beneš by the Russians. I noticed with some interest that the sickle was broken. At that time the attitude of Russia was an enigma and a disappointment to most British people, and I was reminded that, only a day or two before, our propagandists had shown me a new design for the Russian flag in which the sickle had been deliberately transformed into a question mark.

After waiting a few minutes I was taken upstairs to Dr. Beneš's study for the first of the conversations which I was to have with him weekly until he returned to his own country in 1945. I found him well, much better, in fact, than when he arrived in England after Munich on October 22, 1938, having had to depart so secretly by aeroplane that when he landed at Croydon there was no one to meet him. Now he was full of his normal vigour which exceeds that of all but the most super-normal of men. He was disappointed by the attitude of the British and French Governments, but he was not depressed. It is the great and sometimes dangerous virtue of Eduard Beneš that he never gives way to pessimism. In a long war it was to stand his country and his countrymen in good stead, for even in the darkest days his faith in ultimate victory and in the restoration of Czechoslovakia never faltered.

He gave me a graphic account of the Munich crisis and of his personal troubles. The Agrarian Party had been angry with him and believed that Germany was master of Europe and would hold Czechoslovakia for fifty years. It was, therefore, madness, they said, not to collaborate. The Slovaks took much the same line. The French Government, on whom he had pinned his faith, had been very nasty to him and had tried to blacken him in the eyes of his own country-men. He therefore decided to resign, come to England, and begin again the struggle for independence which he had waged so success-fully in the first world war. Before he left, he had held a private meeting of the leading Czechs. He had told them that war was cer-tain, that it had begun, in fact, with the murder of Dollfuss, and that the Allies would win. The old Maffia, the Czechoslovak Secret Society of the first world war, must be revived at once. Before his departure he had formed the nucleus of a subversive organisation with secret cells and secret communications.

His country, he said, had been humiliated by the Munich agree-ment. The army, better mechanised than any other army in Europe except the German army, had wanted to fight. Inevitably the people had reacted against the French and the British. But they were sound at heart, and now all their hopes had been given fresh life by the war. Since March, 1938, he told me, scores of leading Czechs had been smuggled out of the country with the loyal help of peasants and workers. Many had been brought across the frontier disguised as railwaymen.

His conversation was, as almost always, factual and entirely un-emotional. Each point was marshalled in its proper place and, when dealt with, was marked off on his fingers. He himself showed no trace of bitterness. Indeed, he paid a generous tribute to those English-men who had helped him when, broken and destitute, he first reached England. He spoke warmly of Lord Cranborne who had offered him a house and had written him a noble letter, and of Sir Walter Layton who had put funds at his disposal. He inquired eagerly about the prospects of Mr. Churchill and Mr. Eden, for it was on these two men that he had always counted. One of my treasured possessions today is a *Hansard* of the Munich debate. The speeches of Mr. Churchill and Mr. Eden are marked with pencil-lines in the margin. The book was given to me by Dr. Beneš when we had again recognised him as President. Before then, I do not know how often it was produced and put before my eyes in order to point a moral and illustrate a sorry story of delay.

The delays, indeed, were vexatious and unnecessary, for the needs of the Czechs were great. Dr. Beneš wanted and required Allied support to enable him to rouse and maintain the spirit of resistance in his own country. Conversely, the cancellation of Munich and the recognition of Dr. Beneš himself were essential in order to restore the lost confidence in France and Britain of the home Czechs. There was, too, an almost complete lack of funds to maintain the considerable number of Czechoslovak exiles whom Dr. Beneš had gathered round him in England. The total sum available was only twenty thousand dollars; it had been given, not by the French and British Governments, but by the loyal Czechoslovaks in the United States. If I could help him to obtain a loan or a credit and some form of Allied recognition, Dr. Beneš would be grateful. As he stated his requirements, I was impressed by the clear thinking of this remarkable little man.

In the course of my life I have met many political exiles. There is an element of truth in Karl Marx's declaration during his own period of exile in London, that *émigré* life is "a school of scandal and of meanness". My own view is that exile brings out either the best or the worst in a man. It certainly brought out the best in Eduard Beneš. He was now in exile for the second time in his career; yet his faith was undiminished, his patience without limit and his capacity for planning tireless and unremitting. He knew and made no concealment of his knowledge that he had enemies both in France and in Britain. The son of a small farmer, he was never quite at his ease in the presence of certain English Conservatives who, he felt, regarded him as a demagogue and anti-capitalist. During these early and difficult stages of the war I once asked Jan Masaryk for some details of Dr. Beneš's career as a football-player. Jan told me that he had been very good and that, until he broke his leg, he was perhaps the fastest outside left that Bohemia had ever produced. Then he added quickly: "Please don't tell that to your Foreign Office; they'll make a silly joke about it."

It was true that in our Foreign Office there were high officials who were suspicious of Dr. Beneš and who thought him too clever. Yet most of them had never met him or, at best, knew him only very slightly. Admittedly, Eduard Beneš is a difficult man to know well, for his mind is machine-like in its compact tidiness and his reserve is almost impenetrable. But I have been in intimate relationship with him for more than a quarter of a century. I have dealt with him on the most delicate public and personal matters, and I have never known him to break a confidence or fail to carry out a promise.

The British Foreign Office rightly condemns enthusiasm in its servants and, as foreign policy is mainly concerned with the promotion and defence of British interests, it frowns on anything that it chooses to call prejudice. This does not mean that the Foreign Office itself is free from prejudice. What it dislikes are prejudices which do not conform with its own. In 1918 I was labelled a pro-Bolshevik because I opposed the policy of intervention. Now I was suspected of being more Czech than the Czechs. The label appealed to my sense of humour. It also roused my fighting instincts. The Czechoslovaks, I thought, might be mobilised to form a fifth column against Germany. Their geographical position gave added importance to any form of active or even passive resistance that they could show. Although it is a fundamental characteristic of British foreign policy never to commit this country in advance, in total war one must back one's friends and confound one's enemies. Hoping for a Churchill Government, I made up my mind that, if I had to stay in England, I must do my best to obtain recognition for our Czechoslovak friends. If I had a secret ambition in the war, it was that I might be permitted to go back to Prague with President Beneš on the day of liberation.

As I was taking my leave of the President, Madame Beneš came into the room. She had been greatly affected by the fate of her country and sorrow had shaken her nerves. The last time we had met had been in Prague, and with the revival of old memories her eyes filled with tears. She is a gentle and most noble woman and has been, at all times, a wonderful wife to her husband. When they were married, she was comfortably off in her own right. In the first world war she gave every penny of her private fortune to the Czechoslovak independence movement. Although the Austrians imprisoned her in a common jail together with prostitutes and thieves, bitterness has never crossed her lips, nor have I ever heard her make an ungenerous remark about anyone.

The next day the London newspapers printed a sensational story of a rising in Czechoslovakia with large head-lines about rebellion and revolt. Alas! the news was false or grotesquely exaggerated, and the London Czechs, who were then in hourly touch with their compatriots in Czechoslovakia, were bitter, for had they been consulted by the newspapers, they could have contradicted the rumour. The need for closer co-ordination was glaring, but we were to make further blunders before our conduct of the war became efficient. Indeed, lacking a proper lead from the Government, the people of Britain had not yet appreciated the implications of total warfare. In certain political and official circles there were scarcely concealed symptoms of discontent and murmurings of "Chamberlain must go". But appeasement was not yet scotched, and the attitude of the Left-Wing intellectuals during this period was aptly described in a letter to the *New Statesman* from J. Maynard Keynes, himself a director of that newspaper. Dated October 14, 1939, the letter ran:

"The intelligentsia of the Left were the loudest in demanding that the Nazi aggression should be resisted at all costs. When it comes to a showdown, scarce four weeks have passed before they remember that they are pacifists and write defeatist letters to your columns, leaving the defence of freedom and of civilisation to Colonel Blimp and the Old School Tie, for whom Three Cheers."

The letter reflected accurately the confused state of public opinion in the early weeks of the war.

CHAPTER THREE

THE SO-CALLED "PHONEY" period of the war dealt many staggering blows to British pride. The collapse of the Poles whose courage was no substitute for the lack of tanks and aeroplanes was a bitter disappointment, and the Russian occupation of Eastern Poland and of the Baltic States increased the prevailing nervousness. The Ribbentrop-Molotov Pact seemed to be working, and in that autumn of 1939 there were many Englishmen who believed that Russia would come in on Germany's side in order to end the war quickly.

Pro-Russian feeling in Britain was then at a low ebb, and even those Englishmen who were convinced that Stalin could not welcome a German victory held another and possibly accurate view of Russia's intentions. The Russians, they argued, were obsessed with the suspicion that the British and French Governments had intended to appease Hitler by allowing him a free hand in Eastern Europe. In other words, if he attacked Russia, France and Britain would remain neutral. It was a characteristic of Russian policy to meet a thrust of this nature with a riposte in kind. The Russians had therefore struck first by giving Hitler a free hand in the West. Their motive was not to help the Germans to become the masters of Europe. The Russians, so our experts argued, had made a not improbable calculation that France and Britain would hold their own against Germany and Italy. Whoever won the final victory, the war would be long and both sides would be exhausted. In the end Russia, by keeping out of the struggle, would be the strongest Power in Europe. At the same time she was taking no chances and was using the respite of neutrality in order to complete her own rearmament. By occupying the Baltic States and part of Poland, Russia was clearly seizing vantage points and pushing a potential enemy farther back from Moscow. It was an argument which had few loop-holes for refutation. It brought little comfort to the British of whom even those who hoped most from Russia had only the vaguest idea of her military strength or of her capacity for resistance.

Meanwhile, the inactivity of the French and British armed forces had a depressing effect on morale. The early hopes of the neutrals, all of whom except Spain dreaded a German victory, were quickly dissolved, and Allied prestige fell heavily. Even in Britain, feeling throughout the country was not good. The censorship, which afterwards worked most efficiently under the guidance of Sir Cyril

Radcliffe and Admiral Thompson, was then clumsy and inept, and the public received no explanation of our failure to help Poland. My own friends, who admittedly were opponents of Mr. Chamberlain and of Munich, were very critical of the Government. There were, they told me, pacifists in the House of Commons. Vernon Bartlett, who in 1938 had won Bridgewater as an independent progressive by his attack on the foreign policy of the Government, told me that at this time he was receiving pacifist letters from his constituents. Hitler's peace offer after the defeat of Poland was not entirely without effect, and the belief that, if Hitler were replaced by Goering, we could come to terms with Germany was held even in high places. Worse still was the official boycott of men like Lord Lloyd, a potential war leader of Churchillian calibre, who was then breaking his heart and sapping his health and valuable energy as Chairman of the British Council.

In a murky sky there were one or two bright patches. I listened in to Mr. Churchill's first broadcast. Providence, which is supposed to be on the side of the big battalions, was kind to the unprepared Allies, for it gave them in Mr. Churchill and President Roosevelt two natural geniuses of the microphone. Of Mr. Roosevelt I shall have more to say. Mr. Churchill's first broadcast may not have been his greatest effort, but it was a foretaste of better things to come and it gave the country the spark of action that it needed and which, indeed, it wanted. It received a warm welcome in the United States where the Press hailed it with such superlatives as "worth a battery of artillery". During the war Mr. Churchill took only a spasmodic interest in propaganda. "This is a war of deeds and not of words," he used to growl. It was, I recognise, fair comment. The talks of other politicians were only words, but every one of his early war speeches was a deed.

Another healthy sign of these dark days was the huge sale of Harold Nicolson's Penguin *Why Britain is at War*. He wrote it in twelve days. I went to see him on the day he sent it to the printers. He was a little perturbed lest it might be banned because he had been so outspoken in his criticisms. I asked him if he had made a personal attack on individual ministers.

"Oh no," he replied, "only on their policy."

"What did you write?" I asked.

"I just said that Chamberlain and Horace Wilson went into foreign affairs like two curates entering a 'pub' for the first time. They mistook a rough-house for a Sunday school."

I laughed and felt better. The core of the country was better than its political skin. Nearly everywhere I went during those early months I heard the same remark: "The British people will win this war in spite of their Government."

My own work was strenuous and followed a routine pattern. The two thousand words which I wrote for the weekly Intelligence Summary was a regular contribution which had to be approved by the Foreign Office political departments and delivered at a fixed time. I did not dislike the hard work or the difficulties, but I never took kindly to the humdrum vexations of departmental life. I never had been and never should make a good bureaucrat. My main task, I felt, was with the Czechoslovaks, and I devoted most of my time to their troubles. Progress was disappointingly slow. A large section of the British people was Czechophil and there were many members of Parliament who besought Dr. Beneš to furnish them with material for Parliamentary questions. I counselled patience and restraint, and in spite of the irksome delays the President took my advice.

It was a trying period for the Czechoslovaks and, indeed, for all the small nations, for at that time the British Government inclined to the view that small nations who were unable to defend themselves were a danger to peace and that in the new world which was to be built up after the war we must have fewer and larger states. There was therefore a strong reluctance to make any promises about the future of the Sudetenland and of Slovakia, and as a first condition of any form of even *de facto* recognition the Foreign Office insisted that the Czechoslovaks must put their own house in order. I was therefore given the unpleasant task of trying to stop dissensions which the attitude of the French and British Governments could hardly fail to aggravate.

The chief rival of Dr. Beneš was Dr. Milan Hodža, the Czechoslovak Prime Minister at the time of Munich and at that moment an exile in London. I had known him in Prague and had always liked him. Indeed, he was always popular with the British, and during that fateful and ill-starred mission to Czechoslovakia in August, 1939, Lord Runciman had found him far more amenable to what he called reason than President Beneš. Nor was there anything surprising in this preference. Milan Hodža was a man of ripe intelligence and considerable personal charm. Long before the first world war he had been a stout champion of Czechoslovak independence. As a Slovak who had been a member of the Budapest Parliament he had acquired much of the attractive and extravagant nature of the small Hungarian squire. He was a man who found it hard to say no to any important foreigner. Political success in the new Czechoslovakia had gradually undermined his fibre; in exile it broke down altogether. He was now a tired and sick man in whom all power of decision had been sapped. Moreover, although a resolute opponent of Germany, he was an Agrarian, and the Agrarian Party was already in disrepute on account of the collaborationists in its ranks.

In London I had many meetings with Hodža. They were always friendly. They invariably ended with protestations of injured innocence and promises of co-operation. The next day they were withdrawn by letter or evaded by inaction. Unfortunately, his whole mind was warped by his mistrust of Dr. Beneš with whom he had never been on good terms. In his decline Dr. Hodža was a most tragic figure, for in his day he had given splendid service to his country. Now it was impossible for anyone who knew his condition to take him seriously as a political figure. Yet for months he continued to receive the support of the French Government in Paris which he visited whenever he felt that the British Government were leaning towards Dr. Beneš. The British Government therefore marked time, and the deadlock continued.

During this period the official British attitude towards the Czechoslovaks had one unfortunate consequence. The Germans were well-informed about our aloofness and in their propaganda to the Czechs in the Protectorate did their best to undermine the position of the exiles in general, and of Dr. Beneš in particular, by a persistent campaign of abuse of which the most damaging feature was the repeated statement that Dr. Beneš had been discarded by the British and the French.

It was a good propaganda lie, for it contained sufficient truth to make the home Czechs uneasy. To improve their position, they made a premature revolt on November 17. It gained for them the sympathy of the outside world. But the results at home were tragic. Students were shot. Many arrests were made and the universities were closed. Worse still, the security of the underground movement was affected, and the position of General Eliaš, the Prime Minister of the Protectorate and a secret supporter of the Allies, was compromised. The Czechs in Prague were bitterly disappointed by the attitude of the French and British Governments. Although at this stage of the war the Czech secret communications between Prague and London worked with great efficiency, the information which came through by these means was received with scepticism or regarded as Beneš propaganda. Both Dr. Beneš and Jan Masaryk, who was beginning to make history as the most successful Allied broadcaster of the war, were unhappy men.

The Balkan Ministers whom I visited regularly in order to obtain material for my intelligence reports were just as disappointed as the Czechoslovak politicians. Typical of their general attitude were the remarks of M. Subotic, the Yugoslav Minister, who said to me bluntly: "You English do not understand how to handle the Balkans. You say that you cannot do this and will not do that. You hold up our requests for tanks and aeroplanes and even rifles and keep us waiting for an answer. Naturally we think that either you do not want to help us or you are in dire straits. Either way is bad for both of us."

We *were* in dire straits as, indeed, the Balkan diplomatists must have known. There was no secret about the complacency which had put us in this predicament. It had been continuous for twenty years.

During this period I found it hard to understand and to condone the attitude of the Government. Doubtless, it still contained too many men who, as Georges Bernanos wrote of his French politicians, "were ruthless in their search for security because they were impotent to create." Mr. Chamberlain was not the weak man that the public imagined him to be. Indeed, apart from Mr. Churchill, he was the strongest personality in the Cabinet. Moreover, he was guided throughout by principles of moral rectitude. What was wrong was his perspective, and his cardinal error was perhaps not so much Munich as his choice of an adviser who knew nothing of Europe and who owed his reputation to his success in settling conflicts between capital and labour. During the twenty years between the wars there had been a confusion of conflicts; clashes of incompatible ideologies, of over-reaching ambition and greed, of excessive nationalism. But the war had simplified the moral issue. On the one side there was the cause of liberty; on the other the evil cause of tyranny. Mr. Chamberlain narrowed the issue to the cause of British security, and the government departments in Whitehall had perforce to follow his lead.

The immediate consequence of this "phoney" period was reflected in the absence of any sense of urgency in the British public. The plain truth is that at this stage life in England was not as serious as it should have been. At the front there was not sufficient activity to stir the public from its normal round. Business, sport and entertainment continued as usual. In Oxford, which I used to visit occasionally in order to consult the Chatham House experts at Balliol, the Peace Society

had its committee rooms opposite the college gateway. London itself
was not inspiring, seemed to be suffering from a gangrene of the soul
and conveyed a general impression of apathy. Doubtless, in many
places much strenuous work was being done. But the country as a
whole was not yet awake to the gathering danger, and the outside
world was critical of the British Government and more inclined than
ever to believe that the British people were decadent.

Before the end of 1939 the public received a rude shock when on
November 30 the Russians attacked Finland without the formality
of a declaration of war. Indignation was general. There was violent
criticism of the Russian Government, and many people demanded a
rupture of diplomatic relations. All sections of the British people
were eager to help Finland. In particular, the British Labour Movement issued a unanimous declaration recording "profound horror
and indignation at the Soviet Government's unprovoked attack"
and calling upon the free nations of the world "to give every practic-
able aid to the Finnish nation in its struggle". Mr. Philip Noel Baker
and Sir Walter Citrine were sent to Finland to organise the help.
Sir Walter, who is a man of great moral courage, was shocked by
what he saw and did not hesitate to condemn the hypocrisy of the
Russians who in their propaganda justified their action with the pre-
text that they were liberating the Finns for Socialism.

"Socialism!" wrote Sir Walter in his *My Finnish Diary*. "It is a
vile insult to associate the excesses of the imperialist Stalin and his
coterie of despots with a word which has provided the inspiration
and hope of millions of mankind."

His views were shared by many of his countrymen and the number
of people who still regarded Russia as a potential ally now sank to a
tiny minority. At that moment few people dreamt that the Russian
action might have been taken in the cause of security and that Germany, and not Finland, was the real enemy. The Russians themselves
vouchsafed no information. To the British people they remained
more enigmatic than ever.

The end of the year brought a crumb of comfort to the Czechoslovaks. From the beginning the Foreign Office had agreed to the
establishment of a Czechoslovak National Committee provided that
Dr. Hodža, as the most important Slovak exile, would consent to
serve on it. After nearly four months of argle-bargle, I succeeded in
obtaining Dr. Hodža's agreement to co-operate with Dr. Beneš. It
was a reluctant surrender. Its conditions were never strictly observed,
but it served its purpose, and on December 21 the British Govern-

ment recognised the right of a new Czechoslovak National Committee, headed by Dr. Beneš, to represent the Czech and Slovak peoples. The official communiqué was published on December 22. It was cold in content, and of the newspapers only *The Times* gave it any prominence.

That morning there was a blistering frost which ushered in a long spell of wintry weather. At the end of a white Christmas week I went out to Putney to meet the Chief of Staff of the Czech secret organisation. He had just arrived from Prague and was going back early in the New Year. Short, broad-shouldered, thick-set and firm as a rock, he could not have been more than thirty-five. He showed no trace of excitement or of strain. I talked with him for two hours and asked innumerable questions. His answers were factual and convincing. He explained to me how the secret military organisation worked. It was based on the Russian cell system. Only one man in each cell knew the key man in the cell above him. He made light of the dangers of his work and did not attempt to dramatise it. I had to drag out of him the story of Major Klein, the former Czechoslovak Military Attaché in Budapest, who had been arrested in Moravia by the Germans, imprisoned in the sinister Spielburg in Brno and tortured in order to make him speak. He had been kept on the rack for two days. The Germans had put red-hot needles into his testicles. He had died without opening his lips.

This young chief of staff made a most favourable impression on me. His self-control was remarkable in a man who for months had lived in daily danger of detection and whose family had been arrested. I do not think that I have ever met a calmer or less emotional Czech. Later in the war I was to meet similar men from all the occupied countries. They were the bravest of the brave, and their ingenuity in adversity was wonderful. Many made their escape by bribing senior German officials. All were agreed on one point. Nazi Germany was much more corrupt than the Germany of the first world war.

I spent the last day of a grim year in writing an official report of my interview. While I was engaged on my task, the telephone rang. It was a call from the Ministry of Information who wanted me to lecture in Stockholm on January 15. The Swedes had asked for me. It was to be a big show. Reluctantly I had to say no.

That night, which I spent at the P.I.D. headquarters in Woburn, we had a small New Year's party. My friends in Tomintoul had sent me two haggises and a bottle of real Glenlivet which arrived labelled "Tonsil Varnish". We celebrated mildly and at midnight sang Auld

Lang Syne. But I went to bed with a sad heart. I should dearly have liked to accept the Swedish invitation. But like most people of my age and qualifications I was chained to the relentless bureaucratic machine. Never before in my life had I spent a whole winter in England. I was not to leave it until the end of the war.

CHAPTER FOUR

AT THE BEGINNING of the New Year I made the usual good resolutions and reviewed the state of my own affairs. The resolutions remained resolutions; the review gave me little comfort. My financial position was precarious and threatened to be disastrous. My salary as a member of the Political Intelligence Department was small. P.I.D. was still in its nursing-home near Woburn Abbey and seemed to be getting nowhere. So long as it remained in Marylands, it could not count on the full support of the Foreign Office. Official views of the value of its work varied considerably. The Treasury, who had appointed a committee to examine the reports issued by various departments, gave a high mark to ours. Individual critics, including some ministers, took a colder view of our activities. Most of our own staff wished to return to London, but in spite of many rumours we remained where we were.

I was unhappy and felt that I was not pulling my weight. Fortunately perhaps, I had more than sufficient routine work to impose a healthy check on introspection. Indeed, I had recently added to my list of tasks, for, as a Czechoslovak expert, I had been invited to attend the Saturday policy meetings of the propaganda organisation which dealt with enemy and enemy-occupied countries. Thus, although not a member of the organisation, I was indirectly concerned with propaganda almost from the beginning of the war.

Acutely aware of the restrictive dangers of seeing no one but officials, I kept as close a touch as I could with my friends. True it is that my social life was dead—and with it all the pleasures and passions of my past. Occasionally, when Russia and the Far East obtruded themselves into the frame of my work, memories, tinged with melancholy and remorse, returned to disturb for a moment the newly-found equilibrium of my life. They seemed like faint shadows on a distant background, bringing no suggestion that they wished to pursue me, yet real enough to recall vague tremors of the nostalgia in which I have always steeped myself. Of my women friends I saw all too little, for they, like everyone else, were absorbed in the present. "Tommy" Rosslyn was driving for the Red Cross and was bent on going to Finland to nurse the wounded. Others had vanished in the vortex of Whitehall and had passed out of my life. But Moura Budberg I saw regularly. Her circle of acquaintances was extraordinarily varied and ranged from ministers and literary giants to obscure but intelligent foreigners. From her I heard not only the gossip of the outside world, but also its criticisms of the inside world of Whitehall. At this period they were violent. I found her information a useful corrective to official complacency.

Early in the year I had an interesting meeting with Mr. H. G. Wells whom I had known since 1921 as a staunch friend of the Czechs. That day he was in brilliant form and monopolised the conversation with a long dissertation on propaganda. When he started to cudgel the Tories for being interested only in their money-bags, he was pulled up by Captain "Jock" McEwen, a most austere and high-minded Conservative, who said sharply: "Nonsense, choice of Party is purely a matter of the heart." A slightly awkward moment was checked by Sir Orme Sargent who intervened quietly: "Where your treasure is, there shall your heart be also." Everyone laughed.

On propaganda Mr. Wells spoke with convincing effect. He had a clear-cut policy which made great play of a new world and of the coming era of the common man. It would appeal, I felt, to many people, but not to all. Nor could I see how it could be adopted by the Government. We were ruled by a Coalition in which the Conservatives held the key positions. And, even if they paid lip service to the common man, they were looking for uncommon men to pull us through the war. Moreover, there was a weakness, if not in Mr. Wells's argument, at least in his attitude. In the fierce glint of his eye I could see something of the pride of the neglected professional, of the Wells who had worked under Lord Beaverbrook in the Ministry of Information during the first world war and who was now highly critical of the neophytes of this war. For all his international theories, Mr. Wells had always been a nationalist at heart. Without any flights of fancy I could imagine him reverting to the Wells of *Tono Bungay* and as Ponderevo, the propagandist, practising with zest the ruses and deceptions of political warfare. Later in the war, when I was to be more closely connected with political warfare, I was astonished by the easy zeal with which my Socialist colleagues discarded their principles and, in the fight for our existence, indulged with relish in perversions of the truth. Propaganda is a modern evil; in war it becomes the most insidious and easily acquired of all vices.

I also had several talks with Mr. Somerset Maugham who was eager to assist his beloved France, wanted an immediate declaration of our war aims and complained bitterly of the frustration imposed on all would-be helpers by government departments. Like Mr.

Wells, Mr. Somerset Maugham was a severe critic of Mr. Chamberlain, and both men, I think, felt that there was no hope of a new policy without a change of government. Munich divided many families in Britain, but it can hardly have made a deeper cleavage of attitude than that which split the Maugham brothers. Lord Maugham was so devoted to Mr. Chamberlain that, with little or no first-hand knowledge, he wrote a violent attack on the Czechoslovaks. In his *Strictly Personal* Mr. Somerset Maugham describes Mr. Chamberlain as "a man, sincere no doubt and honest, but muddled with self-conceit, who put his party before his country and by his ineptitude and stubbornness brought it to the verge of ruin."

Another sufferer from frustration whom I saw something of at this time was Major Wingate. I had met him first in 1938 and, impressed by his almost fanatical determination and by his passionate Zionism, had taken him, at his own request, to see Lord Beaverbrook. The interview was not a success. Wingate's sole object was to convert Lord Beaverbrook, whom he regarded as pro-Arab, to Zionism. Fixing his deep sunken eyes, bright as a searchlight, on the huddled figure of Lord Beaverbrook, he attacked fearlessly and without favour. When, after listening to a long tirade, Lord Beaverbrook remarked that he had heard other experts argue the case for the Arabs just as eloquently, Wingate became inspired and spoke like a prophet. The other experts were wrong. All that mattered was whose side was God on. Lord Beaverbrook was not converted.

Later, I spent almost a whole night with Wingate in his flat in Hill Street. He told me the full story of his life: how he had been sent to Palestine as an Arab expert, how he had seen the light and been converted to Zionism and how, with official connivance, he had organised and trained a band of Jews to crawl on their bellies in the dark and put paid to the Arab terrorists who were then outwitting all the efforts of the British troops to capture them. A first-class interpreter in Arabic, he told me how he used to creep in disguise into Arab strongholds and discover their secrets. Now that the war had started, he longed for similar work. In certain countries, he explained, his kind of warfare was worth an army corps. He was then engaged on some routine job and chafed bitterly under his enforced inactivity. The spirit of T. E. Lawrence burnt fiercely if conversely in him. There seemed no limit to his ambition. I was not sure if red-tape would make him unusable, but I felt that if he were ever given a job to do on his own, he would make history.

On January 18 I went to Stornoway House to see Lord Beaverbrook. It was the first time that I had seen him since the war. He, too, was suffering from the frustration of inaction. I found him sitting in his armchair. His legs were wrapped in a tweed rug. On the carpet in front of him two huge kettles with spouts as long as golf clubs were pouring out a curiously scented steam, which he was inhaling. Lord Beaverbrook had an attack of the asthma, which later in the war was to undermine his strength but never diminish his fierce energy. His eyes were watery, but he gave me his views with his usual vigour. "This Government", he said, "will never win the war, but no one will ever get them out unless we have big reverses. This is not a real war. Production is bad. A 'phoney' war may land us in a 'phoney' peace. If there's a real war, I'll be in it."

There were others in authority who shared Lord Beaverbrook's views. Sir Walter Citrine, whom I saw from time to time, was not anti-Chamberlain. Indeed, he respected the Prime Minister for his indifference to criticism and to newspaper attacks. But Citrine shared Lord Beaverbrook's view that production was not what it ought to be and that the country was apathetic and only half-awake.

My diary for this period contains several entries of similar opinions by prominent authorities. They criticised the number of old men in high places, the lack of leadership, and the absence of any real spirit of sacrifice, because it had not yet been kindled, among the people. I added comments of my own, comparing our laxity with the fanatical and immense capacity for self-sacrifice of the old-time Russian terrorists. There was something of the same spirit among the Nazis and among the modern Russians who worshipped their leaders like gods. What the world thought of Mr. Chamberlain was expressed cruelly but forcibly in a limerick which was current at this time and which came from the United States:

> "An elderly statesman with gout,
> When asked what the war was about,
> Replied with a sigh
> My colleagues and I
> Are doing our best to find out."

As for the British people they had not yet been given an opportunity to show their mettle.

Meanwhile, my efforts to help the Czechoslovaks were making slow progress. None of the leaders was satisfied with the inadequate recognition of a Czechoslovak National Council which left the Czechoslovaks in an invidious position compared with that of the other Allies. Dr. Beneš was therefore eager to make an official demand for a Czechoslovak Government in London with himself as President. Once again I counselled patience and two bites at the cherry of recognition, the first bite to be at a Provisional Government. The advice was not entirely unreasonable in view of the legal and personal obstacles. The legal difficulties were real. Moreover, I had again received a friendly and valuable hint from Sargent about the necessity of going slowly but surely. "We have accepted Beneš, but in his own interests don't let him force matters too quickly. He has many enemies."

"You mean X?" I said, mentioning the name of an official.

"Oh no!" replied Sargent. "We have snubbed him, but there are far more important persons than X."

We sent in a request for recognition of a provisional government and waited patiently. In the meantime more Czechoslovak leaders were escaping from Prague and making their way to this country. M. Feierabend and M. Nečas, two ministers of the Czechoslovak Government in Prague, arrived in January. Their escape was a great help to Dr. Beneš, for it proved his contention that at least some members of even a German-sponsored Czechoslovak Government were loyal to him. In February came Dr. Drtina, the personal private secretary of Dr. Beneš and his link with the underground movement. He was followed a month later by three Trade Union leaders. All these men had made hazardous escapes. Apart from the initial dangers, all said that the most difficult part of their journey had been to obtain visas for France and Britain! They were in good spirits and gave an optimistic account of the state of feeling in Czechoslovakia which, they said, was much healthier than in France. Paris was free, but its spirit was more defeatist than that of occupied Prague. In the Protectorate the Germans tolerated only one Czech Party, the Narodní Sooručenství or N.S. It had no positive value, but it was useful, for it enabled the Czechs to meet in comparative safety. The Czechs had their own interpretation of the initials N.S. They stood for Němcum Smrt—death to the Germans. Resistance they admitted was difficult, but there were, they said, many weak links in the German propaganda armour if only we could penetrate them. Obviously at this stage of the war the Germans were not yet drunk with victory.

These newcomers were perhaps most interesting on the subject of Russia whom they regarded not merely as a potential ally but as already an enemy of Germany. Their arrival did something to create a more favourable impression of the Czechs in British official circles, but there was no immediate improvement in their status. Sargent, however, was keenly interested in what they had to say about Russia. In Britain anti-Russian feeling was as strong as ever and had indeed been aggravated by the Russo-Finnish peace which had started a fresh crop of rumours of a general peace. The Germans pretended to believe that everything the Russians did was done with German approval, and, claiming Russia as almost an ally, they based their propaganda on their invincibility. Its main theme was: how could Britain win the war, much less help Europe, when Germany had 15,000,000 trained men under arms and Britain not only had no army but was losing all her ships. The argument could be defeated only by long-term assurances. From the British point of view, there was one great difference between this war and the last. In 1914 few people in any section of the community doubted our ability to win. In this war there were men in high places who had no feeling of certainty.

Nevertheless, there were one or two senior officials who had never lost sight of the possibility of a break between Russia and Germany, and, as the latest arrivals from Czechoslovakia regarded this break as a strong probability, what they had to say about Russia was listened to with respect. When I went to see Sargent on March 20, 1940, to urge that our representation in Moscow should be strengthened, he took down a red box from the top of his desk, opened it and handed me a paper. It was a copy of a memorandum written two days before making the same recommendation.

Once again it was a matter of waiting for results, and the first three months of 1940 produced few that were satisfying to us. The Navy, silent as usual, was carrying the main burden of the war. The Royal Air Force, much against its will, was dropping more leaflets than bombs. There had been no major excitements to sound the tocsin for the nation.

For myself I had written some leaflets which had been dropped over Prague, and on March 2 I had felt a minor thrill on hearing the German radio denouncing Harold Nicolson and myself in a violent tirade against the British Council which was said to have supplied funds "to the notorious Secret Service agent, Bruce Lockhart and to the Germanophobe former diplomat Nicolson". Otherwise, my life seemed sterile and a waste of the taxpayers' money. So when my uncle telegraphed me to come to the Tweed for a few days' fishing at Easter, I accepted the invitation without hesitation.

It was a refreshing change. Our fishing was on the Duke of Roxburghe's water just above Kelso. Although Easter was early, the sun shone warmly on banks lined with snowdrops, and on the last day the daffodils came out almost as we watched them. In the spacious grounds of Floors Castle, Tweed looked its most majestic. The water held only two rods and, as my uncle was sharing it with a friend, I fished only intermittently and was a willing "odd man out", for I wanted to be alone.

Fifteen years ago I had spent four months in Kelso. Now the place was full of ghosts. The young gillies of my day were now grey-haired; the old men were dead or long since retired. There was nothing to suggest that we were at war and in the hotel where we lived little mention of it. On the Sunday I went for a long walk along the banks of the Teviot, the loveliest of the Border rivers, and saw again the stumpy ruins of Roxburgh Castle where James II was killed by the bursting of a cannon in 1460. Four hundred years ago these stones had been a royal residence. There had been a flourishing town beside it. It had shared pride of place with Edinburgh, Stirling and Berwick as one of the Royal burghs of Scotland. It had housed the Royal Mint. Now all trace of it had disappeared. Modern war, I reflected, could destroy far larger burghs.

On my way back to the hotel I stood on the Kelso Bridge— Rennie's model for the Waterloo Bridge—and watched the salmon leap in the famous Junction Pool where Teviot joins Tweed. In the past I had known almost every stone in this part of the river, had waded across it in low water and more than once had taken a wetting in following a fish downstream. Now I should never wade Tweed again, but like the old gentlemen in the hotel should do my fishing from a boat.

On the Monday, my last day, my uncle let me do most of the fishing and sent me out with Vivers, the gillie. Not having my own gear, I made a poor showing, hooked three fish, lost two which came unstuck and landed a kelt. I soon tired and devoted my attention to the gillie, a well-known Tweed character and, even at fifty-eight as he was then, a magnificently built man, still tall and erect with powerful arms and long well-shaped hands. In his youth he had served in the Royal Navy and had been a strong-man in a circus. Both in his conversation and in his rowing he was still a great show-man. What interested me most about him was the fact that he had been Mr. Chamberlain's gillie on the same water after Munich. He was an ardent admirer of the Prime Minister who, he said, was the most modest man for whom he had ever "gillied".

Obviously Mr. Chamberlain had been sounding public opinion, for he had talked freely while fishing and had asked Vivers whether the Borderers thought that he had been right at Munich. Vivers had replied that there was not a man from Berwick to the Solway who did not approve. Mr. Chamberlain had been relieved and had told Vivers that he could make nothing of Hitler who was incapable of any form of discussion and never opened his mouth except to make a speech. Gillies are privileged persons, and Vivers was proud of having spent two days alone with the Prime Minister. His pride, however, could not make him say that Mr. Chamberlain was an expert angler. "Man," he said, "he lost six fish in the two days. The plain fact is, he's na hand at the fishing."

The next day a well-known Edinburgh doctor, who was now engaged in military work, gave me a lift to Edinburgh to enable me to catch my train to London. On the way he told me that the war of inactivity was having a very serious effect on the morale of the young men in Scotland. Their first enthusiasm had worn off. Now they not only had no wish to fight but had not even the feeling that there was a job to be done.

On my return to London I went straight to Marylands to make good the arrears of my four days' absence. Nothing had changed, although there was some prospect of excitement in Norway where the Admiralty were trying to force the Germans into action by a more aggressive policy. Ten days later my colleagues and I listened in to the B.B.C. account of the Grand National which was run as usual at Aintree before a huge crowd. Some of my colleagues were angry and perturbed. The war was not being conducted seriously. How could one blame the people, they said, when there was no leadership. Democracy needed and desired a lead. The truth was that the Government did not believe in democracy. I shared their views, with the order reversed. Our democracy did not believe in the Government.

Three days after the Grand National the Germans occupied all Denmark and the chief ports of Norway. It was the first ring of the alarum-clock which was to rouse the nation from the sleep of complacency.

Whitehall is a miniature world, and all kinds and conditions of men make it. There are the honest, selfless and untiring workers; the time-servers and sponges; the intriguers and self-seekers; the bullies and braggarts; and, worst of all, the back-stabbers. All the types are there as Homer and Shakespeare described them: The Nestors, the Ulysses, the Stentors; the good Horatios, the Rosencrantzes and the

Iagos. The strength of a nation depends on the percentage of the men of good fibre and on their ability to maintain the upper hand. During the seven months which composed the period of the "phoney" war, the intriguers and time-servers were on top. Their worst activity had been the whispering campaign to discredit Mr. Churchill who, they said, was too old and too feeble in health to stand the strain of the Premiership. Now all was to be changed. The same wave which was to carry Hitler over nearly all Europe was to sweep Mr. Chamberlain away and to bring to the top the war leader who by word and by deed was to be the symbol of our revived unity.

Nearly fifteen years had passed since I first heard Hitler speak in Munich. Since then he had begun his every speech with one phrase: "Deutschland, erwache—Germany, awake." During the same period a few British statesmen like Mr. Churchill and Lord Lloyd had tried in vain to warn England of her mortal peril. It was true that Hitler had woken Germany. He had done more than that. He had achieved something which had been beyond the power of any Englishman. When he invaded Denmark and Norway, he woke England.

CHAPTER FIVE

NO ONE WHO lived through them will ever forget the feverish, ominous months that followed the invasion of Norway. They were graced with glorious weather. Continuous sunshine showed England at her greatest and rendered her doubly precious to her people. Those months gave new birth to all that was best in her. They brought her to the very brink of complete disaster. They spurred her to the supreme effort in her long history.

If the failure of our expeditionary force in Norway came as a salutary shock to the nation, it spread gloom and pessimism in high places. There was now open criticism of Mr. Chamberlain, whose statement about Hitler's missing the bus exposed him both to ridicule and to fierce resentment. The supporters of a more vigorous war effort were down-hearted. On April 24 I had a long talk with Sargent, who gave me a prognostic of the course he thought the war would take during the next twelve months. Things, he said, would be much worse before they were better. Hitler would over-run Holland and Belgium and the Balkans. Resistance would be feeble. German menaces and German subversive tactics would be successful. The Yugoslav General Staff was already suspect. Russia was an enigma. Certain people in England had hopes of diverting Russia to the side of the Allies, but they were a tiny minority. On the other hand, the French and Americans would be appalled if, after what had happened in Finland, we began fresh negotiations with Russia. "I have always known ", he said, "that it would need a disaster to unite this country. Now I am afraid that Norway will not be enough. We shall have to wait for other blows; perhaps an invasion of Scotland."

It was a dark and, as events happened, a remarkably accurate fore-cast, but not gloomier than the facts warranted or the picture painted by men like Lord Tyrrell and Lord Lloyd. Nor did I receive any comfort from the usually optimistic Dr. Beneš whom I saw the next day. For once he was shaken: he foresaw a joint German-Italian attack on the Balkans with Russia coming in to mop up what she could as she had done in Poland, and predicted the collapse of resist-ance in the oppressed countries. Our prestige had fallen to its nadir. Optimists were scarce, but I found one in Freddy Voigt, who was then working for one of our propaganda organisations. Fearlessly outspoken and a brilliant writer, he was, later in the war, to become editor of the *Nineteenth Century* and in this capacity to incur the censure of the Minister of Information for writing articles which, Mr. Bracken asserted, gave joy to Lord Haw-Haw. Voigt has never been afraid of unpopularity; he can always be relied on to take an original view. And in that April of 1940 he maintained stoutly not only that British morale had risen sharply with the first news of our military set-back, but that it would continue to rise with further disasters. I found considerable comfort in his confidence. Incidentally, he got damages from the paper that printed the Lord Haw-Haw aspersion.

Meanwhile, the politicians were busy with Cabinet-building and, although Mr. Chamberlain had still many supporters, the debates in the House of Commons pointed to a change. In the end Mr. Chamberlain's complacency and self-deception destroyed him, but the crisis did not come until May 10. I awoke at 5 a.m. to a superb dawn, made myself a cup of tea and tried to work. Then I turned on the radio which for days had sadly interfered with most people's concentration. Hitler had invaded Holland, Belgium and Luxemburg. With one exception the British Press presented a united front of national resistance and determination. The *Daily Worker*, which was then opposed to the war, had a long article accusing the British Government of trying to force Holland and Belgium into the war.

That evening at 9 p.m. I listened in to the dramatic announcement of Mr. Chamberlain's resignation. It was a noble effort. Mr. Chamberlain spoke with great emotion but with complete self-command. No one except perhaps his most intimate friends knew that he was then a sick and stricken man. Mr. Winston Churchill was now to have his chance. He took it three days later when he announced to the House of Commons and, through that House, to the country that he had nothing to offer but blood, sweat and tears. Over ninety years before, Garibaldi had used somewhat similar words in an appeal for volunteers to carry on a forlorn struggle. His venture was as dust weighed in the balance against the titanic task of Mr. Churchill, whose call of victory—"Victory at all costs, in spite of all terror; victory, however long and hard the road may be"—was what the country had waited for and longed to hear. Parliament or no Parliament, Churchill was the country's choice.

The new Coalition Cabinet, if not comparable in talent with the Lloyd George Ministry of 1916, was an immense improvement on its predecessor. My Czechoslovaks welcomed it with good reason.

Lord Halifax, it is true, remained at the Foreign Office, but Mr. Eden, Sir Archibald Sinclair, Lord Lloyd, Mr. Duff Cooper, and, above all, Mr. Churchill himself had been stern critics of the Munich policy, and the new Labour Ministers had always been favourable to the Czechoslovak cause. Interesting to me personally, because I had known him and worked for him for many years, was the appointment of Lord Beaverbrook as Minister of Aircraft Production.

On May 15 he asked me to come round to Stornoway House, his London home which looks on to the Green Park. When I arrived, Mr. Attlee and Mr. Arthur Greenwood were the only other guests. They had been dining alone with Lord Beaverbrook. Mr. Greenwood talked brilliantly and gave a dramatic account of Mr. Chamberlain's resignation, in which the two Labour Ministers had played a decisive part. They had seen Mr. Chamberlain alone after the debate in the House of Commons on May 7. Mr. Chamberlain had discussed a reconstruction of the Government and had asked Labour to participate. He had wished to carry on as Prime Minister and had suggested Lord Halifax as a possible alternative. Mr. Attlee and Mr. Greenwood had shown no enthusiasm for either choice, but had undertaken to consult the Labour Party, which was then sitting in Conference at Bournemouth. Mr. Chamberlain had telephoned to Bournemouth on May 10 and had been given the answer that Labour would not enter a Chamberlain Cabinet. As for Lord Halifax, he was, Mr. Greenwood said, a God-fearing Christian gentleman, but no use as a war Prime Minister. Mr. Chamberlain had resigned ten minutes later. The message was sent from the call box in the Bournemouth Hotel.

Mr. Greenwood, who is always at his best when things are going badly, said the new Government was determined to deal ruthlessly with the appeasers. It would win the war, and in order to do so would become unpopular. After the war, he prophesied, the Socialists would romp home in the first election.

I had some talk with Mr. Attlee, who questioned me closely about Central Europe. It was the first time that I had met him. While Mr. Greenwood was talking to Lord Beaverbrook, I took the opportunity of asking Mr. Attlee about his career. He gave me his story quietly and modestly. His early life had begun on smooth lines. His father, a successful solicitor, had sent him to Haileybury and University College, Oxford, where he had taken a Second in modern history. On coming down, he had been called to the Bar. He had also joined the Independent Labour Party. He had not been interested in his legal career, and, after accepting a brief which brought him a fee of ten pounds, he dedicated his life to Socialism. He ran a boys' club in the East End of London and began to practise public speaking. His training-ground was the street-corners of Limehouse. He spoke four times weekly, but met with little success; the public was apathetic. Then came the first world war in which he fought in France, in Gallipoli and in Mesopotamia, beginning as an infantry officer and finishing as a major in the Tank Corps. At the end of the war he had gone quietly back to his politics in the East End. Then had come his first success. In 1919 he was elected Mayor of Stepney. Labour swept the municipality, winning forty-five seats out of sixty. The Labour councillors were one-third Irish Catholics, one-third Jews, and one-third English.

Mr. Attlee has remained faithful to the East End and it has remained loyal to him. He has been member of Parliament for the Limehouse Division since 1933. I took an instant liking to this unassuming man who smoked his pipe and talked as one who because he understood all things could forgive much. He struck me as a man who was not only incapable of any meanness but who was almost too sincere and self-effacing to be a successful politician.

Later in the evening more guests arrived, and the conversation became general. Lord Beaverbrook, who looked tired, but was already applying his fierce energy to his new task, was pleased that his appointment had been received so well by the country. Shortly before midnight Mr. Attlee and Mr. Greenwood left, and a quarter of an hour later the telephone rang. Lord Beaverbrook answered it, got up at once and took me out of the room. He had been summoned by the Prime Minister. He asked me to wait. He came back an hour later; his face was grave. There was bad news from France. The Germans had made a break-through near Sedan.

For most of the next fortnight the sun shone from cloudless skies, but its warmth brought no joy to British hearts. France was in collapse; the British army was in mortal peril. In England men went about their business with grim, earnest faces. Anxiety alternated with an obstinate English hope that the situation could not be so bad as the pessimists feared, and, as always happens when the worst has not been reached, official news of the pending disaster lagged behind events. This was Lord Haw-Haw's opportunity, and during this period he had many British listeners. On May 26 the B.B.C. revealed to the world the full state of our unpreparedness when, acting on an official instruction, the announcer requested everyone who had stocks of cartridges for twelve-bore guns to bring them to the police station.

In the gathering gloom there was one tiny spark of light, visible only to those in the secret; its significance appreciated by none. Sir Stafford Cripps was on his way to Moscow. Stalin, who had thought that time was on his side, was now alarmed by the speed of the German advance and had telegraphed that Sir Stafford's visit would be welcome.

On Wednesday, May 29, I went to the Admiralty at 8 p.m. to dine with Mr. A. V. Alexander, the First Lord, and Commander Fletcher (now Lord Winster). I had known Fletcher for many years and through him had become intimate with Mr. Alexander. The First Lord was engaged, and I waited in Rex Fletcher's room. The news was very grave. We were evacuating our army from Dunkirk. Presently Mr. Alexander sent for us, and we walked across to Fletcher's flat in Whitehall Court. Pipe in mouth and a big black slouch hat on his head, Mr. Alexander had his jaw set. He looked calm enough, but for all his solid front I could see that he was fighting to keep his nerves under control. Fletcher had arranged a cold supper so that the First Lord could talk freely. Fletcher and I sat, but Mr. Alexander took most of his meal standing up and walking about the room. The Navy's responsibility was heavy. It had to evacuate our army and save the lives of as many men as possible. The Government had also to bear in mind the serious, imminent danger of a seaborne invasion which would present little difficulty if the Fleet met with disaster. We were short of destroyers. Saving the army might mean staking our whole existence as an empire.

Fletcher and I tried to distract the First Lord's mind from the crisis by talking of other things. To a small extent we succeeded. Mr. Alexander answered our questions, gave the fullest praise to Mr. Churchill of whom he had always been an admirer, and expressed his determination to see the war won at any cost.

But neither Fletcher nor I could compete against the private telephone to the Admiralty which rang frequently and which, if it did not ring from the Admiralty end, was rung by the First Lord. We stayed in the flat from 8.30 to 10.30. The first hour seemed interminable. Then the reports began to come in. The news was good. It became increasingly better. The night was cool, but Mr. Alexander mopped his brow more than once. When it was clear that the success of the evacuation would exceed all expectations, his face flushed with pride and relief. He had shown a brave front.

We went back to the Admiralty in his car. We drove in by the First Lord's entrance on the Horseguards through the barbed-wire entanglements which had to be pulled back by the naval sentries. Then in the murky darkness we shook hands.

"Bruce," said Mr. Alexander, "you will remember this night: how we waited for the news and how we drove through the wire together."

I replied: "You will endure many nights like this, but I shall remember it all my life."

He was pleased and sent me on to Lord Beaverbrook's house in his car.

At Stornoway House I found Lord Beaverbrook surrounded by his new satellites. The gleam of battle was in his eyes. The scene, in fact, was exactly as it had been in my journalistic days when the senior staff of the *Evening Standard* assembled to submit to cross-examination and to answer "Yes, Sir" and "No, Sir." The replies were mostly "Yes, Sir". Now, however, the satellites were not journalists but big industrialists like Lord Weir, Sir William Rootes, Sir Patrick Hennessey, young Westbrook, Lord Beaverbrook's great discovery, and several others whose names I did not know. All had to face a machine-gun fire of questions:

"How many 'planes are you producing this week?" As each figure was given, crash went the Beaverbrook bullet: "Double it."

If anyone protested, there was a fierce "Why not?"

"Because I am short of mechanics."

"How many do you need?"

"Thirty or forty."

"Which figure do you mean?"

"Thirty."

"You'll have them on Monday. Double your figure."

I noted with quiet satisfaction that the industrialists took this fire as submissively as we journalists used to do. When Lord Beaverbrook was called away from the room, Sir William Rootes mopped his brow and, seeking contradiction from the ceiling, ejaculated: "Isn't he wonderful?"

There was no contradiction from the ceiling or from anywhere else.

I stayed late and heard many stories. Mr. Brendan Bracken, straight from the Prime Minister, told us how Mr. Churchill was determined to deal ruthlessly not only with the Fifth Column but also with defeatism in the Civil Service. He had already drafted a

D

circular for despatch to all higher civil servants warning them that pessimism would not be tolerated. The story was true.

At one moment Lord Beaverbrook took me aside. How was I being treated? If I was making no progress, he had a job for me. I informed him that I could not leave my Czechs in the lurch. I then told him privately what a high official had said to me about his appointment as Minister of Aircraft Production. If we were breaking up the bottlenecks, it would be a good appointment. If not, it would just be another political job. Lord Beaverbrook laughed loudly and slapped his thighs. "Westbrook," he roared, "how fast are we sacking? One an hour or one a minute?" I heard sufficient details to understand that the bottlenecks were numerous.

I stayed late. The telephone rang continuously. Once Mr. Churchill came on. Obviously he was asking Lord Beaverbrook's opinion on some new appointment, for Lord Beaverbrook replied decisively: "I'd give it to the younger man." Before I left, the telephone rang again. This time Lord Beaverbrook said nothing, but as he put down the receiver his face lit up. The evacuation was going marvellously well. We had already saved over 75,000 men. It had been a giddy and inspiring evening. As I walked back to my club, I felt that Ribbentrop had made a slight error in telling his master that we were a decadent and dying race. The fires of British resentment burnt slowly. They had been banked perhaps for too long. Now at last the red was beginning to glow under the fierce breath of a new energy. In his peace offer made after the collapse of Poland, Hitler had not mentioned Mr. Chamberlain, but had singled out Mr. Churchill as the one English statesman who was foolish enough to believe that Germany would be beaten. Expressing his own certainty of a German victory, Hitler had declared: "Destiny will decide who is right." Destiny had not yet spoken its last word.

Although in his propaganda output Goebbels made some capital out of our claiming a victory in what was really a military disaster, Dunkirk was perhaps the turning point of the war, for it brought the nation face to face with stark reality, united it as one man, and galvanised it into new energy.

I spent the next few days in seeing the Balkan Ministers. As usual, M. Momtchilov, the Bulgarian, was the most optimistic. He feared the worst in the Balkans, but never doubted our final victory. He told me that in 1939 a Bulgarian technical mission of air experts had visited Germany and Britain in order to buy or try to buy aeroplanes. In Germany they had been shown everything. Their own sympathies were inclined towards the Germans. But, when they returned to Sofia, their recommendation was: "If possible, order British machines; they are much better than the German." They were. Unfortunately, we had none to sell and all too few for ourselves. I had quiet fun with M. Subotić, the Yugoslav, who regarded the evacuation as the end of Britain. He did not know the figures and assumed that we had saved only a remnant of our army. "Your Excellency," I said, "what do you consider the necessary percentage to save in order to avoid what you call a major disaster?"

He hesitated and then said gravely: "Twenty-five per cent. would be good; fifty per cent. would be a miracle."

I had just been told the latest figures by the Admiralty. At that moment the number saved of all ranks, including French and Belgians, was 264,000. I said to M. Subotić: "Your Excellency, you have got your miracle—and the English have performed it. As a Scot may I give you a sound tip. You must never underestimate the English. They are never more dangerous than when they seem at their last gasp. It's the fog that does it. Anyone who can breathe in this climate has a second wind that lasts for ever." He was temporarily encouraged. Unfortunately, he was one of the few Serbs who had no second wind.

It was at this time that I renewed my acquaintance with M. Maisky whom I met at a small luncheon party given by M. Momtchilov. The only other guest was M. Aras, the Turkish Ambassador. I had known M. Maisky since he first came to the Russian Embassy in London in 1932. Although I had been condemned to death by the Bolsheviks in 1918 as a victim of our intervention which, in point of fact, I had strenuously opposed, M. Maisky did not regard me as a criminal. I was always asked to the parties at the Russian Embassy and saw him frequently alone. I liked this clever, little man. A talk with him was always a lively battle of wits. During the early part of the war, while Russia was apparently an unfriendly neutral, he was in a difficult situation. Nevertheless, I believe that, within the limited power of a Soviet ambassador, he was always anti-German and still hoped and worked for an Anglo-Russian alliance.

At our luncheon I was a little shocked by the conduct of M. Aras who denounced the capitalists with vigour and blamed them for the appeasement which had caused the war. He was obviously playing up to the Russian Ambassador. I was pleased to notice that M. Maisky made no comment on these remarks. His attitude towards me was friendly but guarded. He advised me to read *War and Peace* again. It contained, he said, lessons for the present war. I took it as a friendly indication of his own attitude. A fortnight later he invited me to luncheon. There were other guests, but afterwards I had ten minutes with him alone. He was surprisingly optimistic for the grimness of those days. "If you can get through the next three months," he said, "I think you will win." Until he was transferred to Moscow in 1943, I was to see him frequently.

During that fateful June when France, "stabbed in the back" by Mussolini, was in collapse, and exiled governments were arriving piecemeal at British ports, I was, fortunately for myself, kept very busy. The Czechoslovaks were in dire straits, and even Dr. Beneš's patience was nearly at its end. The Foreign Office had sent an unsatisfactory reply to his request for a Provisional Government. It was not a refusal, but it still insisted on complete unity among the Czechoslovak exiles as a condition of recognition. What it meant in plain language was that Dr. Beneš must re-make his peace with Dr. Hodža, who was again making trouble. Unfortunately, Dr. Hodža had, by some means, acquired knowledge of the contents of Sir Alexander Cadogan's letter and was using his information in order to levy political blackmail. Dr. Beneš was near despair.

"You admit," he said to me, "that I have a big majority. Yet you are trying to force me to accept this insignificant minority of blackmailers. You do nothing to persuade them."

For once he spoke bitterly and talked of going to the United States. What rankled in his mind was the knowledge that the tanks with which the Germans had effected their break-through in France were the Škoda tanks which had been seized after Munich.

My sympathies were on his side, and early in June I came back to the charge in a despatch to the Foreign Office. But even in Dr. Beneš's mind recognition took a back place when the news was received that the Czechoslovak regiments which had been fighting on the French front had reached Sete on the Mediterranean coast and were unable to embark. General Ingr, the Commander-in-Chief, and all his staff were with them. The French authorities had put every difficulty in their way and had tried to stop their departure by force. Fortunately the Czechoslovaks had found one French stand-by in General Faucher who had spent many years in Czechoslovakia as a member of the French military mission. This brave officer had gone up the line to help the Czechoslovak troops and had piloted them to Sete only to arrive after the last ships had gone. Dr. Beneš and M. Masaryk came to me in desperation. The Foreign Office could do nothing. It was not their affair. So making use of my friendship with Rex Fletcher, I went to the Admiralty on my own. As usual, the Admiralty took action and, although many anxious hours passed before the fate of the troops was known, they were brought safely to England. At the height of this crisis the B.B.C. played the hymns of the Allied countries whose governments were now in England. The Czechoslovak hymn was not played. The omission rankled.

The collapse of France brought other Slav jetsam to our shores. During the last days of the Bordeaux bottleneck of escape I had received a frantic appeal from Alexander Kerensky, once the idol of the February Revolution in 1917. He had been living in France, had arrived at Bordeaux and could not go aboard a ship without a British visa. Could I help at once? If he fell into the hands of the Germans, they would deliver him to the Bolsheviks. And that would be the end.

Again I went to the Foreign Office and to the Admiralty. I met with little sympathy in either department. In 1917, when we were afraid that Russia would make a separate peace, British and French ministers had courted Kerensky as rich and aged plutocrats pay court to a ballerina. To his own detriment, for peace was the winning card of the Bolsheviks, Kerensky carried on the war for nine months until the October Revolution. Now he was forgotten, and a new generation did not even know his name. Moreover, every alien who arrived in war-time was an added burden to our own population. I pleaded for a transit visa, pointing out that Kerensky had friends and an Australian wife in the United States. In the end a telegram was sent to Bordeaux, but I had little hope that it would produce any result. But towards the end of June Kerensky arrived. I had saved him in 1918 in Russia by giving him a British visa and by arranging for him to travel disguised as a Serbian soldier. Now he was convinced that I had saved him again, and his gratitude was embarrassing. He stayed nearly a month in London, while I helped him to get a visa for the United States. When we said goodbye, he came out with me to the door of the lift and, shaking me violently by the hand, said in a voice trembling with emotion: "You are a real friend, and I have very few friends nowadays. It is in adversity that you know who are your real friends."

All governments are cruel and Russian Governments are crueller than most. But the individual Russian has more understanding of human nature and more of the milk of human kindness in his heart than any other national. And I like and shall always like Russians.

Money and success mean less to them than to other people. I had been one of the first, if not the very first, British official to meet Kerensky. I had known him in the days of his greatness; I had seen him in the years of adversity and of dwindling hope. I had never once noticed the smallest change in his demeanour or heard from his lips one word of criticism of those who had sought his favour in success and had cursed him in his failure. Yet he was one of the greatest orators of our times and had much cause for bitterness, for his descent from great exaltation had been profound, and few reversals of fortune in history have been more sudden.

In point of fact, the collapse of France was of direct assistance to recognition of the Czechoslovaks in exile, for there was now no anti-Czech pull from Paris. On July 2 the Foreign Office informed me privately that Lord Halifax had approved my paper and that the whole question of recognition would be decided in a day or two. It was. The Cabinet approved without a murmur. But three weeks were to pass before Dr. Beneš was notified and the official announcement made. On July 20 Dr. Beneš's secretary telephoned to me in some excitement. "The President has been sent for by Lord Halifax. Is anything wrong?"

"Of course not," I said. "Why do you ask? Are you afraid of something?"

"We are always afraid of some change here," he replied pathetically.

The official announcement was made three days later by Mr. Churchill in the House of Commons. That night the B.B.C. played the Czechoslovak hymn "Where is My Home" and, although the next day was Budget Day, the Czechoslovaks were done proudly in the British Press, the *Times* devoting a leader to their praise. At eleven in the morning I went to the Czechoslovak offices in Park Street to congratulate Dr. Beneš. I was shown in immediately, and he came forward to greet me with both hands. He started to thank me. "I—we—shall never forget." Then the words stuck, and a film came over his eyes. I felt a lump in my own throat. Then I told him how much I had admired his courage and patience. He smiled and, quite himself again, said gaily: "Well, there have been some bad moments, but, thank goodness, I have strong nerves."

When I came out, the ante-room was full of Czechoslovaks—new ministers waiting to be given office, ex-members of the Czechoslovak Parliament, civil servants and Dr. Beneš's personal staff. The sun, shining through the windows, lit up a sea of smiles.

A fortnight later I was appointed British Representative with the Provisional Czechoslovak Government. My official title should have been British Agent. But I protested. In 1918 I had been appointed British Agent to the unrecognised Bolshevik Government. Once in a lifetime was enough.

CHAPTER SIX

MY NEW POST made a considerable alteration in my life. I now moved permanently to London and took a small flat in Duke of York Street. Nevertheless, I continued to write the Balkan section of the Weekly Summary of the Political Intelligence and to attend the Saturday meetings of the propaganda organisation at Woburn. The change was to my liking. I had now moved from the circumference to the centre.

Simultaneously with my appointment to the Czechoslovaks, great alterations had taken place in the structure of our various propaganda organisations which, like many other temporary war departments, began with anarchy. At the beginning of the war three separate organisations were engaged in propaganda: the Ministry of Information, the Department of Propaganda to Enemy and Enemy-Occupied countries, and the European Services of the B.B.C. The Ministry was housed in Bloomsbury; the Department for Propaganda to Enemy and Enemy-Occupied countries in Bedfordshire. After various vicissitudes the European Services of the B.B.C. moved to Bush House. As Germany began to overrun all Europe, the countries which she occupied passed automatically from the Ministry of Information to the Department for Enemy Propaganda, leaving sore hearts in the Ministry, for the transfer of territory was not accompanied by the transfer of staff. For their respective countries the Ministry of Information and the Department for Enemy Propaganda were supposed to control the foreign broadcasts of the B.B.C. Physical separation, however, made effective control impossible, and the B.B.C. was able to assert a virtual independence. Chaos was therefore inevitable, and the three organisations were constantly at loggerheads. Indeed, during this period there was more political warfare on the home front than against the enemy.

The new Government, overwhelmed with more serious problems, made a patchwork attempt to remedy this state of affairs. The Department for Enemy Propaganda was put under the control of Dr. Dalton, and Rex Leeper was appointed as the official in charge. The change was for the better, but it was only a half-measure. Dr. Dalton's main job was at the Ministry of Economic Warfare. Rex Leeper had also two jobs, for he remained as Head of the Political Intelligence Department. As far as policy was concerned, the Foreign

Office had the last word on foreign propaganda. There was therefore duality of offices and of control from the start.

The right course was to bring the Department of Enemy Propaganda from Woburn to London. This Dr. Dalton did by moving the bulk of the organisation to Lansdowne House which was close to his own Ministry in Berkeley Square. But the difficulties did not cease. Even in London physical separation was still a handicap, and practical experience soon proved the impossibility of controlling the B.B.C. unless the controllers were housed in the same building. The friction with the B.B.C. and the Ministry of Information continued. Moreover, by the time the new plans were ready for execution, the German air-raids on London had started. On account of the accommodation problems created by the raids, the Department of Enemy Propaganda returned to Woburn after one short month in London leaving only a small military wing in Lansdowne House. All the original drawbacks were therefore restored. To make matters worse, the Political Intelligence Department, which had been more or less merged with the propaganda department, disliked the new arrangement, and Professor Woodward, one of its ablest experts, resigned.

For my own part I was well suited with the change. I had established my Czechoslovak office in Lansdowne House and was close to Dr. Dalton to whom I had direct access, for I continued to advise and to co-operate with the propagandists in Czechoslovak affairs. His mental and physical vigour was refreshing. I found him very receptive to new ideas, decisive and quick in action, and a tiger for work. We christened him Dr. Dynamo, and he deserved the compliment. Given full control and undivided time, he would, I think, have made a first-class job of what was almost an impossibility.

I was also in daily and, indeed, hourly contact with General (then Brigadier) Brooks who was head of the Military Wing of the Department for Enemy Propaganda. Tall, well-built and a superb athlete, Brooks was a Marine Officer who, as a youngster of twenty-one, had gained one of the best D.S.O's in the first world war by his gallantry at Zeebrugge. He was an admirable contact man, pleasant in manner, always good-tempered, and at his best in a crisis. My friendship with him was most valuable for he enjoyed the confidence of the Chiefs of Staff Organisation. By pooling our sources of information we were in a position to know nearly everything. He brought me into close touch with General Ismay, the Prime Minister's Military Adviser, and with General Hollis, the Secretary of the Chiefs of Staff. I introduced Brooks to the leading officials of the Foreign Office.

We were to be closely, and I think successfully, associated until the last months of the war. But in that autumn of 1940 the propaganda situation was almost tragic. There was an abundance of real talent at Woburn but the inability of propaganda to disturb the tide of German military successes did not increase the department's prestige, although at that time the task was, in fact, hopeless. And when the raids came, the peaceful security of Bedfordshire invited criticism by Londoners. It was freely given, and Whitehall wits and even the Press made allusions to "Leeper's Sleepers". The criticism was unfair, for the Woburn people worked longer hours than any Whitehall department and were almost too fertile in wide-awake ideas.

My own share in propaganda during this period was small. In September I made my first broadcast in Czech. I wrote a few leaflets to be dropped over Czechoslovakia which was then almost beyond the range of our bombers, and I did my best to ensure a decent share of broadcasting time for the Provisional Czechoslovak Government.

My main work, however, was now political; my first ambition, to obtain full recognition of the Czechoslovak Government in London. I began to see even more of Dr. Beneš, especially as he was without the services of Jan Masaryk who had gone on a long mission to the United States and was doing good work there both for us and for his own countrymen. I was greatly impressed by Dr. Beneš's belief in the inevitability of a clash between Russia and Germany and of Russia's entry into the war on the side of the Allies. His belief had now become a persistent conviction which he buttressed with information from his experts in Moscow and with all the reasoning power of his own well-ordered brain. His information from Russia was excellent. The only trouble was that he produced such a mass of intelligence, some good and some indifferent, from his Czech sources in all countries, that the British authorities, finding some chaff among it, were inclined to neglect the grain and to discard both as Czech propaganda. But on Russia Dr. Beneš's arguments were convincing. His mind was glued on the Balkans where in his view the clash was bound to come. The Russians, he always said, never could and never would tolerate German domination of the Balkan countries. Their whole policy showed how their minds must be working. He pointed to the occupation of Bessarabia and to the clever Russian propaganda. Both were designed to make it impossible for Roumania and Bulgaria to enter the war effectively on Germany's side.

Certainly the propaganda in Bulgaria seemed to be fruitful, for when the Russians sent a football team to Sofia in August, it received a tumultuous welcome from a Bulgarian crowd which our Minister reported as approximately 100,000—or one-third of the population of the Bulgarian capital. Reuters put the figure at 150,000! Russia's attempts to disintegrate and sterilise the Balkans were helped rather than hindered by the pressure which Germany was exerting on the unhappy "bourgeois" governments of Yugoslavia, Bulgaria and Roumania, and when on August 30 the unfortunate King Carol preferred to cede Transylvania rather than fight, I felt that the wages of surrender would be abdication.

Dr. Beneš's capacity for work kept me more than busy. Having achieved provisional recognition, he had already prepared a complete case for full recognition including the juridical continuity of his own position as President. He was eager for me to present it to the Foreign Office, but I begged him to wait. In August and September the attention of the Government and, indeed, of every British subject in the world was rivetted on the air-battles which almost everyone felt must be, in the event of failure, the prelude to an invasion of this country. Since my return to London I had been on several occasions to Lord Beaverbrook's house and had met some of the young airmen who were defending so desperately and so successfully the life-line— now no longer the sea but the air—of Britain. They inspired everyone by their modesty, their seriousness, and their confidence in victory. I remember one young Spitfire pilot who came to see Lord Beaverbrook on August 24. He had been in the thick of the fighting and was going back. He told his story very simply. Shooting down the German bombers was easy. The German fighters were not very good, although there were some clever German squadron leaders. But the fighters were troublesome, for they kept our men away from the German bombers. And we had too few squadrons to engage both bombers and fighters.

Lord Beaverbrook had many stories of the heroism of our pilots. One which pleased him greatly was the exchange of telegrams between the Prime Minister and Squadron-Leader Peel. This officer, who already had a fine record, had been in a dog-fight over the sea with ten Hurricanes against fifty Messerschmidts. All was going well, when suddenly Peel found himself wobbling. His tail-piece had been shot away. A stormy day was an uninviting prospect for a parachute landing so far out at sea. So he decided to make for the coast. Six miles out he had to make his jump from a low height. The force of his parachute descent carried him several feet under the water. His life-jacket kept him down, and he had to take it off. He had swallowed much sea-water and was sick. He lay for an hour in the sea before he was picked up. A few days later Lord Beaverbrook told the story to Mr. Churchill who invited Peel to luncheon. Lord Beaverbrook sent the telegram. By this time Peel had returned to his squadron and once more was in the van of the fighting. Back came his telegram of acceptance: "Greatly honoured to lunch with the Prime Minister. Last week my stomach was full of salt water; tonight it will be full of champagne." As I listened to the story, there flashed through my mind King Lear's apostrophe to the storm: "Rumble thy-bellyful: spit fire, spout rain." But for our Spitfires and Hurricanes in that autumn of 1940, many of us would not be alive today and none of us would be free men.

I was glad and proud to have the opportunity of seeing so much of Lord Beaverbrook during this period, for it was indubitably the greatest period in his own life. No one who knows him would ever dismiss him as little in anything except physical stature. On the contrary, he has the qualities of greatness, and in the Battle of Britain he played a decisive part by providing aeroplanes by inimitable methods of his own. His energy was daemonic. He spared neither himself nor his subordinates. In his own sphere he was given the powers of a dictator, and he used them with piratical ruthlessness. He broke bottlenecks; he ruffled the dignity of senior officials. But where no other man would have succeeded, he produced the aeroplanes for the Battle of Britain.

Although he looked, and undoubtedly was, physically tired, his nervous energy was amazing. He slept little, ate sparingly, and worked sixteen hours of every day in every week. Never have I seen a man drive himself and others with such relentless speed. Yet almost all the time he was puckishly cheerful, filling his house with people, inspiring them with the magnetism of his own determination and always ready to cap their stories with a better one of his own.

I remember one night at Stornoway when Mr. Hore-Belisha held the general attention with an account of his visit to Mussolini before the war. Mussolini had asked him what he thought of the French army.

Mr. Hore-Belisha replied: "The best in the world."

The Duce said: "I agree about the soldiers, but not about the generals. French strategy and French theories are out of date. If there is a war, we shall see many surprises. The French generals will be unable to cope with them. The Germans will go far and quickly."

Thereupon Mr. Hore-Belisha asked Mussolini when the Germans would reach Trieste. Mussolini had turned red and had replied sourly: "That is a question for discussion."

At this Mr. Hore-Belisha retorted: "Yes, Duce, but unfortunately the Germans never discuss."

It was a fragment of history. Not to be outdone, Lord Beaverbrook then told the story of *his* meeting with Mussolini. The Duce had begun the talk as one newspaper man to another. "I started my life as a journalist," he said, "I never forget that I may end my life as one." Then the name of Sir Stafford Cripps cropped up in the conversation. Mussolini wanted to know who he was.

"I hear he is very clever."

"Tolerably so," replied Lord Beaverbrook.

"Is he honest?"

"Certainly."

"I hear he is rich."

"Tolerably so."

"Where did he get his money from?"

"Eno's Fruit Salts," said Lord Beaverbrook puckishly.

"Ha, ha," roared Mussolini, "I owe *my* success to castor oil."

The story is typical of Lord Beaverbrook's lightning changes of mood. He can laugh and cry or be ribald and serious almost at the same time. But he has always the speed of action of the New World, and his successes and failures have been largely determined by the fact that, although he has lived so long in England, he has never been able to anglicise himself. The dominants in his character are a restless ambition and a ruthless love of power. Both spring from the materialism of the New World. Both have made him enemies among the British public who dislike newspaper proprietors and, more particularly, among the Tories who mistrust his methods and who always suspect clever people, especially when they are not English.

Although he can be tough in a fight, he has performed many kind acts, of which the public hears nothing, and he has always had the knack of inspiring great loyalty in those who are nearest to him. He has been the confidant of three British Prime Ministers: Lloyd George, Bonar Law, and Winston Churchill, and many prominent men have sought his advice which is almost always shrewd, wise, and generously given.

Yet in spite of the material successes of his life, I have no doubt that he counts himself a failure if only because his ambition has always outrun achievement. He dislikes the privileged position of the English upper classes, and nothing will rid him of the feeling that if he had not been born a poor boy in Canada he would have reached still greater heights. There is in his character a strong streak of Presbyterianism which makes him prone at times to melancholy. He is, in fact, a Scot of the New World, and his attitude towards the English is typical of that of many Dominion Scots. It is best expressed in a phrase which I have heard him use more than once in a moment of frustration; "I dislike these damned English, but I hate like hell to hear anyone else hating or criticising them." In his conversation with Americans he acts vigorously on the second part of his dictum.

The revolution of 1945 has left him in a backwater. But, whatever the future may hold for him, he has left an indelible mark on the Press and politics of his time, and nothing will ever rob him of a place in British history for his part in the Battle of Britain. Combined with the skill and courage of our pilots, it was decisive, and it was performed with all the physical and mental vigour, ability and sacrifice of self that few others could command.

Looking back on the Battle of Britain, I find it hard to recapture my reactions. My diaries show that I had very little idea of what was coming to us in the form of indiscriminate air-raids. I felt an emotional exaltation and a fierce pride in the heroism of British youth which once again had refuted the pessimism of the arm-chair critics. On the other hand, I found it hard to concentrate on my work. For total war middle age must discipline itself and must train as if for a long-distance race or a rugby football international. My self-discipline was poor; it became instinctive to fortify my nerves with more alcohol than usual. There were others who did the same. I envied the stoical phlegm of the senior civil servants, most of whom worked longer hours on a shorter and more abstemious diet. On the afternoon of Saturday, September 7, I had my first sight of a big air-battle over London. Although the aeroplanes were high up, they could be followed easily with the naked eye. The azure sky looked like the Pacific, the 'planes themselves like silver tropical fish. I watched the scene from the balcony of my club in St. James's Square. It never occurred to my mind that soon—very soon in fact—German aeroplanes would be attacking the heart of London and that every sound of the sirens would bring with it a sickening feeling of personal dread.

That night the whole of dockland was ablaze, and, for miles around, the sky was a sea of molten lead. The German radio announced the attack as the beginning of the end, and the rest of the world believed it. During that first fortnight of September I received several telegrams from friends in the United States and in the Balkans. They conveyed prayers and good wishes for Britain's safety. In my diary I find the entry: "Very kind of them, but we are not near destruction—at least not from the Germans, although I personally may be from my creditors." The last statement was true. My income from books had ceased. My official salary was small, and I found I had to divide my scale of living by five. My innocent optimism about the air-raids was soon dispelled by Air Commodore Groves, the first, the most consistent and the most accurate prophet of air power. He explained to me that the present tactics of the Luftwaffe were an integral part of military strategy. When and if they failed, the Germans would launch full-scale attacks on the civilian population. His forecast was correct. After the Battle of Britain the bombing became indiscriminate.

At first the day raids caused a serious disturbance of work, for the official rule was that everyone must take shelter as soon as the sirens sounded. In Lansdowne House, where I had my Czechoslovak office on the same floor as the military wing of the Enemy Propaganda Department, the rule was enforced with military precision. It was soon killed by ridicule. On the morning of September 13, I arrived at the office to find everyone down below. The raid was a long one. During our enforced incarceration a little Czech girl of sixteen arrived with a letter marked "To be delivered to Mr. Lockhart personally." It was from Dr. Beneš. The girl had walked from Grosvenor Place to Berkeley Square and, raid or no raid, was setting out nonchalantly to walk back. After this lesson the shelter order was revoked.

Every Londoner has had his or her long tally of bombing experiences, and today most people probably try to forget them. One experience of my own is perhaps worth recording. On October 14 I dined at the United Services Club with Dallas Brooks. It was the night of the raid on Club-land. During dinner a near bomb crashed, shook the building, and rattled the chandeliers. The always cheerful Brooks said gaily: "Well, that's all right. We shan't get another as close as that." After dinner we went into the smoking-room which was full of generals and admirals. After a short talk with General Ismay I sat down with Brooks at a table by the window overlooking the garden. Soon there was another whizz and a crash, and I was shot off my chair on to the floor. I looked up slightly dazed. The generals and admirals—and, indeed, everyone else—were flat on their stomachs. The only standing figure in the room was a naval captain. He was very erect. In his right hand he held a full glass of port. As I raised myself, he asked me if I were hurt. I told him no. He lifted his glass and emptied it slowly.

"Thank God," he said, "that didn't spill."

Fortunately the bomb had landed in the garden plot and not on the concrete path outside the window, but the blast killed Admiral Tower who had left the club a few seconds before.

I had received a few tiny punctures on my arm from glass and after minor repairs I set out with Brooks to walk to the East India and Sports Club where, having previously been bombed out of my flat, I was now living. There were several fires between Pall Mall and Piccadilly. In the club all the front windows had been smashed, but the bar was open. After a stiff whisky I wanted to stay where I was, but Brooks dragged me out again away from the target of fires. We walked to Berkeley Square and after more bombs had made us go down twice on our faces, we found the underground Lansdowne Restaurant. We looked like Negroes. We sat late and were charged four pounds for whisky and sandwiches.

During the winter of 1940–41 the underground restaurants near our office—the Lansdowne, the Mayfair and the Ritz—were our night shelter. They were crowded with officers, officials, young girls driving canteen vans, American correspondents like Quentin Reynolds, and occasional ministers. Afterwards the chief shareholder of Lansdowne House explained to us that the underground restaurant was anything but safe. But we did not know and perhaps did not care. The guns and bombs could not be heard; the music and the alcohol gave at any rate the impression of security.

During that year our life was a curious and monotonous ritual. We worked till 9 p.m. Then we would walk round the corner to the Lansdowne. By ten o'clock it was crowded. The scene was different from the gilded squalor of the big hotels. Here nearly everyone was a war-worker. At dinner we met officials from other departments and discussed our common problems. Intermittently I watched the dancing and studied the sea of faces and the sway of human bodies. In Europe I had had my fill of night-life. Apart from the gipsy music in Russia it had followed a stereotyped pattern. But here was something different, decorous, orderly; infinitely more restrained than the riotous night-life of the first world war, and yet slightly sinister. Certain memories will remain with me always. In the Lansdowne, at least, the tune of the Blitz was Jerome Kern's "All the Things You

Are". It was played a score of times every night, and on each occasion a tall, pale consumptive-looking saxophonist would lay down his instrument and, taking up the microphone, would croon the words in a plaintive and appealing voice:

> "Some day my happy arms will hold you
> And some day I'll know that moment divine,
> When all the things you are, are mine."

On me the melody had a strong nostalgic effect, and as a Scot I felt the full loneliness of a London which I had never known until middle age. I noticed no similar reaction in my English friends or, indeed, in the dancers. Doubtless, their emotions were the same as mine, but they were never allowed to appear. I admired and envied this English self-control. I saw no sign of strain in any face. Perhaps I guessed wrongly that it was hidden under the surface. My own sense of loneliness was I think greatest when I walked back through the deserted streets to St. James's Square.

Londoners were at their best during the first month of the Blitz, and the office girls were wonderful. They came early and worked late. They arrived and left to the cacophonous chorus of bombs and guns and sirens. Poorly paid, they never complained. They rarely, if ever, arrived late. Grimmest and bravest of all were the charwomen who cleaned the offices and who, as they worked, swopped gruesome details of the previous night's blitz. The lady from Camberwell would say her piece. The bloody recital would be taken up by Battersea who, not to be outdone, would preface her account with a contemptuous "Lor, that was nuffin". Then the competition in horrors would continue to the accompaniment of violent scrubbing and equally violent oaths. It was horrifying, but it was magnificent. As Lord Beaverbrook said to me one night: "You are a Scot; I am a Canadian Scot. We know what courage is. But when it comes to sheer guts you have to give the palm to the English."

One of my chief concerns at the beginning of the Blitz was to find a secure residence for Dr. Beneš. The little villa in Gwendolen Avenue was ridiculously unsafe. After some trouble I succeeded in getting a house for him at Aston Abbots which was only four miles from Woburn. It suited the President very well and me even better, for its proximity to Woburn enabled me to attend my Saturday meeting of the Enemy Propaganda Department, to see Dr. Beneš the next day, and to spend a blitz-free week-end.

The house was in the heart of the country with a clear view of the

Chilterns. It had once belonged to Sir John Ross, the Polar explorer, who discovered that the Eskimos had no word for war and did not know what it meant. It was now to be Dr. Beneš's headquarters for the planning of the worst form of war: resistance and sabotage by an enemy-occupied country. We found the house just in time. Soon after Dr. Beneš moved to the country, the shelter in the Gwendolen Avenue villa received a direct hit.

Although I had a hard fight for recognition of my Czechoslovaks, working with Dr. Beneš was an exhilarating experience, and I was confident from the start that of all the exiled leaders in this country he would be the one who would be welcomed back. It was not the view of the Foreign Office at that time, and the unfortunate Czechoslovaks were subjected to irritating delays and unnecessary, if minor, humiliations. At the first Inter-Allied Conference they were originally placed bottom of the list because they were only a Provisional Government. I protested on their behalf, and the sitting was altered to alphabetical order.

October 28 is Czechoslovakia's Independence Day and I accompanied Dr. Beneš when he laid a wreath at the Cenotaph. This time the Foreign Office did the unrecognised President full honour. The Vice-Marshal of the Diplomatic Corps and representatives of the War Office were present, and the ceremony was simple and dignified. But I felt the irony of celebrating the Independence Day of a country that was no longer independent. It was two years ago almost to a day since the great little man had been forced to flee from Czechoslovakia, and the full burden of his tragedy weighed heavily on me. In the afternoon I attended his reception for the diplomatic corps which was represented by two minor figures: the Norwegian Chargé d'Affaires and myself. Following the example of the British Government, the other Allied Governments in exile did not recognise the poor provisionals. It was at this time that, by way of reminder, the otherwise patient Jan Masaryk sent me a letter signed: "Yours provisionally."

Fate was against the Czechoslovaks in 1940, and the attempted bombing of the Škoda Works, which they had urged continuously, was a real disaster. It was announced by the Air Ministry as a success. In point of fact, the pilots missed their target by twenty miles. The effect on the Czechs in the homeland was unfortunate, for they assumed that our communiqués were as false as the propaganda of Dr. Goebbels.

Dr. Beneš, however, never lost heart, and gradually his affairs began to mend. A week before Christmas I recorded another broadcast message to Prague. Soon, however, the home Czechoslovaks were to receive vastly more welcome tidings. I spent Sunday, December 22, with the Leepers near Woburn. The other guests were Sir Orme Sargent and M. Masaryk. At 7 p.m. we received the official announcement that Lord Halifax was leaving the Foreign Office to go to Washington as Ambassador and that Mr. Eden had been appointed Foreign Secretary. It would be a perversion of an obvious truth to pretend that the Czechoslovaks were not pleased. From Dr. Beneš to the smallest office boy in the Czechoslovak Government offices they were radiant, and after dinner we had a rare treat. I persuaded Jan Masaryk, who when he is in the mood can draw from a piano the whole gamut of human emotions from bitter tears to paeans of rejoicing, to sit down and play to us. He was in the right mood.

He sat in silence for a moment with his head bowed over the keys. Then he started to improvise a symphonic poem which symbolised the hard road which the Czechoslovaks had trod since Munich. It began with minor Slav melodies. The song was old, but it was deathless. It told more poignantly than any words the longing of the exile for his home-land. I could see the solitary Slovak shepherd standing on the hillside and sending the notes of his reed-pipe out to the vastness of the Tatra mountains. Next came a prayer motif, perhaps intended as a heart-felt plea for a higher standard of morality in international relations. Then, as nostalgia yielded place to hope, the theme changed. Negro spirituals heralded the translation of Lord Halifax to Washington. Spanish music with the angry jealous clatter of castanets expressed the disappointment of Sir Samuel Hoare who, as the first President of the Anglo-Czechoslovakian Society, had in turn bitterly disappointed the Czechoslovaks by his attitude at the time of Munich.

As he introduced Mr. Eden, Jan worked himself up to a triumphant finale which ranged in rapid succession from "Rule Britannia", "Annie Laurie", with bagpipe imitation thrown in as my special reward, and the plaintive Czech national hymn "Where is My Home", to the five last majestic chords of "God Save The King". It was a brilliant performance which would never be repeated. Jan was not only inspired; he was exalted. More perhaps than any of his compatriots, he had fixed his hopes on Mr. Eden. They were not misplaced. After a quiet Christmas I went to see him on December 27 at the new Czechoslovak Government offices in Furzecroft. While I was in the room one of the private secretaries telephoned from the

Foreign Office. "Would it be convenient for M. Masaryk to see Mr. Eden at 3.30 p.m. on Tuesday?" Jan was delighted. Mr. Eden had lost no time.

The year 1940 ended with the disastrous raid of December 28 when, during the absenteeism of an English week-end, a high wind fanned the flames started by incendiary bombs into a raging fire which created havoc throughout the City and nearly destroyed St. Paul's.

Yet in spite of the horrors of the bombing, the muddles and delays in Whitehall, and the desperate race to catch up with armaments, the nation and I think everyone in it, had gained a new spirit under Mr. Churchill's leadership. Confidence was restored.

On New Year's Eve I received a warm and hopeful letter from Dr. Beneš and, although at that time I knew Mr. Eden only very slightly, I felt sure that my task would now be easier. My instinct was correct. From September, 1939, to December, 1940, I had never once seen Lord Halifax and, with but little official encouragement, had to make out on paper the best case that I could for the Czechoslovaks. Mr. Eden was always accessible and my relations with him became increasingly cordial and intimate.

CHAPTER SEVEN

THE MORE I see of the inside making of history, the more I realise how haphazard it is. There is, in fact, no law of destiny except chance. Mr. Eden had not wished to return to the Foreign Office, where he had already spent the major portion of his political career. He had been very happy as Secretary of State for War and has always liked soldiers and got on well with them. Indeed, there is no tie in life which holds his heart more closely than his association with his old regiment, the Sixtieth Rifles, once known as the Royal Americans. His transfer to the Foreign Office was determined, partly, by the sudden death of Lord Lothian, the most successful of all British ambassadors to the United States, and, partly, by the desire of Mr. Churchill, in his capacity of Minister of Defence, to hold all the reins of strategy in his own hands.

The change completely altered the fortunes of the Czechoslovak Government in exile. I have already referred to the unfailing optimism of Dr. Beneš. It can be further emphasised by one simple illustration. In their secret communications with Prague all the leading Czechoslovak exiles used pseudonyms. Dr. Beneš's *nom de guerre* was Pan Navratil which means in English Mr. Come-Back. Hitherto, his confidence had been the courage of a man who resolutely refused to despair in adversity. Now it became the optimism of rational and justifiable expectation. From Mr. Eden the Czechoslovaks received not only sympathy but also official backing, and my own work now acquired a live and inspiring interest because every project received immediate action. Mr. Eden has rightly acquired an international reputation as a negotiator, but perhaps his greatest virtue as a minister is the speed with which he deals with paper. He is a tireless and rapid worker.

For some time past I had been trying to assist the promotion of Polish-Czechoslovak Confederation. From the beginning the project had received the official blessing of the Foreign Office. Now it was given a fresh stimulus by Mr. Eden, and a Polish-Czechoslovak Committee was set up which after several preliminary discussions held its first official meeting on January 11, 1941. Superficially it was a success, but none of the difficult problems was discussed. Although I favoured a project which every dictate of common sense recommended, I was never very hopeful of a successful result. Combination and compromise are not the strong virtues of the Slavs; they are the weakest qualities of the Poles. Although Dr. Beneš and General Sikorski had always been on good terms, there were many Poles who disliked the Czechoslovak President. There were others who did not hesitate to intrigue against General Sikorski.

At the end of January I met General Sikorski at Aston Abbots where he spent the night with Dr. Beneš. The next day the two men motored to Leamington to attend the manoeuvres of the small Czechoslovak army. I went with them, together with Victor Cazalet who was Mr. Churchill's personal aide-de-camp to the Polish Prime Minister and Commander-in-Chief. During the long drive I had a good talk with Victor whom I had known since my Russian days. As a member of Parliament he should have done better than he did, for he knew everyone, had travelled much, and understood the problems of Europe better than most politicians. His political banner, however, carried too many devices. He had been pro-Munich and pro-Habsburg. He was a convinced pro-Zionist. Now he was pro-Polish and also pro-Czech. His loyalties were therefore not only too numerous but also too conflicting. On the Polish-Czech problem, however, he had sound views. The Poles, he said, were popular with the British Right; the Czechoslovaks with the British Left. If we could induce them to combine, they would command the sympathies of all Britain. I was in full agreement with him. General Sikorski made himself very affable to me and talked very sensibly on Polish-Czech co-operation. His views were the same as Victor's, and I guessed that Victor had been helpful. General Sikorski's political make-up seemed to me to be twenty-five per cent. charm, twenty-five per cent. flair, twenty-five per cent. vanity, and, compared with that of his Polish colleagues, only twenty-five per cent. ultra-nationalist.

The manoeuvres took place near the battlefield of Edgehill. I understood little of what was happening. The day was bitterly cold, and I was greatly relieved when some Czechoslovak orderlies appeared carrying trays of huge sandwiches with layers of sausage, sardines and cheese, and an imposing array of bottles and glasses. The liquid in the bottles was clear as water. Vodka or slivovice, I thought, and my heart warmed. General Sikorski took half a tumblerful and tossed it down. My turn came next. I threw the liquid down my throat in the best Russian manner, spluttered and spat out what I could. It was neat gin!

The real luncheon, however, which followed the manoeuvres was a great success. The Czechoslovaks had decorated their mess for the occasion with appropriate texts and a picture of a Pole and a Czechoslovak shaking hands. General Sikorski, whom Dr. Beneš had decorated with the Czechoslovak War Cross, made a brilliant speech in which he emphasised the advantages of a Polish-Czechoslovak alliance. Dr. Beneš spoke in the same vein, and, fortified by a potent claret, I made a completely successful speech in a language which the Poles thought was Czech and the Czechoslovaks thought was Polish. There were presents for everyone. A military band played the national anthems. The generalities of a Polish-Czechoslovak Confederation were well and truly formulated. For the moment I felt quite optimistic.

Then I drove back to Aston Abbots alone with Dr. Beneš. The little man's enthusiasm had evaporated. He alone had imbibed no alcohol. He was even more serious than usual. He had, in fact, been much upset by his talk with General Sikorski. The Polish Prime Minister had requested him formerly to recognise the Eastern frontiers of Poland. He had refused to discuss the handing back of Teschen which the Poles had seized at the time of Munich. Sikorski was the most pro-Czech of the London Poles. If this were his real attitude, what hope was there of any understanding, let alone formal co-operation, between the two nations?

Teschen was a black shadow between these two Slav cousins. Yet, had Sikorski lived, even this difficult problem might have been solved. Unfortunately there was an even more serious obstacle to co-operation than the Teschen question. This was the general attitude of the Poles who regarded the Czechs and, more particularly, the Slovaks as an inferior race. In this respect they had the same Herrenvolk instincts as the Nazis. Many of them desired not a Polish-Czechoslovak confederacy but a Polish-Czechoslovak state in which Poland as a Great Power would be the dominant partner. In the end Russia destroyed the London Polish Government and with it all the preliminary work of the Polish-Czechoslovak Committee. But, in point of fact, co-operation was strangled almost at birth by the intransigent attitude of some of the London Poles. A congenital megalomania, based more on romanticism than on realities, has been the chief cause of Poland's tragedy in history.

Another activity which occupied much of my time was the formation of the Czechoslovak Institute in London. This project was sponsored and financed by the British Council which performed an excellent and most useful service in providing these cultural and social homes for the Allied exiles in Britain. I presided at the meetings which brought the Czechoslovak Institute into being and was bitterly disappointed when an attack of influenza prevented me from being present at the official opening by Mr. Eden on January 22. He received a rousing welcome from the Czechoslovaks.

In spite of the persistent cold weather everyone in Britain, I felt, was better both in body and spirit during the first months of 1941. General Wavell's offensive in the desert was bringing us the first taste of military victory, and the nation was united in a healthier and quieter optimism. In my own work I was greatly stimulated by Jan Masaryk who, fortified by Mr. Eden's encouragement, was now doing a splendid job on the radio. In those days the home Czechs were still able to fool the Germans, and, strange as it may seem, Jan's broadcasts from London were advertised in Prague. The king of good "mixers", he is known to every Czech by his pet name of Honza. In Czech literature there is a famous fairy story, often acted as a play, which is called *The Tale of Honza*. Placards were therefore posted in Prague with the following notice: "Hear the Tale of Honza tonight at 9.30" or at whatever hour Jan's broadcast was to be delivered. Some months passed before the Germans realised what was meant. This was the peak period of Czech secret communications. By the end of January, 1941, more than 14,000 secret messages —filed and registered—had passed between Prague and London.

Our own propaganda, too, was beginning to develop on better lines, and Dr. Dalton infused into it all the drive and stimulus of his abundant energy. His views on foreign policy did not differ from those of Mr. Eden, and, as he was sympathetic to the Czechoslovak cause, I took a keener interest in this side of my work. At one of our week-end propaganda meetings at Woburn I met again Mr. Attlee whom Dr. Dalton had brought down to visit the establishment. He stayed for twenty-four hours, and I had some conversation alone with him. He asked several leading questions, but expressed no opinion. As he has the knack of putting everyone at his ease, I asked him a question to which I had long sought the answer. Was the story of his famous shooting match with Mr. Bingham, the former American Ambassador, an invention or a fact? He gave me the story in his quiet, matter-of-fact manner. Mr. Bingham had asked him to luncheon together with several Labour leaders. The Ambassador had talked throughout the meal about shooting, about his guns, about his grouse moor in Scotland. Mr. Attlee had listened with outward patience but inward boredom. Finally the Ambassador had asked him:

"And do you shoot, too, Major Attlee?"

"I have shot."

"And when did you last shoot?"

"In 1918."

"And what was your bag?"

"Germans," said Mr. Attlee grimly.

Meanwhile Dr. Beneš's hopes of full recognition were rising buoyantly. They received a strong fillip when on February 10, Mr. Eden came to luncheon with Dr. Beneš and Jan Masaryk at Claridges. There were only the four of us, and the two Czechs put their case modestly but firmly. Mr. Eden listened most sympathetically, asked some questions, and made some notes on his menu-card in the red ink which British Foreign Secretaries have used since the days of Lord Salisbury, if not indeed before.

When Dr. Beneš began to complain that the other Allied Governments had no diplomatic representatives with the Czechs and that Mr. Roosevelt had just appointed Mr. Biddle as Minister to all the other Allied Governments except the Czechs, Mr. Eden asked me sharply: "What on earth is the reason for this?"

Jan Masaryk answered for me. "You have recognised us only provisionally; the other countries follow your example."

Mr. Eden came back at me: "What is the trouble about full recognition?"

I told him that our legal advisers had had difficulties to contend with. He promised to look into the matter at once. He would, he said, find a way. Dr. Beneš is a man of immense self-restraint, but there was no mistaking the light of new hope in his eyes. Jan was openly rapturous.

I drove back to the Foreign Office with Mr. Eden. He took immediate action, and the Central Department put in a long list of objections. Their action was proper and correct. It is the duty of permanent officials to point out the consequences of ministerial action. The objections were real and serious. The British Government was a partner in the Munich Agreement. Dr. Beneš had resigned the Presidency legally and had been replaced legally by a President whom we had recognised legally. For us now to recognise the juridical continuity of Dr. Beneš as President would mean denying a legality which had received the approval of Parliament and might entail all kinds of legal consequences. Nevertheless, the Czechs had full confidence in Mr. Eden, not without good reason, for he gave them immediate encouragement by making arrangements to see Dr. Beneš regularly and by requesting Mr. Churchill to invite the

President to luncheon. Dr. Beneš was delighted by his meeting with Mr. Churchill to whom he expressed his conviction that Russia would be in the war before the summer was over.

Then, just when the Czech fortunes seemed to have emerged from the disasters of the last two and a half years, fate pushed them back into the gloom. With the signing of the Bulgarian-Axis Pact on March 1, the German path to Greece was open. To meet the crisis that was clearly coming, Mr. Eden and General Dill were sent to the Middle East. Mr. Eden was to be absent from England for six weeks. Obviously none of the legal difficulties about recognition would be settled in his absence. Dr. Beneš was downcast and wanted to approach the Prime Minister. I advised him strongly not to worry Mr. Churchill at this moment. The best and, indeed, the only step that he could take was to invite Mr. Churchill to visit the Czechoslovak army. Perhaps, if he had a spare afternoon, he would come. The invitation was sent. For six weeks nothing happened, and I myself had lost all hope.

On April 16 I left for a long week-end in the North of England where I had an official job in Manchester. For some time the British Council had been trying to amalgamate or at least co-ordinate the activities of three separate Czechoslovak Societies. I had agreed to deliver a goodwill talk and had twice postponed my visit. I took the opportunity of spending two days with my brother at Sedbergh in the hope of casting a fly on the swift, clear waters of the Rathay. Scarcely had I arrived when my secretary telephoned. Number 10 Downing Street had been asking for me. The Prime Minister proposed to visit the Czechoslovak Army on April 19. Had I been twenty years younger, I should have cancelled my Manchester visit and returned by the first train to London. Instead, I telephoned to the Foreign Office who at once put a damper on my enthusiasm. There was no need to cancel my Manchester business. There was a job to be done there and it should not be postponed any longer. The Greek crisis was at its height. Our troops there were in grave peril. The public, dismayed by the double setback in North Africa and in Yugoslavia, was disturbed and critical. It was all the favourites and the field to a single lame outsider that the Prime Minister would be unable to leave London at such a moment. Whether he went or not, the visit was of no great importance.

Uneasy in mind and sad at heart, I carried out my Manchester engagement on April 19, and in the evening left for Bletchley and Aston Abbots. I was with Dr. Beneš at 9.30 a.m. the next morning.

He was gaily, almost sportingly dressed in well-cut grey flannel trousers and a smart double-breasted blue coat. He had a daffodil in his button-hole. The sun was shining warmly; it was reflected in his eyes. The clothes and the smiling eyes were unusual. Obviously something unusual had happened. Dr. Beneš told his story badly. The Prime Minister had come to Leamington with Mrs. Churchill, Mr. Harriman, Mr. Bracken and the American General "Happy" Arnold. He had inspected the army. He had stayed a long time. Dr. Beneš had lunched with him and had taken the opportunity to mention the matter of recognition. Mr Churchill had said at once: "This must be put right; I'll see to it."

All seemed well and I left for London at once in order to brief myself for the nth time on all the arguments for recognition.

The next morning I was called early to the telephone. Could I come at once to the Foreign Office? The Central Department had received a communication from Dr. Beneš. It was not at all a good document. Did I know anything about it? I went at once to the Foreign Office. I was shown the offending document. It was a short memorandum on recognition which the careful President had handed to Mr. Churchill during his visit. Unfortunately, Dr. Beneš had inserted one sentence in which he had referred to the slowness of the Foreign Office. I felt a little crest-fallen. Had I gone to Leamington with Dr. Beneš, I should have been shown the memorandum and I should have advised him to leave out the disparaging sentence. I read on to the end and then my eye caught the bold writing of the Prime Minister: "I do not see why the Czechs should not be placed on the same footing as the other Allied Governments. They have deserved it." Underneath, Mr. Eden, who had just returned from abroad, had written: "I agree."

That afternoon I heard the full story from Jan Masaryk, and nothing of the drama was missing from his lips. On Jan's suggestion the Czechoslovak army had been taught to sing English songs, and, as Mr. Churchill stepped into his car after tea to set out on his long drive home, the Czechslovak troops, drawn up to wish him godspeed, broke into "Rule, Britannia". Nearly all of them superb singers, they sang the words in English with a full-throated fervour which stirred the emotions of all present. They loosed the heart-strings of Mr. Churchill. He descended from his car. He sang with them. His eyes welled with tears.

He remembered Munich. The singing was a reminder that reparation was long overdue. He was grateful to the Czechoslovaks.

They had good cause to be satisfied with him. As is his wont, he had taken immediate action.

Here the story of recognition should end, and I should have become, as I had always hoped, Minister to the fully recognised Czechoslovak Government. But nearly three months were to elapse before the final act of recognition was signed. Many difficulties had to be overcome, quite apart from the problem of juridical continuity. The Dominions had to agree, and some of them were difficult. Mr. Winant, the American Ambassador and a staunch Czechophil, wanted concurrent recognition by the United States, and in the State Department in Washington there were men of Munich who were therefore opposed to the Czechs.

Yet the delay was caused not so much by these political obstacles as by the series of critical military events which occupied the full time of the Prime Minister and the Cabinet. Indeed, in the dangers that had to be faced and in the possible consequences of disaster May and June of 1941 bore some resemblance to the May and June of 1940. The situation in the Aegean was desperate, and for the Navy the evacuation of Greece was a more hazardous and more costly operation than Dunkirk. Indeed, in the Battle of Crete, so heavy were our casualties in ships that during the action Sir Andrew Cunningham's officers thought it their duty to call his attention to the disproportionate balance of tonnage against us in the Mediterranean. Every British ship had been hit. The Italian Fleet was in harbour and intact. Admiral Cunningham gave his answer at once: "It takes two years to build a ship; it takes two hundred years to build a tradition. The action goes on."

There was also the arrival of Rudolf Hess, an event which at the time caused considerable excitement not only in the country, but in the Cabinet. Whether or not Hess was a pathological case is of little importance. The object of his visit was clear. As a convinced believer in the Herrenvolk idea, he wished to share the world between Germany and Britain, Germany to be given a free hand in Europe and presumably against Russia. His statement was regarded as a probable confirmation of Mr. Churchill's view that Germany intended to attack Russia very soon. Mr. Churchill was exceptionally well informed about this attack and warned Stalin who probably thought that we were trying to push Russia into the war.

In addition to the hazards of the war situation, the squabbles of our various propaganda organisations had now become a preoccupation of the Cabinet, more particularly as Mr. Duff Cooper, the Minister of Information, was at loggerheads with Dr. Dalton. The right and obvious course was to put all propaganda, as distinct from information services and publicity, under one minister. But in a Coalition the right course in smaller matters may cause serious conflict in bigger matters, and an unsatisfactory compromise becomes the only solution. After various wrangles in the Cabinet which ended without decision, I heard rumours that my name was being mentioned in connection with propaganda. On May 30 Lord Beaverbrook, who was advising the Prime Minister on these matters, sent for me and told me that Mr. Eden wished to make me an Under-Secretary in order to co-ordinate policy and propaganda. He advised me to accept. I told him frankly that unless the friction between the Minister of Information and the Propaganda Department was removed on what is called in Whitehall language the highest level, my task would be hopeless. Lord Beaverbrook still advised me to accept, saying: "This is only a beginning; I want you to get on." Lord Beaverbrook himself was in favour of putting propaganda under single control.

After further delays Mr. Eden sent for me and gave me the Cabinet's final decision. It was a thoroughly bad compromise. Propaganda was to be placed under the control of a Ministerial Committee composed of himself as Chairman, Mr. Duff Cooper, and Dr. Dalton. The actual work would be done by an operational committee. He wanted someone to preside over the second committee and to advise him. I could have the job. He would appoint me an extra Deputy Under-Secretary of State. I should have direct access to him at any time.

I asked for time to consider the proposal. I was thoroughly unhappy. I did not want to leave my Czechs. I felt not so much that I was making a mistake as taking on a job for which I was not fitted. My fears were confirmed by Sargent whom I consulted. He advised me to refuse. His view—and it was mine, too—was that I was being produced, like a rabbit out of a conjurer's hat, in order to provide an easy and temporary solution to a silly ministerial squabble. I should be of more use to the Foreign Office and to the country as an expert on Slav matters.

I waited for several days and went to spend the week-end of June 22 with Lord Beaverbrook. It was a great moment. Germany had attacked Russia, and Lord Beaverbrook was off early to Chequers to see the Prime Minister. At 9 p.m. we listened-in to Mr. Churchill's broadcast speech. It was perhaps his most important speech of the war, and it was admirable in content and in delivery. He had with him during that day Mr. Eden in the morning, Lord Beaverbrook all day, Mr. Winant and Sir Stafford Cripps part of the day. From all four I have had first-hand accounts of the conception, birth, and delivery of the speech. Lord Beaverbrook, Sir Stafford Cripps, and Mr. Winant made suggestions, some of which the Prime Minister accepted. But what is clear from the story is that Mr. Churchill had conceived the general lines of what he was going to say within half an hour of receiving the news of the attack.

Lord Beaverbrook did not come home till nearly ten o'clock at night. He looked tired, but he gave me at once his memorandum on the reconstruction of our propaganda activities and again urged me to accept. Then we went into his private cinema theatre to see a film. It was called *Dust is my Destiny*. I felt that it was mine also. I knew already that, if the proposal was put to me as a duty, I should accept. Nevertheless, I still hesitated.

Meanwhile, in spite of this disturbing intervention of fate, I was devoting all my energies to accelerating the process of Czech recognition. The delays were becoming vexatious. Now that Russia was in the war, I felt instinctively that many of the Czechoslovaks would begin to look East instead of West. I wrote another memorandum urging the necessity of speed. This time I was a little intemperate and had written, "Morality pays; immorality has always to be paid for." I showed it to Sargent who advised me to take the sentence out. I did so—wisely, as it proved, for Mr. Eden sent for me and promised immediate action. I then informed him that I would accept the propaganda job provided that I could stay with the Czechoslovak Provisional Government until recognition had gone through. He agreed at once. The Cabinet approved, and my appointment was announced in Parliament on July 3. It could hardly have been more vague. I doubt if anyone knew exactly what I was supposed to do, and my doubts proved to be substantially correct. The job had to be made by a long period of trial and error.

The day after my acceptance I went to tell Dr. Beneš that I should soon be leaving him. Jan Masaryk was present during what was a painful interview. Both were dejected, not because I was being transferred, but by the long delay in the granting of full recognition. Dr. Beneš was puzzled and almost silent; Jan, as usual, more temperamental and emotional. Dr. Beneš could not understand what the difficulties were. Jan wanted to know if the Czechoslovak aviators who had died fighting for Britain were to be regarded as provisionally dead. He had been told that day that the Foreign Office did not propose to appoint a full diplomatic Minister, although Mr. Eden had assured him that a Minister would be appointed. I was sad and very uncomfortable and felt like a deserter leaving his friends in distress. As I went away, I vowed to make a last appeal to Mr. Eden. That night I wrote him a private letter in which I let my feelings run freely. He sent for me the next day.

I told him first the news I had just received; namely, that the Russians were going to recognise the Czechs and that they would waste no time in drafting and re-drafting a treaty. I also gave him an account of my interview with Dr. Beneš and Jan Masaryk and asked him was it really true that we were not going to appoint a fully accredited Minister. He seized the telephone impatiently and rang through to the Department. Jan's story was true. The Department's plan was to appoint someone of ministerial rank but still to call him "British Representative".

Mr. Eden's eyes flashed: "What is all this about?" he said. "I don't understand these nuances. The Czechs must have a Minister. You have no time to waste."

That time was urgent was only too true. Two days later there was a garden party at Buckingham Palace for the Allied Governments. As the skies were leaden and full of rain, it was held indoors. The government representatives were lined up in a long train in the corridor in order of seniority. They were accompanied by their British ambassadors and ministers. The provisional Czechoslovaks came last, and I went with them like a whipper-in in a paper-chase. After the official reception by the King and Queen, both the Prime Minister and Mr. Eden engaged Dr. Beneš in friendly conversation and told him that recognition was now settled and that the documents would be ready almost at once.

The next day Jan Masaryk gave me a copy of another treaty to read. It was the Russo-Czechoslovak Treaty. It was to be signed the next morning. It was now a race between the Russians and ourselves. The Russians won. They signed at noon on July 18. I had been requested to bring Jan Masaryk to Mr. Eden at 4 p.m. Jan called for me with his car at 3.45, and in heavy rain we set out for the Foreign Office. We were received at once.

Mr. Eden was alone, and we drew our chairs close up to his desk. He was smiling and at his most informal best.

"This is a day of treaties for you, Jan," he said. "You signed one this morning, I understand. Well, here is another."

He handed to Jan the note according full recognition and gave me the official communiqué. Jan was very emotional, and the paper trembled in his hands as he read. Once he paused and ejaculated, "Thank God." There were tears in his eyes when he started to thank Mr. Eden who, feeling embarrassed, cut him short.

"I've done very little," he said, "but you owe a great deal to this fellow here." He pointed to me. Then he went on quickly: "There's one fly in the ointment. Phil Nichols whom I am giving you as Minister has developed a duodenal ulcer and will not be able to take up his appointment for some weeks. In the meantime, as far as high policy is concerned, I hope that you will be content to rely on this violent anti-Czech here"—again he pointed to me—"and for current affairs I'll give you Frank Roberts."

We all shook hands. When we came out into the corridor Jan put his arms round my neck and kissed me on both cheeks in front of the office-keeper. Then we went off to Grosvenor Place where Dr. Beneš was awaiting us. When we came into his study, he was working at a mass of papers. He looked up with a quizzical smile as if still not certain that all was well. I made him a little speech in Czech: "For the first time I have the honour to greet you officially as the President of the Czechoslovak Republic and to hand you on behalf of Mr. Eden this letter."

The little man made no sign. He took the paper, sat down at the desk, and, crossing his legs, began to read. His face was impassive, but I noticed that his crossed leg was trembling. I waited patiently. Through my mind flashed the phrase which he often used to say to me: "A man may be the greatest genius in the world, but he'll never get anywhere without hard work." Never had he shown a more admirable thoroughness than now.

When he had read the paper twice, he put it down. "There is a mistake in the last paragraph," he said.

There was, but it was soon altered.

Then he thanked me quietly, and I left him alone with Jan and walked to the St. James's Club. The long Odyssey of the Czechoslovaks was not yet over, for their country was still under the heel of the brutal oppressor. But at any rate they were now on the right road, and a great wrong and much cruel indifference had been righted. I had been flattered by Jan's gratitude, but now the emotions of the afternoon had left me deflated like a pricked balloon. I had no illusions about my part in the struggle for recognition. The plain truth was that, had there been no Churchill and no Eden, there would have been no Czechoslovak Government, no President Beneš, no Foreign Secretary Masaryk, and no gratitude from any Czechoslovak to Britain and still less to the United States who in the matter of recognition had lagged behind us all the way.

When I reached the club, I felt strangely alone. Then I was called to the telephone by George Malcolm Thomson, the able and gifted principal secretary and right-hand man of Lord Beaverbrook. We were brother Scots and saw alike on most questions. George had been very much opposed to my having anything to do with propaganda. He himself was being worked almost to death, for Lord Beaverbrook had just been made Minister of Supply and was tackling his new problems with his usual frenetic energy. I told him that I had accepted the propaganda job.

George's voice was strident. "God!" he said. Then he added consolingly: "What are you doing to-night? Let's have a wake before our funerals. I am being murdered by Beaverbrook, but *you've* committed suicide."

We had our wake.

E

BOOK III

WORDY WARFARE

"AS THEMISTOCLES SAILED along the coasts, wherever he saw places at which the enemy must necessarily put in for shelter and supplies, he inscribed conspicuous writings on stones, some of which he found to his hand there by chance, and some he himself caused to be set near the inviting anchorages and watering-places. In these writings he solemnly enjoined upon the Ionians, if it were possible, to come over to the side of the Athenians who were risking all in behalf of their freedom; but if they could not do this, to damage the Barbarian cause in battle, and bring confusion among them."

PLUTARCH'S LIVES

"DEMOCRACY IS THE one form of human society which not only is un-afraid of truth but looks to truth as its ally." R. B. PERRY

CHAPTER ONE

WHEN ONE ACCEPTS a difficult job, the only thing to do is to make the best of it. And I determined to do mine with good grace. My first task was to find out exactly what I had to do. I was given little time to think, for even before I had taken leave of the Czechoslovaks I was summoned to a meeting at the Foreign Office. With the entry of Russia into the war, trouble had arisen over the playing of national anthems by the B.B.C. The Russian *hymn* was "The International"; there was strong opposition in the Cabinet to its being played. The Foreign Office sought the advice of the propagandists. I was in favour of including "The International" in the programme. Throughout the country there was a wave of enthusiasm for the Russian Army. There would be resentment both in Britain and in Russia if the national anthem of our new ally were omitted. On the other hand, the tune itself was unlikely to stir Anglo-Saxon emotions. It was a dismal dirge which, as Mr. Shaw once said, "was hardly fit to be the funeral march of a fried eel."

The sentiment of the meeting was in favour of "The International", but in view of the attitude of the Cabinet a typical British compromise was recommended and approved by the Prime Minister. On Sunday, July 13, "The Kutuzov March", an almost forgotten tune, was played together with the national anthems of our other Allies. Two days later I met M. Maisky at an official reception. He greeted me warmly. "I have great hopes of your appointment," he said. "I believe in youth." I was then fifty-four! Then he added with a twinkle in his eyes: "I trust that you will be able to stop this comic opera about 'The International'." After some delay "The International" was eventually given its place in the programme. Later, the Russians produced a new hymn which both in its words and in its martial air conformed fully to the patriotic pattern of national anthems.

This difficulty settled, I devoted my full time and energy to the study of my new job. Our two main tasks, which had been approved by the Foreign Office and the Chiefs of Staff, were clear enough. They were (1) to undermine and to destroy the morale of the enemy and (2) to sustain and foster the spirit of resistance in enemy-occupied countries. The principal instruments of our propaganda or of our political warfare as it was now beginning to be called were radio and leaflets. By arrangement with Bomber Command leaflets had been disseminated regularly since the first days of the war. A voluntary agreement with the Governors of the B.B.C. gave us policy control over all foreign broadcasts to enemy and enemy-occupied territory.

On paper the position seemed satisfactory. But there were serious defects in the internal organisation. Control of propaganda to enemy and enemy-occupied countries was vested in the three Ministers. As Chairman Mr. Eden had the final word on policy, but he had no propaganda machine of his own. Dr. Dalton controlled the original department of enemy propaganda. Mr. Bracken, the new Minister of Information, was responsible to Parliament for all broadcasting. The Cabinet decision on the new organisation was vague, and at first Dr. Dalton assumed that he would continue to be solely responsible for his section. As a counter-move Mr. Bracken asserted his rights over the B.B.C., although from the first he was a strong advocate of unification of ministerial control.

Moreover, the original difficulty of geographical separation was now aggravated, for, while the department of enemy propaganda still remained at Woburn, with its military wing in Lansdowne House, I now had my own offices in the Locarno Room of the Foreign Office. As the European Services of the B.B.C. were lodged in Bush House, sectional jealousies were intensified rather than relaxed by the new arrangement.

Obviously the two main tasks of reorganisation were (1) to obtain unification of ministerial control and (2) to house under one roof all the component sections engaged in propaganda to enemy and enemy-occupied countries.

This first problem was partially settled by the end of August. The three Ministers agreed to act as a trinity. Under them they established an Executive Committee of three officials composed of Mr. Leeper, General Brooks and myself. I was appointed Chairman. The new organisation was given the high-sounding and baffling title of Political Warfare Executive and in Whitehall soon became known as P.W.E. or, more vulgarly, the Peewees. The Executive Committee of officials ran the new department and at weekly meetings received the necessary guidance and approval from the Ministerial Committee.

On September 11 the formation of the Political Warfare Executive was announced in the House of Commons. Little information was given, and answers to questions were refused on the ground of secrecy. The Government's attitude provoked a sharp query from

Mr. De la Bere who asked the Prime Minister to define the difference between a secret and an awkward question. Without hesitation Mr. Churchill replied: "One is a danger to the country and the other a nuisance to the Government."

For the moment the secrecy was an advantage to us, for the new arrangement was awkward and far from tidy. We had made a slight advance, but further changes and reforms were necessary. The most serious mistake at this stage was the omission of Mr. Ivone Kirkpatrick, the able and experienced Controller of the European Service of the B.B.C., from the Executive Committee. I had been in favour of his inclusion from the start, but had not then the power to enforce my will. The mistake was not to be rectified for many months, nor for an even longer period was it possible to house the whole organisation under one roof owing to accommodation difficulties and to the reluctance of the Treasury to bring back any large number of officials from the country to London.

Much of our teething trouble would have been modified if only the Prime Minister had been interested in political warfare. Unfortunately for us, this great man, himself our greatest war propagandist, attached at best a secondary importance to all forms of propaganda. Yet words counted. In 1940 the words of Winston Churchill counted very much for Britain's advantage and in June, 1945, in that fateful blunder of his election broadcast, they dimmed the destiny of the greatest of all the Churchills. At the time of great operations, he would show a transitory interest in our activities, would want a certain line to be taken in our broadcasts or would ask for leaflets to be dropped at once on some important target, as if by opening a drawer we could produce a couple of million leaflets on demand. But mostly he lived up to his reputation as a man of deeds, and the truth was that, when he spoke or wrote a message, it was always a deed; when other ministers spoke, it was often only words.

During this experimental period when I had position without power and when even the most obvious reforms took weeks and even months to effect, Dallas Brooks was a great support. His patience was unlimited. In Whitehall, if you pegged away, kept your head and maintained a steady pressure, you eventually reached your goal. And Brooks certainly took me to one most useful and important place. It was, in fact, entirely through him that I was able to establish friendly and most valuable relations with the Chiefs of Staff organisation. This was the best piece of machinery in Whitehall and probably in any country and was the main reason why the recent war was so much more efficiently conducted than the first world war. It acted as an effectual and necessary check on the inter-departmental jealousies of the three services. By its careful insistence on the proper division between strategy and policy it not only won the full confidence and co-operation of the Foreign Office, but also prevented a repetition of the unseemly quarrels between the politicians and the generals which in 1914-1918 were a serious handicap to the successful prosecution of our war effort.

With the Prime Minister, the three Chiefs of Staff constituted the Ministry of Defence which, in conjunction with President Roosevelt and the American Combined Chiefs of Staff, ran the war. The efficiency and success of this machinery owed much to General Sir Hastings Ismay, the Prime Minister's military representative, and to General "Jo" Hollis, the secretary of the Chiefs of Staff. From the point of view of work alone, the two men had the hardest war imaginable, and if they averaged four and a half hours sleep a night during the six years the figure is probably on the high side. They were at one and the same time the servants of the Chiefs of Staff and the slaves of the lamp of an exacting and temperamental Prime Minister. Their position was not easy. General Ismay was, in a very real sense, a buffer between the Prime Minister and the Chiefs of Staff and during moments of tension the buffer was likely to get knocks from both sides. Minor crises were not infrequent, nor could even the most prescient foretell when a storm might arise. Ismay, an Indian army officer, would be sitting at a Chiefs of Staff meeting. A message would be brought in. The Prime Minister wished to see General Ismay at once. The General would make his excuses. Up would go the eyebrows of the Chiefs of Staff. What did the old man want now? Even the Greek gods were human, and the Chiefs of Staff were neither Greeks nor gods.

General Ismay would soon find out what the "boss" wanted. He had received perhaps some mildly critical comment by the Chiefs of Staff on his latest strategic proposals. He would have their paper in his hand. "What is this?" he would ask. The papers would rustle like a leaf before a gale. "I thought that you were there to defend my point of view." And backwards and forwards General Ismay would have to go until the two views were reconciled and peace reigned.

Only a man of supreme tact, great ability, penetrating insight into human nature, a profound experience of the administrative machinery of a modern state and the temper and patience of an angel could have, held the post for long, let alone for a period of six years. Fortunately,

General Ismay possessed all these qualifications in abundant measure. He not only had a great personal affection for Mr. Churchill but, together with the Chiefs of Staff, he fully recognised that in his politico-strategic conception of war and in his historical under-standing of the broad sweep of events the British Prime Minister far excelled any soldier. At the same time, he knew that Mr. Churchill's knowledge of the technical side of war was on a considerably lower plane, and by steering a careful course between the expostulatory gusts of genius he would persuade the great man to temper his politico-strategic brilliance with the practical mechanics of the Chiefs of Staff.

When General Ismay, who would have made a better ambassador than most of our professional diplomatists, was away in Moscow or Washington, General Hollis took over his duties in addition to his own. The Prime Minister who almost always had two hours sleep in the afternoon liked working late. The Ministry of Defence met at night; the Chiefs of Staff had their daily meeting in the morning. Hollis had to attend both meetings and had to get his minutes out and despatched to a score of interested parties within an hour or two of each meeting. The work was done with amazing speed and efficiency.

Each of these two men saw more of the general conduct of the war than any other single individual. I maintained regular and friendly relations with them until the end of the war. Like all really first-class administrators, they were never flurried and, although probably the busiest men in Whitehall, always seemed to have time at their disposal. Their wise counsel saved P.W.E. from many mistakes, and above all, they made its way smooth with the Chiefs of Staff.

I made my first appearance before them soon after the establish-ment of P.W.E. Admiral Sir Dudley Pound was in the chair; the C.I.G.S. (then Sir John Dill) was on his left with General Ismay and General Hollis beside him. On his right sat Sir Charles Portal, the Chief of the Air Staff, myself and Dallas Brooks. I was given twenty minutes in which to give an account of our work. Sir John Dill looked, and was, a sick man. Sir Dudley Pound puffed his pipe. It was impossible to deduce from his face whether he was interested or bored. Sir Charles Portal, another constant pipe-smoker, listened. Hardly had I started when he pushed a piece of paper to me. On it he had written: "The First Sea Lord is rather deaf." Thanks to this kindly hint I spoke up, said my piece, and was thanked.

Afterwards, Brooks and I went before the Chiefs of Staff from time

to time. We did not overburden them with requests, conducted ourselves, I hope, modestly, and rarely failed to receive some benefit in
the form of either sound advice on what to avoid or of backing for
some risky action. I found these meetings the most practical, the
most business-like, and the least formidable of any that I attended.

Although I had a full-time job in my attempts to reorganise our
propaganda service, this was only one of my activities. I continued
to see President Beneš regularly. I found his advice on propaganda
matters invaluable and his information on Russia more optimistic than
our own. Some British ministers and officials make a great mistake in
neglecting and under-estimating the small nations. In order to survive, their representatives have to be far more efficient than those of
the Great Powers. As the late H. A. L. Fisher always said, Czechoslovakia was the first state in the world to be created by propaganda.
Moreover, the Czechs, who were neither Communists nor capitalists,
had always made it their business to know both East and West.
President Beneš was therefore well worth consulting both on propaganda matters and on Russia. But our intelligence services, the best
in the world in technical matters and not infrequently the most
erratic in political sense, were sceptical.

At that time Whitehall had little faith in Russia's capacity to resist.
General Ismay, who was what might then be called an optimist on
Russia, said that the high figure for Russia's resistance had been six
weeks. Every day after August 3 was therefore a gain for the Allies.
As August drew out into September, a new hope and a new fear
suggested themselves to the Cabinet. Russia was still resisting, but
the Germans were still advancing towards Moscow. Was it possible, was it even probable that the Russians could hold out until the
Russian winter came to their rescue? Mr. Churchill was excited.
Lord Beaverbrook, who was preparing to visit Russia, was excited.
The Chiefs of Staff were excited. Above all, the Prime Minister
wished to know when the Russian winter started. Like other so-
called experts on Russia, I was rung up by members of his staff to ask
if I could give the date! I made a blunder. By pointing out rather
pompously that the task was impossible and that, if by winter the
enquirers meant snow, it might come at any moment from October 1
to January 1, I did no good to myself or to anyone else. Had I given
boldly and without reservation a fixed date, I should have given
great pleasure to the Government and added greatly to my own
prestige as a prophet for, since the Russians held out anyway, I
should have been right.

I also had to entertain, and be entertained by American acquaintances who, amazed that we had survived, visited Britain in August
and September in considerable numbers. First there was Dorothy
Thompson whom I had met in the days when she was not even
Sinclair Lewis's wife and had never seen a microphone, let alone
received two dollars a second for talking into it. For several years
before the war she had consistently foretold its inevitability and with
eloquence and fervour had warned her countrymen of the dangers
which threatened the civilised world. When she visited London in
August, 1941, she was already an international figure enjoying all the
success of an honoured prophetess. She moved in a stately and almost
ponderous manner and expected, and was given, free access to the
great. When Mr. Churchill granted her a special interview before
going off to sign the Atlantic Charter with Mr. Roosevelt, the other
American journalists were angry and stormed Mr. Bracken's office
at the Ministry of Information. But Mr. Churchill was right.
Dorothy had performed a great war job. In the United States she was
the high priestess of intervention—not for Britain's sake, but for the
safety of her own country—and was well worth Mr. Churchill's
time and attention. She was disappointed by the Atlantic Charter
which, given in its advance publicity that suggestion of mystery
which always ensures the public's attention, came as an anti-climax.
Like many other people, she wanted a clearer and more detailed
statement of our war aims.

Then there was Paul Patterson, the publisher of the *Baltimore Sun*,
who also saw the great by entertaining greatly, but gathered his
information from all quarters. He was a much shrewder man than
most of the English took him for, and he had the knack of picking up
one little item of inside knowledge here and another there and
moulding the bits into a pattern which would have horrified the
different divulgers of the separate pieces by its accuracy. He asked
Brooks and me to his farewell party in the Patience Room at the
Savoy. We sat down about sixteen strong. The women included the
four loveliest ladies in the land. All were war-workers; all had put on
their best powder and paint to do honour to generous, warm-
hearted Paul. The men included several officials and two future
ministers in Sir Walter Monckton and Lord Winster, but indubitably
the big guns of the occasion were Mr. A. V. Alexander and Mr.
Bracken. The food was sumptuous; for drink there was champagne
and, better than champagne, the choicest of German Moselles. In
the midst of such plenty what matter if the speeches were long or if

the host himself spoke too often. Good humour glowed with a brightness which no black-out could dim. At great length and with skilful flattery Mr. Bracken enumerated the virtues of the First Lord and ended his eulogy with the announcement that Mr. Alexander was the minister whom above all others Winston Churchill loved. Not to be outdone the First Lord volleyed the ball of compliment back to the Minister of Information and, pleased with Mr. Bracken's statement about Mr. Churchill's affection and dwelling on the heavy burdens of his own task, declaimed with becoming modesty that "whom the Lord loveth he chasteneth". It was an exhilarating performance, and when later a piano was brought in and Mr. Alexander, the post-pluperfect master of the impromptu sing-song, began to crash out the strains of sea-shanties and old music-hall ditties, I almost felt that the war was over. When from the other private rooms and from the main restaurant other cheerful souls flocked to join in the acting of:

> "We don't want to ride like the cavalry;
> We don't want to fly over Germany,"

and to swell the final chorus of "We are the King's Navee", I realised that for bureaucrats who are fair targets for a long suffering public it was time to go. So, gathering Brooks, I made a discreet withdrawal. It was my gayest evening of the war.

Thirdly, there was long, lanky Bob Sherwood, slow in speech, lugubrious in countenance, but eloquent enough on paper to be the most successful and inspiring dramatist of modern times. I had met him some years before he had become world-famous, had been placed next to him at luncheon and had thought him speechless until he suddenly caught up with some question that had long drifted out of the conversation and began to answer it. Although the United States was not yet in the war, Bob, who ran away from Harvard to fight for us in the first world war, was doing his best to ensure that his countrymen wasted no time in getting into this one. He stood close to Franklin Roosevelt and helped him with his speeches and fireside chats. Now, in the guise of an information officer, he had come to England to provide for Anglo-American co-operation in political and psychological warfare in the event of the United States' participation in the war. For three years he was to be my American opposite number, and he will appear later in these pages. At this moment he was very confident that the Americans would be fighting by our side before the end of the year. He had only one reservation: what with Russia's resisting better than anyone expected, the isolationists were already on the up-grade and were making some headway with the cry: "Well, we're sending them the stuff, aren't we?"

Occasionally, too, one or two of our fighting commanders would descend on us, make some propaganda demand and depart in peace or in displeasure. The calmest and the kindliest was that noble and great-hearted soldier Lord Gort who, after Dunkirk, had been rewarded with the Governorship of Gibraltar. I had first met him in that tragic summer of 1940 when with the honour of a back-to-the-wall and typically British retreat fresh upon him he had been persuaded by Lord Halifax to give an address in the B.B.C. religious service on August 4. The incident inspired one of the best stories of the war. Lord Halifax had taken great interest in this special service and had worried his secretaries for weeks. He had given even his own personal time and study to the choice of a suitable hymn and, finding decision difficult, had consulted his favourite henchman, Mr. Charles Peake.

"I am at a loss to find a suitable hymn for the Gort service," said Lord Halifax.

"Surely", replied the gallant Mr. Peake, "the choice is obvious: O Gort, our help in ages past."

His Lordship reflected for a moment. Then a pale and watery smile lit up his face.

"Excellent, my dear Charles, but I fear that the Prime Minister might not like the second line."

The remark was apposite. Lord Gort had been our shelter in the stormy blast. All that courage could do, he always did. He had superb qualities of simplicity, of devotion to duty, of great strength in adversity, but intellectually he could not appeal to Mr. Churchill as "Our hope in years to come".

At this particular moment Lord Gort was interested in propaganda. At Gibraltar there was a transmitter which was about to be erected and which could cover North Africa. Its strategic importance was considerable. We must therefore send a fully-equipped broadcasting mission to Gibraltar. Its members would have his special protection.

With some difficulty we found the broadcasters, the script-writers and the translators, and a professional diplomat in Mr. Gordon Vereker, now H.M. Minister to Uruguay, to shepherd them. But we could not overcome the local technicians or the general shortage of radio equipment. The mission was sent out to Gibraltar. No sooner had it arrived there than Lord Gort was transferred to Malta. Meanwhile, the transmitter made no progress, and the mission had to do its best with a small local transmitter of very limited range. After a few months the new Governor, a more impatient and more ruthless administrator than his predecessor, sent our team back to England.

This fiasco made no difference to Lord Gort's interest in propaganda or in his personal relations with myself. From Malta he used to send occasional projects for setting up a new transmitter on the island and sensible suggestions for the improvement of our propaganda to Italy. When, later, he went to Palestine, he again came to see me, although the area was not included in the countries for which P.W.E. was responsible. He was a charming man who was as unconscious of rank or of side as he was of fear.

September, 1941, was a sobering and serious month. Administrative problems continued to be troublesome, mainly because the Woburn organisation was fighting a protracted battle against central control, and on my first visit there as Chairman of the Executive Committee I was met with threats of revolt and resignations. Administration, however, was not my only preoccupation. We were eager to establish co-operation in propaganda with our new Russian allies. The moment was favourable. Mr. Harriman, President Roosevelt's special representative on supply matters, and Lord Beaverbrook were on the point of leaving for Moscow in order to discuss with Stalin what help we could furnish. With Kiev captured and Moscow threatened, the Beaverbrook-Harriman mission was, in fact, Mr. Churchill's answer to Stalin's appeals for aid. The Russians certainly needed all the help we could give them. If, at this critical stage in their fortunes, they were not receptive to proposals of collaboration, they never would be.

Fortified by Mr. Eden's approval, I had a long talk with M. Maisky, but we did not make much progress towards genuine collaboration. We should, of course, keep one another informed, he suggested, but there was no need for both countries to take the same line in their propaganda. In fact, there was a distinct advantage in separate lines. In this manner we should make two breaches in the German propaganda defences. The implication was that we should appeal to the German Right and the German officer class and leave the Left and the ordinary soldier to the Russians. Indeed, M. Maisky went out of his way to point out how bad our Left Wing propaganda to Germany was and how much better the Russians could perform this task.

In other respects M. Maisky was eager to please and kept me for an hour, plying me with questions and paying compliments to the British war effort and to individual British leaders. Clearly he hoped great things from the Beaverbrook-Harriman mission, for there was high praise of Lord Beaverbrook with whom he had recently been in frequent touch. There was also warm commendation of Mr. Eden who, M. Maisky said, was easily the most popular Englishman in Russia. Stalin's attitude towards Mr. Churchill, he told me, was the recognition of one great man by another. There was also favourable mention of Dr. Beneš and of General de Gaulle and a querulous query about the London Polish Government. Why did we single it out for special favours? It was a very poor government both in ability and in loyalty to its Prime Minister. The most satisfactory feature of M. Maisky's discourse was his sturdy and obviously genuine optimism about Russia. Moscow would not fall. There would be no Russian collapse as in 1917, because there was now a new Russia. Victory was certain, but the price would be high.

This Russian optimism was worth something at a moment when most British people were resigned to the fall of Moscow and to a collapse similar to that of France. Even that incorrigible optimist, President Beneš, was shaken, but he at any rate had some excuse for his temporary lapse. The home Czechs were in serious trouble. The Germans had discovered some of the threads of the underground movement and had acted quickly. Freiherr von Neurath, the weak and contemptible German Protector, had been dismissed and had been replaced by Heydrich, the most notoriously brutal of the Gestapo Chiefs. Many arrests had been made among the Czechs, and the brave and venturesome General Eliaš, who as Prime Minister under the Germans was really guiding the underground and was in constant communication with President Beneš, was taken to Berlin and condemned to death.

This blow to Czechoslovak hopes was severe, but there was little that we could do to repair the damage, and early in October I took a week off and went to stay with my schoolmaster brother at Sedbergh. Situated in the heart of the fells the little village lies in a broad dale which is watered by four fast-running trout streams. The mixture of moor and crag and torrent are the nearest approach to Scottish Highland scenery that England can offer. It would be an arrogance of Scottish nationalism at its worst to say that I consider these delectable dales and fells inferior to the Scottish Highlands. They have found a place in my affection for their own sake. But true it is that, every time I visit Sedbergh, the drive across the moor recalls memories which tug at my heart strings and create a fierce desire to go farther north to my own country. Throughout the war I was travel-sick, so travel-sick that I had to lock up my vast store of guide-books and sternly deny myself the heart-ache which came from reading C. E. Montague's *The Right Place* or Romilly Fedden's *Golden Days*. The first day at Sedbergh always reawakened this nostalgic restlessness, but after twenty-four hours the feeling passed, and I was grateful not only for the rest but also for the sight of the hills and the scent of the heather.

On this occasion I was too late for the trout fishing, but I walked by the riverside with my brother's dogs. The air brought the colour back to my cheeks, and the sun shone serenely and steadily for three out of the seven days—a rare kindness on the part of the weather god in a corner which boasts one of the highest rainfalls in England.

It was a peaceful and pleasant week enlivened by first-hand information of the school-life of one of my three ministers. The best-known of living Old Sedberghians is Mr. Brendan Bracken, who is a whole legend in himself at Sedbergh where he arrived from Australia in 1919 with a shock of red hair, a pocket-full of bank notes and a self-assurance which carried him straight into the headmaster's study and, with the headmaster's approval, into the Lower Fifth.

Sumner, then the second Master of the school, remembered him well. "B.B.", as all Whitehall called him during the war, must then have been between fifteen and eighteen. There is a discrepancy between the entries in the school register and *Who's Who*. The school register gives the date of his birth as 1904; in *Who's Who* the year is given as 1901. Be his age what he will, what is certain is that at that time he was his own master, for in the register under the heading of Guardian or Parent is the bold and clear signature "Brendan Bracken". There is a well-founded local belief that he paid his first term's fees direct to the headmaster from a wad of bank-notes.

Coming from Australia, he was a difficult boy to place. In certain subjects he was far ahead of his contemporaries; in others he was below the standard of the lowest form. Even then he had the photographic memory of figures, the passion for information, and the knowledge of quaint subjects which have been the adventitious aids of his subsequent successful career. At school he was a member of a club at which informative papers were read on subjects not included in the curriculum, while the boys drank cocoa and ate stodgy cake.

On one occasion Sumner, a brilliant historian who had also studied economics, was reading a little essay on paper currency. Scarcely had he finished when a shaggy-headed figure uncurled itself from a rug in front of the fire and began to tear the essay to pieces, illustrating his arguments with verbatim quotations from the currency regulations of India, Australia, China, Siam, Czechoslovakia and Uzbekistan. The young know-all was of course Brendan Bracken who retains today a strong affection for his old school, has become a member of the governing body and, when he revisits the scenes of his youth, alters his whole mode of life, goes early to bed and rises with the sun to scale the fells or walk prodigious distances. The antechamber of 10 Downing Street and the financial gossip of the City are temporarily forgotten, and Nature claims her own when, at the end of a long day, he leans his arm on your shoulder and looking westward, declaims ecstatically: "My dear Bruce, what have you in Scotland to compare with that?"

To explain the "that", the arm is released in a wide sweep which ranges from the Home Fell across the valleys of the Rawthey and the Lune to Lambrigg Fell. It is, indeed, a fair vista, and it brings out the best in Brendan whose own nature retains much of the "old school-tie" spirit including a nobility and a capacity to stand up for, and to take, all the knocks on behalf of his own staff even if they are past defending. He possesses this endearing quality in a higher degree than any other minister or politician that I have known.

At Sedbergh there were moments when the war seemed hundreds of thousands of miles away. There were no alerts, no sirens, no real need for a black-out. Yet even in this remote dale it made its presence felt in a score of different ways. There were the boys themselves, drilling now two days a week instead of playing football. The school had already won two V.C's and had suffered losses. There were my brother's sons. The youngest, still little more than a schoolboy, was then spending his last days at home before going to Sandhurst. Here too, where one was cut off completely from all inside information, the radio never stopped. I found myself listening-in with the same vicious lack of self-control which afflicts nearly everyone who is solely dependent on radio for news. And the news was tense and of course bad. The Germans were within forty miles of Moscow.

On October 9 the German radio announced that the Russian armies had been annihilated and that the war in the East was over. Later, we were to learn that this statement was Hitler's greatest blunder, for it was published in every German newspaper including the official *Voelkischer Beobachter* which in its edition of October 10 had huge headlines announcing: "The Great Hour has struck; the War in the East is Over." Afterwards, on every anniversary of October 10, my department published as a leaflet a facsimile copy of the front page of the *Voelkischer Beobachter* with a red strip across it with the words "What Hitler said in 1941" and dropped it in millions of copies all over Germany and over the German troops. But at the time most British people believed the news was true, and on the night of my return to London the B.B.C. included in its religious service a special prayer that Russia might be given strength to withstand the danger which threatened her.

The prayer echoed the heart-felt anxiety of the whole country.

CHAPTER TWO

I ARRIVED AT Euston in the cold grey dawn of October 16 to find the official news from Russia greyer still. The diplomatic corps and most of the Russian Government had evacuated Moscow for Kuibishev on the Volga, and, although Stalin had remained to defend the capital, the British public was depressed and inclined to assume the worst. Fortunately inside information was more encouraging, and Lord Beaverbrook and General Ismay who had just returned from Russia believed that Moscow would hold out.

I went to Cherkley on the Sunday of October 19 to dine and spend the night with Lord Beaverbrook. The other guests included Mr. A. V. Alexander, Colonel Ralston, the Canadian Minister of Defence, and M. and Madame Maisky. The procedure at Cherkley week-ends during the war followed a regular pattern. Lord Beaverbrook, who worked seven long days in every week, was at his Ministry all day, and his guests were free to roam the grounds and to enjoy the superb view across the Downs to Ranmore Common. There was a strict adherence to the rationing rules and considerable austerity. Breakfast, in fact, was a severely frugal meal, and the single pat of butter had neither length nor breadth nor depth. At night the household staff, reduced to a minimum and scarcely visible all day, came to life. There was a simple but excellently cooked dinner strictly limited to three courses with good wine to drink and much lively and interesting political talk. Then, almost before they had time to swallow a cup of coffee, the guests were marched off to the small private cinema theatre to see a film. After the film there was more good talk until the host, in peace-time a late sitter, would suddenly jump to his feet and with an abrupt "Goodnight to you" go off to bed. According to their mood, the guests would either follow his example, or sit up, if the spirit moved them or lasted long enough, until the early hours of the morning.

On this particular occasion the talk was exceptionally interesting, because, although Lord Beaverbrook looked tired and ill, the success of his mission with Mr. Harriman to Russia had galvanised all the reserves of his energy. At the first meeting Stalin had made impossible demands, and they had told him frankly and almost brutally that the demands could not be met. He was, they pointed out, a man of intelligence and could read for himself the story of our early military failures. They were the result of unpreparedness. We were short of nearly every military supply ourselves. We would do all that was humanly possible to provide supplies for Russia, but the Russians themselves must realise the cold truth of the situation. Stalin, of course, was disappointed, but he saw reason, and at the next meeting he had reduced his demands to a point at which practical negotiations could begin. Then all had gone well. Stalin had been grateful, and Lord Beaverbrook and Mr. Harriman had come back loaded with gifts of fruit and signed photographs of Russia's man of steel, and, what was more important, with a new confidence in Russia's capacity to resist.

My attention, too, was absorbed by a fascinating study of the Maiskys, who were now fairly regular visitors to Cherkley. Madame Maisky, who knew how to dress, was entirely at her ease and fully held her own in the general conversation. M. Maisky took longer to adapt himself to the peculiar atmosphere of Cherkley and at first he seemed embarrassed by Lord Beaverbrook's banter which is always direct and amazingly frank. "Maisky," Lord Beaverbrook would say in front of everyone, "you told Uncle Joe that I was a quarrelsome fellow," and at first the unfortunate Maisky would wriggle and blush. I have no doubt that the story was true and that Stalin had told Lord Beaverbrook. Gradually, however, the Russian Ambassador found a defence to this form of bombardment and gave as good as he got. When on another occasion Lord Beaverbrook said to him bluntly: "Maisky, you must have Mongolian blood in your veins," the eyes of the little Russian sparkled, and he replied at once: "Yes, I have Chinese ancestors. And who would not be proud to have in his veins the blood of the most civilised race in the world!"

M. Maisky was brought up on Mayne Reid and Fenimore Cooper at Omsk where his father was an army doctor, but both his parents came from South Russia. He had a genuine respect for Lord Beaverbrook both on his own account and also because, as he himself told me, Stalin had been deeply impressed by his Lordship's energy and decisiveness. M. Maisky saw in him a valuable ally who could be relied on to ensure that the supplies to Russia were promptly delivered. He therefore humoured him, kept him well informed, and responded readily to all his moods and humours.

In spite of his progress in the game of back-chat, M. Maisky was at his best when alone. Then he was comparatively easy to draw out, if not on current events, at least about his revolutionary past. An intellectual who as a student wrote poetry and won the gold medal at the

Omsk High School, he entered the revolutionary movement before he was twenty and like many of his contemporaries suffered prison and exile for his opinions. At pre-war banquets at 13 Kensington Palace Gardens, where the best food and drink of Russia were served in profusion, no one ever saw M. Maisky as much as look at caviare. Exile in Siberia, where for two years sturgeon's roe was the staple dish of the political prisoners, had created in him such a dislike and nausea that for years he could not bear even to see a caviare tin. The little slate-coloured beads, he told me, were like myriads of eyes which reminded him of all that he wished to forget.

During the first world war he was in exile in London and contributed articles to the anti-war newspaper *Golos* which was produced in Paris for several months until the French Government stopped it early in 1915. For his contributions to this revolutionary sheet M. Maisky was honoured with a special mention in the archives of the Okhrana, the Tsarist secret police. In these archives he is listed under the names of Maisky and Liachovetsky.

A great reader with a fertile and subtle intellect and a genuine appreciation of the best in world literature, he was by far the shrewdest and most able of the Russian ambassadors whom the Kremlin has sent to this country. He gave me considerable help in my political warfare work, and his criticisms of our leaflets were always valuable. He did not believe in subtlety in propaganda and found our leaflets too long. A leaflet, he said, was like a bullet. One argument was enough for one target. Figures and facts were the best propaganda; the best facts were victories and the best figures dead Germans.

On all matters concerning purely local problems M. Maisky was always extremely frank and outspoken. But when any question of policy was involved or when, for instance, I tried to establish with the Russians some form of collaboration in propaganda and sought his help, I came at once to the dead-end which frustrates all Russian diplomats abroad. "Personally I am in favour," M. Maisky would say, "but your people must raise the matter in Moscow."

For all his knowledge of England and the greater freedom of movement which he enjoyed in comparison with most Russian ambassadors, he could not settle the simplest political problem or give even a visa without reference to Moscow. Yet not even M. Molotov could be more obstinate in defending the official policy of the Kremlin, and in the long agitation for the Second Front he was a skilful and at times over-reaching propagandist of the Russian case and a persistent and vexatious barb in the flesh of the Foreign Office. Like all Bolsheviks and, indeed, nearly all Slavs he was an extremist who, even if he understood, was always irritated by the infinite capacity of the Anglo-Saxon for compromise. Although by the rules of the Party an atheist, he could use the Scriptures to support his argument, and he was never tired of quoting to me the sixteenth verse of the third chapter of *Revelations*:

"So then because thou art lukewarm, and neither cold nor hot, I will spue thee out of my mouth."

It was a sentiment which was fully shared both in theory and in practice by the Canadian-Scot in Beaverbrook.

As I had spent most of my life in Slav countries, I was passionately interested in the whole Slav problem. Indeed, from the beginning of the war it was clear that, if we won, the Polish-Czech-Russian triangle would be the corner-stone on which the future peace structure would stand or founder.

Having acquired with increasing age a degree of caution which I should have despised in my youth, I was very careful not to interfere in matters which were not my immediate concern and never to proffer advice unless it was sought. But as the war progressed, I was brought more and more by the Foreign Office into Russian affairs, and it was on the subject of Russia that I had my most intimate conversations with Mr. Eden. I had hoped secretly that he would take me with him on one of his various visits to Moscow. I think that he would have done so but for one insurmountable obstacle. In 1918, when I was diplomatic agent with the Bolshevik Government, I had opposed our intervention with a violence which destroyed my credit with the interventionists in Britain. Then, when the intervention took place, I had remained at my post and done my best to support it. I had fallen heavily between two stools and had lost the favour both of the Russians and of the British authorities.

Always I had held a favourable view of Russia's capacity to resist and I was therefore immensely heartened by Lord Beaverbrook's confidence which was shared in considerable measure by Mr. Averell Harriman. A few days after my visit to Cherkley I saw General Hollis who offered to lay odds on the Russians being still in Moscow at Christmas. Incidentally, General Hollis was amazingly sound on the whole campaign in Russia. I used to consult him regularly on the strategic situation on the Russian front, and I cannot remember a single occasion when his appreciation was wrong.

Nevertheless, it required an almost reckless courage not to be alarmed about the Eastern front in October and November of 1941. There were many anxious moments, and the telegrams of Sir Stafford Cripps from Kuibishev hovered rather bewilderingly between optimism and pessimism. Nor were signs of panic entirely lacking in Moscow itself. The evacuation of industrial plant from the capital was not accomplished without some initial disorder, and one factory started to scuttle without awaiting instructions. Stalin took the most ruthless measures to stop what might have been the beginning of serious trouble. The factory was surrounded by troops and the management taken out and shot before the workers. In the end all was well, but the Russians had had only a narrow margin of safety. They owed their escape partly to their own courage, partly to the mistakes of German strategy, but most of all perhaps to the Yugoslav *coup d'état* of April, 1941, which delayed the German attack on Russia by an inestimably valuable fortnight.

Meanwhile, our political warfare activities continued to be hampered. The committee of three officials worked reasonably well, but the committee of the three ministers was never satisfactory, and the weekly meetings, at which the three officials were present, frequently ended in a wrangle between Dr. Dalton and Mr. Bracken which might have been amusing if it had not deterred all progress so seriously.

Much good work was done both by the European Service of the B.B.C. and by the organisation at Woburn where the training of propagandists was to prove of great value for the future. Indeed, the first two years of the war may be described as an experimental period of trial by error, and we were fortunate in being able to improve our technique at a time when our propaganda was not only inefficient but could, in fact, have little effect on a seemingly victorious enemy. Good propaganda can help to minimise the pessimism which results from failure. It can keep alive the spark of hope in ultimate victory. With increasing military success it can swell the tide of triumph. At all times, however, it must keep in step with military progress. Nothing angered our troops so much as exaggerated accounts of German weakness at a time when the German armies were fighting with undiminished determination. Such reports were regarded inevitably as a reflection on the valour and prowess of our own men.

From the first I tried to insist on one principle: that the efficacy of our open propaganda was in direct proportion to the accuracy of our statements. I do not think that at the beginning our propagandists realised this fundamental truth. They were immensely keen on their work. To some extent they were influenced by the apparent success of Dr. Goebbels's technique, although all the early so-called triumphs of German propaganda were directly due to the apparent invincibility of the German military machine. In extenuation of this early weakness of our propaganda I must point out that during the period of our military failure the propagandists were encouraged by the service departments to go to extremes. It was, I think, a bad policy and a manifest example of desire outrunning the possibilities of performance.

A case in point was the beginning of the Libya offensive in November 1941. The first official communiqué from Cairo was lyrical in its optimism, which was properly and inevitably exploited in our leaflets and in our foreign broadcasts. The offensive ended in failure, and the Germans and the Italians made capital out of the initial optimism of our propaganda.

Our propagandists felt depressed and needed encouragement. It came on November 19. Some time before, the Woburn organisation had acquired the services of Mr. David Bowes Lyon, the youngest brother of the Queen. He possessed great drive, a mind fertile in ideas, administrative ability, and a much-needed courage and capacity to take decisions. Through his influence the King and Queen made an official visit to Woburn on November 19. A special show—a kind of March of Time of our propaganda activities—was staged for their benefit. Their Majesties stayed for over three hours and seemed to enjoy the proceedings. Their visit was a great stimulus to the Woburn organisation and undoubtedly gave a fillip to our propaganda, but even so the importance of our work was never fully appreciated in certain government circles.

The next day I had a curious experience in the visit of a member of the American Embassy who came to consult me privately about the merits of an idea which had come from President Roosevelt's agile mind. The President proposed to fly a Glen Martin bomber from Newfoundland to Germany and back in one trip and to drop American newspapers over German territory as a token of the visit. Mr. Roosevelt's proposal was not based on any desire to impress Germany. His main object was to bring home to the American public that, if an American bomber could cross and re-cross the Atlantic in one flight, German bombers could do the same.

Of course we welcomed the idea, even if it meant a breach of the neutrality rules by the United States. It was never put into execution.

American neutrality was to be ended in a far more dramatic manner. On the Sunday afternoon of December 7, 1941, I went to Cherkley to dine with Lord Beaverbrook. Shortly before 8 p.m., while his guests were drinking cocktails in the long living-room, Lord Beaverbrook, who had been called to the telephone, poked his head round the door and announced, "The Japs have attacked Pearl Harbour."

The effect was electrical. We had been discussing the war which was going badly for us everywhere. On the Eastern front the Russians were holding their own, but the Germans were still within striking distance of Moscow. Gloom had settled on all our prospects in Libya. Now the whole course of the war had changed, and in one flash deferred hopes of victory had given way to absolute certainty. Mr. Churchill must have been in his seventh heaven, for during the evening he telephoned repeatedly to Lord Beaverbrook. Then and there he made up his mind to visit Washington at the earliest opportunity. For the first time in the war I felt an exhilaration which I have experienced perhaps only once previously in my life when with the sentence of death hanging over me I was released from my Bolshevik prison.

My joy evaporated with the morning which brought a more sober realisation of the immediate consequences of the Japanese attack. It was a busy day for me. The treatment of the news required guidance from the Cabinet. The big problem was how Germany would react to the breach between Japan and the United States. If the United States did not declare war on Germany and her war was confined to the Pacific, we should be—temporarily at least—much worse off, because the United States would need all her supplies for her own unprepared forces.

The Prime Minister was to speak at 3 p.m. in the House of Commons. His speech would be the official guidance for our propaganda. At 2 p.m. President Roosevelt telephoned from the White House to request Mr. Churchill to postpone his statement until Mr. Roosevelt had made his. He said that his reasons for this request were psychological. Postponement of Mr. Churchill's speech was technically impossible at such short notice, but the President's message must have put a damper on the Prime Minister's initial exuberance. When, later in the day, President Roosevelt spoke, he made no reference to Germany or to Britain. The omission caused some disappointment to the British public, but it showed Mr. Roosevelt's almost uncanny knowledge of his own countrymen. Had he declared war on Germany, he might not, and probably would not, have had a united country behind him.

On December 9 I went to see General Ismay in order to consult him about the problems of collaboration with the United States. He gave me one of his admirable appreciations of the general situation. The entry of the United States into the war made ultimate victory certain, but, he said, we must expect things to be worse before they were better. Our Eastern possessions, almost undefended, were now open to the Japanese. Some weeks before we had sent the *Prince of Wales* and the *Repulse* to Singapore in the hope of deterring the Japanese from entering the war. These ships would now be exposed to a combined attack from sea and air. He asked General Brooks and me to lunch with him and General Hollis at the United Services Club next day. At 11 a.m. on December 10 Ivone Kirkpatrick telephoned to me. His voice rang cold. "The *Prince of Wales* and the *Repulse* have been sunk off the East coast of Malaya—official," he said curtly. A little later, with dismay in our hearts, Brooks and I went off to our luncheon at the Senior. Going into the smoking-room, crowded with high-ranking naval and military officers, was like entering a Scottish house in which the will is being read after a funeral. There were drinks on the tables, but gloom on every face. Officers spoke in low tones. The atmosphere was heavy with the dead weight of tradition. Military defeats are the initial fate of the English in almost every war and can be borne with stoical courage. A disaster to the Navy is unthinkable and unbearable.

During luncheon there was some talk of the construction of our ships and parallels were drawn between our difficulties in sinking the *Bismarck* and the apparent vulnerability of the *Prince of Wales* and the *Repulse*. Rumour, too, was busy with suggestions of some wonderful new Japanese explosive. The real tragedy, however, was the same as all our naval and military tragedies: our criminal unpreparedness for a war which every European from Cape North to Cape Matapan had predicted with assurance. Of this there was a poignant personal example in the fate of Admiral Tom Phillips who went down with his ship.

At the time of the Abyssinian war, when the Chiefs of Staff were weighing the chances of possible action in the Mediterranean against Italy, Tom Phillips was a member of the Planning Committee. One of his colleagues was Air Marshal Sir Arthur Harris. The two men were good friends, but wrangled fiercely over the respective merits of air and sea power. Although the Fleet was unequipped for air defence, Phillips was quite confident of the Navy's ability to take on the Italians. Harris demurred and began to put awkward questions:

"What do you propose to do in a narrow sea like the Mediterranean, when you are attacked from all sides from the air?"

"Dodge," said Phillips resolutely, "and keep on my course."

Eventually Harris became exasperated. "Tom," he said, "one day you'll get a lesson. You'll be standing on your quarter-deck in wartime. The air will be black with bombers and torpedo-bombers. You'll be hit from above and from below, and as your ship staggers before she goes up in pieces, you'll just have time to glue your eyes to the water and say, 'Another blasted mine.' "

The only relief to a gloomy luncheon was Ismay's conviction about Russia. Contrary to the general opinion that the Germans were withdrawing in the East in order to prepare another offensive, he declared confidently: "I am convinced that the Germans have suffered not only a check but a real defeat."

The very next day brought great tidings. Elated by the early successes of the Japanese, Germany and Italy declared war on the United States. The restraint of President Roosevelt and the Prime Minister had been rewarded. In the folly of their megalomania Hitler and Mussolini had saved us from what might have been a most awkward situation.

Coming in such close sequence, the entry of the United States into the war and the sinking of the *Repulse* and *Prince of Wales* provided a remarkable example of the fickleness of popular favour. On December 8, the day after Pearl Harbour, Mr. Churchill's stock was at its highest. Two days later, with the news of the loss of the great battleships, complaints began. The criticisms reached their peak in the secret session of the House of Commons on December 19 when Mr. Churchill who had already left for Washington was strongly attacked for the first time. I was reminded of Voltaire's remark when at the end of his life he returned to Paris where he was welcomed as a hero by a cheering mob. "What crowds to greet you!" said one of his attendants. "Alas!" replied Voltaire, "there would be just as many to see me on the scaffold." On more than one occasion during the war Mr. Churchill must have been tempted to echo Voltaire's words.

The last fortnight of 1941 was one of the black periods of the war. Fortunately, we propagandists were stretched to our fullest capacity by work. There was little we could do to counteract the flood tide of disaster in the Pacific, but we had one mild score off Mussolini who, when Italy declared war on the United States, announced bombastically that the Italians would be "proud to fight alongside the brave soldiers of the Rising Sun". Luckily for us he had used almost the same words in 1917 when, as editor of the *Avanti*, he had written: "The Italians will be proud to fight alongside the brave soldiers of the United States, the only nation in history which has never gone to war except in a just cause." Our Italian experts had the quotation in their files, and the European Service of the B.B.C. used it in their Italian broadcasts with good effect.

At the moment our two most important problems were what line to take towards Japan in our propaganda to Russia and whether or not there should be a bombing truce at Christmas. Official guidance with regard to Russia was clear and concise. We were instructed to avoid any suggestion that Russia should declare war on Japan. This policy, I think, was right. At that moment Russia was bearing the full brunt of the German attack.

The question of Christmas bombing was always a difficult one. We propagandists were in favour of no bombing. We had raised the matter with the Air Ministry the previous year some time before Christmas. Then, while we were still waiting for a decision, Hitler had announced that Germany would not bomb during the Christmas festival. The Germans had therefore won a propaganda point. In 1941, I put the case to the Foreign Office on the following lines. It was bad propaganda for us to bomb on Christmas Eve and Christmas Day. It was also bad propaganda to announce a truce because it might be misinterpreted in Russia. I therefore recommended no bombing for two days and no announcement, and the Cabinet approved this action. The Germans followed our example. In point of fact, German bombing of Britain had been on a smaller scale for some months, and on Christmas Day Dallas Brooks, my deputy, won a bold wager from Frank Owen, then editor of the *Evening Standard*. Brooks had laid odds of two to one against the Germans ever having a hundred aeroplanes at one time over London from August 25 to December 25.

The last day of the year was cold and misty. There was little warmth in Whitehall where in their few moments of relaxation the high officials speculated on the decline of the Prime Minister's fortunes and on the slow progress of the war. Our bastions in the Far East were falling like rotten fruit in a storm. We were barely holding our own in the Libyan desert. From a military point of view Russia was the one bright star in a murky sky, and Hitler's dismissal of General Brauchitsch was a confirmation of the German failure in the East. But in Moscow Mr. Eden was having difficulties in his negotiations with Stalin who was already demanding large territorial compensations in Finland, the Baltic States and Bessarabia. A sudden cloud, too, had darkened the new Anglo-American alliance, for, without informing the Americans, General de Gaulle had sent Admiral Muselier with the submarine *Surcouf* to seize the islands of St. Pierre and Miquelon at the mouth of the St. Lawrence. The appearance of a French submarine so close to American waters enraged the American people. Their indignation was violent. It took the form of suspicion of British connivance, and the impulsive action of General de Gaulle cost him the favour of President Roosevelt and of the State Department for many months to come.

I myself felt down. I was worried about my son who was then flag-lieutenant to Admiral Layton, the Commander-in-Chief of our tiny naval force at Singapore, and from whom I had had no news except that he was safe for the moment. Nor was I happy about my work. I had been six months in my new job and, as far as I could see, I had made no progress whatsoever towards any improvement in our propaganda services. I made puerile excuses for myself by blaming Whitehall with its bureaucratic methods. I still felt that the people of Britain, who had celebrated their war-time Christmas with their usual calm and their innate genius for adapting themselves to any circumstances, were better than their government and their bureaucracy. I was not pessimistic about the outcome of the war, although obviously General Ismay had been right when he said that things must be worse before they were better. But I was thoroughly disappointed with myself. I had worked hard enough. On the other hand, I had wasted endless hours in fruitless negotiations. I had excused my failure to take decisions on the ground of frustration from above. I had fortified my lack of courage by self-indulgence.

On New Year's Eve I retired to bed before dinner and re-read Petronius's *Satyrikon*. I found admonishment and consolation almost on the first page: "If any man seeks for success in stern art and applies his mind to great tasks, let him first perfect his character by the rigid law of frugality. Nor must he care for the lofty frown of the tyrants' palace nor scheme for suppers with prodigals like a client, or drown the fires of his wit with wine, or sit before the stage applauding an actor's grimaces for a price."

The warnings were timely. They seemed to be directed against the subservience of many Whitehall officials to the higher officials and of some of the higher officials to ministers. I took them to my own particular address and made them my resolutions for the New Year. Of course I did not keep them.

But 1942 was to see a great change. Frustration was to be replaced by the tense excitement of action. Order was to be brought into the chaos of our propaganda. It was to be the year of the Anglo-Russian Treaty and the invasion of North Africa.

CHAPTER THREE

THE ACTUAL OPENING of the new year brought little sign of the better things to come. Throughout January and February public attention was focussed on Malaya and Indonesia where the success of the Japanese, inevitable in view of their overwhelming superiority, was nevertheless startling in its speed. Disasters which Parliament and the people had taken philosophically in 1940 came now as a severe shock to public confidence, and when the Prime Minister returned on January 17 from a most successful mission to Washington he found a sullen House of Commons. Criticism reached its peak in the middle of February when Singapore fell almost without a fight and the *Scharnhorst*, the *Gneisenau* and the *Prinz Eugen* slipped out of Brest and, escorted by destroyers, mine-sweepers and fighter aeroplanes, succeeded in reaching Germany. Both misfortunes caused widespread gloom. Few people perhaps expected that we could hold Singapore indefinitely, but the manner of its fall seemed inglorious. The escape of the German men-of-war came as a shock to the whole nation, and faith in the conduct of the war was severely shaken.

The reactions of the public were curious. Enthusiasm for Russia as the one successful combatant increased enormously, and to some extent her military success was attributed to the Russian system of government. Popular opinion about our own war effort was sullen, and there was a marked slump in the stock of the Conservatives whom the public regarded as mainly responsible for the conduct of the war. The general attitude was reflected in a story which was popular at the time.

Two Englishmen were sitting opposite each other in a railway carriage; both were reading newspapers. After a time one laid down his paper, smiled and said to the stranger opposite, "Well, we're not doing so badly."

The other looked up in surprise and replied politely, "You talk remarkably good English for a Russian."

Expressed in terms of personalities, the public reaction denoted a distinct increase in the popularity of Sir Stafford Cripps, whom many people regarded—quite erroneously—as the man who had brought Russia into the war, and a temporary decline in the fortunes of the Prime Minister. Partly because he was still flushed by his Washington triumph and partly because he was suffering from a bad cold Mr.

Churchill handled a critical House of Commons with less than his usual skill. Bowing to the storm, he was forced to make changes in his Government.

As usually happens when the Government are in trouble, the critics seize on any available stick with which to beat them. On this occasion the Political Warfare Executive was subjected to an attack, mainly on account of our broadcasts to Germany which many members of Parliament considered as altogether too friendly. In January one of our German experts had made, on his own responsibility, a broadcast in which he had expressed admiration of the qualities of the German people and of the German soldier whom, he said, "we respect even in war." Not unnaturally, in the Parliamentary criticisms the objectionable phrases were removed from their context. Since that occasion certain members of Parliament had followed our German broadcasts very closely. Now in February, when the Government was in difficulties, political warfare came in for its share of hard knocks in the House. If the debate, which filled many pages of *Hansard*, produced no concrete results, it served to focus attention on our activities.

The criticisms, if somewhat inexpert, were certainly justified. The Political Warfare Executive was deservedly in bad shape. We had few supporters in Whitehall, and even they made it quite clear that we should do no good until the whole organisation was concentrated in one building. Even our best friends thought that we made far too extravagant claims for what propaganda could achieve. I felt acutely the accuracy of these criticisms. But the decision lay with the ministers, and the ministerial committee of three was out of gear. The Woburn organisation, backed by Dr. Dalton, was determined to stay at Woburn. Mr. Bracken, who had tried by methods, which were sometimes more violent than diplomatic, to establish both geographical and ministerial unity, had reached the end of his tether. He had had even then more than his fill of the Ministry of Three, but in his devotion to Mr. Churchill he was not prepared to worry the Prime Minister at a time when he was beset with other troubles.

Admirable, as I have said, in standing up for his staff and defending them in Parliament, Mr. Bracken has a temperament which is as fiery as his aureole of flaming Celtic hair. On first acquaintance he seems to be a prey to every human emotion. Certainly he has more than a dash of Celtic exuberance, and, when it is in the ascendant, the words flow from his lips in a torrent which seems as tempestuous as a Highland stream in spate. The illusion of emotional lack of control is dangerous, for underneath he possesses a self-restraint which his opponents often fail to appreciate. In his verbal duels with other ministers, he possesses one great advantage, for when he seems to be hitting hardest, his temper is always under control. At such times his anger is feigned. He is, in fact, playing a part which is sometimes carefully rehearsed, but more often than not is extemporised to suit the impulse of the moment. On the other hand, when he is hurt, he is silent and like most Celts yields easily to depression. A few days before the debate in the House of Commons, he sent for me. He had, he said, a cure for our troubles. He would resign, and Sir Stafford Cripps could take over P.W.E. We should then have single ministerial control.

I said nothing. For an official, silence is often the best answer to ministerial despondency. But I went away feeling a little desperate. I could see no way out of the impasse. What I feared most was that Mr. Eden, who had many other preoccupations, would be only too glad to be rid of the trammels of a tiresome committee and would agree to Mr. Bracken's suggestion.

When our outlook was at its blackest, the changes in the Government were announced. Sir Stafford Cripps was appointed Leader of the House of Commons; Dr. Dalton was promoted to the Presidency of the Board of Trade. In the re-shuffle the Political Warfare Executive was given a new charter by the Prime Minister—and two Ministers instead of three. Mr. Eden was made responsible for policy and Mr. Bracken for administration. I was appointed Director-General. It was not an ideal arrangement, for in practice it is impossible to separate policy from administration. It did not fulfil the requirements of single ministerial control which I had always urged, but it was a great improvement on all the previous schemes.

My main preoccupation now was to bring the skilled propagandists from Woburn to London and to place the whole organisation in one building. At the end of February Brooks and I moved our sections from Fitzmaurice Place and the Foreign Office into Bush House where we had accommodation directly above the European Service of the B.B.C. By going to Bush House we were now able to exercise the policy control, granted to us by the Governors of the B.B.C., over broadcasts to enemy and enemy-occupied countries. In order to win the confidence of the B.B.C., I at once made Mr. Kirkpatrick a member of our Executive Committee. The former fortnightly meetings of the two Committees of Ministers and officials were abolished and, instead, I dealt direct with Mr. Eden and Mr. Bracken.

F

Bringing the Woburn organisation back to London was a slower process, mainly because of accommodation problems and the Treasury rule against the return of large numbers of civil servants from the country to London. But by the end of the year we had brought nearly everyone back to Bush House except the section engaged in secret work.

At first it was uphill work, but with some creaking the machine began to run more smoothly. Our department was organised on a central and regional basis with inter-regional directors for each country or group of countries. The general lines of policy were laid down by the central authority at weekly meetings with its own regional directors and with the central controllers of the European Service of the B.B.C. Within this framework of general policy considerable latitude was allowed to the regional directors who worked very closely with the corresponding regional sections of the B.B.C. Under one roof this scheme of organisation was workable.

One of my first efforts was to eliminate an undesirable eagerness on the part of our experts to indulge in wordy warfare with the German Propaganda Ministry. However entertaining and occasionally useful it may be to score off the enemy, propaganda is not and should not be a duel of dialectics between the political warriors of the rival propaganda organisations. It should be addressed to the masses. German propaganda may have inspired fear of Germany. I do not believe that it made a single friend for Germany apart from Germans.

For this tendency the new title of political warfare was largely responsible. Certainly the name was not always an advantage, for both the ministers and the government departments on whose goodwill P.W.E. was dependent did not appreciate the difference between propaganda and political warfare and merely assumed that the new name was a misguided attempt by the propagandists to increase their own importance.

In point of fact, many new technical methods of propaganda were introduced during the war, of which perhaps the most valuable was the deduction of enemy intentions from enemy propaganda. Some of the new methods were overdone. For instance, after one or two initial successes the practice of committing the Germans to the capture of a key position (for example, Stalingrad) by a date, which from the best military opinion we knew was highly unlikely, was carried to an excess which defeated its own ends. An essay could be written on the differences between propaganda and political warfare.

Perhaps the truest definition of the latter is that political warfare practises every form of overt and covert attack which can be called political as distinct from military. It seeks both to counter and by intelligent anticipation to forestall the political offensives of the enemy. It demands a highly specialised intelligence service of its own and, above all, an accurate estimate of the enemy's intentions. It relies not only on open and truthful propaganda, but also on a whole series of secret or "black" operations which can be suitably classified under the headings of subversion and deception. These operations include so-called "secret" broadcasting from stations supposed to be operated in or close to enemy and enemy-occupied territory by subversive enemy or enemy-occupied elements.

I cannot say that P.W.E. was an easy team. Every good propagandist must possess the qualities of a prima donna or, as Ernst Toller once said, must be born with one eye. The department was composed almost entirely of temporary officials who had plenty of *esprit de corps* but considerably less knowledge of official procedure. There was no lack of brains, especially in the organisation at Woburn where Rex Leeper had assembled and trained a varied array of talent which gave the form and shape to the propaganda policy which was finally adopted. But at all times, and particularly during the first two years of the war, there was a tendency to try to make foreign policy by means of propaganda instead of being content to support policy by propaganda. This tendency was strongly resented by Ministers and by the Foreign Office and the service departments.

Actually political warfare is neither an exact science nor a separate art. As the handmaid of official policy and of military strategy, it is dependent on the calculations and errors of government. At the same time it must be supple with an instinctive feeling for the element of chance in human affairs. Above all, it must on occasions act with great speed in order to kill an enemy lie which otherwise might do great harm. It has therefore to take its directives not only from ministers and Chiefs of Staff who are not always readily available but also from the incidence of time and events.

Inevitably, therefore, the propagandists chafed under the restraints of official policy and were inclined to regard Whitehall as an obstacle which had to be circumvented by intrigue rather than eliminated by persistent persuasion and argument. Most of these attempts to by-pass the permanent departments were detected, caused an infinity of trouble, and did great harm to P.W.E. Early in February, 1942, the Joint Planners, a section of the Chiefs of Staff organisation composed of members of the three service departments and the Foreign Office, were considering a request from the War Cabinet for a paper on the state of morale in the occupied countries of Europe. One member suggested that P.W.E. should be asked to prepare the memorandum. The suggestion was rejected on the ground that P.W.E. was "wild and irresponsible".

To be fair, there were faults on both sides. The permanent departments, especially the Foreign Office, were slow to realise the importance of broadcasting to a Europe that was cut off from every other means of communication, and without constant pressure by P.W.E., even if at times it was unwisely exerted, it is doubtful if we should ever have progressed beyond the cramping limits of excessive caution. Having been a permanent civil servant in the first world war and a temporary one in the second I think it fair to say that in war-time the temporary departments suffer from lack of experience and excess of enthusiasm and that the reverse applies to the permanent departments. In P.W.E. I made it my principal task to try to hold a fair balance between the enthusiasm of the propagandists and the caution of the permanent officials.

The composition of P.W.E. was extraordinarily varied. It contained a handful of professional soldiers and civil servants. The rest were drawn from almost every walk of life and included journalists, business men, advertising experts, schoolmasters, authors, literary agents, farmers, barristers, stockbrokers, psychologists, university dons, and a landscape gardener. I do not think that any one profession provided any initial advantage of training. A propagandist is born and not made. The journalists were undoubtedly the best exponents of propaganda. They wrote the best leaflets. They had the best understanding of the value of the spoken and written word, and in a department which had always to work at top speed they alone had the requisite sense of urgency. Being used to ephemeral work, they were not so good on policy and sometimes felt frustrated by the hampering necessity of consistency. Our schoolmasters were excellent. The dons included some brilliant men, but were inclined to resent criticism. With one exception the advertising experts were a disappointment. I have an open mind about psychologists. We employed three, and one, at least, did useful work for our German section. Psychological analysis has undoubtedly a place in political warfare, but it was not sufficiently tested in the war to justify any firm conclusion. My personal view is that in propaganda an ounce of first-hand experience of a country is worth a ton of theoretical knowledge, and this theory applies not only to our psychologists but to all the propagandists we employed.

On account of the shortage of men we relied for staff mainly on women who were vastly in the majority. Taken by and large, they were admirable in efficiency and in conduct. Two were expert propagandists who ran their own section with men under them. Several excelled in administrative work. All showed a spirit of cooperation and loyalty which to me at any rate was always a consolation in times of trouble. Brooks's secretary and my own were entrusted with all our Top Secret information, and, as far as security is concerned, I believe firmly, and I think the belief is widely held in Whitehall, that women keep official secrets far better than men including most ministers. Pessimists, who take a gloomy view of the future of this country, may reap a morbid satisfaction from the German theory that the first sign of decadence in a country is when the women become superior to the men. Personally I shall be satisfied if Britain continues to be served by her women-folk as well as she was during the war.

Our activities, apart from our secret work, were mainly concerned with broadcasting and the dissemination of leaflets. With the exception of a short interval for maintenance purposes, broadcasting went on by day and by night. Every twenty-four hours 160,000 words went out over the air in twenty-three languages. Twenty-two per cent. of this total of over a million words weekly went to Germany. It was perhaps too high a proportion, for in my opinion the best work of the European Service of the B.B.C. was done in the occupied countries. Leaflets were distributed by the Royal Air Force from the first day of the war and also by balloon. They ranged from single sheet leaflets to miniature illustrated newspapers and long before the end of the war they had set a new high standard for this form of production. A special feature of our work was the production of miniature magazines and even books which were distributed, partly, by air and, partly, by secret methods. Reviews like *La France Libre* and a book of Mr. Churchill's speeches were reduced to the size of a folded lady's handkerchief and, nevertheless, were so beautifully printed that the text could be read with ease and comfort by the naked eye. Both in content and in attractiveness they were, I think, the best propaganda productions of any country.

Both broadcasting and leaflets to the occupied countries presented no great difficulties. We were appealing to friends who were eager—sometimes, indeed, too eager—to listen to our broadcasts and to pick up our leaflets and miniature magazines. In our task of maintaining morale in these countries we collaborated closely with the Allied Governments in London. That we achieved excellent results is borne out not only by the evidence of the oppressed peoples themselves but also by the fierce penalties which the Germans imposed with increasing savagery on listeners to the foreign broadcasts of our European Service.

In our propaganda to Germany, however, we were handicapped from the start by a problem which was never solved. This was the vexatious question of what we called a "hope clause" for Germany. For a long time there was no official policy about the future of Germany, and we were left to grope our way as best we could. But we were never allowed to make any promises in our propaganda. When eventually the policy of unconditional surrender was officially announced, it imposed a severe restriction on the opportunities for successful propaganda. Indeed, it was undeniably a propaganda asset to Germany, and Dr. Goebbels employed it constantly in his propaganda to his own countrymen. Put in plain language, the argument he used was: "Some of you Germans may not like us Nazis, but if the Allies win they will wreak on us all a peace of revenge in comparison with which the Treaty of Versailles will seem Utopian." To enforce his point, he plastered the walls of the chief German cities with huge posters containing extracts from Lord Vansittart's *Black Record*.

The problem with which the Government were faced was: "Were there sufficient so-called 'good Germans' to justify a promise of a reasonable peace provided that they turned against Hitler before the end of the war?" On the proper answer to this question the House of Commons and, I imagine, the whole country, were divided. It was a personal and not a Party issue, and even in the Labour Party there were deep cleavages of opinion. After the debate on political warfare in February, 1942, Mr. Eden and sometimes Mr. Bracken used to receive two separate Parliamentary Propaganda Committees. I attended as adviser on the current affairs of our department. One Committee took what I may call the Vansittart line and complained querulously of P.W.E's softness towards the Germans. The other Committee, of which Commander King-Hall was the mainspring and which advocated a hope clause, took exactly the opposite line and with equal vigour protested against the harshness of our German propaganda.

We propagandists favoured the hope clause, but the difficulty was to win approval for a formula which would not conflict with the official policy of unconditional surrender. Many attempts were made both by the British and the Americans, but they came to nothing, and with the understandable object of preserving national unity at home the Government did their best—and in war-time it is a powerful best—to avoid public discussion of the problem.

Certainly nearly all members of Parliament regarded themselves as experts on propaganda, held strong views on the subject, and more often than not had their own pet German *émigré*.

For what it is worth, my own opinion is that, so long as a German victory or even an inconclusive peace seemed possible to Germans, the "good Germans" were powerless to cause any serious disruption of the German military machine.

Nevertheless, there is now a considerable amount of evidence, taken mainly from captured German documents, which indicates that anti-Nazi Germans, including high officers of the army, listened-in assiduously to both our "white" and our "black" broadcasts and that until the official announcement of "unconditional surrender" our propaganda was having an increasing effect. Obviously its big chance would have come at the moment when German hopes of winning the war were beginning to wane. This moment coincided with the formula of "unconditional surrender".

The absence of a hope clause was, therefore, a severe handicap to our German propaganda. I do not cavil at the Government's policy or lack of policy. It is difficult to prepare for peace when one is fighting for very existence; doubly difficult when a country is as unprepared for war as ours was. But the fact should be noted that in January, 1941, when Mr. Harry Hopkins came to England to find out how we proposed to win the war, he was informed that the three lines of our attack on Germany were (1) blockade; (2) bombing and (3) propaganda and subversion. There was then no prospect of attacking the Reich itself by land. These lines of the politico-strategic conduct of the war were confirmed by the American Chiefs of Staff during Mr. Churchill's visit to Washington in December, 1941.

Yet at the time no serious impetus was ever given to our propaganda efforts from on top. It was due, I think, partly to the pressure of graver events and partly to ignorance of the subject in Whitehall. The ignorance bred scepticism, and together they were a formidable hurdle. The Chiefs of Staff were always willing to help us to solve our problems but, to begin with at least, they erred on the side of over-simplification. When we explained to them our difficulties about the hope clause for Germany, one of them, assuming that all propaganda was deception, provided an admirable solution. "Why don't you take the King-Hall line in your propaganda and keep the Vansittart line for the peace terms?"

Unfortunately, open propaganda is always a responsibility of the Government's and—to Mr. Eden's credit be it said—we were never allowed to make in our propaganda any commitment which the Government were not prepared to fulfil. If we approached even the borderline, I was certain to be rebuked. But in the first years of the war the Foreign Office were no better educated in the technique of propaganda than the service departments, and even those officials who wished most to help us sometimes tumbled into traps. When Hungary and Roumania were restive about the ultimate fate of Transylvania, I would receive a suggestion: "Why don't you tell the Hungarians in your Hungarian broadcasts that Germany is going to let Roumania keep Transylvania and tell the Roumanians in your Roumanian broadcasts that she is going to give it to Hungary." With patience and good humour I had to explain not only that in Transylvania there were people who spoke both languages but also that Dr. Goebbels employed a large staff of linguists to listen in to all our foreign broadcasts in the hope of discovering inconsistencies in our policy and exposing them to the world, and that of course we did the same.

I do not think for one moment that during the period of German military ascendancy our propaganda, even if given greater support, could have achieved more than it did. And that was very little indeed as far as Germany was concerned. You cannot undermine morale in the hour of military success, and not even Hitler himself could have stopped the German people from shrieking *Sieg Heil* in unison when after twenty-five years the bitterness of defeat seemed to have been wiped away by the most resounding of victories.

Nevertheless, Whitehall's ignorance of the technique and possibilities of propaganda and, more particularly, of broadcasting was unnecessarily prolonged. This was a minor misfortune for which the pre-war planning of our propaganda activities was responsible. Apart from the defects of organisation, an initial mistake was made in establishing the enemy propaganda department at Woburn, and this defect was aggravated by the obstinacy of a department, which had done most valuable pioneer work, in resisting for so long every attempt to bring it back to London. I have always felt that, if it had been established from the beginning in or near Whitehall, its efficiency would have been increased, its merits more quickly recognised, and many vexatious delays and inter-departmental wrangles avoided. I am no lover of the bureaucratic state, but the senior officials of the British civil service bring to the study of most problems the knowledge of a vast experience, nor are they lacking in goodwill. On the other hand the initial attitude of the propagandists was ostrich-like, and surely never in Whitehall has there been a better example of a situation in which great possibilities were sacrificed for petty considerations.

CHAPTER FOUR

MY QUARTERS IN the Foreign Office had been a set of temporary cubicles hastily erected within the frame-work of the great Locarno Room. They reminded me of war-time cabins in a giant liner. They were stuffy in summer and cold and draughty in winter. The walls were not sound-proof, and if I was carrying on a secret conversation we had to talk in whispers.

Urgent business was conducted by personal contact. I locked my door, put my key in my pocket, and walked down the long, high corridor to Sir Orme Sargent's room. I would find him surrounded by a vast pile of red boxes. If I required an immediate decision, it was given with a plain yes or no. If my problem was complicated and concerned other departments, the answer would be longer and more cautious. The advice was nearly always sound.

The administration of the Office was crusted with the cobwebs of a fusty tradition, but in matters of policy the senior officials had a confidence and a surety of touch which compelled both respect and admiration. If they showed a tendency to be cautious, it was prompted, not by an exaggerated respect for the principle of safety first, but by a dislike of rashness based on insufficient knowledge. Long experience had taught them that crises in foreign affairs are far from simple and that ministers and even Prime Ministers not infrequently take decisions which, in the light of further information, they may regret the next morning. Foreign affairs are not like football matches and mediaeval battles which start at a given time and by sundown have produced a conclusive result. That is perhaps why soldiers and a football-mad public rarely understand them.

Doubtless, reforms are needed in the Foreign Office, for today its functions are no longer confined to the narrow limits of pure diplomacy. The real weakness is in connexion with appointments. As in other permanent departments there is an almost maternal unwillingness to eliminate the inefficient members of the service. I do not know what providential guardian watches over appointments in other departments, but in the Foreign Office it has been for many years the ghost of Charles the Second, the principle governing all senior appointments being that monarch's dying words: "Don't let poor Nellie starve." When a post is vacant, the diplomatic list is produced, and the man at the top, irrespective of his qualifications, is rarely passed over.* It is a pernicious system which in spite of red tape and civil service rules should be remedied without delay. In Russia an official who makes a mistake disappears and is never seen again. In the Britain of today he is eliminated by promotion. Common sense should be able to find a suitable compromise between the two systems.

Apart from this weakness, which imposes a heavy strain on the better officials, the Foreign Office has a high standard of efficiency within the limits of the present system. The main burden falls on a comparatively small number of men, who, although overworked, deal rapidly with an ever-increasing mass of telegrams and minutes, and shoulder their heavy responsibilities with a fine disregard of uninformed criticism. They receive plenty of it, but the fact remains— and it is a significant one—that whenever a Cabinet Committee is seeking trained personnel its first request is always for a Foreign Office man, and for its greater glory the Foreign Office supplies him. Sometimes I felt that these sacrifices were made at the expense of efficiency, for, if the good Foreign Office men are the best in White-hall, they are not too numerous. Indeed there is much truth in Mr. Bevin's remark, made not long after he had become Foreign Secretary, that there is nothing wrong with Foreign Office men except that there are too few of them and that they are underpaid.

I did not leave the Foreign Office without some regrets. Thirty years before, I had begun my career there, and, although I had come back as a stranger, the place gave me a feeling of security. Whatever happened to the world, the Foreign Office, like the Church of Rome, would always be there. An easy and most vulnerable target for any bomb, it was the one building in which the sirens aroused no fear in my stomach.

The change to Bush House was like a journey from an old-world English home into a brand-new skyscraper in a Middle West American township. But the move was necessary and the site convenient, for I was half-way between Mr. Eden and Mr. Bracken and could reach both within five minutes by car. The offices which we occupied were spacious but strangely un-English, for they were designed on the United States business pattern with a few small rooms and one large central hall in which all the staff could be under the constant watch of the management. We converted this space into

---

* Since the Eden reforms came into force, this system has ceased, and the Foreign Office is now the one department of the Civil Service in which promotion is by merit and not by seniority.

cubicles and, to meet the requirements of the security officer, we wired the entrances from the lifts with heavy netting. In this zoo I remained until the end of the war. Most of my work was done by telephone. On my desk I had two instruments and a house telephone with switches to all the chief officials of my department. In addition, I had a private line to my bedroom in my club in St. James's Square. They were rarely inactive. I worked long hours, and the demands on my time were constant.

My private life, already heavily restricted by the war, now ceased to exist. My world was bounded by an ellipse of which the four points of the compass were the East India Club in St. James's Square, Whitehall, Bush House and the Ministry of Information. I saw few of my old friends, and these only rarely. I went to no theatres or cinemas. I read no new books except those connected with my work.

In the first world war there was a purpose in my life—a purpose that seemed to me noble and inspiring. We were fighting not only for freedom but also for a better world in which war would be no more. A League of Nations would see to that. My faith in the ultimate goodness of humanity was unquestioning. Now the faith and the nobilities were gone, and not only from me and my contemporaries, but also, it seemed, from the younger generation. We were fighting for our existence, but for what else? The foe was no longer Germany, but the more sinister enemy of a totalitarianism which was not confined to one country.

True, my Socialist colleagues insisted that, more and more, we were fighting for a better world. I tried to believe them and, when I drove through Camden Town on my way to Woburn and saw the long drab rows of wretched houses, my sense of justice was outraged by the inequalities of our social system. But very soon I saw clearly that my friends, whether they realised it or not, were as totalitarian in their hearts as the Germans or the Russians, for the things that they wanted—state socialism, planned economy, and centralisation—could be obtained only by a totalitarian régime. I accepted my job as a duty, and did it, I hope, none the less efficiently because I had no dream vision of a Utopian future. I was too old to be a convert to new mythologies. London was my prison and the office was itself my life-sentence. I had no time for personal reflections, and I was content that it should be so.

Even my meals were part of my duties. At them I talked "shop" with my colleagues or lunched and dined out with officials whose affairs had some connexion with ours and whom it was difficult to see at other times. Relaxations were therefore few and simple, and such as presented themselves I accepted gratefully. During the first weeks of the Blitz a pigeon was blasted into the smoking-room of my club through the open window. It was dazed and had a broken leg, but it was otherwise unhurt. One of the valets tended it and mended its leg. It became the club pet. In the day-time it went abroad, like the members, on its own business and returned in the evening to take its place in the smoking-room. It was wonderfully tame and friendly. Several times I took it to sleep with me in my bedroom. It was a quieter companion than any cat or dog, sleeping peacefully on the mantelpiece or on the wooden ledge at the end of my bed and paying no attention to the sirens. If a bomb fell near, it would flutter round the room for a moment and then resume its place. In the mornings, when it woke it would strut majestically along the bed clothes and take its place on my arm or shoulder. Unfortunately it was not house-trained, and eventually a long-suffering secretary banned it both from the smoking-room and from members' bedrooms. It remained, however, with the valet and, more regular in its hours and habits than the members, lived to celebrate the final victory over all our enemies. To one nervous Scot who did not like to be alone and who welcomed any diversion in the Blitz, it will always be a pleasant memory.

Like many elderly officials, I did with extraordinary little sleep during the war. I worked late, sat up late and woke early. In the morning I prepared my agenda list and at nine-thirty I set out for Bush House. Sometimes as I made my way down the Strand I would contrast its war-time dinginess with the romantic glory of its old associations. But my mind was not troubled by the ghosts of its literary giants. Much as I admired the Londoner, I had never shared the views of Lamb and Johnson about London itself. I vastly preferred Skiddaw to Lamb's Strand and, if Dr. Johnson chose to say that anyone who was tired of London was tired of life, then I was ready for the worms. If I thought of the spectres of the past, it was of the failures; the Dowsons, the Lionel Johnsons, the Richard Middletons and the other Bohemians who, mistaking a minor talent for genius, had wasted their substance in irregular living.

Sometimes I made calculations of the sums I had squandered on night life between 1909 and 1939. At the most conservative estimate the figure was unpleasant to contemplate. It would have bought me a comfortable annuity for the rest of my life and been a guarantee against the loss of earning power which comes with old age and against which I had made no provision. But mostly my mind was concentrated on the long list of problems on my agenda. All these morning reflections were futile. As soon as I arrived at the office, my agenda list had to be laid aside in order to enable me to deal with some new internal or external crisis which had arisen and which had to be solved immediately.

Admittedly, inter-departmental disputes were a plague and a curse, but even in the darkest moments there was always one unfailing spur to optimism. All that was best in British youth was in the fighting line. We in the rear had no right to our own time or to our personal reflections. Whichever way one looked at it, work was either a duty or the best form of escapism from a war which had to be won. It was easier and more flattering to one's conscience to regard it as a duty, and for myself I found both consolation and usefulness in President Eliot's old maxim: "Things seem to be going fairly well now that the spirit of pessimism prevails in all departments."

Apart from giving political guidance and forecasts of the situation, I contributed little to the output of our department. The actual propaganda was planned and executed by the regional directors and by the planning section. More by necessity than by choice I was from the beginning more of a salesman than a propagandist, my self-imposed duty being to "sell" the department to ministers and to the permanent departments on whose goodwill our existence depended. In this task I had an admirable deputy in Dallas Brooks. He had been connected with propaganda since before the war, possessed considerable expertise and great tact, and by his sound knowledge of Whitehall was able to temper the exuberance of the propagandists with the more sober judgment of official experience. I have already referred with gratitude to the help we received from the Chiefs of Staff and from General Ismay and General Hollis. Thanks to Brooks we were also on excellent terms with the Admiralty from whom we received great assistance throughout the war. Our relations with the Air Ministry were not quite so satisfactory. Partly through our own fault, we suffered permanent frustration from a cumbersome and somewhat inhuman War Office.

With the abolition of the two committees of Three, my weekly meetings with Mr. Eden and Mr. Bracken became a pleasure instead of an affliction. Almost simultaneously with the changes in the Political Warfare Executive, Sir Stafford Cripps was sent on a hopeless mission to India. It was doomed to failure from the start and its ultimate results were a reduction of his prestige in the Coalition

Government and the removal of a possible rival to Mr. Churchill in popular esteem. It caused me great anxiety, for Mr. Eden took Sir Stafford's place as Leader of the House of Commons, retaining at the same time his functions as Foreign Secretary. It was a dual task which would have taxed the strength of a young athlete, and I assumed with justifiable apprehension that now, when P.W.E's affairs seemed likely to run more smoothly, Mr. Eden would have no time to spare for us. I was entirely mistaken.

The public has made its own picture of Mr. Eden. It is taken from the popular Press and assumes the form of a well-dressed and good-looking young man who is the mould of fashion and the creator of the Eden black hat. It is, of course, a caricature of the real man. He is, in point of fact, a lonely man who dislikes most forms of social life and is at his happiest in his country home where he wears the shabbiest of old clothes and can work with his hands, chopping wood, grubbing weeds, digging his border or spraying his fruit trees with a contraption on his back which looks like an infantryman's flamethrower. He is a man who cultivates his garden both mentally and physically. This passion for the simple life has given him a robust health and a reserve of physical energy which enable him to stand the strain of public life better than any of his colleagues. The passion is genuine. He has his roots deep in the soil of England. He has three great qualities as a politician: an immense capacity for work, a natural courtesy and an integrity in public life which is unequalled. The courtesy is a compensating virtue, for it implies respect for the opinions of others and a gift of listening which makes him countless friends among the young men who sooner or later chafe under the monotony of ministerial monologues. It is his courtesy, combined with his integrity, which makes him so successful a negotiator, for it wins him the confidence of even the most suspicious foreigner. In most successful ministers there is something of the buccaneer. There is none in Mr. Eden.

During the war he had a particularly difficult task in dealing with a Prime Minister who was as nearly a dictator as this country has ever had since Cromwell and who intervened constantly, always daringly, and sometimes rashly in foreign affairs. Whenever Mr. Churchill's genius for improvisation outran discretion, Mr. Eden was not afraid to make a firm stand, for he possesses both physical and moral courage in abundance. But he lacks ruthlessness, and if this is a fault in politics he will never cure it. He has set himself certain standards in public life, and he will never willingly fall below them.

I saw a great deal of Mr. Eden during the war, and, even when, as happened more than once, I disturbed his sleep in the early hours of the morning on some matter of urgency I never heard a complaint from his lips. I learnt very much from him. His advice was always good. His decisions were firm and quickly given. He was open to argument and, if he said "go ahead", I was sure of his backing. In spite of the excessive demands on his time, he came to inspect our organisation at Bush House and visited Woburn more than once. His handling of the Parliamentary Committees on propaganda was an object-lesson in tact and firmness. To a man of his experience the task was perhaps not difficult. Parliamentary Committees come to ministers either for information or to state grievances. The grievances about us invariably took two forms: complaints against the Right Wing or the Left Wing tendencies of our propaganda and attacks on the extravagance of the Woburn establishment. The complaints on policy were easy to answer. They raised inevitably the problem of the "good Germans", and on this subject even a Left Wing Committee was sure to be divided. Peace and honour were generally satisfied by Mr. Eden's declaring that while we sought to divide the Germans we must not go too far in the way of promises. The attacks on the Woburn establishment were trickier and sometimes directed against individual officials. They used to alarm me by their venom. But Mr. Eden took the right line by declaring: "You can go for me as much as you like, but it is most unfair to attack officials." The answer generally turned away wrath. But Mr. Eden did not like the attacks and was doubtless relieved by the knowledge that the administrative problem of bringing Woburn to London was not his.

This task was Mr. Bracken's, and he had three war jobs, for, in addition to his duties as Minister of Information and as Minister responsible for the administration of the Political Warfare Executive, he was also the faithful attendant of Mr. Churchill and had his own room in No. 10 Downing Street, in which a fine portrait of a naval rating by Mr. Eric Kennington and a somewhat florid-looking cigar-cabinet were the chief ornaments. Nevertheless, he, too, devoted a portion of his remarkable energy to our affairs, and soon after Dr. Dalton's departure I found myself in the Bracken Bentley with Mr. Ronald Tree and Lord Birkenhead on our way to Woburn. The Minister wished to inspect the establishment.

It was a wet and depressing morning in March, but the journey was enlivened by the sparkle of the conversation. Mr. Bracken has an almost encyclopaedic knowledge of a surprisingly large number of subjects. He is an authority on Burke, English architecture, head-masters and bishops, blue-books and finance and, of course, Mr. Churchill. He also possesses a most retentive memory, a lively and vivid imagination which transports him on occasions into the realms of decorative art, and a fine and selective choice of words acquired from much reading and perhaps from an unconscious imitation of his hero. In the right mood and on the right occasion he gives there-fore very good value for his loquacity.

For our Woburn visit both the mood and the occasion were har-monious, and after we had passed St. Albans we were regaled with a feast of wit and pungent comment. He had once owned and re-decorated a charming Queen Anne house in the Dunstable district. We were given the history of the house and of the fate of all its previous owners. As we drew near to stately Woburn Abbey we were enthralled by a series of brilliant bijou biographies of the various Russells beginning with John Russell, the young favourite of Philip le Bel, Archduke of Austria, and of Henry VIII, to whom the Russell family owes its fortunes and, incidentally, its share of the monasterial spoil, and finishing with the present pacifist Duke of Bedford.

The inspection of our organisation gave me some quiet amuse-ment. We began with the Abbey itself, where in large rooms and picture galleries, which contained a mixture of priceless treasures and family junk, were the main offices of the country section. Rex Leeper, eager to impress the Minister with the excellence of his work which, in truth, was not properly appreciated in London, was our guide. Aglow with enthusiasm, he would open a door and reveal a fine room in which heavy Victorian furniture was incongruously jumbled with typewriting tables and steel filing cabinets. "Here", he would say proudly, "is where our French Region works." But Mr. Bracken's attention was elsewhere. His practised eye had spotted a treasure on the wall and, turning to Lord Birkenhead and Mr. Tree, he would exclaim with rapturous enthusiasm: "Freddie! Ronnie! Look at that Canaletto—absolutely first-class. Just about the best in England." The other sections suffered much the same ordeal, with this difference that when the glance of the Minister lighted on a sickly portrait of Lord Odo Russell, the junior hero of the Berlin Conference, praise would be tempered with a scornful, "Gosh! what junk."

But when we came to the production unit, Mr. Bracken was all attention, and the merit of our leaflets received its proper meed of recognition. The Minister, too, was enthusiastic about the so-called "black" broadcasting and was impressed by the quality of the voices of the various announcers which he pronounced as much more virile and effective than those of the B.B.C.

The inspection was long and rather tiring. But Mr. Bracken's wit continued to scintillate, and at luncheon he delighted all present with a firework display of epigrams the best of which was his answer to a question regarding the merits of a certain politician. "He's the kind of man", said Mr. Bracken, "who prefaces every new sentence with 'You know what I mean'. You don't, and in a very few seconds you know that you don't want to."

The visit was a great success, and at the end Rex Leeper took me aside and said to me privately: "That was all right, wasn't it? He asked no difficult questions." I felt unhappy. For a moment I imagined that he believed that I had been misleading him by my frequent warnings of the Minister's desire to bring the Woburn organisation to London. Rex was one of my oldest friends. This was what made the situation so difficult. It would have been a thousand times worse if Mr. Bracken had changed his mind.

But Rex Leeper was wrong and I was wrong. Mr. Bracken is nothing if not perceptive, and for all his pleasant manner and apparent nonchalance he had shrewdly assessed the two main defects of the Woburn organisation: the distance from London and the high consumption of petrol for motor-transport between London and Woburn at a time when the whole country was being severely rationed.

On the way back to London he spoke to me very seriously. All the country establishment, except the officials engaged in really secret activities, must be brought to London. The petrol consumption must be reduced by half. He promised to do his utmost to obtain the necessary accommodation in London for the returning officials. He ordered me to arrange for an immediate enquiry into the transport situation and himself nominated the man who should conduct it. I was no longer amused. I was impressed. The functions of a Minister in relation to his department are to lay down the main lines of policy and not to get bogged in detail. If he would consent to concentrate on one job, Mr. Bracken, who has already made a successful career both in politics and in business, could reach almost any goal. His weakness is that he wants to have an iron in every fire. And for all his battery of invective he has too kind a heart.

In view of his numerous other activities Mr. Bracken's interest in

P.W.E. was inclined to be spasmodic. He was like a volcano which erupted frequently and sometimes violently. The eruptions, let it be said, were stimulating. Not only did he keep us well informed, but he gave invaluable aid by introducing me and other members of my department to the people who mattered most to us.

It was through him and with him that I first met Air Marshal Sir Arthur Harris. In that spring of 1942 he was at the height of his fame, for Bomber Command was then our most spectacular arm, and it alone was bringing the war to the very heart of Germany. As it was his bombers that carried our leaflets, it was all-important for us to convince him of the value of propaganda. We never converted him although Mr. Bracken did his persuasive best. Heavily built with blue eyes, fair complexion, firm jaw and broad shoulders, the Air Marshal was burly in appearance and tough in mind, and one look at him convinced me that nothing would ever shake him from his fixed purpose. He believed in bombing Germany relentlessly and unremittingly. He was convinced that this was the only method by which the German people could be brought to their senses. He told me that, when we could send out a thousand bombers a night, the war would end very quickly. He was not, he said, opposed to leaflets. He recognised their value, but he objected strongly to exposing his bomber crews to danger in order to drop what he called "pieces of bumph".

At that time (April, 1942) the arrangements for dropping leaflets were primitive. The rear-gunner of the bomber had to leave his gun for several minutes in order to release the leaflets. As they had to be dropped over targets protected by German night-fighters, the rear-gunner could not afford to take his eye off his gun for ten seconds, let alone five minutes. He would do all he could to help, the Air Marshal promised, but he wanted a mechanical dropping device. Of course, in the state of our unpreparedness, it took months to obtain it.

Three months later, Sir Arthur Harris was to be indirectly responsible for my most unpleasant experience of the war. True to his promise to give us all possible aid, he had agreed to put his name to a leaflet which was to be dropped over Germany. It was prepared with great care, was shown to the Air Marshal and received his approval. It took the form of a message to the German people. It emphasised the immense productive capacity of the Anglo-American aircraft industry, the determination of the Anglo-American people to end the dictators' rule of force, and the futility of German resistance. It told the German people that, if they did not overthrow the Nazis and make peace, they would be bombed "every night and every day, rain, blow or snow". It was a good aggressive leaflet, and it was dropped in millions of copies. The Air Chief Marshal, I think, was satisfied. We were over-pleased, for one of our leading German experts tried to make good better. Contrary to the arrangement with Sir Arthur Harris, who had given his name to a leaflet only, our bright enthusiast wished to broadcast the message. Just to what extent he obtained the permission of the Air Ministry was never satisfactorily established, and at the best the permission could have been given only by a junior official. What was certain was that Sir Arthur Harris was never consulted.

The message was duly broadcast, and the next day several hells gaped simultaneously. On reaching the office I received a message from Mr. Eden. He wished to see Mr. Bracken and me as soon as possible and in any event before the morning meeting of the Cabinet. I arrived first and received part of the blast which had already blown over Mr. Eden. He had just received an indignant letter from Sir Archibald Sinclair, then Secretary of State for Air. It accused P.W.E. of having broadcast to the wide world a message expressly intended for a leaflet only. The Prime Minister had been on the telephone. He did not object to the contents of the message, Mr. Eden told me, but was annoyed that a leading Service Chief should broadcast a political message without ministerial approval. On learning the facts of the case, he had wished to issue a statement white-washing Sir Arthur Harris and therefore discrediting our propaganda. Mr. Eden was angry—not without reason. His whole morning had been wasted by our folly. Administration was not his affair, but, he suggested, it was time that an example should be made. Where was Mr. Bracken? He summoned a private secretary and asked him to find out.

I had to think quickly. The first essential was to prevent, if possible, the issue of a statement which would give a winning hand to Dr. Goebbels and incidentally, provoke serious trouble in a House of Commons that was still restive about the debacle in the Far East. The second was to save my man whom I could ill spare.

I did my best to argue the case against the public statement. With one eye on the clock I pleaded for time for an investigation. I did not know all the facts. Both sides should be heard. The minutes passed with painful slowness. Mr. Eden did not relent. Then his private secretary came in: Mr. Bracken would not be available till later. He had been summoned to Buckingham Palace. Mr. Eden had to leave at once for his Cabinet meeting. I mopped my brow, and, as I left the room, whispered fervently to myself, "God Save The King."

The respite gave those priceless moments of time which cure all ills. I saw Mr. Bracken in the afternoon. He, too, was angry, but was helpful and promised to speak to the Prime Minister. The next morning Mr. Eden telephoned. The news was good. Mr. Churchill had read the message, had found it good, and had agreed that it would be a mistake to issue a public statement. But he wanted a full investigation of the incident.

I spent four laborious days hearing evidence and writing my report. During this interval Providence came to my help in the form of messages from the Allied Governments and from the resistance leaders in the occupied countries who had been delighted not only with the aggressive tone of the message but with the confident note of victory which it sounded. It was what they had been waiting for months to hear. In the end the incident was allowed to fizzle out, and my expert escaped with a reprimand and, I hope, a salutary fright. He remained to do good work and to earn high praise from General Eisenhower. He is now a public figure and may well reach great heights. I hope that he sings "God Save The King" with fervour, for, if Mr. Bracken had not been summoned to an audience on the day the crisis broke, an irrevocable decision would undoubtedly have been taken and a promising career checked.

CHAPTER FIVE

THE SPRING AND early summer of 1942 had a decisive influence on the course of the war. It was then that our future relations with Russia took their definite shape and that the agitation for the Second Front entered the first stage of its acuteness. The success of the Russian winter campaign had aroused the greatest enthusiasm among the British people, and throughout the country there was a fervent desire to help the Russian armies who were then facing almost the full military strength of Germany. The Russian Government, with a very vivid memory of the success of the initial German attacks in 1941, viewed with alarm and misgivings the renewal of what might be a decisive German offensive in the summer of 1942 and in its anxiety demanded with increasing insistence an Anglo-American attack in the West which would relieve the German pressure on Russia. Already in Moscow the old rumour of 1915 was going its dangerous round: the British and Americans would fight to the last drop of Russian blood. The hullaballoo of the Second Front had begun.

The dangers of the situation were very obvious to Mr. Churchill and Mr. Roosevelt and to the Anglo-American Chiefs of Staff, from whose minds the possibility of a Russian collapse and a separate peace with Germany was never absent. Our desire to help was therefore inspired as much by national interests as by natural sympathy with a gallant ally. Our own fortune of war was inextricably linked with that of Russia.

Early in April Sir Archibald Clark Kerr, who had succeeded Sir Stafford Cripps as our Ambassador in Moscow, was well received by Stalin and was given the longest audience that the Russian leader had ever granted to a foreigner. The audience, it is true, was unduly prolonged by a German air raid, but there was no mistaking either the friendliness or the anxiety of Stalin. He expressed his gratitude for the punctual delivery of the promised supplies of material. His one wish, he said, was to see Hitler dead. But he did not conceal his fears of the coming German summer offensive.

The gratitude was not an idle compliment. We had made great sacrifices in order to deliver material assistance by the perilous Murmansk route. About this time I had a long talk with Mr. Averell Harriman in his country cottage near Dorking and there, with two paintings by Mr. Churchill—a still life of a flower vase and another of a small table with a background of blue curtains—looking down on us, he gave me a full account of his mission to Moscow with Lord Beaverbrook. It was during this mission that the agreement about supplies had been concluded. He gave great praise to Lord Beaverbrook who, he said, not only had promised the supplies to Stalin but had convinced him that they would be forthcoming. On their return to England Lord Beaverbrook had watched over these supplies like a pouncing cat. If there were any signs of delay, he harassed the offending department and, if this pressure failed, went straight to Mr. Churchill. But for this constant vigilance, Mr. Harriman said, we should have been short on our deliveries.

Nor was Stalin's anxiety about the summer offensive the result of any unreasonable pessimism. President Beneš, whom I continued to see regularly, was very well informed about the Russian military situation by his military advisers in Moscow. Their reports were more sympathetic than ours, but, while praising the comparative success of the Russian winter campaign, they emphasised the probability of reverses in the summer.

The problem of the Anglo-American leaders was not whether to help but how to help most effectively. In April General Marshall and Mr. Harry Hopkins came to London to discuss the situation with Mr. Churchill and the British Chiefs of Staff. A decision was taken to come to Russia's aid if she were in extremis or, conversely, if she were so successful that the date of a landing in Western Europe could be advanced with reasonable prospects of success. As events turned out, the decision was inconclusive. There remained the opportunity of removing Russian suspicions by political action.

For some time Mr. Eden had been eager to conclude a Treaty of Alliance with Russia. The difficulties were considerable. If Russia was suspicious of her Allies, there were also deep-rooted suspicions of Russia in London and in Washington. The Tories disliked Bolshevism. The Labour leaders in the Coalition Government were opposed to Russia's seizure of the Baltic States. The Ribbentrop-Molotov Pact and the war against Finland had made an impression which was difficult to eradicate. Russia's Realpolitik, in fact, conflicted with the Atlantic Charter to which Stalin had adhered. In England, it is true, the people were enthusiastically pro-Russia, but their enthusiasm sprang mainly from a sentiment of gratitude for the unexpected Russian resistance. In the United States the people were even more anti-Russian than our own Tory Die-Hards, and the Russian attack on Finland, which by Americans was regarded as the best European democracy, had caused widespread resentment. Indeed, the British and American attitudes towards the Treaty were not unfairly generalised in a wisecrack which was popular at the time: in Britain the people wanted the Treaty, and the Government held back; in the United States Mr. Roosevelt wanted the Treaty, and the people were against it.

With little or no first-hand knowledge of Russia, my department was strongly in favour of an Anglo-Russian understanding. Although Russia as an ally did not come within the orbit of my work, I was frequently consulted on Russian matters both by Mr. Eden and Sir Orme Sargent. Early in March, when Washington was still hesitating, Sargent, who was working for the Treaty, asked me to prepare a memorandum for submission to the Foreign Secretary. I took an entirely realistic view of the situation. I knew all the arguments against the Treaty, and I was well aware that the Russians regarded any agreement with a capitalist state as temporary and opportunist. Between Britain and Russia there had been a long period of serious misunderstandings. Moreover the opponents of the Treaty made much use of the moral argument. It might have been convincing if all the rights had been on one side and all the wrongs on the other. But they were not.

After 1918 we had tried to make a European peace without the co-operation of the largest country in Europe. We had done more. We had intervened in the internal affairs of Russia. We had given financial and material support to the Russian White Army in the Civil War. Our motives may have been good or bad, but we had backed the wrong horse.

There had been a long list of other wrongs culminating in the Munich agreement from which Russia had been excluded. With this background it was not difficult to guess what must be the Russian attitude towards Mr. Churchill who after 1918 was the great white hope of the anti-Bolshevik Russians. The present rulers of Russia obviously disliked his past. They welcomed his present, because they knew that he was determined to fight the Germans to the last. They almost certainly suspected his future. In these circumstances sentiment could have no place in any treaty. The only question to be decided was: which was better, to carry on as we were without a treaty and with the certainty of increasing suspicions or to make a treaty which would see us through a war that both sides must win and which, with all reservations, might serve as a sheet-anchor for the future? The hopes for the future might be over-optimistic, but the immediate advantages of a treaty were obvious. I went all out for the Treaty, and in my memorandum I recommended that Russia be granted immediately (1) her security demands, (2) an equal say in the strategy of the war, (3) an equal say in the pooling of supplies, and (4) an equal say in the peace settlement. I based my arguments on the conviction that if Russia were treated like the Government of a Great Power, that is, on a par with the Government of the United States, it would respond to this treatment.

There was some opposition to my paper, but Mr. Eden, who had always wanted the Treaty, supported it. A delay of several weeks followed while telegrams went backwards and forwards between Washington, London and Moscow. In April Mr. Roosevelt gave his blessing to the project, and Mr. Eden sat down to await the arrival of M. Molotov, while the Foreign Office prepared the drafts for a Treaty of Alliance and a Military Convention.

What followed was a serio-comic drama which nearly ended in tragedy. At the request of the Russians the visit of M. Molotov was kept in the closest secrecy. He was expected on May 11, and, two days before, Sir Alexander Cadogan left for Scotland in order to welcome him on his arrival. On May 12 we were informed that M. Molotov had been unable to leave Russia on account of bad flying conditions. Three more days passed, and still there was no sign of the Russian plenipotentiary. Sir Alexander Cadogan returned to London, and then, as usual, delay gave birth to apprehension. Perhaps, after all, the incalculable Russians had changed their minds. The German offensive in the East had begun; the German armies were moving forward in the Crimea. I refused to yield to despondency and worked hard at repolishing my knowledge of the Russian language. On Sargent's suggestion Mr. Eden had requested me to act as interpreter during the negotiations. But having been condemned to death in 1918 for alleged participation in a plot to kidnap Lenin and Trotsky, I felt a little doubtful of my welcome and suggested that M. Maisky should be consulted. If anything went wrong in the negotiations, the Russians might say that we had insulted them by asking them to meet the arch-criminal Lockhart.

All doubts were ended on May 20 when M. Molotov arrived out of an ominously dark sky so suddenly that Mr. Eden and Sir Alexander Cadogan were late in arriving at Brooklands Park and the only British to welcome him were three correspondents who were not allowed to approach the aeroplane. Fleet Street knew the secret, but kept it securely. The question of my modest participation as interpreter had been settled the previous morning when Mr. Eden informed me that my services would not be required. As I surmised, M. Maisky had said "Better not". The same evening the German sponsored "New British Broadcasting Station" put out a fantastic story about me to the effect that I had recently paid a secret visit to Russia and had written a book which had been banned in England because it gave a picture of the war in Russia which would have shocked the British public! The timing may have been a coincidence, but was certainly curious.

The negotiations began on the morning after M. Molotov's arrival and, although they started badly, finished well. When matters were at their worst over the difficult problem of the Baltic States, the original draft treaty was withdrawn and a second draft was produced which, after reference to Moscow, the Russians accepted. The new draft avoided all mention of the Baltic States. M. Molotov, who could not have come to London in war-time unless he was prepared to sign, was more amenable than first appearances had seemed to indicate, spent a week-end at Chequers after his bodyguard had inspected his bedroom, and smiled pleasantly at the luncheon at No. 10 Downing Street when Mr. Churchill proposed an amended Marxist toast: "Workers of the world, unite; Hitler is forging you new chains."

The Treaty, providing for a twenty-year alliance and for postwar collaboration, was signed on May 26 after less than five days of pourparlers with an English week-end thrown in. It was a speed record in Anglo-Russian negotiations, but the secret had to be kept for another fortnight. M. Molotov left for Washington as soon as the Treaty was signed and insisted on no publicity until he returned to London.

On June 10 I was summoned to a meeting in Mr. Eden's room in the Foreign Office. M. Molotov had come back. Mr. Eden was to announce the Treaty in the House of Commons the next day, and he wished to make the final arrangements for the release of the news to the world. All went well, and in the House of Commons Mr. Eden, who made his statement—after a debate on fuel!—had a great personal triumph. The Treaty was welcomed by all sections of the House and, in congratulating Mr. Eden, Lloyd George made one of his last appearances in the House of Commons.

Mr. Eden was pleased by the almost unanimous support given to the Treaty. In the early stages he had met with considerable opposition not only from Tory Die-Hards, but also from Labour leaders and prominent members of both liberal Parties. Most of it had come from ex-Ministers who, when they were in office, had not hesitated to make all kinds of shameful surrenders and submissions and who now in opposition discovered hitherto unrevealed scruples of conscience. Fortunately Mr. Eden had stood firmly by his intentions, and his success was well and truly deserved.

There was, however, a last minute surprise which was to have serious consequences. During the morning of the day on which Mr. Eden made his announcement in the House of Commons, the Russians handed to the Foreign Office a copy of the joint Russo-American communiqué which had been prepared during M. Molotov's visit to Washington and which was to be released simultaneously with the announcement of the Treaty. This Russo-American communiqué contained the phrase that "full understanding was reached concerning the urgency of the arduous task of creating a second front in Europe in 1942". The communiqué was given to me for comment. I pointed out that this one phrase would attract more attention and more interest than the Treaty itself. The Foreign Office had to decide at once whether it should be included in the British communiqué. No one knew exactly what had happened between the Russians and the Americans. There was no time to consult Washington. M. Molotov was due to leave for Russia in a few hours. Rightly, I think—because the alternative was worse—the phrase was included in our statement.

The reaction of the public was immediate. The next day the newspapers welcomed the Treaty with great enthusiasm, but in the popular Press chief prominence was given to the Second Front. In a confused situation one fact was clear. In the eyes of the Anglo-American public and, indeed, of the whole world we were committed to the creation of a Second Front in Europe in 1942. To most people this meant a landing in Western Europe. Unless Germany collapsed, we were not in any position to make such a landing. Now not only could Russia urge us to fulfil our promise, but the Second-Fronters in Britain could turn the phrase to good account in bringing pressure to bear on Mr. Churchill. The *Daily Express* set the pace for the advocates of the Second Front. It handed a bouquet of compliments to Mr. Eden for the Treaty, but its headline banner was: "Second Front in Europe in 1942."

If the unfortunate phrase was meant to mislead the Germans, it was the most dangerous form of deception, for it raised false hopes in the hearts of the Allies at a moment when the war had again taken a bad turn. In South Russia the Germans were making considerable headway. A serious situation had developed in Libya where Rommel's offensive was assuming alarming proportions. Within ten days of the announcement of the Anglo-Russian Treaty Tobruk fell. A week later the Russians were forced to evacuate Sevastopol after an eight months' siege. As happened more than once when a serious set back disturbed the equanimity of the British public, Mr. Churchill was out of the country. He was, in fact, in Washington where he was trying to devise with President Roosevelt some means of implementing the promise of a Second Front in 1942 other than by an unfeasible landing on the open beaches of Western Europe.

During his absence the fall of Tobruk roused a storm of hostile criticism, and on June 6, Mr. Tom Driberg, standing as a Left Wing Independent in the Malden by-election, won what had been considered a safe Conservative seat by a majority of over six thousand. The next day Mr. Churchill returned to England and almost at once had to face a vote of censure on the Government. He had an easy triumph. The malcontents were divided among themselves and commanded little respect. The debate lost all seriousness when Major Wardlaw-Milne, the chief critic, declared that the proper course was to make the Duke of Gloucester commander-in-chief. The suggestion, which was most unfair to the Royal Family, was greeted with jeers and guffaws of laughter, and the Government received an overwhelming majority.

The military set-backs, however, had a depressing effect on British prestige everywhere. Once again hopes had been raised only to be dashed to the ground. The modern English character is a mixture of phlegm and grousing. The grouses are the oil which lubricates the phlegm. The disappointment was natural, even if it vented itself in such false directions as attacks on the conduct of the war, the failures of our strategy, and the apparent inactivity of the Americans whose entry into the war had been expected with grossly exaggerated optimism to yield immediate results. What was wrong with our war effort was not our leadership but the continued consequence of our unpreparedness, for which both politicians and public were to blame.

The unreasonableness of the public attitude is well illustrated by an American story which was current in England at the time. An

American officer in England, eager to establish good relations with an English brother officer, greets him cordially. "Well, we must do our best to get together. After all, we're relations I suppose."

English officer, coldly: "I am not aware that I have any relations in the United States."

American officer, still cheerfully: "I dare say it's a long way back, but at any rate we've this in common: we're both sure descended from Ethelred the Unready."

The grousing mood, however, had to have its outlet, and the public, eager for action, was restive and on the look-out for scape-goats. As usually happened when things were going badly, our propaganda became a target for criticism, and on July 7 there was another debate on this most inexact of sciences in the House of Commons. Fortunately for us, Mr. Bracken handled the critics with great skill, and we emerged comparatively unscathed. The chief attack was on our Woburn organisation which, as Woburn itself could not be mentioned, was accused of "resting at Hogsnorton!"

I did not resent criticism which is good for all departments, but it had not been an easy spring and early summer for the propagandists. In order to help the Russians who were being sorely harassed by the German summer offensive we had been instructed by the military authorities to give a series of warnings to the French on the Atlantic seaboard to evacuate their homes. The object of this deception was to pin down as many German troops as possible in Western Europe. But the deception worked two ways, and when two members of the French resistance movement came over to England and told Mr. Eden that all France was expecting the British in August we had to modify our tactics. The truth was that we were in a real jam over the Second Front, because we could not bluff the Germans without deceiving both the French and the Russians.

We were also in difficulties with the Americans with whom our relations were most friendly but severely restricted by the vagaries of an uncertainty for which we were in no way responsible. In making their propaganda arrangements the Americans had repeated and, indeed, aggravated our mistakes, for two separate organisations, the Office of War Information and the Office of Strategic Services, were competing with zeal and with ill-concealed hostility for the doubtful privilege of collaborating with us. Until their differences were settled, we had to be co-operative with both organisations and at the same time to sit back very carefully on a most uncomfortable fence. Both organisations mobilised their forces in Washington in order to obtain the support of President Roosevelt whose interest in propaganda was keener than Mr. Churchill's, but whose methods of settling interdepartmental disputes were dictated more by political considerations than by administrative needs. He did not make matters easier by giving to both organisations new charters which were so vague in definition that even our legal advisers could not say with any certainty which organisation had the overriding authority to conduct political warfare. The delicacy of our own position was accentuated by the fact that the Office of War Information was staffed mainly by New Dealers, while the Office of Strategic Services was a stronghold of Republicans. Eventually we found a workable compromise. In the planning and execution of our open or white propaganda we co-operated with the O.W.I.; in our secret or black activities we worked together with the London Staff of the O.S.S. But before this happy ending was reached, much valuable time was wasted in tiresome negotiation.

With the Russians we had at this stage no contact whatsoever except with M. Maisky to whom we sent copies of our directives and from whom I received occasional pieces of sound advice when he was not afraid to give it. But from the Czech reports and, indeed, from our own sources it was clear that, at this period, the Kremlin had overplayed its hand. During the winter campaign it had boasted continuously to its own people that the Red Army was the master of the Germans and that Germany would be defeated before the end of 1942. Doubtless the object of this propaganda was to maintain morale, but exaggeration always defeats its own end. The successes of the new German summer offensive had been rapid and considerable. They had come as a surprise to the Russian people whose disillusionment was in proportion to the height to which their hopes had been raised. The Soviet authorities were now the victims of their own propaganda and for the first time were flustered. Their anxiety did not lessen their demands for a Second Front.

Meanwhile, I was kept even more than usually busy by the affairs of my own department, and, if our propaganda still suffered from the lack of military success, the work itself was now absorbingly interesting. At the end of May, Brooks and I had had a useful meeting with the British Chiefs of Staff at which the whole problem of resistance in the occupied countries had been fully discussed. In reporting on the state of morale in the various countries I made the point that some considerable measure of Anglo-American military success was a necessary condition to any stronger action by the oppressed peoples. General Sir Alan Brooke (now Field-Marshal Lord Alan-brooke), who had replaced Admiral Sir Dudley Pound as Chairman, gave us what we badly needed: a clear and concise directive. What the Chiefs of Staff wanted from a military point of view was: (1) the formation and support of organisations in the occupied countries which could take charge at the moment of Germany's collapse; (2) sabotage activities by these organisations in connexion with our military operations, and (3) a continuous sabotage of a "go slow" nature by all possible means of passive resistance. As to the first two directives we should co-operate with the British organisation specially charged with these functions; the third was our direct concern.

And here I should like to pay a tribute to Lord Alanbrooke. On the various occasions on which I went before the Chiefs of Staff, he seemed to me the most admirable of chairmen. He had the great art of giving you just sufficient time to state your case. He never allowed you to wander from the point. In his own answers he was always quick, decisive, and helpful. On a matter of principle no politician or soldier could be more firm. He was one of the few men in Whitehall who was always fit. Indeed, with his rosy cheeks, his short robust figure exaggerated by the long tunic which he always wore, and his brisk, active gait, he looked as if he had spent all his life in the open air. If his words were few, they were invariably courteous. Towards the end of the war, he found time and the kindly thought to write me a few lines in his own handwriting to thank me for the help given by our department. Such little courtesies, trivial in themselves, help to dispel the frustration from which every well-meaning temporary official suffers from the slow motion of a war-swollen bureaucracy.

At General Ismay's suggestion I repeated my Chiefs of Staff report to the American Staff officers in Grosvenor Square. It was a curious scene. I spoke from a large walnut desk in the corner of a room which had obviously been someone's library. About twenty American officers of various ranks sat in two rows of chairs just opposite me. On a chair to my left sat General Chaney by himself. While I was talking, a young staff officer entered and handed a slip of paper to the General who rose to his feet, apologised for interrupting me, and announced in a staccato voice: "You may be interested to know that Heydrich has died of his wounds. The news is official." There was a moment's silence. With the afternoon sun beating on them, the American officers sat stiffly in their chairs. No word crossed their lips, but a grin lit up each face to signify their satisfaction that the butcher of the Czechs had met the fate which he deserved.

In point of fact, the assassination of Heydrich, carried out by Czech agents dropped by parachute, brought no comfort to the Czechoslovaks and no value to the Allied cause. The German revenge was swift and relentless. Its outward sign was the holocaust of Lidice; its more serious effect the disruption of the Czech underground movement and of the system of secret communications between Czechoslovakia and Britain.

In June I spent an evening with Sir Stafford Cripps who, having returned from India, had resumed his functions as Leader of the House of Commons and as a member of the War Cabinet. He had been very critical of our propaganda, and, in conformity with my usual practice, I had asked to see him in the hope of convincing him, by putting all my cards on the table, that we were not as black as he had painted us. It was my first meeting with him. I liked him at once. Tall, with a good figure, he was well-dressed in a dark grey suit with carefully pressed trousers. He wore rimless, half-glasses which to my mind somewhat marred his fine features. A teetotaller and a vegetarian, he is quite a heavy smoker and that evening indulged in turn in cigarettes, a cigar, and several pipes. His complexion was a little sallow, but otherwise he looked very fit. His smile was pleasant and dangerously disarming, for I soon found that he was more set on making converts than on being converted. He struck me as an aristocratic missionary, a Christian Socialist, who had set himself the highest moral standards and lived up to them and whose mind was rigidly clear on nearly every subject.

He was remarkably well-informed about our propaganda to Germany which he followed very closely. He was strongly opposed to our secret activities which he thought were dangerous and conducted on the wrong lines. He was almost as critical of our open propaganda in spite of the fact—which he knew well—that the director of our German section was a member of the Labour Party. He made out a good case for his own point of view which was that we should concentrate on making connexions with the anti-Nazi groups in Germany: the Catholics, the Liberals and the Social-Democrats. Obviously he believed in the existence of a considerable number of "good Germans".

I tried to point out to him that, assuming that he was right, we could achieve little unless we were allowed to hold out some hope of a better future to the anti-Nazi elements. At present we were severely restricted in this respect. Even the Atlantic Charter could not be implemented in our propaganda because it gave too many freedoms to the propagandists who, like himself, believed in the good Germans and in their ability to make trouble for the Nazis. The sentiment of the country was overwhelmingly anti-German, and, even if reason were on Cripps's side, in war-time common sense was always swamped by popular emotion. The Political Warfare Executive did not make policy; it executed it.

He was sympathetic about our policy difficulties, but was not convinced that our propaganda was as efficient as it ought to be. If I could not alter policy, I could at least expedite the return of the Woburn organisation to London. With the increasing tempo of the war it was more hopeless than ever to conduct efficient propaganda from a place fifty miles distant from London. With this I agreed and begged him to urge the authorities to provide us with the necessary accommodation.

He spoke with great conciseness and without a trace of passion or impatience. He had disliked very much the policy of Mr. Chamberlain, but he had, he told me, no hates. He was, he added with a smile, going to breakfast with Lord Baldwin the next morning.

I enjoyed our talk. Sir Stafford would have made a good Minister of Political Warfare, for he had a policy. It was not, however, the policy of the British Government.

Even at this stage of the war it was clear that there were divisions of opinion, if not of purpose, in the coalition and in the country, and that, indeed, inter-Allied unity was held together only by the cement of a common danger. It was not difficult to foresee that, as the danger receded, the divisions both in Britain itself and between the Allies would become accentuated.

Fortunately, our work was now to become more and more an adjunct to military operations demanding careful planning and special political and strategic guidance. July was a month of important decisions. General Marshall and Admiral King came to London to discuss with Mr. Churchill and the British Chiefs of Staff the problem of the Second Front, which in view of the severe and indeed highly dangerous pressure on the Russians in the Don area, had become a matter of vital urgency. General Marshall arrived with plans for the creation of a Second Front in France at the earliest possible moment, but of the various technical arguments, which inevitably protracted what was possible to a period which could bring no

G

immediate help to the Russians, one consideration was at this stage paramount. The American army had not yet received its baptism of fire. To attempt a hazardous assault on the open beaches of France with inexperienced forces was, apart from all other risks, to court disaster. Mainly at the instigation of the British experts, agreement was reached to precede the invasion of France by a combined Anglo-American assault to be launched both from East and West on the German and Italian forces in North Africa. The operation, known as Torch, possessed the double advantage of affording immediate help to the Russians and of giving to the combined Anglo-American task force the necessary battle experience under a single command.

When President Roosevelt had given his approval to the plan, General Eisenhower was appointed Supreme Commander, and at the beginning of August Mr. Churchill went to Moscow in order to "sell" Torch to Stalin. It was perhaps the most difficult and most important of his numerous missions abroad. His initial talk with Stalin was encouraging. The next day Russian suspicions reasserted themselves and threatened to create, if not a rift, at least profound disappointment and a permanent grievance. The final conversation was a success in so far that Stalin accepted a second best with good grace.

On his way back from Moscow the British Prime Minister stopped in Cairo where he took all-important decisions. General Alexander was appointed Commander-in-Chief of the British forces in the Middle East in succession to General Auchinleck. On August 7 General Gott, who had been appointed Commander of the famous Eighth Army, was killed when, on its way to Cairo, his aeroplane was shot down by two German fighters. The loss seemed irreparable. General Gott was not only our greatest expert in desert warfare, he was the popular choice of the Eighth Army itself. After reference to London, General Montgomery was appointed his successor. Destiny which has been described as the euphemism for chance in the game of war plays strange and sometimes fortunate tricks with the careers of generals. But for the tragic death of General Gott, it is possible and even probable that General Montgomery would never have received an important war command. Yet Gott, who had never spared himself, was already a tired man. Montgomery came fresh to a task for which he had trained himself from his first days at Sandhurst and for which he felt with a deep religious conviction that his Maker had called him.

All was now set for Torch which was originally fixed for October, 1942. Brooks and I were early apprised of the secret and were instructed to prepare immediately a comprehensive plan for the political warfare needs of the operation.

Before devoting myself to this new problem, I enjoyed a pleasing and memorable experience. Although the Czechoslovak Government in London had received full recognition in July, 1941, it had one grievance. The Munich Agreement still stood on the Statute Book of the British Parliament. From a juridical point of view the British Government were still committed to the truncation of Czechoslovakia, and until this sinister bar was lifted President Beneš could not feel happy. Mr. Eden had long been eager to remove this restriction and in spite of his numerous other activities kept pegging away at the most difficult of tasks: to find a formula which would enable the British House of Commons to go back on an agreement which it had previously approved.

On August 5, at the invitation of Mr. Law, then Minister of State in the Foreign Office, I went to the House of Commons with Jack Wheeler-Bennett, the historian of Munich, to hear Mr. Eden renounce the Munich Agreement on behalf of His Majesty's Government. A not very full House was at its best. Mr. Eden's statement was lucid and concise. As the Germans had not observed the terms of the agreement, we considered ourselves no longer bound by it. Sir Derek Gunston congratulated every member of the Government on having got rid of the incubus of Munich. Mr. Eden's references to the courage of the Czechs and to the horrors of Lidice moved Mr. Gallacher, the Communist deputy, to express the hope that the Foreign Secretary's remarks might be brought to the notice of the Honourable Member for the Sutton division of Plymouth (Lady Astor). This indirect reference to the so-called Cliveden set caused some guffaws, and the House broke up in laughter. Everyone seemed pleased. If there were any men of Munich present, they were discreetly silent.

Afterwards I went with Mr. Law and Wheeler-Bennett to the House of Commons cocktail bar, where Mr. Eden gave a small party for M. Masaryk and Count Raczynski, the Polish Ambassador. As usual, the warm-hearted Jan Masaryk was emotional in his gratitude, but, since I no longer had any direct concern with Czechoslovak affairs, I was agreeably surprised to receive the next day the following letter from President Beneš:

"On Wednesday, August 5th, 1942, the House of Commons

finally settled the question of Munich. I cannot let this occasion pass without remembering our collaboration during the last three years and without saying to you: my sincere and friendliest thanks."

The thanks of the President and, indeed, of the whole Czechoslovak nation were due to Mr. Eden. Without him their fate would have been very different.

CHAPTER SIX

THE PLANNING OF propaganda for Torch gave a new zest to my life. Working to a fixed date and having more frequent meetings with the practical-minded military authorities, put an end to, or at least, a brake on, the constant theoretical speculations of our propagandists. The secrecy of our work imposed a new discipline on those members of my staff who were "ticketed" for the operation; that is, formally cautioned by the security officer, given a special card and warned not to mention the subject to any person who could not produce a similar card.

This special secrecy inside a secret department created something of the atmosphere of a conspiracy and reminded me forcibly of those days in Moscow in 1918 when it was impossible to trust anyone and when I had to spend long hours in ciphering my own telegrams. The increased responsibility gave to me personally what I had long wanted: the feeling that at last we were giving direct aid to the men who were doing the fighting. If I could not go abroad, and this was still my fervent desire, this new task was the best substitute. It meant, above all, the closest collaboration with the American propaganda organisations and direct access to General Eisenhower and his senior officers who, as far as the operation was concerned, were now our masters.

Although the psychological warfare responsibilities of the American Office of War Information and of the Office of Strategic Services had not yet been clearly defined, we had been instructed to collaborate with O.W.I. who had established a special European division under Robert Sherwood for this purpose. At the beginning of August, two of the senior officials of O.W.I. came to London to discuss plans for Anglo-American co-operation in political warfare for the Torch operation. These were Mr. Archibald MacLeish, the famous American poet, and Mr. James Warburg.

Tall, good-looking, and possessed of a golden voice, MacLeish was a master of words. With little practical experience of politics he believed in the coming century of the common man and desired an Anglo-American declaration of war aims which would go farther than the somewhat indefinite generalities of the Atlantic Charter. American-born, he was the youngest son of a Scot who had been forced to emigrate to the United States nearly a hundred years ago and who gave the name of Glencoe to the suburb of Chicago in which he lived. On Independence Day he used to thunder against tyranny in the softest of Highland accents. Archie himself retained many of the prejudices of a father who all his life had nursed a hatred against the privileged class of Britain. A firm believer in Anglo-American co-operation for the creation of a better world, he was shocked by some of our Tories to whom a return to the golden past was the highest future desideratum. His eloquence and the charm of his manner endeared him to those members of my department who shared his idealism.

Jimmie Warburg, however, was the more practical man of the two and was, indeed, as far as our special work was concerned, the ablest American who came to London. A hard and quick worker with an agile mind and a sound knowledge of Europe, he had a shrewd sense of all political and economic problems, knew what he wanted and fought hard to get it. As he had a host of important friends in Washington, including the White House, he was able to present his requests to the highest authority.

Collaboration started at once, and on August Bank Holiday, Brooks and I went with MacLeish and Warburg to lunch with General Eisenhower in a private room at Claridge's. He gave us an hour of his time, showed an intelligent interest in political warfare, and asked us to explain how we thought we could help. Brooks gave an excellent exposition of political warfare as an auxiliary aid to a commander in the field. While he was saying his piece, I had time to study General Eisenhower. Blond, with clear, blue eyes, bullet-shaped head and firm jaw, he reminded me at once of Castagno's picture of "The Condottiere". Yet there was nothing of the European about his appearance. He certainly bore no resemblance to the modern Italian or to any Latin. Although his name was German, he had none of the cold arrogance of a German commander, none of the stiff awkwardness of the new Russian. He looked what he said he was: a Middle-West American, Texas-born and Kansas-bred, amiable, frank and direct. At first I thought he was almost too amiable and that he lacked ruthlessness. I knew his early career. He had begun the war as a colonel and, although he had been ear-marked for promotion by General Marshall from the first, I doubt if he himself had ever dreamt that within a year of America's entry into the war he would be commanding the combined armies of the United States and the British Empire.

He let Brooks have his say. Then he turned to me. Did I agree

with Brooks's exposition? If anything, Brooks had been too optimistic, so I gave the reverse side of the picture and warned the General
that we must not expect too much from the oppressed peoples who
were our friends. In the Russian revolution of 1905-06 the workers,
although defeated, had been able with their rifles to make an effective
resistance behind barricades. With the technical progress in modern
weapons it was now much easier to control and prevent revolts.
General Eisenhower intervened at once: "I've got you," he said,
"the era of small arms was good for the democracies. Tanks and
aeroplanes help the totalitarian dictators."

Then he gave us a short talk. He never hesitated for a word and at
once put his finger on our weak spot. We could help, and he would
use us. But he did not understand what all our damned initials—
O.W.I., O.S.S., P.W.E.—meant or how he could fit them all into
his scheme. He must put this right first. He ended by telling us
briefly how he proposed to run his organisation. In his headquarters
there were to be no British and no Americans. It was to be an integrated Allied force in the fullest sense. If a Britisher and an American
did not get on together, both would have to go.

When he had finished, he shook hands and was away without
wasting a word. It was an impressive performance which completely
erased my first impression of diffidence and lack of ruthlessness.
Here was a man who knew exactly what he wanted to do. I felt that
he would succeed, although I did not then realise what a gift Destiny
had bestowed on us by sending to Europe a man who with no ties of
blood or of sentiment with this country was not only to become the
greatest advocate of Anglo-American unity but also to impose it on
the field of battle by the sheer force of his own character and by a
sense of fairness which would have been remarkable in the best
judge.

Inspired by General Eisenhower's encouragement, we began our
operational planning at once. The start was inauspicious and, indeed,
almost chaotic, for if the Americans introduced healthy gusts of
energy and a spirit of bold empiricism, they were new to the job.
Our own propagandists, too, had to adapt themselves to a new technique. Here Brooks was a valuable stand-by, for he knew both the
form and the language of military planning.

The planning section itself was composed of civilians, two of
whom won my special respect, gratitude and affection by their tireless devotion to duty and by the selflessness of their determination
to create harmony out of what threatened to be permanent disson-

ance. They were not only our chief planners but in a very practical sense our most effective peacemakers in internal troubles and, apart from their invaluable contribution to our work, they, more than anyone else, provided the oil which made a clumsy and complicated piece of machinery work. They were a remarkable pair, devoted to each other and, by a curious combination of contrasts, each providing the complement to the other.

Peter was an idealist, a convinced Socialist, and a dreamer whose lively and fertile imagination occasionally needed an anchor to keep it on the stony ground of official reality.

Harry was also an idealist but at the same time a practical business man who before the war had been a partner in a well-known private banking firm. Neither was robust. Both paid dearly for their long hours of overwork. The Socialist collapsed a month after D-day with a serious haemorrhage of the brain. Fortunately, he recovered. Harry, who was consumptive and who might be alive today had he spent the war in Switzerland, insisted on working until he had to be carried to his bed. He lingered on for seven months in hospital, but did not live to see the final victory, although he knew before his end that the war was won.

On January 7, 1945, I went to see him for the last time with Mrs. Eden at the Pendean nursing-home in Sussex. Sleet was falling, and the day was bitterly cold, but when we entered the sick man's room the sun came out. He had shrunk to nothing and could speak only in a whisper. He did not seem unhappy. He was eager that we should admire the view from his window which was, indeed, the fairest that Sussex and perhaps all England had to offer—a stretch of heath lined by warm pines and rolling in an undulating sweep towards the glorious background of the Goodwood Downs. His mind was as clear, his courage as undaunted, as ever. Three days later he died, having killed himself by overwork as surely as if he had made the supreme sacrifice as a soldier.

While our long-term operational plans were being drafted, submitted, sent back for correction and constantly revised, our ordinary activities continued as before, bringing almost daily a new crisis or an unforeseen demand. Almost before we knew where we were, the great attack on Dieppe had been launched. It was a big-scale raid, but never intended to be more than a raid. The task force which carried it out was strongly supported by ships of the Royal Navy and by fighter aircraft. The landing operations were successful, but our forces ran into trouble on the beaches. The Germans had been forewarned and were on the alert. For the size of the force the Allied losses were heavy, especially among the Canadians who supplied the bulk of the troops.

Unfortunately, like all offensives, the raid came as a surprise to the British and American publics and was misunderstood. My department had received strict instructions to keep the raid within its proper perspective in our propaganda, and, above all, to avoid calling it a dress rehearsal for a Second Front. The early news was well handled by P.W.E. and by the European Service of the B.B.C. which put out its first bulletin in French at 6 a.m. and warned the French that the attack was only a raid. These precautionary measures were frustrated by the American Press which, in spite of official guidance, announced the raid with banner head-lines:

"British and American troops Invade France."

The whole treatment of the news indicated an attempt to form a second front. Naturally Dr. Goebbels made the most of his opportunity and, after dismissing the raid as "an amateur's undertaking", defined it as a desperate venture undertaken at Stalin's order as the price for keeping Russia in the war. As the raid coincided with the announcement of Mr. Churchill's return from Moscow, the German Propaganda Ministry had a field day. In the United States and throughout the Empire there was considerable disappointment.

Yet the raid provided lessons which were to prove their value later. At this time the general attitude towards the Second Front can be defined very simply. All the Allies wanted the Channel to be crossed as soon as possible. The Russians wanted action immediately; the Americans were eager to take chances; the British experts required the fulfilment of certain conditions. These were (1) that the American armies should have some previous battle experience; (2) that the Anglo-American Air Forces should have the necessary time and opportunity to destroy German communications so thoroughly as to prevent the rapid transport of large numbers of German troops from East to West or from West to East; (3) that the necessary landing-craft should be tested and provided in sufficient quantity, and (4) that, if an assault had not only to be made on open beaches but also to be maintained from England, May and June were the only months which offered a reasonable chance of success. It was because these conditions were far from being fulfilled in 1942 that operation Torch had been decided on. The Dieppe raid proved incontestably the sound common sense of the British view. Its final effect was to fortify the supporters of the Mediterranean strategy in their conclusions and to retard the launching of the Second Front to a date which would previously have seemed too remote to the Americans and would undoubtedly have angered the Russians.

As it was, the failure of Dieppe was a bitter disappointment to the Russians who in August were entering into the most critical phase of the second German summer offensive. I saw M. Maisky on the day after the raid. He had of course been informed of Mr. Churchill's conversations in Moscow and knew at any rate that the Allied attack in North Africa must precede a landing in France. He was quite polite, but he was not pleased. He was, he told me, very much afraid that our failure to form a Second Front in Europe at once would permanently endanger Anglo-Russian relations. He admitted that M. Molotov had not been deceived by the joint communiqué issued at the time of the announcement of the Anglo-Russian Treaty in June, but the British and Russian publics had been misled, and this, he said, was a bad background to future relations. He did not add that, although Stalin himself was fully informed about Torch and had, in fact, given it his blessing, he was, for internal propaganda purposes, encouraging his own people to expect an invasion of France.

President Beneš was also worried by the deterioration in Anglo-Russian relations. In his eagerness to hold a straddling position between East and West he was an ardent Second-Fronter. His reasons, however, were different from those of the British Second-Fronters who feared that without immediate aid Russia would collapse or make a separate peace with Germany. Apart from one or two anxious moments Dr. Beneš was consistently confident of Russia's ability not only to hold out but also to spring surprises on the Germans. It was, he said, foolish to assume that, because Russia had her back to the wall at Stalingrad, she would be too weak to launch a counter-offensive and eventually to invade Germany. He was afraid not of Russia's being too weak but of the Allies being too slow and too late. In this respect his attitude, which by and large proved to be right, was very different from that of the London Poles who believed that Russia was finished because they needed a weak Russia in order to create a Greater Poland.

The agitation for the Second Front grew in volume as the battle for Stalingrad increased in violence. It reached its most abusive height at the end of September when the Germans had forced their way into the streets of Stalin's city. The vehemence of the Russian propaganda was encouraged by considerable backing both in Britain and in the United States. On September 23 the indefatigable Wendell Willkie had a two hours' talk with Stalin to whom he brought a letter from President Roosevelt. He left the Kremlin a convert to Stalin's strategy and in a written statement handed to the American correspondents declared that he was now convinced that the best way the United States could help Russia was "by establishing a real second front in Europe with Great Britain at the earliest possible moment our military leaders will approve". And to this declaration he added the dangerous words: "and perhaps some of them will need prodding."

The prodding came immediately from those sections of the British and American Press which favoured the immediate creation of a Second Front. But it was overdone in Moscow when in answer to a written questionnaire from Mr. Henry Cassidy, an American correspondent in Moscow, Stalin criticised the aid given to the Soviet Union as "so far ineffective" and requested "the full and prompt fulfilment by the Allies of their obligations".

This was going too far, and the criticism caused considerable resentment, although it was published in full, and in some newspapers with favourable comment, throughout Great Britain and the United States. Doubtless, Stalin was working to a carefully reasoned plan, and he certainly knew how to take advantage of the freedom of the democratic Press. It was another matter when Anglo-American newspapers ventured to criticise Russian shortcomings. Stalin would then complain to Mr. Roosevelt and Mr. Churchill. When on one occasion Mr. Churchill explained that his power over the British Press was severely limited, Stalin replied with sour but genuine surprise: "Then I don't see how the democracies can ever hope to win a war."

The agitation for the Second Front had undoubtedly a bad effect on Anglo-Russian relations, because it was to last intermittently for more than a year and a half. But it did not and could not effect the Allied conduct of the war at that moment. The die was now cast for Torch. All that remained to be done was to complete the preparations with the greatest possible speed and efficiency.

In this connexion the Political Warfare Executive was given quite a variety of assignments which were formidable mainly because they could be entrusted to only a severely limited number of people. We had to prepare, translate and print the proclamations of President Roosevelt, Mr. Churchill, and the Allied Supreme Commander; to record them for broadcasting; to write and print in large numbers a small handbook for our troops instructing them how to treat the French and native populations of North Africa and, not least in importance, how to get on with their American brothers in arms; to select and train a special political warfare unit to accompany the invading forces, and, finally, to prepare and submit a comprehensive plan showing how we proposed to execute the politico-strategic aspect of the operation in terms of propaganda. We were also asked to carry out both in our foreign broadcasts and in our leaflets various instructions designed to deceive the enemy as to the exact whereabouts of the intended landing. Fortunately, in Torch the operational field for deception extended from Norway to Dakar.

All this work had to be done not only in the greatest secrecy but also concurrently with our strenuous daily routine. Much of it depended on decisions of the highest policy by President Roosevelt and Mr. Churchill, and, as frequently happened in the mounting of the great Allied offensives, there were many minor changes in policy before finality was reached. Every step, too, in connexion with our own work had to be taken in line with our American colleagues. But the main burden of technical preparation fell on the Political Warfare Executive.

For a long time I thought that order would never emerge out of chaos. Although we were on good terms with both O.W.I. and O.S.S., these two American organisations were still wrangling over their respective functions, and, with O.S.S. claiming the right to conduct all propaganda in the field of operations, General Eisenhower was unable to implement his promise to fit the propagandists into his organisation scheme, until Washington had taken a decision on the O.W.I.— O.S.S. dispute. In the end General Bedell Smith, the Chief of Staff, grew tired of waiting and, with General Eisenhower's approval, settled the problem by creating an integrated Anglo-American Psychological Warfare Branch of his own and by putting it under one of his senior staff officers. The Psychological Warfare Branch would be a military unit and would be responsible for the execution of propaganda in the theatre of operations. It would take its political guidance from O.W.I. and P.W.E., the two civil agencies in London. Here at last was order. In the circumstances it was the right decision, but this new creation imposed an extra strain on us at one of our busiest periods in the war, because we had to supply the British staff to the new unit.

The whole burden of these preparations fell on a handful of my colleagues who worked like slaves. My own task was confined mainly to obtaining official guidance on policy, to getting our plans and mass of material approved, and to establishing good relations with the new authorities, mostly Americans, who now had some dominion over us. Fortunately, I was on friendly terms with General Bedell Smith who, as General Eisenhower's right hand, could make or mar the effective co-operation between the civil agencies in London and a Psychological Warfare Branch controlled by the military in a distant theatre of operations. Unlike many of General Eisenhower's closest American colleagues, he did not belong to the West Point vintage year of 1915, but had begun his career as a ranker in the militia. Thick-set with a typical fighting face and brown eyes that looked you straight in the face, he was rather fearsome in his office. Terse, efficient and business-like, he said what he thought with brutal frankness and expected you to answer with equal directness. He worked long hours, husbanded carefully a constitution which for all his appearance of physical robustness was not too strong, received you to the second and dismissed you with similar promptness. If you had a good case and made it firmly, you received the fairest treatment. Generous, large-minded, devoted to General Eisenhower, and determined to make a success of Anglo-American co-operation, he combined a genuine consideration for others with a fiery temper. Once when I was shown into his room he was giving an order to one of his staff officers and was letting himself go with expletive force.

"Get that order out at once," he said, "and see that the next offender is punished. What the heck do you think we would say if we saw British despatch cyclists riding our public off the Washington side-walks!" He had just come into his office from a visit to Whitehall and had seen American despatch riders careering through the streets and scattering the public in all directions. Both the thoughtfulness and the vigorous action of the man were typical.

Luckily I had met him first at a luncheon given by General Eisenhower and had had some private talk with him. I found that he had two great relaxations in his life: an exuberant enthusiasm for angling and an absorbing interest in military history. He had a poor opinion of the professional historians' handling of military matters. They did not understand topography. There was one Britisher who did, a fellow called Hilaire Belloc. Had I read his *Six British Battles*? It was great stuff. He wanted a copy now. His own was in the States; he had been unable to find one in London.

Later on, although Mr. Belloc was seriously ill at the time, I was able to obtain a copy from his daughter. "Beedle" was delighted. He also professed to be an admirer of my Russian book, *British Agent*. There was therefore an angling and literary bond between us.

He took all the Torch preparations with admirable calm, making his own plans and suffering with an outward show of good humour the sometimes vexatious interventions of the politicians. Early in October, when we unfortunate propagandists were showing a not unreasonable anxiety lest finality between Washington and London should be delayed too long for us to complete our printing obligations in time, he gave a much needed moral tonic to our flurried American chief planner by lying back in his chair and ejaculating with the greatest show of cheerfulness: "My dear boy, don't go away with the idea that yours is the only section of this outfit which is being messed about by Washington." He was a great man and the perfect complement to General Eisenhower. I rarely troubled him afterwards, but I never failed to obtain his support whenever I sought it.

During the preparation period of Torch I went down, by invitation of course, to address the senior officers of a command headquarters on the possibilities of political warfare as an aid to military operations. I had been told more than once that in the early stages of the war, when things were going badly, our senior officers had been irritated by the extravagant claims of the propagandists and, more particularly, by some indiscreet boasting of the power of the fourth arm. I had been forewarned by General Ismay that a decent modesty was the civilian's best road to the military heart. The urgency of our own affairs had given me no time to prepare a proper talk, but during a longish train journey I was able to make a few notes and think out a suitable opening. My train was late, and I was hurried to the lecture ground—a flat sward of English grass with leafy elms for walls, a trout stream behind me, the noblest of English country-houses in the foreground, and below my improvised platform three rows of senior officers with the commander-in-chief in the centre. I plunged straight into my subject.

"You have probably heard," I began, "that there are four arms in this war."

"There is the sea arm; there is the land arm; there is the air arm—and there is the hot-air arm. I've come to you today to talk about the hot-air arm."

After this all went well, and I travelled back to London in a more comfortable frame of mind than I had come down.

By Saturday, October 24, we were as near to readiness as we could be. The proclamations were in type. Our propaganda team, armed with literature, had gone off to join the huge armada that was transporting the greatest combined Anglo-American force in history to its destination. Our appreciation plan, which had been revised a score of times and had been rejected by the Prime Minister as late as October 15 on the ground of indecent length, had received its final approval. The radio record of Mr. Roosevelt's address had arrived safely from New York. The necessary arrangements had been made to record Mr. Churchill's broadcast in French. New valves had been provided for our various transmitters. The engineers of deception had led the Germans up and down the Western Seaboards of Europe and Africa. In Egypt General Montgomery had taken the offensive in the engagement which was timed to be the prelude to Torch and which, after its victorious conclusion, was to be known to the world as the Battle of El Alamein. Now if we could not rest, we could look forward with mingled hopes and fears. The uncertainty was over. The Torch armada was on the move.

It was time for everybody; time for the cognoscenti who for four months had dreamed, planned, built and lived with Torch; time for the troops who had been kept on leash, knowing they were going into action but with no idea of when or where, and time for the still unwitting British people. It was time, too, for the ticketed officials of my department who were over-excited by the knowledge that they were co-operating directly for the first time in a great military operation.

In war the democracies suffer from a multiplicity of control, from the delays, none the less vexatious because inevitable, resulting from consultations between heads of governments separated by thousands of miles of land and sea, and from the irksome necessity of "squaring" so many different departments before any action can be taken. And the lower the standing of the department, the greater the delay, the frustration and the pile of rejected plans. The preparatory period had imposed a strain on everyone connected with the operation. Nerves were frayed. Tempers too had begun to show ragged edges. Now the vast armada was assembled and ready to start. Although twelve exciting days were to pass before the success or failure of the landings would break the news to the world, the period of uncertainty was past. Operation Torch was "on".

The attitude of the general public was, I think, one of impatience. The secret of the operation had been well kept, and in my notes, made at the time, of an always fluctuating morale I registered a distinct depression and more criticism than usual of the conduct of the war. The British people, inspired by the fighting spirit and defiant eloquence of Mr. Churchill, had risen to their greatest height in the first year of disaster. They had been galvanised into unity and action by Dunkirk, by the Battle of Britain, and by their own experience of the Blitz. They had not expected a second year of failure, and a long period of deferred successes had been hard to bear.

The very optimism of Mr. Churchill had caused irritation. The man in the street had heard one general after another being exalted in terms of high praise until the inevitable promotion to a post far removed from the battle-line announced his failure. In this manner General Wavell had made his exit. The sudden dismissal of General Auchinleck caused widespread disillusionment. The public was suspicious. Characteristic of the general attitude were the comments made in many quarters at the time of the appointment of the new commander of the Eighth Army: "Who is this fellow Montgomery? Is he any good?"

It is true that the public then knew little or nothing about General Montgomery, but their comments would have been the same about any new appointment. They had become cynical and were not prepared to "buy" generals on pre-operational publicity. They wanted physical success. Torch was to give them the victory for which they had waited so long.

CHAPTER SEVEN

THE COURSE FOR North Africa was now set, and the days during which the armada was at sea were tense with expectation. Every section concerned with the operation—and doubtless the Cabinet itself —had its optimists and its pessimists. Most prominent among the optimists was the Prime Minister, who on the eve of every great offensive refused to admit the possibility of failure and encouraged the commanders in the field with last-minute messages of forceful eloquence. His optimism had the virtue and defects of all optimism. The pessimists were to be found mostly among the Second Fronters who disliked the Mediterranean strategy, objected to the dispersal of the Anglo-American forces, and feared lest it might strengthen the hands of those Pacific-minded Americans who wished to see all the might and energy of the United States concentrated against Japan.

President Roosevelt had accepted the thesis that Germany was the main enemy and must be tackled first. He had sent a large army to Britain in order to create a Second Front. If the Second Front were to be delayed indefinitely, and obviously the adoption of the Mediterranean strategy meant an indefinite postponement, would there not be an outcry in the United States against the waste of American men and materials on operations which diverted the strength, resources and shipping of the Anglo-American Allies from, instead of to, Europe? So the pessimists argued. There were others—and they were assuredly the majority—who tried to steer a middle course between the alternating currents of hope and fear.

I did my best to qualify for this third category and tried to think as little as possible about the operation and to concentrate on my daily work. One experience helped me in this practical form of escapism. General Smuts had come to England in the middle of October. I had seen him several times during both the first world war and the period between the two wars and had, indeed, a tenuous claim on his attention. Bertrand Marchand, the grandson of Napoleon's valet who had migrated from St. Helena to South Africa after his master's death, had married my aunt. A Huguenot and a pro-Boer, he had become Treasurer of the Dutch Church in South Africa. He had held that office during the Boer War, had contributed to the Boer war-chest and had earned the esteem and friendship of General Smuts.

Soon after his arrival General Smuts was invited to deliver a broadcast address to the Dutch. He asked me to prepare some suggestions. After it was delivered, he sent for me and I had a talk with him at the Hyde Park Hotel.

He looked considerably older than when I had last seen him and his voice, which was always rather weak, sounded feebler. But his cheeks were aglow with the colour of health, and his mind, scholarly and severely analytical, was as clear and as tidy as ever. I had guessed that he wished to talk to me about Russia. But no—his subject was our propaganda to Germany. After greeting me with a cheerful "Well, Mr. Lockhart, here you are in the thick of it again", he went straight to his point.

Germany, he said, would crack sooner or later. A hope clause was therefore necessary in our propaganda. No new Europe would be built, no permanent peace established, if we merely ignored the German problem. Germany must always be an integral part of any European polity. We should not say too much at this stage. We could develop and enlarge on the Atlantic Charter. But we must get away from national concepts. Above all, we should avoid saying to Germany the things which played into Goebbels's hands. What was rightly or wrongly called Vansittartism was wrong. It was sheer folly to exploit war-hate. Mr. Churchill, he said, was sound on this aspect of the problem. The curse was the minor politicians. It was so easy to inflame hate on a public platform. There were so many politicians who were afraid of being labelled pro-German.

He spoke wise words. He was full of confidence in the success of Torch, eloquent and moving in his admiration of Mr. Churchill whom he described as the greatest war-leader of any country.

These two men, I reflected, had been through three wars: on opposite sides in the first; together in the two world wars. Their experience of the politico-strategic conduct of warfare was un-rivalled. I recalled Mr. Churchill's exemplary words after the first world war: "In war—resolution; in defeat—defiance; in victory—magnanimity; in peace—goodwill." General Smuts himself was the living embodiment of the practical benefits of a policy of magnanimity and goodwill. Yet I wondered if the South African had interpreted correctly Mr. Churchill's present attitude towards a people who twice within twenty-five years had plunged the world into war. Doubtless, at all times, and especially in war, the real inclinations of statesmen in office are restrained by considerations of public expediency—of what the French call *le tact des choses possibles*. That may explain why we were never allowed to enlarge in our propaganda on the Atlantic Charter, the effect of which was heavily counteracted by the policy of unconditional surrender.

Writing a report on General Smuts's lucid statement helped me to tide over the last few days of waiting. Then there were one or two last-minute alterations which demanded changes in our propaganda directive. The most important concerned the relation of the operation to the Second Front. In the British directive both the Foreign Office and the Chiefs of Staff had approved the ruling: "The operation must *not* be represented as a Second Front." On November 2 President Roosevelt telegraphed the text of the statement which he proposed to release to the Press after the landings. The text contained the statement that the operation would render "effective second-front assistance to Russia". The Prime Minister and Mr. Eden liked this amendment, and we were requested to suppress or amend the "second front" sentence in our directive. After consulting Mr. Wallace Carroll, who had replaced Mr. Warburg as the London head of O.W.I., we adopted a compromise which Mr. Eden approved. It was that "the operation should not be represented as a second front unless mentioned as such in official statements".

We were now ready for our part in the great day which was fixed for the early hours of the morning of November 8, and on November 5 I had a final meeting with Mr. Eden and Mr. Bracken in order to go over again all our arrangements for the release of the news in every European language. It was a gay and almost light-hearted meeting. After an anxious period of waiting, great news had come from General Alexander in Egypt. Rommel's forces were in full retreat, and in an Order of the Day to the Eighth Army, General Montgomery had declared: "Complete victory is almost in sight and we shall have the whole German African Panzercorps in the bag."

Mr. Bracken was twenty minutes late for our meeting. He had been lunching with the Prime Minister with whom he had been discussing the vexatious problem of our prisoners of war in Germany who were still being manacled as a reprisal for the handcuffing of a few German prisoners by our Commandos during a raid on the island of Sark. We had not given way, but had informed the Germans that we should manacle a German prisoner for every British prisoner manacled in Germany. This unpleasant situation had lasted for a month, and both Mr. Eden and Mr. Bracken were eager to put an end to it.

When he came into Mr. Eden's room in the Foreign Office, Mr. Bracken was beaming with joy. Apologising for being late, he explained that he had been having "a heated tussle with the boss" over the prisoners of war. Mr. Bracken dramatised the scene in three crisp sentences:

Mr. Bracken: "Now in the hour of our strength is the time to un-
chain."
Prime Minister, obdurately: "You want me to grovel in the mud
to the Nazis!"
Mr. Bracken: "No, Sir, they are grovelling to you now in the
sand!"

Mr. Churchill had smiled and had promised to reconsider his decision. Mr. Eden was pleased. Mr. Bracken was pleased. All was well and better than well in Egypt. The portents for Torch were excellent. Mr. Eden told us the dramatic story, now so well known, of the visit to Algiers of General Mark Clark, with a team of British and American officers, in a submarine in order to "square" the French generals in North Africa. There was, Mr. Eden said, good ground for assuming that French resistance would be insignificant. The two Ministers passed P.W.E's programme without demur. At that moment they would have approved a broadcast to Paradise.

As far as P.W.E. was concerned, the part which we had prepared with an excess of zeal was played during the week-end of November 7 and 8. The instructions given to me by General Bedell Smith, who had remained in London in order to control all the details of supply, shipping and eventual reinforcements, were that we should be informed at 5.30 p.m. on the Saturday whether the operation was "on" or not; in other words, we should know by then if all had gone according to plan. A second message would give us the exact time to release the whole battery of our broadcasts and leaflets. In point of fact, the Americans were a little late with their first message which reached us at 6 p.m. The operation was "on". The second arrived at 8.30 p.m. It instructed us to begin our broadcasting programme as soon as the radio stations in the United States had given out the first communiqué of General Eisenhower. This was to come at 1 a.m. It meant a longish wait. Our small Torch staff, who had slept little during the past few days, were tired.

To relieve the tension I took them to dinner at the Savoy on the one condition that they were to relax and not mention our special task which had been discussed *ad nauseam*. We had a competition in war stories. Only one was new to me, but it was amusing and was brilliantly told by our chief radio expert. A Polish airman, who had done splendid work from a distant airfield, was rewarded for his prowess with ten days' leave in London. It was his first visit. Being alone, he sought female companionship and found it in Piccadilly. He took his platinum blonde to dine, treated her with true Polish courtesy, and, as he had been unable to find a room in any hotel, was delighted to accept her invitation to share her flat for the night. He treated her like a duchess, she responded gallantly to this unwonted politeness and in the morning cooked and served him with a real English breakfast. Then the time came to say goodbye, and, bending low, the Pole kissed her hand and began to walk towards the door. The lady now revealed her true colours and pulled him up with a husky cry: "What about some dough, duckie?" The Pole looked bewildered. So with icy articulation she explained: "Cash. M-O-N-E-Y—money." The Pole smiled gracefully, drew himself up to his full height, and clicked his heels.

"I, Polish officer," he said, "I, man of honour. Polish officer never take money."

After dinner we went back to Bush House and, after a last word with Ivone Kirkpatrick who was in charge of the broadcasting arrangements, I went home to my club to try to snatch some sleep.

All went well enough, but not quite perfectly. The American broadcasting stations were twenty minutes late with the first proclamation. They also caused some confusion by changing the order of the official communiqué, but Kirkpatrick, always at his best in a crisis, was the complete master of the situation and, by keeping pace with the spoken word of the Americans, was able to carry out the programme without a hitch.

London awoke to a Sunday of beautiful sunshine to learn the news for which the people had waited so long. The first communiqué merely announced the fact of the landings in North Africa. Having been written and approved before the operation started, it gave and could give no details. But the news in itself was sensational enough to make everyone happy, and the streets were full of smiling faces.

I saw little of the sunshine, for we were engaged all day in conferences and in waiting for official news of the actual course of the operation. Soon after midday I was summoned by Mr. Bracken. General Bedell Smith had proposed a Press Conference at the Ministry of Information at 4 p.m. that afternoon. Mr. Bracken wanted a brief for what he was to say. I suggested that he should confine himself to the political aspects of the operation and leave the technical details to

Bedell Smith. So far so good. But worse was to come. At 3 p.m. Mr. Bracken telephoned to me. Would Brooks and I come to the Ministry of Information immediately? For once we found Mr. Bracken a little agitated—not without reason. The Conference was "on", but General Bedell Smith, who had not been to bed for three days, was asleep, and there was no American who dared to wake him. Mr. Bracken had therefore to take the Conference himself. Brooks and I must attend.

Our presence was highly irregular. We were members of a secret department. The home front was no concern of ours. It was, indeed, laid down in our instructions that we were to have no official contacts with the Press. Most instructions, however, are made to be wisely disregarded, and in we trooped to the large hall of the Ministry of Information. Taking my seat at a high dais beside Mr. Bracken, I looked down on a sea of faces in many of which I recognised old friends. Suddenly I was embarrassed. I should have been, I felt, in the body of the hall. I had heard beforehand that there was likely to be some excitement, for the Press was disappointed by the arrangements made for it by General Eisenhower who had imposed severe restrictions on the activities of the journalists and had insisted for the initial stages on what is known as a pooling system. It meant that several newspapers had to share one correspondent.

There was no fresh news to offset the discontent. I foresaw trouble, but was wrong. The joy over the landings had infected the editors and correspondents with good-humoured tolerance, and Mr. Bracken handled them beautifully by promising the speedy abandonment of the pooling system and quick release of news. By revealing to them that he knew as little as they or, indeed, anyone else in London, he won their confidence. During question-time there was one awkward moment when a correspondent asked: "What is the position of Noguès?" Mr. Bracken did not know, and the journalists knew he did not know, but his answer came like a pistol crack: "Very uncomfortable." A roar of laughter ended the meeting.

With a quiet sigh of relief I went off to see Mr. Eden who also had no news. Then, thinking that all was serene, I dined early and went to bed at nine o'clock. Within an hour I was disturbed by a violent assault from my telephone. It was Mr. Bracken who was ringing me on the private line from No. 10 Downing Street. His voice was angry. He was with the Prime Minister who wished to know at once whether a broadcast message, alleged to have been delivered by General Giraud and to have been put out by the Algiers radio, was "phoney" or genuine. He, Mr. Bracken, had telephoned to Bush House to the Director of the European News Service. This man, Newsome or Grisewood—he could not remember the name—had kept him waiting. When he had rung a second time, the fellow had lost his temper and had replied that his business was to get on with his job and not answer questions which concerned the radio engineers. He, Mr. Bracken, did not like the fellow's manners or his voice. He had never seen his face, but would I ensure that it was not there the next day.

The trouble had been caused by General Giraud who, after being rescued from Germany, had been brought to Gibraltar for the Torch operation. Regarded as a key man to ensure the co-operation of the French in North Africa, he had undertaken to deliver a broadcast from Algiers immediately after the landings. Unfortunately, the General was temperamental and, instead of going in with the landing forces, had remained in Gibraltar where for a whole night he had wasted General Eisenhower's time in an unseemly wrangle over his own position. With little regard for the realities of the situation he had tried to insist on being given the appointment of Supreme Commander of all the Allied Forces.

Mr. Churchill knew that General Giraud was still in Gibraltar. He was therefore surprised to hear a broadcast message from General Giraud on what was alleged to be the Algiers radio. Not unnaturally his suspicions were aroused. The Allies were not the only combatants who practised deception.

I dressed and got busy. In a few minutes I discovered from the B.B.C. engineers that the broadcast had gone out on the Algiers radio. It had been delivered by General Mast in General Giraud's name. Fortunately, the script had been sent beforehand to Algiers, for, while he was still in his tantrums, General Giraud had wished to withdraw it.

This problem settled, I lay down again—this time in my clothes. I read and dozed for about forty minutes. Then the telephone went again. Another radio message had been received. Algiers had capitulated. The message had been put out by Vichy. Mr. Bracken, who was still with the Prime Minister, wished to know whether we should give it further circulation on our own network. I asked for five minutes' grace in order to consult my staff. The military experts were against further circulation. I favoured immediate circulation on the ground that, even if the story were untrue, no harm and possibly some good could result from our circulating it provided that it was announced as a Vichy message. Mr. Bracken approved. He was right. The French in Algiers had, in fact, capitulated.

Mr. Bracken and I played telephones until long after midnight. I guessed that the Prime Minister was impatient at the absence of news from General Eisenhower. At one moment my private line went out of order while I was talking to Mr. Bracken and I had to go downstairs, ring up Bush House on an ordinary telephone, and beg Peter Scarlett, my personal assistant who was spending the night in the office, to check the answer to Mr. Bracken's question, telephone it direct to him at No. 10 Downing Street, and then, if possible, send an engineer to put my private line right.

Fortunately, this was the end of my telephonic exchanges with No. 10. The engineers arrived with remarkable despatch at 2.5 a.m. They soon corrected the defect and, all hope and, indeed, all thought of sleep now being gone, I took them down into the club hall, gave them a bottle of beer and made them tell me the story of their lives. They had no story or were too shy to tell it, but it helped to pass the time. Before the morning dawned, Bush House was receiving both radio news and code messages from North Africa. The information was good. Algiers was quiet. There had been some fighting at Oran and Casa Blanca and some French ships had been knocked about. Most promising of all was General Montgomery's talk with a captured German general who with great frankness said that not only was Germany beaten and Hitler's strategy responsible for her failure, but that Italy was in a bad way and could be quickly knocked out.

I stayed until the newspapers arrived, had a bath and went to my office where presently a somewhat bedraggled Noel Newsome, the Director of the European News Service, came to see me. His eyes were bloodshot with tiredness. He had not been to bed for forty-eight hours. I congratulated him on his work, but the praise gave him no joy. He smiled rather wanly and began to explain: "I made a fool of myself last night. I got rattled . . ." I suddenly remembered and cut him short. He was the guilty man of the incident with Mr. Bracken during the night. I rang Mr. Bracken and told him that Newsome was contrite. He had worked himself to a standstill. In turn the big-hearted Mr. Bracken cut me short. "Forget it," he said, "tell him he's done a good job." In the next Honours List Mr. Newsome was given an O.B.E. I do not know for certain, but my guess is that the recommendation came from Mr. Bracken.

Tuesday, November 10, remains pleasantly clear and vivid in my memory. The morning brought me a letter from Mr. Eden. Sent at the Prime Minister's request, it conveyed to P.W.E. the official thanks and congratulations of His Majesty's Government for its work in connexion with the operations in North Africa. The message was evoked by a letter from General Bedell Smith to Mr. Eden in which the American Chief of Staff, after emphasising the importance of our contribution, stated:

"We have kept them on a series of rush jobs often working all through the night, and to each of our orders for vast quantities of printed texts the most stringent time-limits have had to be imposed. But they never failed us, and all their work, excellently produced, has been delivered on time. I am conscious of how much we shall owe them when the operation is successfully completed."

These tributes were not, I think, undeserved. Our team had never spared itself. All the work had been done by the specialists: by Brooks, by Kirkpatrick, by the Planners, by the French Region, and, not least, by the Production Unit. To them belonged the real credit.

After communicating the substance of these tributes to those members of P.W.E. and of the European Services of the B.B.C. who had borne the main burden of the day, I went down at noon into the Strand to watch Mr. Churchill pass on his way to the Lord Mayor's luncheon at the Guildhall. The streets were lined with crowds to welcome him. As he drove past, his face, still marvellously cherubic, was one big smile. He made the V. sign, and opposite the European Service of the B.B.C., which had started the V. campaign, was the right place to make it. He was in his happiest mood, and the crowd, forgetting the disappointments of the last few months, remembered the dark days when his voice was their voice, his resolution their resolution, and his defiance their defiance. And in their cheers they gave full expression to the joy and gratitude which was in their hearts. It was a great day for Mr. Churchill who doubtless had felt the long trail of disappointment more keenly, more poignantly, than any of his critics. It was a great day for the Allies and, above all, for Britain. British brains had planned the gigantic and perilous undertaking. A British admiral had organised the greatest armada that till then the world had ever seen. Another British admiral had been in charge of it. A British air marshal had commanded the air force which protected it. A British general had led the Eighth Army whose successful offensive had eased the task of the landing forces. Later, the Americans were to prove themselves the masters of land and sea and air, but at this stage they were new to the job.

Experience was on the British side, and British experience had

won an astounding triumph. The Germans had been deceived. Their
submarines had concentrated on Dakar. The landings had been
accomplished with infinitesimal losses in men, ships and material.
Assuredly it was an occasion for rejoicing and justifiable pride, and
its memory will not be dimmed by the disappointments which followed.

CHAPTER EIGHT

THE INVASION OF North Africa was brilliantly executed, a portent of better things to come, and a convincing proof that the technical organisation of the Allies was far more efficient than in the first world war. It was another turning point in the long struggle. It meant that the darkest days were past, that we had now passed from the defensive to the offensive. But the initial optimism which it aroused was unjustified, and those who thought that the end was in sight were soon to be disillusioned.

Torch, in fact, was the beginning and not the end of a gradual German collapse which was to be protracted by a determination worthy of a better cause. Its primary object was the expulsion of the German and Italian forces from North Africa, and the task of the Allied armies was to be hampered not only by a formidable German resistance but also by political difficulties which were to create divisions in public opinion both in the United States and in Britain.

The political complications, which began even before the landings, arose from a fundamental difference in attitude between the Anglo-American Governments and a large section of the Anglo-American people. The first preoccupation of the Anglo-American Chiefs of Staff had been to ensure the military success of the operation irrespective of political considerations. In this aim they had the full support of President Roosevelt and Mr. Churchill, and to this end the American Government had maintained, with the approval of the British Government, a representative at Vichy, had entered into negotiation with Vichy generals, and had taken every possible precaution, if not to win the support of Vichy, at least to neutralise its opposition.

To the majority of British people and to a section of the American public these tactics seemed very much like shaking hands with the devil of collaboration. The storm broke when on November 13 General Eisenhower recognised Admiral Darlan as head of the French administration in North Africa.

It was true that the Admiral had been instrumental in stopping French resistance in North Africa. True it was, too, that by his action the Allied losses had been one-tenth of what the Anglo-American military experts had anticipated. More doubtful was his claim to have prevented the Toulon fleet from falling into German hands. He had, in fact, ordered it to proceed to North Africa, but, although orders had not been obeyed, he could assert with some justification that he had rendered valuable services to the Allied cause.

There were some 400,000 French in North Africa. Their attitude was at the best highly uncertain. General Eisenhower was dependent on them for the huge task of unloading stores and guns. If they were to go over to passive resistance or to commit a few acts of sabotage, the Allied forces would be in grave peril. General de Gaulle's name was not popular in North Africa. As for the French officers, their oath and their pension rights weighed heavily with them, and even Admiral Darlan had failed to win over Admiral Esteva who, by letting the Germans into Tunis, had immensely aggravated General Eisenhower's task. Darlan alone had some semblance of authority, and political and military expediency demanded that his status should be recognised.

As far as the British Government were concerned, this recognition was not the result of any high-handed action by Mr. Churchill. Admiral Darlan had Labour supporters in the Coalition. He had, indeed, given material assistance to the Allies on a previous occasion. At the time of the collapse of France in June, 1940, the last British Minister to set foot on French soil was Mr. A. V. Alexander, the First Lord of the Admiralty. He had been sent at the eleventh hour to do his best to prevent the French naval ships at Brest from falling into German hands. At Brest was the French battleship *Richelieu*. Mr. Alexander did a great best. He went to Admiral Darlan and appealed to his patriotism. Every minute was of value. On account of the tides the huge man-of-war could leave port only at certain hours. Admiral Darlan gave his word and kept it. Mr. Alexander, who himself had some difficulty in getting away from Bordeaux in time, paid full credit to Admiral Darlan for his action. There were, he told me more than once, two sides to the Darlan issue. It was, he said with undeniable truth, easier for a Frenchman to be the complete patriot in England than in France. Undoubtedly many of those, who knew the military situation, thought as he did.

These considerations, however, weighed little with the vast bulk of the British public which, Gaullist in sympathy, saw the issue in one light only. For the sake of military expediency the man who had stood alone for France in her darkest hour was being sacrificed to a clique of admirals and generals who had preferred the easier path of collaboration, and true or untrue, there were ugly stories not only of Darlan's collaboration with the Germans, but also of his persecution of the resistance groups. Democratic instinct told the public that, whatever short-term advantages might accrue from this policy, the policy itself was immoral and would have disastrous long-term consequences.

General de Gaulle was bitterly disappointed and did not fail to show his displeasure. With his eye always on the French resistance movement on which he relied for his real support, he was not the man to accept a compromise which he knew would be disastrous to his own fortunes, in order to win the favour of the President of the United States and of the Prime Minister of Britain. He stood for France. She had been and would be again a Great Power. He must not betray her. The character of this tall, stern Norman was at all times little given to yielding; in a moral issue it was as firm as the hardest rock. And morally he felt himself outraged by the elevation of Darlan to the position of a head of state. An even greater grievance to General de Gaulle was the use of the word amnesty in connexion with the liberation of his imprisoned followers in Algiers. Amnesty meant an act of oblivion, a general pardon. It was applied to enemies. Was this, he asked, a word which should be used to cover the liberation of men whose only crime was that they had remained loyal to the Allied cause? He protested violently, remained obduarate to all appeals for patience, and, when Mr. Churchill banned one of his broadcasts, showed his displeasure by surrendering the free time on the air which the British Government had given him. Meanwhile, his London followers fanned the flames of his displeasure among the British public.

His obstinacy was an inconvenience to President Roosevelt, to Mr. Churchill and, not least, to General Eisenhower who, though not himself easy in his mind about Darlan, was guided on policy matters by his political advisers. But General de Gaulle had the backing of large sections of the British and American public. And not only of the British and American public. The resistance movements in all the occupied countries were not only Gaullist in sympathy but were horrified by Allied collaboration with Frenchmen whom they regarded as little better than Quislings.

These conflicts of opinion affected P.W.E. acutely and made our propaganda exceedingly difficult. How were we to explain Darlan and his régime to our friends in France and in the occupied countries? By now the character of the resistance movements had acquired a more or less clear pattern. In all the occupied countries with the exception of Poland resistance had been organised and maintained largely by the democratic elements and by the Communists, and, although a common desire to be rid of the Germans united men of widely divergent views, the general trend of active resistance was to the Left. The bourgeoisie, because it had more to lose, tended towards collaboration.

This generalisation will doubtless be contested, but it is based on the best intelligence that is available. Moreover, its truth was recognised at the time by the greatest living man of letters among French Catholics. Writing in secret during the occupation, M. Mauriac noted with some disillusionment that "only the French working class in its whole will have remained faithful to a profaned France".

Admittedly, it was much easier for the worker to go underground. He was a cipher among millions. The rich bourgeois was known to the Germans from the start. Apart, however, from these material considerations, most of the resistance leaders were men who wanted a new Europe and wide measures of social reform in their own countries. In a world, which was visibly undergoing one of its periodic cataclysms, they wanted changes and for these changes they risked their lives. For us to try to ram a Darlan down their throats was to court the greatest of all disasters: an accentuation of the social divisions in the resistance movements and a strengthening of those elements which looked only to Russia for their salvation. In the absence of an agreed post-war policy between the Russians and the Anglo-Americans there would be increasing competition between the Eastern and Western Great Allies for the control of the body and soul of the oppressed countries.

Most of the Allied governments in London were well aware of this danger, and no one more so than President Beneš. The unexpected successes of the Russians, who were the first to show that the German armies were not invincible, had given a powerful impetus to Russia's prestige. This impetus had been particularly strong in Czechoslovakia where Munich was not forgotten. Nor had President Beneš failed to note that in his homeland his compatriots had been deeply stirred by a popular ballad written by a Czech poet soon after the failure of the first German winter campaign in Russia. It was entitled: *The Ballad of the German Soldier's Bride*. It began with: "And what did he send you, my bonny lass?" Then each verse described what the soldier lover had sent back to his bride from the cities which the German armies had conquered. I give the last verse in full:

> "And what did he send you, my bonny lass,
> From the deep, deep Russian snow?

From Russia he sent me my widow's weeds,
For the funeral feast, my widow's weeds,
From the deep, deep snow, my widow's weeds,
From the deep, deep Russian snow."

Even in Britain there was a strong instinctive tendency to assume that the military successes of the Russians were due to some inherent virtue in the Russian system of government. Mr. Chamberlain's policy had divided the British people. When it failed to prevent war, it became bankrupt. During the year when we stood alone, the ranks had been closed. But the divisions were still there, and with the optimism engendered by the North African offensive they began to reveal themselves unmistakeably. Irrespective of party politics, two main lines of demarcation were evident. There was one group which, holding that Britain was the best of all possible countries, demanded nothing better than an "as you were" policy and a return to the past. The other and, I think, even at that time the larger group wanted not only a new and better Britain, but also a new and better world which would not be dominated by nationalist ambitions. The first group supported Mr. Churchill both for war and for peace; the second recognised his great qualities as a war-leader, but regarded him as a dangerous peace-maker. Doubts of Mr. Churchill's ability to create a satisfactory post-war world were by no means confined to the Socialists.

The majority of the Political Warfare Executive belonged to the second group, although the department could show every shade of political opinion from die-hard Toryism to intellectual Communism. In particular, the younger and more energetic men were Socialists. Moreover, they had the best brains. Very strong, too, throughout the department and in the European Service of the B.B.C. was the feeling against privilege. On the other hand, the loyalty of the staff was unimpeachable. All were desperately eager to make their contribution to the winning of the war. But their enthusiasm, essential in propaganda work, was sometimes inclined to soar to dangerous heights. It fell the more heavily when they were confronted with a problem like the Darlan episode. Then faces drooped, and the sense of frustration was complete.

For me personally the first week after the landings was the most depressing of the whole war. My sympathies were with the anti-Darlanists in our department. I envied the confidence of our young Socialists who believed in progress and who were so sure of themselves. Fundamentally they were right. The history of man's efforts to better himself might make poor reading, but it was the belief that counted. That gone, man might as well write his own death warrant. I, too, wanted a better Britain, but with increasing age I had lost the faith to see the world through a veil of self-generated illusion. I had always been a romantic, but in the soulless machine of a swollen bureaucracy ideals had to be pursued with realism. It was a crime and an expensive, long-term blunder on the part of the democracies to sacrifice a moral principle for a temporary military expedient. But, as far as Darlan was concerned, such a conclusion came better from the men who were doing the fighting than from chair-borne propagandists, some of them of military age, in London. We were in a nasty mess, for, once committed to Darlan even temporarily, how could the Allies undo a harm that had already been done?

One example will suffice to show the confusion of the Allied propaganda. On Sunday, November 15, I went to my office at ten o'clock. The morning was foggy, but not so bewildering as the news. There was a clear instruction from General Eisenhower: "Keep off all personalities for the present." The morning newspapers contained a message from Algiers stating that Eisenhower and Darlan were co-operating for the defence of North Africa. In the evening the B.B.C. Home Service repeated statements from Radio Algiers to the effect that Darlan had appointed Giraud Commander-in-Chief of the French forces, that Darlan himself took full responsibility for what he had done and was carrying out Pétain's wishes, and that the French were fighting Germans in Tunisia. On the Brazzaville radio the Gaullists attacked the Americans for employing traitors. Then, before I went to bed, Brooks brought me a message from General Eisenhower's headquarters. Our picture of the situation was wrong. General de Gaulle had no following in North Africa. The god to the French officers was Pétain. Darlan, Noguès and the other generals must be used. Otherwise more Allied troops would have to be sent.

The picture was now clear enough, but it merely added to the difficulties of our propaganda. For once I felt a little envious of Dr. Goebbels who was enjoying himself at our expense and adding points almost hourly to his score.

Nor was the actual output of propaganda our only worry. The first wave of enthusiasm over the landing operations had spent itself, and with the inevitable slowing down of military progress there were no immediate successes to distract the grumblers from their political obsessions. The anti-Darlanists in Britain blamed the Americans for the Darlan expedient, and their outspoken criticisms caused some friction in our relations with our American friends. Fortunately, P.W.E. was on the best possible terms with the London representatives of O.W.I. who themselves did not like the policy. But naturally they resented attacks on the American Government.

Much more delicate were our relations with the new Psychological Warfare Branch at Allied Headquarters in North Africa to which we had provided the British personnel. It was under military control, and inevitably its propagandists had to carry out the instructions given to them by General Eisenhower's political advisers. They were the men on the spot. They assumed very naturally that they could appreciate the local situation much more accurately than people who were fifteen hundred miles away. They were inclined to accept the local American view that the British were jealous because American diplomacy had won a triumph by obtaining the all-important co-operation of the French.

There was during this period another fly in the Anglo-American ointment. For political reasons, determined mainly by the desire to interest the American people in the war in Europe, the chief credit for the successful landings had been given to the American forces. This seeming injustice caused some resentment on the part of the British who showed a regrettable *Schadenfreude* over the subsequent military set-backs to the inexperienced American troops. It was accompanied by foolish quips like "How green are our Allies", a play on the title of the popular novel, *How Green Was My Valley*. At this stage the British public, never properly conscious of the fact that the United States had won the first world war by the mere act of coming in, had not yet realised that she would win the second war by the material might and magnificent fighting of the American forces on land and sea and in the air.

These somewhat trying circumstances, which were more in evidence in Washington and London than in North Africa, imposed a severe test on General Eisenhower's qualities as a Commander-in-Chief. He emerged from it with remarkable success. The conception of an integrated Anglo-American force was his. He fought for it until he obtained his desire. It was his great qualities of tact, organising ability, leadership and, not least, complete impartiality and fairness, that made it the most successful experiment in military co-operation since the beginning of history. Time, I think, will prove that anything short of complete integration would have been attended by serious difficulties. In sending this quiet, unassuming American to the

H

European theatre of war, Providence and General Marshall made their greatest contribution to the Allied cause.

In spite of the political imbroglio, the initial optimism of the British and American publics was slow in subsiding, and on November 29 Mr. Churchill, in a broadcast to the world, issued a salutary caution against wishful thinking. Although he foreshadowed an offensive against Italy, he was careful to fix no date for the expulsion of the Germans from North Africa. In point of fact, the original estimate had been December 31, but bad weather, mud and the unresisted occupation of the Tunisian tip by the Germans, were to delay the final victory for four months. The truth was that the Allies had gone forward too fast with too small forces and had to retire and remount their offensive.

The slowing down of operations was now evident to the public who realised that Tunisia was not going to be the walk-over that they had expected. It was a thousand pities that they had ever been encouraged in their hopes. The Press, the Home Service of the B.B.C., and to some extent the propagandists were to blame. In war there is no greater mistake than raising the hopes of the public to a pitch which your military effort cannot reach. In a contracted world, radio is an open weapon. It cannot be used indiscriminately to depress the morale of the enemy without encouraging the hopes of the home public. Exaggeration therefore is always wrong.

As the war progressed, I noted with increasing apprehension a marked change in the character of our people. Twenty years of headlines and of broadcasting had made the public far more mercurial than in the first world war. But if the British public was momentarily depressed by the delay in North Africa, there was a more dangerous disappointment in another quarter. Soon after the landings in North Africa, Stalin, relieved of his anxieties concerning Stalingrad, had heralded the Allied campaign as "an outstanding fact of major importance which created conditions for putting Italy out of commission and for isolating Hitlerite Germany". At this moment, with Mr. Eden's approval, I had had a long talk with M. Maisky. It was nominally on the subject of collaboration with Russia in political warfare, but it covered nearly every aspect of Anglo-Russian relations. M. Maisky was less complaining than usual and, apart from the stock appeal for more convoys and more supplies, was most amiable. He, too, had been impressed by Torch, but warned me that the Russians would expect a Second Front in the West in the spring of 1943.

But in December, when the set-back in North Africa must have made it plain to Stalin that there could be no Second Front in 1943, the Kremlin volcano began to rumble again. To start with, the rumblings were not very serious, because the Russians were doing well, but they were sufficiently loud to give some anxiety to Sir Archibald Clark Kerr, our Ambassador. Throughout the war the Russians could never stifle their suspicion that the Anglo-Americans were letting Russia bear unnecessary sacrifices in order to leave her weak at the end of the war. Their attitude towards the Second Front was apostrophised in Stalin's blunt remark: "Three things are required for this war: blood, materials and time. The Russians give the blood, the Americans the materials, and the British the time." Obviously the rumblings were a clear sign of louder explosions to come.

As the year drew to its close with little prospect of any solution to the Darlan problem, I heard the good news that the Government was sending Mr. Harold Macmillan at once as Minister-Resident to Algiers. I had known him slightly for some years and admired his intellect. He had a clear, logical mind, knew what he wanted, and had a talent for getting it in a quiet tactful way. It was a certainty that his relations with the Americans would be happy; like Mr. Churchill, he had an American mother. I felt relieved and asked to see him. He received me at once, gave me an outline of the situation on which he was already well briefed, and suggested that we might make a fresh start by sending him a first-class political warfare expert from London. But, he told me, he proposed to go slow until he had taken his bearings.

Destiny acted with dramatic swiftness before he had left England. On December 24 I spent a long and fatiguing day at my office examining with my administrative officer the final details for the return to London of the bulk of the Woburn organisation. In the evening I went to eat my Christmas-Eve dinner at my club. It was fairly full and we had a better dinner than usual. I was just preparing to have a drink with the Canadian staff officers who lived there, when at eleven o'clock I was called to the telephone. It was General Hollis. Could I come to the War Cabinet offices at once?

When I got there, I found Dallas Brooks who had also been summoned. Jo Hollis, calm, business-like, and unemotional, tossed me a telegram. Darlan had been assassinated in Algiers. There were so far no details except that in his recent broadcasts and telegrams Darlan had called on all Frenchmen to unite and had suggested to Eisenhower that General Noguès and M. Yves Chatel, the Civil Governor of Algeria, should be dismissed.

We did not waste much time talking. Whatever else happened, we had to take action at once and issue special guidance to all our Regional Directors and to the European Service of the B.B.C. Hollis and Brooks suggested that I should ring up Mr. Eden, but I demurred. It was, I argued, certain that he had already been informed of the assassination. He was exceedingly patient about taking calls at any hour of the day and night, but if I were to disturb him every time there was a piece of news he would get no sleep. Jo Hollis thought that it was quite probable that Mr. Eden had not received the news and that this time the occasion justified a call. I therefore compromised by pulling Sargent out of bed, told him what we proposed to do, and he agreed. He said that Mr. Eden had already been informed.

Actually the guidance directive was quite simple. It was composed entirely of negatives: (1) Don't allow the Germans to drive a wedge between the Americans and the British. (2) Don't do anything which might compromise the difficult negotiations on which General Eisenhower is engaged. (3) Don't condone assassination. (4) Don't enter into polemics with the German propagandists.

On Christmas Day, Dr. Goebbels excelled himself. His story was that the long quarrel between de Gaulle, the hired assassin of Churchill, and Darlan, the hired traitor of Roosevelt, had reached its climax and that the British Secret Service had been ordered to remove Darlan. The secret thugs had done it in their usual way. Darlan's alleged last words were given as: "You can do nothing more for me now; the English have achieved their object."

Had he made a better job of his effort to create bad blood between the Americans and the British, Goebbels might have had a temporary triumph, for General Eisenhower was away at the front when the assassination took place and, although he returned at once, it was 6 p.m. on Christmas Day before he reached Algiers. The facts were therefore slow in coming out and not suitable for publication when they arrived. Darlan was shot by a young Frenchman who, as a passionate Gaullist, regarded the Admiral as a traitor. There was also some uncomfortable evidence of a plot to murder Mr. Robert Murphy, the American State Department's political adviser to General Eisenhower. The assassin was executed after a court-martial. Some arrests were made, and fortunately the excitement died down more quickly than might have been expected.

Whether Darlan was a true patriot or not, there can be no doubt that his removal, however regrettable the manner of it, brought relief to a deep and dangerous political impasse. The way was now open for the necessary rapprochement between General Giraud, who succeeded Darlan, and General de Gaulle, and when Mr. Macmillan left London on the last day of the year he carried with him to North Africa the first proposals of the Foreign Office for the establishment of a French Provisional Government with headquarters in Algiers.

On New Year's Eve I dined quietly at my club with a brother Scot, saw the New Year in, and heard the midnight news. It was good. The Russians had taken 137,000 prisoners during the past six weeks.

BOOK IV
ANNUS MIRABILIS

"THERE WAS AMBITION, there was sedition, there was violence; but no man shall persuade us that it was not the cause of liberty on one side and of tyranny on the other."　　　ATTRIBUTED TO CHATHAM

CHAPTER ONE

THE THIRTY-FIRST OF December, 1942, marked the end of the most
exacting, the most strenuous and perhaps the most inspiring period
of the war. It had been a time of stress and strain; a time of military
disasters, of sustained threats of invasion, and of gnawing anxiety
about Russia; above all, a time of many muddles while an unprepared
Britain tried to gear herself for war. It had also been a time of trials
manfully endured; a time of successful military preparation; a time
set to every purpose of victory. We were now entering the penultim-
ate stage of that victory. From now on the armed forces of the Allies
were to come more and more into their own and bring the war to
the inmost fortress of the enemy.

The new period would also witness the second triumph of the
British Commonwealth over the implacable foe that was Germany
—a triumph in which the glory of millions would be the glory of
each. In particular, it would be the triumph of the man whose
leadership had united a divided country and inspired it to work with
an energy so dogged, so persistent that, man for man and woman
for woman, no other country was to equal it in productive results.
Winston Churchill has earned great distinction as an historian, and
the writing of history has been one of his main peace-time avoca-
tions. In the war he made history by his essentially practical skill as a
geographer. A zealous and proficient map-reader, he saw the world,
as no other did, as a strategic whole, and the knowledge enabled him
to foresee the course of events, to forestall them by action instead of
following them, and to conceive the broad lines of strategy and the
daring political combinations which drew from General Eisenhower
the tribute that the British Prime Minister was worth an army to the
Allied cause. It was, too, his personal magnetism which won the
admiration of President Roosevelt and which galvanised the
Americans into genuine respect for a Britain which so many of them
thought decadent and already defeated before the first shot was fired.
His prestige was now at its highest. Henceforth it would wane
slowly with the sagging of his own remarkable physical and mental
powers. But when the hour came none of those who disliked his
politics would grudge him the laurels of victory.

The new year opened to a damp dawn and to an air so mild and
balmy as to suggest the first breath of spring. I lay abed rather later

than usual and relaxed. I made no good resolutions, having, indeed, discarded that pleasant but unprofitable pastime as an unnecessary labour in a war in which, like millions of others, I was not master of my destiny. Instead, I took stock of P.W.E. and of my own stewardship of its fortunes. The result gave me no gratification. Eighteen months had passed since I had been appointed to co-ordinate our propaganda. For the last nine months I had been the chief executive of a new department. From the beginning I had been convinced, as I have repeatedly said, that the right policy was to bring the Woburn section to London. To that end I had received the full support of Mr. Eden and Mr. Bracken. But only now had I effected the necessary reforms. It had been a most unpleasant business.

From the start there had been a conflict of opinion between Rex Leeper and myself. He was, and I hope still is, one of my best friends. I owed my present position to him. Indeed, without him it is unlikely that I should ever have been given a war job. I saw eye to eye with him on most policy matters, but on one issue we were divided. He believed in the Woburn organisation. He insisted that propaganda and political warfare were more effectively conducted from the country, where there was time for thinking and planning, than from London. Admittedly there was some sense in what he said, but in my opinion the arguments in favour of having the propagandists under the same roof as the European Service of the B.B.C. were overwhelming. Instead of strength, I had shown the worst form of weakness. I had tried gentle persuasion instead of taking a firm decision. I had whittled down the Woburn staff piecemeal and the process had been painful. Now with the recent arrival in London of the last big batch there was nothing left at Woburn except the sections engaged in secret work. It was an important activity, but hardly enough to occupy the full time of a man of Leeper's calibre and standing. I should have liked him to come to London, but we both felt that the position would be difficult. He was a permanent Foreign Office official, an Assistant Under-Secretary and an old friend of Mr. Eden's. And yet in London I alone had direct access to the Foreign Secretary.

This personal problem was still unsolved. As for me, I should have been delighted to go myself—either to another job or out altogether. For better or worse I had completed my task of co-ordinating. It had taxed all my energies and had kept me tied to London. Robert Sherwood, my opposite number in O.W.I. in Washington, travelled constantly to visit the O.W.I. missions in London and in the Mediterranean. I had been unable to make similar trips. More serious still was the effect on my health.

In the summer of 1942 I had developed a severe type of eczema. I had neglected it. I had seen a specialist, but he had been too busy to give me more than the proper advice and I had been too busy to take it. Now it was interfering with my sleep and wasting an hour a day of my time for the bandaging of my legs. Whitehall, moreover, was a machine which absorbed thousands like myself whose peace-time means of livelihood had been suddenly ended by the war. My job was not only my subsistence; it was also an escape from myself and from sombre thoughts of what I was going to do after all was over. If the streak of Scottish obstinacy in my character told me that, having put my hand to the plough, I ought to complete my furrow, I was unconscious of the telling. I hated the work but could not keep away from it. I answered fully, I felt, to Santayana's definition of a fanatic as a man who redoubled his efforts when he had forgotten his aims. There were hundreds of similar fanatics in Whitehall. Some of them slept with the aid of hypnotics; others, on alcohol; and some again, with the aid of both.

With these thoughts in my mind I went to my office. On my desk was a letter marked *Personal and Secret*. It was from Leeper. It was a noble letter. He had taken his decision. He was going back to the Foreign Office. If he felt any bitterness, there was no trace of it in his letter. Yet the wrench must have been severe. Woburn, if not his creation, owed to him its reputation as the only school of trained propagandists in the Allied countries. Its influence was to impregnate the whole Anglo-American propaganda effort in the war. Now the structure which he had built had been removed. My emotions were deeply stirred. I was losing not only a friend but also a colleague whose understanding of the difficult relationship of propaganda to official policy was unrivalled. But I had no doubt that his decision was right. I received his official resignation two days later. Shortly afterwards he was appointed Ambassador to the Greek Government.

His departure put an end to my own hopes of another war job for myself. There was also another and even more compelling reason which had kept me chained to Bush House. Five weeks before, there had been changes in the Government. Sir Stafford Cripps had left the War Cabinet and gone to the Ministry of Aircraft Production. Mr. Eden had succeeded him as Leader of the House of Commons. This additional burden to his duties of Foreign Secretary meant that he would have less time to devote to our work. Indeed, he sent for me at once and told me frankly that I possessed his full confidence and that in future I must assume greater responsibility.

The Government changes gave me a curious insight into the mutability of human affairs in a world which no man can set to his own wishes. When the changes were announced, I was spending the night at Lord Beaverbrook's house at Leatherhead. The only other guest was Colonel "Jay" Llewellin, who in order to make way for Sir Stafford Cripps had been transferred from the Ministry of Air-craft Production to the post of Minister Resident in Washington for Supply. He drove me back to London the next morning. I knew that he had been passionately devoted to his job in the Ministry of Aircraft Production. As Parliamentary Secretary in 1940 he had been Lord Beaverbrook's right-hand man in the latter's "magical" drive to produce the fighter aircraft for the Battle of Britain. During the critical year of 1942 he had carried on the good work as Minister. I wondered how he liked his transfer to Washington. His face had given no indication. Finally I put a direct question to him. He gave a wry smile. "Heigh-ho," he said, "the life of a politician is queer: here today and gone tomorrow. On Saturday night everyone in M.A.P. went home thinking that I was still their Minister. Now to-day I have to go back to say goodbye, and the officials have to start all over again explaining things to a new Minister."

He might have added that this particular change had been made, not for the sake of efficiency, but to enable the Prime Minister to carry out a piece of political expediency.

The first big event of 1943 was the Casa Blanca Conference at which President Roosevelt and Mr. Churchill, attended by the leading British and American service chiefs, took a number of important decisions affecting both the conduct of the war and the kind of peace that would follow it. To ensure the complete co-ordination of all the Anglo-American forces in North Africa, General Eisenhower was appointed Allied Commander-in-Chief with General Alexander as his Deputy. As regards peace terms the formula of "unconditional surrender" was adopted and published as the official declaration of the policy of the Allies towards the Axis. At this Conference, too, President Roosevelt and Mr. Churchill arranged the first meeting between General Giraud and General de Gaulle. The two Frenchmen were photographed shaking hands, and a statement was issued declaring that both men had agreed to fight the Axis. The atmosphere, however, was freezingly cold. It sank almost to zero when M. Peyrouton, a former Vichy Minister, was appointed Governor-General of Algiers and Mr. Roosevelt delegated to General Giraud the right to conduct all propaganda to metropolitan France. Public opinion both in the United States and in Britain had expected the Conference to put an end to the Vichy policy, and the Peyrouton appointment evoked indignation and strong criticism, some of which was vented most unfairly on General Eisenhower.

The Casa Blanca decisions had serious consequences. The policy of "unconditional surrender" squashed once and for all the use of any hope clause in our propaganda to the Axis Powers and nullified any benefits that might have accrued from the Altantic Charter. Indeed, the very words "unconditional surrender" seemed almost designed to prevent the application of the Charter to Germany. The strong support given to General Giraud was merely an unfortunate postponement of the inevitable. It meant that General de Gaulle would have to wait a little longer; and even his patience was not proof against recurring delays. It also meant that local considerations were given precedence over the general trend of French aspirations and that the task of explaining Peyrouton to the resistance movement in France would remain a difficulty of our propaganda. Taken by and large, the Casa Blanca decisions revealed only too clearly the absence of any definite peace proposals in the policy of the three major Allies. This was to remain a fundamental weakness.

Co-ordination between Washington, Moscow and London was complicated by geographical distance and was never easy, and temporary agreement could be achieved only by a series of expedients. At Casa Blanca the decision on unconditional surrender was taken in order to placate the Russians who were as suspicious of Anglo-American overtures to Germany as the British and Americans had been of a separate peace between Germany and Russia. The failure to enforce on General Giraud the fullest co-operation with General de Gaulle was a sop to Mr. Roosevelt and to the American State Department. Until the end of the war improvisations continued to take the place of a clear long-term policy, at conferences held in exotic surroundings and in the atmosphere of Hollywood. The conferences were necessary, but, only too often, were badly prepared. In politics the Anglo-Saxon genius consists in an infinite capacity for compromise. Like the Russian climate the Russian character moves between extremes: extremes of hot and cold, of laziness and energy, of political indifference and political fanaticism. Eighty years ago,

Alexander Herzen, half-Russian aristocrat, half-Jew and whole-hearted revolutionary, wrote:

"Where, in what corner of the Western world of today, do you find such groups of devotees of thought, of zealots of learning, of fanatics of conviction—whose hair turns grey but whose enthusiasms are for ever young? In the Europe of today there is no youth and there are no young men."

Since 1917 the zealots and the fanatics had been in power in Russia. In the war a new faith, whose orthodoxy was carefully guarded by the pontiffs of the Kremlin, had enabled the Russian armies to move mountains. The same faith, while sanctioning an alliance with the democratic Powers against the more immediate danger, never lost sight of the conflicting ideologies of capitalism and Communism. The Russian policy towards co-operation was one of "so far and no farther". Stalin's farthest was Teheran. He made the Allies come to him; otherwise, he stayed within the confines of his own territories. The Russian Press told the Russian people only what Stalin wished them to know. The prestige which accrued to him was universal.

Meanwhile, although the Anglo-American forces were still pinned down in North Africa, the Russian armies were winning a remarkable series of successes. The genuine nature of these victories was revealed in Germany's propaganda which was clearly preparing the German public for further withdrawals on the Eastern front.

On January 30, the tenth anniversary of Hitler's accession to power, our own propaganda enjoyed a minor triumph when a daylight raid on Berlin by British Mosquitoes made Goering take shelter and postpone his speech for over an hour. P.W.E. could claim some credit for this raid, for it was an important part of our work to call the attention of the Cabinet to the psychological value of these and other anniversary raids. For the first time since the war the Fuehrer did not address his people, but we spoke for him when on the eve of the anniversary the German section of P.W.E. and the European Service of the B.B.C. put on the air a composite record of extracts from those speeches of Hitler's in which he had boasted that Russia was defeated and victory already in sight.

This broadcast repetition of Hitler's voice was well timed, for on January 31 the Russians announced their greatest victory when General Paulus, who had been trapped at Stalingrad two months before, surrendered with 91,000 men. They had also relieved Leningrad and cut off the Germans from the Caucasus. These Russian successes were welcomed both in Britain and in the United States with perfervid enthusiasm. But in the Kremlin, where the sense of urgency was always stronger than in Washington and London, the victory revived the pressure for a Second Front in Western Europe. The agitation caused considerable anxiety among the Russian experts in this country to whom a new danger had now presented itself. This was that, whereas until two months ago both the British and the American Governments had assumed that Russia would need abundant Allied help during and after the peace because, although she would have been the main instrument of victory, she would be badly crippled, there was now at any rate a possibility of her winning the war without us and not needing our help at all.

I had several talks with Sir Archibald Clark Kerr, our Ambassador in Moscow, who was then in London for consultation. Tall, with iron-grey hair and clean-shaven rugged features, Clark Kerr is the most unconventional of British diplomats, going about London hatless and wearing a yellow Jaeger sports overcoat with belt. His eyes, rather small and deep-set, give no indication of his thoughts. His physiognomy, in fact, is slightly Mongolian. Indeed with his slow, deliberate speech and cultivated capacity for seclusion he reminded me of a Chinese sage and, doubtless, during his long residence in China, where he first made his diplomatic reputation, he had acquired some of the impassive detachment of the Chinese scholar. An able and intelligent Scot, he made himself very popular with our propagandists by his interest in our work, proved by several visits to our various establishments, and by the broadness of his views. He was in every respect the complete antithesis of what the Americans call the striped-pants diplomat.

He described to me his lonely life in Moscow. Although he was on good terms with the Russian high officials, he saw them only a little more frequently than other less favoured ambassadors; the diplomatic corps he avoided as far as possible as a hotbed of anti-Russian rumours. He expressed full confidence in Russia's capacity to resist and, indeed, to defeat the German armies, but he was apprehensive of the spring. If there were no Second Front by then—and obviously there could not be one—he would have the unpleasant task of convincing Stalin of the necessity for postponement. He foresaw trouble. He said to me jokingly: "You can have my job in April; I'll recommend it."

Averell Harriman, whom I also saw at this time, was even more outspoken than Clark Kerr. As special representative of President Roosevelt in Great Britain, he had accompanied Lord Beaverbrook to Moscow in September, 1941, and had taken part in the meeting at which the agreement had been negotiated for supplying the Soviet Government with the war materials which they so sorely needed. He had made two subsequent visits to Moscow and had seen more of Stalin than any other Allied minister. Like Clark Kerr he was convinced that Russia would never make a separate peace. Stalin, he told me, always spoke with great frankness and made no concealment of the fact that he had signed the 1939 pact with Germany because he dared not risk a war for which France and Britain, on their own confession, were unprepared. He had been equally frank and even brutal about the inequality of the Allied sacrifices and about the necessity for a genuine Second Front. But always he had come back to his main preoccupation. Whatever happened, Russia, which had been ravaged twice in twenty-five years, must be rid for ever of the German menace.

Mr. Harriman believed that this determination was genuine. He was critical of the Anglo-American policy towards Russia. We should stop making promises which we could not fulfil. We should put away the irritating spoonful of "jam tomorrow" which merely aggravated Russian suspicions and should tell the Russians bluntly and truthfully exactly what we could do and could not do. Otherwise, he feared that Anglo-American relations with Russia would suffer permanent harm and that Russia would revert to isolationism and pursue an independent policy in the post-war Europe.

This remarkably accurate prophecy was made on February 11, 1943.

Lord Beaverbrook and President Beneš, both of whom I saw regularly, differed slightly from Mr. Harriman's views. Both were ardent Second-Fronters; both believed that by postponing the Second Front the Western Powers were increasing the difficulty of their own task. Both were critics of the Mediterranean strategy, which they predicted would prolong the war unduly and would lead to dangerous and perhaps permanent misunderstandings with Russia.

Outwardly, however, all seemed well. The Russian victories continued throughout February, and on February 23, the twenty-fifth anniversary of the creation of the Red Army, an immense throng of ministers, members of Parliament, service chiefs, high officials, and British notables filled to capacity the large premises of the Russian Embassy in order to congratulate M. Maisky. As I drifted with the slowly moving phalanx of visitors, I reflected with nostalgic regret that I was almost certainly the only person in the building who had been present at the first parade of the Red Army on the Red Square in Moscow in 1918. I had stood near Count Mirbach the German Ambassador, whom the Soviet Government had been forced to accept as a direct consequence of the Treaty of Brest-Litovsk. I had watched with sympathetic pity the ill-armed soldiers as they marched past. Unshaven and ill-clad, they were little better than a rabble. Then I had seen the German Ambassador bristle. Two battalions in field grey were passing before his eyes. They bore a banner with the device "Workers of the World Unite" and the title "First and Second Battalions of the German Social-Democrats". They were, in fact, battalions formed from German Socialist prisoners of war who had accepted service in the army of the world's first Socialist Republic. Instinctively I remembered the warning words of General McReady when I was setting out on my last mission to Moscow: "When an army of seventeen millions has broken, it cannot be reformed within a generation". Now a generation had passed, and the Red Army had astounded the world.

As I floated helplessly on the slowly advancing wave of people, I came near M. Maisky. He was talking to Mr. Eden. When he noticed me, he called me over to him, and, greeting me warmly, said: "Our celebrations would not be complete today without Lockhart. He is the only man here who saw the beginnings of the Red Army." I was pleased that he remembered. He was all smiles. It was, indeed, a great day for him and for Russia; very different, in fact, from his first ambassadorial receptions, when the great rooms at Harrington House were half-empty and a few minor officials, some thirty journalists, and a handful of long-haired intellectuals with red ties were the only visitors.

Obviously Maisky enjoyed his triumph. He could afford to be gracious. But, I reflected, Stalin's Order of the Day for the great occasion contained only an indirect reference to the Western Allies. "The Red Army", he stated, "had borne the whole brunt of the war."

Every day it was becoming increasingly evident that Russia, conscious now of her final victory, was determined to have her say— and a big say at that—in the future settlement of Europe—either in agreement with her Western Allies or without it. As President Beneš had been preaching for some months past, we should have to recognise an entirely new situation in Eastern Europe. If the recognition were ample and timely, all would be well. If not, there would be trouble.

I felt that he was right. It might be true, as our soldiers said, that the two turning points of the war were the Battle of El Alamein and the Battle of Stalingrad, but there could be no doubt which battle had the greater political significance, not only for Russia and Britain, but for the whole world.

CHAPTER TWO

MARCH OF 1943 opened like a lamb. Rarely, if ever, has London known such an early and clement spring of blue sky and warm sunshine. March was to be a favourable month for us until the end of the war. The fine weather was a godsend to Mr. Churchill who at the end of February had had the first of his disturbing pneumonic attacks. Indomitable in determination and insistent on keeping abreast of his work no matter how high his temperature, he was a difficult patient. In my journalistic days Lord Beaverbrook used to explode if anyone on his newspapers ever referred to "doctor's orders". "Doctors give advice, not orders," he used to say. Certainly no doctor could give orders to Mr. Churchill, and Lord Moran, who handled him beautifully, could only guide his obstinate patient. What, in fact, could any doctor do with a man who, when "ordered" to inhale Friar's balsam, would be found the next morning with the inhaling cup in one corner of his mouth and a large cigar in the other? As a patient Mr. Churchill was to cause much anxiety to his doctors and to his colleagues.

This first illness forced Mr. Eden to postpone for ten days his visit to the United States where he was to discuss post-war problems with the Americans. When he finally left, Mr. Churchill, who had been "ordered" to go slow, took over the Foreign Office in addition to his other duties! He seemed to thrive on the extra work in which he took a keen interest. We even received a word of praise for our leaflets. More helpful to us still was his intervention in a tiresome dispute which was a relic of the early days when half a dozen different organisations were indulging in propaganda. We had achieved unity in London, but in the Middle East another organisation persisted in carrying on an independent propaganda. Profiting by Mr. Churchill's presence at the Foreign Office, we pleaded again for single control. The mere knowledge that the Prime Minister was taking the matter up was sufficient to bring the offending department to reason.

Our affairs in the whole Mediterranean area now began to take a tidier shape. In March Robert Sherwood, the head of the psychological department of O.W.I., came to England and visited Algiers, where he saw Mr. Harold Macmillan who by now had established the happiest relations with General Eisenhower and Mr. Murphy, the American Minister. On his advice we agreed to strengthen our representation in General Eisenhower's Psychological Warfare Branch, and in April we sent one of our best and most energetic experts. His knowledge and technical skill appealed strongly to the Americans and, although we were heavily outnumbered, our influence was paramount.

Personally I owe very much to Bob Sherwood whom I now learnt to know intimately. Immensely tall and slow in speech, he needed time to develop his thoughts. He was completely unspoilt by his immense success as a dramatist. Indeed, he was at times almost painfully diffident. And yet, for all his outward reserve, he was mercurial and highly emotional in temperament, and at moments the tragedy of the war itself and the cares of his own job weighed heavily on him. When he was gay, it was with a full measure which infected all present. He would yield easily to depression. He could celebrate success with the abandon of a schoolboy. Indeed, one of my happiest memories of an unhappy war was the sight of this tall, lanky giant shuffling his long legs round the room in a war dance and crooning, "When the Red, Red Robin comes bob-bob-bobbing along."

Sherwood's status was different from mine, for he had no Minister, being responsible, not to the State Department, but to President Roosevelt whom he worshipped and to whom he had direct access. The position had certain advantages over mine, but probably more drawbacks, for inevitably he could see the President only on very important occasions. In our day-to-day work I had the advantage of immediate consultation with Mr. Eden and Mr. Bracken. But on matters of the highest policy and in moments of crisis, notably when the American Chiefs of Staff wished to take over the control of all propaganda, Bob was able to go direct to the President, and on those occasions his intervention was decisive. As he was also an intimate friend of the late Harry Hopkins, he was not only very well-informed about the supreme conduct of the war, but could also by timely knowledge forestall the intrigues against O.W.I. in Washington. He had two principles to which he stuck like a limpet: the cardinal virtues of the four freedoms and the supreme importance to the world of Anglo-American co-operation.

As a combination Sherwood and I worked in complete harmony and, I think, with fair success. Certainly there was no problem affecting either policy or Anglo-American differences which we could not discuss with a frankness which was invaluable and, indeed, indispensable to two men who were in charge of large teams of temperamental propagandists. He paid his first official visit to London in September, 1941, that is, three months before Pearl Harbour, and laid then the foundations of our co-operation in the event of America's entry into the war; incidentally, an event of which he was so sure that in June, 1940, he took advertising space in the American Press at his own risk and expense for the only poster which he has ever written. It had the huge headline of "Stop Hitler Now". President Roosevelt gave it the greatest support consistent with neutrality by hanging it over his desk in his Press Conference Room in the White House. From 1943, Bob Sherwood made London his headquarters until he resigned in the autumn of 1944 in order to assist President Roosevelt in his presidential campaign for the Fourth Term.

Incidentally, many of Mr. Roosevelt's best speeches came from the combined pen of Bob Sherwood and Harry Hopkins. I have several letters from Bob which I shall always treasure. A reluctant modesty forbids me to quote more than one, and that one is given only because it shows the spirit of co-operation which existed between us from first to last:

> American Embassy,
> London.
> *April 2nd*, 1944.

"My dear Bruce,

The other day I sent information to Washington concerning recent developments here and I emphasized the great improvement that you had achieved in the whole situation since you returned from your long illness. I said that you had stepped vigorously into a situation that had become sluggish and, as a result of your vigorous intervention, our combined work is now going forward at a good pace.

Having expressed these views to Washington, I can see no reason why I should not express them to you, and I am doing so herewith, adding a word of gratitude for all the generous co-operation you have given to me and my associates in the last three years. It is a source of great satisfaction to me to realise that in political warfare we achieved combined staffs long before the armed forces thought of doing so.

> Ever yours,
> Bob."

Although Anglo-American co-operation was now running comparatively smoothly and I myself was satisfied that our work was in better shape, March brought trials as well as triumphs. The public was chafing at the slow progress of our forces in North Africa. With the recapture of Kharkov by the Germans a new wave of pessimism swept London, and once again the grousers or "girners", as we call them in Scotland, were in full cry after the propagandists. On March 16 I had a bad time when I had to face a Parliamentary Committee in the House of Commons without the support of my ministers. The Committee, composed entirely of Tories, was obsessed with the idea that our propaganda was dominated by Left-Wingers. In their search for scape-goats some of the members exceeded the bounds of propriety in attacking individual officials of my staff. Eventually I appealed to the chairman, Sir John Wardlaw-Milne, who, although he doubtless shared the views of the critics, at once supported me. I am glad to admit that, in my various experiences of Parliamentary Committees, I found that, however hard they sometimes hit, they were generous and scrupulously fair to officials, very properly reserving their attacks for the responsible ministers.

We were not, however, out of the wood, for a House of Commons motion had been put down—by Mr. McGovern of all people—accusing the European Service of the B.B.C. of proletarianism. The debate took place on April 8. By this time the First and Eighth Armies were on the move in North Africa, and at home the pendulum had swung back full length to the rosiest optimism. In the prevailing good humour of the House, Mr. Bracken had a field day. One or two members made attempts to create a bogy of a Socialist-dominated B.B.C., but in the end only three went into the lobby in favour of the motion. These minor troubles were more than offset by generous recognition of our efforts from the best of all sources, the Allied nationals in the occupied countries to whom our propaganda was addressed.

About this time I met M. Massigli who had recently arrived in London in order to join General de Gaulle and to apply his diplomatic skill and experience to achieving French unity. I listened to him while he gave a brilliant, concise and cold analysis of the French situation. It was frank and not wholly optimistic. He was depressed by the political atmosphere of London and by the lack of any serious preparation for the difficult post-war period. He admitted the almost inhuman character of General de Gaulle, but gave full praise to his long-range political judgment which he described as uncanny. Metropolitan France, he said, was predominantly on the General's side and resistance was excellent. Then, to my delight, he went on to extol our propaganda and to say that its influence had been very great. I was pleased by this unsolicited tribute to the French sections of P.W.E. and the European Service of the B.B.C. I was greatly gratified that it should have been given in front of Sir Orme Sargent who was our firmest supporter in a Foreign Office by no means wholly converted to the possibilities of political warfare.

It was now time for me to take some heed of my own affairs. For four months I had neglected my skin trouble. It had now become much worse. My arms and legs were badly swollen, and the pain made sleep almost impossible. I went to see another specialist who told me that I must rest; otherwise I should break down altogether. Perplexed and wondering whether I should resign or carry on in spite of the doctor's advice, I went to Cherkley to consult Lord Beaverbrook. I owed much to him. During the years that I had worked for him he had been an exacting taskmaster, but underneath the hard exterior there was a core of emotional sentiment which, try as he might, he could never suppress. In his public life he had the hard-boiled attitude of the New World, regarding politics as a game in which every friend was a potential enemy and every enemy a potential friend, but in his private life he was capable of extraordinary kindness—a kindness that was the more impressive because it was spontaneous, undemonstrative, and never mentioned. During the war his house was always open to me. It was a valuable resort, for not only did he keep me well-informed about the course of events, talking to me freely about Russia on which we had almost always seen alike, but under his roof I met nearly all the more important American and Dominion visitors in Britain. In trouble or in sickness he was a real friend and could be relied on to give wise and disinterested advice. I feared him. At times he drove me nearly mad, but in my heart I had a genuine affection for him which I knew would last my days.

During the first week-end of April, 1943, I found him among a small party of guests and had no opportunity of talking to him alone. He was dressed in a dark blue suit, a soft white shirt open at the neck and tie-less, white socks, and neat black slippers. A son of the manse, he looked quite the Scottish Presbyterian. Now that he was temporarily out of the Government he had recovered from the severe asthma which had developed as a result of his frantic energy before the Battle of Britain and which in the winter of 1940–1941 had nearly killed him. He was going through a bookish period, was collecting first editions of Scottish authors, and talked of buying a bookshop.

On the Sunday we had a Scottish evening, for after dinner he went to his lectern and, without the book, gave us a series of Burns recitations. It was a remarkable performance, tense and compelling in its dramatic fervour. He had regained or perhaps never wholly lost his Scottish accent. My mind skipped the centuries and in that black and white figure I could see the preacher on the hill-side. This was not the puckish, the violent, the forceful Beaverbrook. This was Max Aitken, the minister's son in whose veins ran the blood of the Covenanters. What impressed me most was the prodigious memory. He went on for the best part of an hour. Once or twice he would turn to me and ejaculate solemnly: "Great stuff, Bruce, isn't it? The finest lyric poetry in the world."

He was never at a loss for a word; never, as far as I could judge, did he make a mistake. I have often wondered how far this accuracy of memory, which enables him to quote appositely and always with effect, is responsible for his success. For, whatever the public may think of the merits and defects of his character, there is a strong and rare streak of genius in the man. Many people have been puzzled and sometimes perturbed by the close friendship between Churchill, the proud aristocrat of Norman blood, and Beaverbrook, the grandson of the poor Torphicen crofter. Yet, apart from the emotionalism and buccaneering spirit which is common to both, those who know the two men best will readily agree that it is the agile brain in Beaverbrook which appeals to Churchill and which the Englishman likes to use as a whetstone on which to sharpen his own remarkable wits.

On the Monday morning I saw Lord Beaverbrook alone and told him my trouble. He was kindness itself. Had I the right doctors? Did I need help? He told me to go away. The war would be long. Ill—I was of no use to anyone. Well—I could still play my part. He advised me to see Mr. Bracken at once.

I determined to take his advice, but postponed it for a week. The next day there was a minor propaganda crisis over General de Gaulle who, with events now moving swiftly to their close in North Africa, was itching to get to Algiers. French unity had not yet been achieved, and the Prime Minister had requested the General to postpone his visit until after the battle for the Tunisian tip was over. The General had taken the request—it was virtually an order, since we controlled all movements out of England—with bad grace and gave vent to his disappointment by putting out a communiqué to the Press, although he had previously undertaken not to do so without consultation. The Prime Minister was annoyed and refused to allow the communiqué to be broadcast in French on the European Service of the

B.B.C. I had to smoothe the ruffled feelings of General de Gaulle—not a very easy or pleasant task for he had been subjected to unreasonable delays, although at that particular moment the Prime Minister's request was in itself not only reasonable but dictated by common sense.

This recurrent crisis temporarily sealed off, I went to see Mr. Bracken and discussed my personal problem. As always, he was helpful and sympathetic. I was to put all idea of resigning out of my head. The battle in Tunisia was going well, but it would be another month before we got the Germans out of North Africa. General Alexander, modest in forecasting events and seldom inaccurate, had given May 15 as the probable date. The next step was the invasion of Sicily. It would take six weeks or more to mount the offensive. P.W.E's plans for Sicily and Italy were already in good shape. I had two clear months and probably more in which to get well. I was not to come back until I was completely recovered. Brooks would act for me. He, Brendan Bracken, would give more personal attention to our affairs. Before I left I should arrange a weekly meeting at Bush House which he would attend.

On April 15 I went to Sedbergh, nominally on a month's leave. The specialist had said that a week in bed and three weeks in the mountain air of the Yorkshire village would put me right.

The advice was not good. Sedbergh, remote from the war, was a haven of rest and peace. My brother and his wife, with whom I stayed, did everything humanly possible for my comfort. I was able to relax, to read again, to think more clearly than had been possible in a full-time administrative job in which quick decisions had to be taken more by instinct of experience than by contemplation. My general health benefited by the rest, but my arms and legs showed no improvement. I was immobilised, and, as I looked on the Yorkshire fells, my thoughts turned to the hills of Scotland. There was a brilliant dermatologist in Edinburgh. A heavy fall of snow at Sedbergh on May 11 made up my mind for me, and on the 14th I took train for the North. When I arrived in Edinburgh, the newsboys were shouting: "Final victory in North Africa." For once there was no exaggeration in the headlines. General Alexander's promise to clear the Germans from North Africa by May 15 had been fulfilled to the very day.

Dr. Percival, my Edinburgh specialist, put me to bed for a month in a nursing-home on the outskirts of the city and gave me a trained nurse. I needed, he said, skilled and constant attention. It was not an exciting month. The Edinburgh weather did its worst, for it rained nearly every day. But I was not unhappy. From my window I could see the Pentlands and, with nothing else to do, I read voraciously, plunging myself into *War and Peace* which I had first read in Moscow during the war of 1914-1918. Fortunately, I had brought with me the four volumes of the Russian edition which I now re-read with a new and absorbing interest inspired by the further experience of a second war. No other book—certainly none of the literature written under the Soviet régime—gives so clear an insight into the Russian character. When I first read it, I had been wholly captivated by the superb sweep of the narrative. Now I realised that everything that could be said about war had already been written by Tolstoy. The artificial building up of great men, who were not so great, in the needs of nationalism, the faking of history—again in the cause of nationalism, the disastrous defeats disguised by the defeated as masterly withdrawals carried out in perfect order, the characteristics of the different European races, the British suspicion of the Russians, the Russian suspicion of all foreigners, the Russian hatred of the Germans and Austrians, the Russian capacity for changing sides, the slowness of the British in getting under way, the planning of a better world, the war to end all wars, with Napoleon as Hitler, and France instead of Germany as the enemy of mankind—all were there in *War and Peace*. Even the poison of propaganda was the same, and the venomous accusation, which I myself had heard in two wars, that Britain would fight to the last drop of Russian blood was first started by Napoleon.

Everything that the English had been taught to regard as sacred had its Russian counterpart. Even Pitt's classic exhortation, "England has saved herself by her exertions and Europe by her example," was offset by Alexander's commendation of his staff officers at Vilna: "You have saved not only Russia; you have saved Europe." Doubtless, Mr. Churchill and Stalin would indulge in similar eulogies after the present war, if indeed they had not done so already.

I was excited and at the same time depressed. There was so much in the dialogue which seemed like a record of our own discussions in Whitehall. When Peter Bezukhov points out that the time has come when senseless wars will cease, the old prince replies quietly: "Let the blood out of men's veins, pour in water, and then perhaps there will be no more war." In P.W.E. we had several Bezukhovs and at least one old prince. Here was the conflict, old as man himself, between the cynical realists and the idealists whom the cynics dismissed con-

temptuously, unfortunately not always without reason, as the uninformed men of goodwill. No one had ever decided or ever would
decide who was right. All that was true was that the human brain
had changed very little in four thousand years.

My room in the Ettrick Road nursing-home is stamped indelibly
on my memory for the re-reading of *War and Peace*. It changed my
whole attitude towards the war. Although officialdom frowned
rightly on wishful thinking, in my heart I was more on the side of
the idealists than ever. It was not a blind faith, as it had been in
1918. It was a reasoned faith, because any faith was better than none
at all.

At the end of three weeks Dr. Percival was so pleased with my
progress that he allowed me to leave the nursing-home. But he
would not hear of my return to London. Before I could go back to
the turmoil of Whitehall, I must see how my legs would stand up to
walking. He prescribed a gentle and gradual course of exercise. He
recommended a fortnight in the Highlands. There was a hotel at
Dalwhinnie in the heart of the Central Highlands where the food
was wholesome and where there was no Spey or Avon to tempt me
to the too strenuous exercise of salmon fishing.

Dalwhinnie, where I arrived on the 9th of June, was not a success.
The hotel was all that my doctors had promised. The view of Ben
Alder where Cluny Macpherson once sheltered Bonnie Prince
Charlie, not to mention David Balfour and Alan Breck, was superb.
But I saw it only once, for throughout that dreadful summer the
rain fell incessantly. Walking, too, soon showed that I was not so
well mended as I had hoped, and if I went more than a few hundred
yards angry red patches flared up on my ankles. Moreover, I was
worried by my long absence from work and was eager to get back
to my desk. I therefore wrote to Mr. Bracken. In my letter I described the barrenness of Dalwhinnie, the mournful cry of the
curlews on the sodden moor, and the dank mists which blotted out
the mountains. I told him that the only building of any size for miles
around was a distillery—and that the distillery was not working. In
order to obtain his acquiescence to my return I worked up to a fine
crescendo of woe.

My letter produced a startling reply. On the night of June 15
everyone in the hotel, including myself, had gone to bed. At midnight I was wakened by a series of knocks at my door. I was wanted
on the telephone. An official telegram marked Urgent Priority had
arrived at Kingussie, the nearest township. The Kingussie exchange

wished to read it to me at once. I went downstairs, and a soft Highland voice read out the words with mechanical precision:

"Bruce Lockhart,
        Grampian Hotel,
            Dalwhinnie.
Open the distillery and stay till July first.

                            Bracken."

I laughed and thought no more of the matter. The next morning brought a forcible surprise. Up and down the line the rumour had spread that a high official had arrived to re-open the Dalwhinnie distillery. It was a matter of national importance. Scotland was short of whisky, and during the morning I was in constant demand on the telephone. The episode gave much amusement to the hotel guests and some inconvenience to myself.

The telegram was hotly followed by a visit from Jack Wheeler-Bennett, my personal assistant, whom Mr. Bracken had sent North in order to give me all the news of my department and to keep me quiet.

Being ordered to stay where I was, I promptly decided to make a move. Dalwhinnie was only the gateway to my Highlands. Less than forty miles round the corner of the local hills were the Cairngorms, Strathspey and Tomintoul, the original home of my Macgregor forbears. Here I had spent the happiest years of my youth. Here I had written most of my books. Here, too, in 1939, I had left my dog Betty, a clever and gentle wire-haired terrier who had been my constant companion in the years before the war. In a long life of wandering this was all the home I had.

The temptation, welcome and irresistible, forced me to immediate action. The day after Wheeler-Bennett left, I was in the train on my way farther North. At Grantown I was met by Duncan McNiven, a crack sniper of the last war, the best fisher in the Highlands and now owner of the Tomintoul hotel which I had made my headquarters before the war. As we set out by car for Tomintoul, a miracle happened. As we climbed the high mountain road, the bank of clouds rolled away, and the sun came out in the clearest of blue skies, flooding the whole scene with brilliant light. We stopped at the fork, where the Grantown road and the road to Nethy meet. Far below our feet lay the fertile strath of the Spey winding its course through woods of pine and birch interspersed with patches of green corn and pasture fields and with the silver waters of Loch Garten glistening in the sunshine. Closing in the whole scene was the great range of the Cairngorms, the Blue Mountains of Scotland, which today still form the sometimes sinister but always majestic barrier between Gael and Saxon. Here and there the war had left its mark upon the scene. Canadian, Newfoundland, and Indian lumber-jacks had been busy on the hill-side and with indiscriminate and in some instances unnecessary zeal had wrought their havoc on famous beauty spots. But, thank God, no hand of man can destroy the solemn grandeur of what to me has always been the fairest sight in all the world.

My welcome at Tomintoul was more than I had dared to expect. I had only one disappointment. As soon as I arrived I went across the square to see my dog which I had left with the local banker. She had become a great favourite and was now an elderly and much spoilt lady. At first she did not recognise me, and I felt selfishly unhappy. During tea I fed her, making her beg in the old way that I had taught her. She responded at once. When I left the house, she followed me hesitatingly to the hotel, and then trotted slowly back to the bank. The next day I took her for a short walk to the rabbit warren by the burn-side where we had spent many happy days together. When we came back, she followed me into the hotel and went straight up to our old room. The next morning she was waiting for me at the hotel door. I pulled myself together. I was being selfishly cruel. I had to go South within a week. It was brutal to woo her away from the banker's family where she was obviously not only well-cared for but perfectly happy. With a heavy heart I decided to leave her where she was. I never saw her again. She died some months before the end of the war.

There were other friends at Tomintoul who also claimed my time and attention. On my first night, and I fear on several other nights, I sat up late talking to Duncan McNiven. A West Highlander with a remarkable gift of second-sight, he was full of Celtic fire, hated all politicians and multiple shops with an equal fervour. Since 1929 he had prophesied the inevitability of war with Germany with the fierce conviction of an inspired seer. Now that his prediction had come true, there was no holding him. In Tomintoul he *was* the war, the Air Warden, the head of the National Fire Service, the local commander of the Home Guard, and the liaison with the military. He was still a prophet of gloom. Like most educated Highlanders, he read deeply and seriously through the long winter months. Secret weapons had long been his hobby, and he predicted with almost inspired accuracy the engines of destruction which Germany was afterwards to unloose. With little faith in Governments he saw our war effort as the last convulsive throe of a giant whose strength had been sapped by luxury and idleness. Many people laughed at his warning of approaching doom. Others like myself who had Celtic blood in their veins and who in the uncanny atmosphere of Avonside believed in kelpies took him seriously and thought him fay.

Dr. Percival had warned me against taking any too violent exercise and, above all, against fishing, since a stumble might easily break the slender film of new skin which had formed on my ankles. Avon, swift-running, rocky with huge granite boulders and shelving cliffs, was a man's river and no place for an elderly crock like myself. My intentions, fortified by the remoteness of the temptation, were therefore of the best. But of course I fell. On my last day an Air Force officer arrived on leave. He had a car and wanted McNiven to go far down the river with him to fish, and "Mac" suggested that I should accompany them, not to fish, but to watch. There was a new hut by the Boat pool where I could rest if I were tired. I went, dressed in my thin London shoes and a pair of flannel trousers. Lazily I watched the two men put up their rods. To please me McNiven had a cast or two down the Boat pool. Then the two anglers went their separate ways, leaving me alone by the river's edge. The air was soft and balmy and, as the sun went down and the long Highland twilight set in, the pool, heavily wooded on both banks, seemed to close in on me until it and I seemed one. The dancing waters were eerily inviting, and even a few fish began to move—not like taking fish, for the water was low and gin clear, but with lazy splashes which seemed to imply a knowledge that no danger threatened from the stranger on the bank. I went into the hut where McNiven had left a fly rod and a bag. I soon found a cast and a Blue Charm and in a few minutes I was by the water's edge. A cast or two from the grassy bank could do no harm. The rod suited me well, but I could not reach the fish which were lying beyond my range. The swirling waters beckoned me, and then time and the war and the outside world passed into oblivion. When McNiven came back after midnight, he found me up to my waist in the water. I had caught no fish, but my heart was full. I had fished the Avon again—perhaps for the last time. I had heard the soft melody of its swift waters, and the lost youth that was still in me had responded to the call. It was two a.m. by double summer-time when we got back to the hotel, and the drive across the Fimoussac moor with the Cairngorms standing out in the gloaming—massive, mysterious, with a wraith-like mist creeping slowly like an advancing barrage over the mountain tops—was a worthy curtain to an act which I shall never regret.

These returns to Tomintoul have always satisfied me completely and, indeed, as nothing else has in a life of much travelling. I have never been able to explain the fascination. It does not come only from seeking the traces of ancestral footsteps, although this quest is strong in me. Here for two centuries my savage Macgregor ancestors tramped the hills and moors, eked a bare living from an unfriendly soil, quarrelled with their neighbours, fought the excise-men, and made and drank whisky. From them I inherit my love of the mountains and of solitude. But the place gives me something more than the recapture of my lost youth. Had this district been ravaged and spoilt by the march of modern materialism, there would have been no rapture in these returns. It is because there has been no change or so little change that, when I look up the valley of the Avon or across the moors to the Cromdale Hills, I can feel and see the living link with the past. It is this visible continuity which gives to Tomintoul its real charm. And, wherever he may be, the exile is consoled by the mere knowledge that, when he returns, he will find again the everlasting hills and the same little huddle of grey houses on the village square and will relive the same sensation of walking on the top of Scotland that I have always felt ever since I can remember. Time has stood still in Tomintoul. That to me is its charm and its magnet. It is a retreat to keep ever in one's mind, to visit not too often nor for too long, and to seek when one needs physical regeneration and spiritual comfort.

The next day I left for Edinburgh and stayed a day there in order to see my doctor. He expressed himself as satisfied and passed me fit for work provided that I never exceeded six hours, put my legs up regularly every evening, and avoided all worry. I am afraid that I deceived him by assuring him that what was quite impossible was, in fact, possible. My legs were better, but I knew that they were still far from right. I knew, too, that my daily hours of work were more likely to be sixteen than six. I left the next evening for London where I arrived on the morning of June 30. I had carried out Mr. Bracken's instructions to the day. Soon after my arrival he telephoned to me to ask how I was. I gave him an optimistic answer, saying nothing about Percival's reservations. He was pleased and asked me if I could dine with him that night. He was entertaining some important American visitors. I could get away early. He himself had an appointment at ten-thirty.

With some misgivings I went and found a large party with seven Cabinet Ministers and a bevy of big American newspaper proprietors and authors including John Knight, the owner of the Chicago *Daily News*, Roy Howard, the boss of the Scripps-Howard Press, Bill Shirer and John Steinbeck who had just sold the film rights of his *The Moon is Down* for a fabulous sum. Of course the dinner did not finish at ten-thirty. My neighbour was John Steinbeck who at first seemed very tired. He had arrived only recently and had, he told me, been entertained for three days without rest. As I greatly admired his work, I was satisfied with the dinner placings. Nor was I disappointed, for he gave full value. Curiously foreign in appearance, he has a round and rubicund countenance which gives the impression that the moon, so far from being down, is very much up. He informed me proudly that he had Persian blood in his veins. Like many authors, he was a jerky conversationalist, but all the jerks were full of pithy comment, and one on Glasgow which he had visited and on which I had asked his opinion, was all embracing in its succinct conclusiveness. "In my own country", he said quietly, "I have seen much of what greed has done for the world, but Glasgow is the worst example."

I realised that, like many other people, Mr. Steinbeck did not share Mr. Churchill's view that all Britain needed was a return to a Tory past.

It was after midnight before I got to bed. There was a red patch on my leg which showed that my skin was not proof against late hours. But I was back in good time for "Husky", the code word for the invasion of Sicily.

This was my first return from sick-leave. It was not to be the last.

CHAPTER THREE

I CAME BACK to Whitehall to walk straight into the biggest trouble that I had yet encountered. It arose from the dual ministerial control of P.W.E. During my absence the propaganda plan for the invasion of Sicily had been completed. It had been co-ordinated with General Eisenhower's Psychological Warfare Branch and had been approved by the British Chiefs of Staff. It was a highly secret document, and by a ruling of the Prime Minister secret operational plans were not divulged to the Minister of Information. In its planning for forward operations P.W.E., therefore, worked direct to the Chiefs of Staff Organisation and to the Foreign Office and, acting on instructions, ignored the Minister of Information, although he was also one of the two P.W.E. Ministers. It was an impossible situation, for Mr. Bracken, whose personal relationship with the Prime Minister was one of daily intimacy, was well-informed about the future course of events. When, as occasionally happened, he saw for the first time in the Cabinet a finished plan which had been prepared perhaps months before by a department for which he was administratively responsible, he, not unnaturally, showed considerable resentment against both the Foreign Office and the Chiefs of Staff.

What made matters worse on this occasion was the fact that the propaganda plan for the invasion of Sicily contained a deception scheme which cut right across the principles for which we were fighting. The scheme, approved by the Chiefs of Staff, was that, simultaneously with the invasion, we should announce to the Italians that their leaders had concluded an armistice. In return for a possible temporary military advantage, we were to run the certain risk of compromising the veracity of the whole Allied news service. At this very moment, too, the Foreign Office decided to recall Mr. Kirkpatrick who, although he was a regular member of the foreign service, was the key man in the European Service of the B.B.C.

Mr. Bracken had therefore more than one good cause for legitimate grievance. He sent for me on the morning after my return and for a quarter of an hour he gave full vent to his indignation. What was this secret plan? We were going to announce a bogus armistice. That was no secret. It would be denounced in a few hours and would be known all over the world. Our news services would be compromised for the rest of the war. We should be no better than the

Germans. What did the soldiers understand about a delicate matter like news? As for the Foreign Office wishing to take Kirkpatrick away at a time like this, that showed what this moribund institution cared about propaganda.

I agreed with him. The bogus armistice seemed to me a crazy scheme. The withdrawal of Kirkpatrick would leave us cruelly handicapped. I begged him to let me investigate the matter. Things could not be as black as he painted them. He agreed, but said that, if the armistice scheme were not dropped and Kirkpatrick left where he was, he would go direct to the Prime Minister.

I spent the next two days seeing all the parties concerned and going first to General Ismay, who, wise in the ways of Whitehall, was most helpful. It was, he said, impossible to worry the Prime Minister with such minor problems on the eve of a great operation. He himself had never liked the bogus armistic scheme. I could discuss this with Mr. Eden. As for Mr. Bracken, obviously it was improper that he should not be informed of what P.W.E. was doing. I must use my own discretion. It was, in fact, what I had always done, but, when events were moving fast, it was not always easy to keep pace with two Ministers who were fully occupied with the prior claims of their own departments. I then saw Mr. Eden who quickly smoothed our troubles. He liked the bogus armistice proposal even less than Mr. Bracken. He agreed to leave Mr. Kirkpatrick at Bush House.

All therefore ended well. The bogus armistice was ruled out. Mr. Bracken's naturally sunny disposition returned. Fortunately for me, the two Ministers genuinely liked each other. Had they been antagonistic I should have resigned, for the root cause of all our difficulties, dual ministerial control, remained, and only good personal relations made an impossible piece of machinery work reasonably well.

Our next task before the invasion was to prepare a draft for a joint declaration to be made by President Roosevelt and the Prime Minister. An American draft was also being prepared in Washington, and several days passed while by telegram and Atlantic telephone Mr. Roosevelt and Mr. Churchill sought to weld the two texts into one whole.

July 10 was a day of triumph. Two thousand seven hundred and eighty ships and barges were employed in the invasion, and the landings were effected with great smoothness and small losses. We had our usual crisis in the release of news from London, for the signal "Operation on" never reached us and we had to pick up General Eisenhower's communiqué from the monitored report of the

Algiers radio. Once again Ivone Kirkpatrick, who was not only used to these aberrations but always anticipated them, kept our end up with complete success, and the outside world had no idea that anything untoward had happened. Later in the day the telegram from General Eisenhower's headquarters arrived. It had not been marked "Most immediate!"

The Sicilian operations followed the course of most of our offensives. The advance was not so rapid as the optimists hoped and not nearly so slow as the pessimists feared. For P.W.E. it was the most trying period of the war because of the difficulty of co-ordinating propaganda policy between London and Washington and General Eisenhower's headquarters. In general, it may be said that the soldiers in the theatre of war regarded propaganda solely as an adjunct to military operations. If it could lessen Italian resistance, it was doing a good job. They counted, too, on quick results and were prepared to back a Badoglio or any Italian general who could give them military support. The British and American Governments in London and Washington, although eager to facilitate the task of the soldiers, had to give consideration to the political consequences of military expediency. Inevitably the propagandists under General Eisenhower used all their ingenuity to assist the military. In London O.W.I. and P.W.E. were the servants of their Governments.

Our next excitement arose from the Churchill-Roosevelt declaration which was to be released simultaneously from London, Washington and Algiers at 11 a.m. British Summer Time on July 16. It had been agreed that the authorised Italian text should be the responsibility of the Americans. The text reached us shortly before midnight on July 15. It contained one major mistake in translation, the phrase "to bring home to the Italian people the tragic devastation of war" being rendered by "to bring the tragic devastation of war to the homes of the Italian people". Fortunately, one of my most zealous assistants was working late at Bush House and, receiving the text from the duty officer, checked it and discovered the mistake. We had just time to make the necessary correction and inform Algiers and Washington!

This was merely a technical difficulty, although it illustrates the kind of problems we had to tackle at short notice. It goes without saying that, had the mistake gone out on the air, we should have been blamed.

Much more complicated to follow were the fluctuations of policy. Sicily itself was only a springboard. The real strategic objective in the Mediterranean was the elimination of Italy from the war. And it was to the Italians as a whole that our propaganda was addressed. To be successful it required a consistent policy. Mr. Churchill, always hopeful of obtaining effective military aid from the Italian armed forces, was inclined to support Marshal Badoglio and the House of Savoy. Mr. Roosevelt agreed with him, but was much criticised in the United States. In Britain a large section of the public, fearing another Darlan problem, suspected and disliked Mr. Churchill's tendency to support bankrupt monarchies. In Italy itself the partisans, who were the strongest anti-Fascist element, would have nothing to do with the King or with Badoglio. At the same time the official peace terms of the American and British Governments were unconditional surrender.

It was a confusing and difficult situation. It was not made easier when General Eisenhower's propagandists, elated by minor successes and eager to take their own initiative, began to make promises and appeals to the Italians which went far beyond the limits of official policy. Confident that they were better informed of the state of feeling in Italy, they resented political guidance from the far-distant rear. They overreached themselves. Washington and London were annoyed, and the Prime Minister sent a sharp telegram to Mr. Harold Macmillan, the Minister-Resident, telling him that there had been too many appeals to the Italians and that the soldiers should attend to their own business. The original Churchill-Roosevelt declaration had denounced the Fascists in no uncertain terms, but it had offered the hope of honourable treatment and a democratic government to the Italian people provided that they overthrew Mussolini. It was the policy of "working their passage". It was followed ten days later by Mr. Churchill's speech in the House of Commons where he spoke in much harsher terms and threatened to leave the Italians "to stew in their own juice".

There was no easy line for our propaganda to follow, for clearly Italy itself was divided into many factions. We did our best to make the official line as acceptable as possible to the Italian people, but our Italian section, being itself pro-Italian, was suspect to ministers and to the Foreign Office. On July 22 I had a meeting with Mr. Eden and Mr. Bracken in the Foreign Secretary's room in the House of Commons. I had with me the text of a leaflet which I wished the two Ministers to approve. On one side were the cold official terms on which the Allies were prepared to make peace; on the other, a somewhat softer explanation of the terms themselves. I handed the leaflet to Mr. Eden. He read it and frowned. "What on earth does this mean?" he said, pointing first to one side and then to the other. "Unconditional surrender here and 'honourable capitulation' there!" I foresaw trouble and thought quickly. "Oh," I said innocently, "honourable capitulation is the Italian for unconditional surrender." They both laughed, and all was well.

Altogether July was a month of frustration in regard to policy and of optimistic anticipation of Italy's early surrender. Hopes rose high when on July 25 Mussolini resigned under pressure from his own Fascist Council and Marshal Badoglio became head of a new government pledged to restore democratic institutions. The Italians were already in touch with the Allies through secret agents, and, although their overtures were regarded with suspicion, it was clear that Marshal Badoglio wished to withdraw the Italian armed forces from the war. General Eisenhower was empowered to conclude an armistice, and the British Foreign Office and the American State Department worked day and night on the drafting of the terms. Their unenviable task was complicated by the difficulty of keeping pace with the feverish round of telegrams between London, Washington and Algiers, for differences of policy continued. Very naturally General Eisenhower now more than ever desired a hope clause in the terms in order to facilitate his military tasks. Mr. Roosevelt, in full agreement with Mr. Churchill on the necessity of supporting Badoglio, complained testily of the same tiresome people who had criticised his support of Darlan in North Africa. It was, in fact, the Darlan issue over again. We were fighting to destroy Fascism and Nazism, and public opinion, both in the United States and in Britain, resented support of men who, if not Fascists, had at any rate accepted service under Fascism. As far as our propaganda was concerned, I could see that, as usual, uncertainty would prevail almost to the last minute and that we should be given little time to prepare.

With the policy problem still unsettled, Mr. Churchill and the British Chiefs of Staff left early in August for Quebec where they were to meet President Roosevelt. Mr. Eden and Mr. Bracken, who were also going to this conference, remained in London for ten days. It was a fortunate dispensation for P.W.E., for, while Mr. Churchill was on the high seas, the American Chiefs of Staff sent a telegram proposing that, in view of the obvious confusion between London, Washington and General Eisenhower's headquarters, the Combined Chiefs of Staff should take over the co-ordination of all propaganda policy. If accepted, the proposal meant that the virtual control of all propaganda to Europe would be exercised from Washington. It seemed a wholly impracticable proposition. I had just time to enlist the support of Mr. Eden and Mr. Bracken for an alternative scheme in which I recommended the establishment of three high-power Committees in London, Washington and New Delhi in order to deal with emergency propaganda problems arising in connexion with operations in the three main theatres of war. Mr. Eden and Mr. Bracken took this scheme with them to Quebec and promised to do their best to ensure its acceptance.

On the day they left England—August 17—the Allies completed the conquest of Sicily and General Castellano, the official peace delegate of Marshal Badoglio, arrived in Madrid. He gave a full account of the military *coup d'état* organised by the Italian armed forces and said that Badoglio was prepared not only to surrender but also to come over to our side provided that we landed in sufficient strength on the mainland. General Eisenhower immediately sent General Bedell Smith, his Chief of Staff, and Brigadier Kenneth Strong, his British Chief of Intelligence, to Lisbon to meet General Castellano. Brigadier (now Major-General) Strong, who was afterwards to become my Deputy and eventual successor in P.W.E., has given me a graphic account of the Lisbon meeting at which Sir Ronald Campbell, the British Ambassador to Portugal, was present. The four men began their talks in the evening. They lasted until 7 a.m. General Castellano, who gave much valuable military information, had come to offer an alliance. General Bedell Smith, who conducted the negotiations, said that he was there to receive unconditional surrender. To reach a point of agreement between these two distant poles of approach was no easy task, but Bedell Smith performed it with masterly skill, standing firm on the necessity of unconditional surrender, but making it more palatable by tactful references to the humaneness and fundamental decency of the Anglo-American way of life. Sir Ronald Campbell told Brigadier Strong that in a long experience of diplomacy he had never seen a negotiation more ably conducted. Perhaps that is why Bedell Smith is today the United States Ambassador in Moscow.

In the end General Castellano gave way, but said that he had no power to sign. He left the same day on his long and difficult journey back to Italy, and Bedell Smith and Strong returned to Algiers. In spite of my forebodings, we would now have time and to spare to study the armistice terms and to prepare a suitable propaganda.

During this period of waiting I had one inspiring experience which had no connexion with my work. I was sitting one evening in the hall of my club talking to some friends, when in, like a gust of fresh air, burst a Canadian naval officer. His cheeks were aglow with health. His eyes were sparkling. It was Commander MacLachlan, the former Canadian Deputy Minister of Defence. During the first two years of the war he had lived in my club, and I had seen much of him. A man of great ability and in his country a successful business magnate, he had come over to Europe at the age of fifty to do his bit. It included the right to criticise the English, and in those early days the criticisms were friendly but pungent. The English were too slow; they had not kept pace with the march of time. They must learn from the New World. It was, he said, his privilege as a Canadian to say these things. I noted quietly and with some amusement that he allowed no American to make similar criticisms without challenging him fiercely. In spite of his Canadian accent he had still a good deal of the Highlander in him. He was in every way a grand chap, and I was sorry when in the spring of 1942 he disappeared from the club.

Now he had just returned from Sicily on some special mission and at once he plunged into a dramatic account of his adventures. He had been with Admiral Troubridge. He had helped to land General Montgomery and the Eighth Army at Syracuse. With the experience he had undergone a conversion. The British, he said, had the Americans and the Canadians licked for improvisation, organising skill and coolness and efficiency in action. All Canadians and all honest Americans in Sicily said so. He became lyrically eloquent as he described General Montgomery's visit to his troops during the battle. The General had been accompanied by Admiral Troubridge who had taken MacLachlan with him. The Canadian had travelled thirty miles or more with the General, had seen him address from his car scores of groups of men, make over a hundred little speeches and give inspiring encouragement and packets of cigarettes to his troops. MacLachlan had been enthralled. Troubridge was a man in a million; Montgomery was the greatest general of all time. Be that as it may, it was abundantly clear that the British General had cast a spell on this sober, hard-bitten Canadian who travelled everywhere with the Book of Common Prayer and a copy of Rupert Brooke's poems.

MacLachlan's eulogy was obviously sincere. I had no doubt that it would be repeated to his fellow Canadians and that the story would be handed down in his own family from generation to generation. It would do great good, for MacLachlan himself was no ordinary man. Indeed, Admiral Troubridge told me that, as an organiser and administrative officer, this vigorous Canadian was one of the best subordinates he had ever had.

Meanwhile, the Quebec Conference was proceeding in the usual blaze of publicity and absence of real news. Necessary as these conferences obviously were, they were not popular with the high officials of Whitehall who disapproved of diplomacy by circus. The public, too, was apprehensive of the Prime Minister's frequent comings and goings and, fearing for his safety, was inclined to question their usefulness.

The journeys also roused suspicion in another quarter. Stalin, still pressing privately and sometimes publicly for a real Second Front, disliked the Quebec talks and already saw in the close co-operation of the British and the Americans a post-war Anglo-American grouping against Russia. And, as always happens when Russian susceptibilities are hurt, he had begun to make his own counter-moves. Freed from his fears of a German victory, he had already broken off relations with the Polish Government in London and was moving forward his own Polish pawns from Moscow. Now he showed his disapproval of Quebec by demanding a joint commission of control for Italy and by withdrawing M. Maisky from London and M. Litvinov from Washington. It is true that both in Washington and London there were experts who believed that the return of the two ambassadors to Moscow was an advantage and that, as victory loomed in sight, Stalin rightly wished to have his best English and American experts at his side. But the writing on the wall, I think, was plain. If Russia were not to be brought wholeheartedly into the Anglo-American counsels, she would go her own way. Earlier in August I had, at Sargent's request, submitted a memorandum recommending a straight round-table talk with the Russians with a fully prepared agenda and no shirking of difficult problems. Mr. Eden had read the paper and, before he left for Quebec, had told me that he approved it in principle.

Mr. Eden came back from Quebec at the end of August—three weeks to a day before the return of Mr. Churchill. He saw me the next day at the Foreign Office. On the whole his news was good. A three-Power Commission of Control for Italy had been approved. A meeting of the Foreign Secretaries of Britain, Russia and the United States had been arranged for an early date in October. He had taken action in Quebec on the problem of propaganda control by the Combined Chiefs of Staff in Washington and hoped that the idea would be quashed. General Castellano had arrived in Rome. It was believed that Marshal Badoglio had agreed in principle to the terms of unconditional surrender.

Two days later I went to Harrington House to say goodbye to M. Maisky, with whom my relations had always been friendly, and spent three-quarters of an hour with him alone. He was in a subdued mood, and there was a queer distant look in his Mongolian eyes which seemed to indicate that he was sad to leave London. He was in the throes of packing his books of which he had many and was anxious about their safe arrival in war-time. His tastes were bookish. In his youth he had edited a highly intellectual review in St. Petersburg, and his knowledge of European literature was comprehensive. Rather shyly he produced a copy of my *British Agent* and asked me to autograph it.

We had a serious discussion about the forthcoming meeting of the Foreign Secretaries. His views were succinct and firmly stated. All outstanding problems must be fully prepared and frankly discussed. The Americans and the British must recognise freely and without secret reservations Russia's new position. She was no longer the Russia of 1919. She had emerged from this war as at least equal to the greatest Power in the world.

Our farewell was quite emotional. It was preceded by an exchange of reminiscences and by nostalgic references to the many changes that had taken place during his long stay in London. I reminded him that in his early days he had once asked me how he could get to know more people in London. I had expressed surprise and had pointed out that he must know our Socialists better than I did. He had replied quite seriously: "Yes, but I want to meet more of the people who are running this country."

In those days his receptions at Harrington House had been filled with Leftists dressed in queer clothes. Gradually the guests had progressed from red ties to stiff shirts and evening dress, until one evening Mr. H. G. Wells who had come to a large party in an ordinary day suit found himself the only person so dressed.

Maisky was always a stout and sometimes tiresome defender of his own country, but I firmly believe that within the limits of his powers he was a convinced advocate of an Anglo-Russian understanding. He certainly knew his England thoroughly, indeed too thoroughly for some people. But when I said goodbye, I thought that we might wait long before we were sent as good a Russian ambassador.

12

On September 3 we received the news that General Castellano had arrived in Sicily with Marshal Badoglio's acceptance of "unconditional surrender". The armistice itself was signed on September 3, but for operational reasons—we were invading Italy in the early hours of the morning of September 9—the news was not to be released to the world until the evening of September 8. On September 7, I was summoned to attend the Cabinet meeting which was to review and approve the final arrangements for the release of the news.

It was the first time that I had been present at a Cabinet meeting since December, 1917, when in urging the necessity of establishing relations with the six-weeks-old Bolshevik Government I had to say quite a piece. Now I had to answer only a few questions about our propaganda arrangements. Mr. Eden presided and, as everyone was in good fettle over the armistice and over the pending invasion, all went well. There was some uncertainty as to the relation of the 18.30 hours in Eisenhower's telegram to British Summer Time, and to ensure no possibility of a mistake a telegram was sent to the Allied Commander asking him to confirm that his time for the release of the armistice was, in fact, 5.30 p.m. British Summer Time. The procedure was that General Eisenhower and Marshal Badoglio should announce the armistice by simultaneous broadcasts from Rome and Algiers and that London and Washington should follow immediately afterwards.

The next day began quietly and ended in high tension. Confirmation of the time of release—5.30 p.m. British Summer Time—was received early, and, as all our preparations had been made, I anticipated a smooth release. Fate, however, decided otherwise. At 2 p.m. a long telegram was received from General Eisenhower. Badoglio was showing cold feet. The Germans, who had considerably strengthened their forces in Italy, were near Rome. The Italians could not hold the city. Badoglio demanded a postponement. General Eisenhower had refused to agree to Badoglio's request. He recommended that the Allies should go ahead with their arrangements and put Badoglio on the spot. In London a special Cabinet meeting was held at once and General Eisenhower's line supported. Badoglio must be held to his promise.

The suspense of the next three hours was highly trying. Mr. Eden and the Foreign Office were now full of suspicions, more particularly as General Eisenhower's headquarters had reported that they were uncertain what Badoglio would say. The long delay since General

Castellano's visit to Lisbon had increased the risk of a leak to the enemy. I was instructed to take all measures to check the announcement and to ensure that the voice from Rome was, in fact, the voice of Badoglio. I ordered all our Italian experts, including one who knew Badoglio's voice well, to glue their ears to their radio sets. It was a hectic afternoon. My telephone rang unceasingly. The Foreign Office had new suspicions and new ideas for precautions. At 5.30 p.m. Algiers released General Eisenhower's announcement. Then for an interval, which seemed like eternity, there was silence. Our Italian listening-in staff, temperamental by nature and over-excited by the occasion, gave two false alarms. Then, after a triple check and a report by the monitors, came the confirmation. Badoglio had spoken. He had followed more or less the wording of the agreed text. Tired but relieved, I went off with Sir Percy Loraine, our Ambassador in Rome up to the time of Italy's entry into the war, and celebrated. There was no "mafficking" in London. The heavy rain did not encourage street processions. But everyone was delighted, and later at night, when the skies cleared, youthful enthusiasts danced round the barricaded site of the Eros monument in Piccadilly Circus.

The next morning the newspapers gave the news of the Allied landing at Salerno, and once again optimism ran riot both in this country and in the United States. The *Daily Telegraph* carried a story that a Czechoslovak minister had bet his colleagues a hundred pounds that the exiled government would be back in Prague before Christmas. In the United States, American Senators, confident that the Allies would be on the Brenner in next to no time, predicted that the war would be over by the end of the year. In the general joy over the collapse of Italy everyone seemed to have forgotten the Germans.

Disillusionment came swiftly and decisively. Within twenty-four hours the Germans had taken action. Their troops, now computed at nineteen divisions, had moved into all the key centres including Milan, Turin and Pola and, as a result of a threatened air bombardment by Marshal Kesselring, Rome had capitulated. Breaking a long radio silence, Hitler spoke the same evening from his headquarters. The speech, raucous and bombastic, abused Badoglio and his backers, praised Mussolini as the greatest Italian since classical times, extolled what Germany had done for Italy, and declared that in Germany there would be no "July 25" (the date of Mussolini's enforced resignation). Germany would never surrender even if she had to forgo some of her conquests.

Worse calamities were to follow. On September 13 came the news that the Germans had made a daring rescue of Mussolini. At the same time General Clark's Fifth Army had run into serious difficulties at Salerno and was in danger of being driven back into the sea. To the British public which had never realised and, indeed, had never been told that the armistice did not mean the end of fighting in Italy these set-backs came as a bitter disappointment. Now it was clear to everyone that the struggle would be long and costly, and, as hopes of an early finish dwindled, resentment became open and found its expression in the Press. Once again Mr. Churchill, whose travel fever was the subject of increasing comment, was to come home from a conference abroad to face hostile, if only temporary, criticism.

It was certainly curious how disaster seemed to dog him every time he went abroad. He would win a triumph at some conference, feel justifiably elated, and return home to find the British public despondent and critical. He had been abroad when Malaya was falling, when Tobruk was lost, and now again when Mussolini had escaped. No man, however, knew better how to disconcert his critics, and on this occasion the fortuitous timing of his return favoured him. When he arrived in London on September 19, the Salerno crisis, the seriousness of which had driven all thoughts of Mussolini out of most people's minds, was past its worst.

Two days later the Prime Minister addressed the House of Commons and delivered one of those fighting speeches which he alone can make. In point of fact, he made several concessions, although at the time neither the House of Commons nor the public realised them. The Prime Minister had been the chief advocate of "unconditional surrender" by Italy; he had expressed a personal objection to Count Sforza, the veteran Italian champion of democracy. General Eisenhower had wanted to make Italy a co-belligerent and to go easy on the armistice terms. Mr. Roosevelt, who had several million Italian voters on his doorstep, was prepared to make even greater concessions. Mr. Churchill, therefore, compromised. He was prepared, he said, to support the King of Italy and Marshal Badoglio, but this support was contingent on Badoglio's broadening the basis of his government by bringing in the six Italian democratic Parties including the Communists. The full terms of the armistice must stand, but they could be relaxed as and when Marshal Badoglio "delivered the goods".

Although there was some criticism from Labour members of the failure "to support the people who had been on our side from the beginning", the speech was well received both by the House and by the public.

Once again Mr. Churchill had triumphed over the grumblers. But there was to be no rapid conquest of Italy, no attack on Germany through the Brenner. Not until the end of the war in Europe were the Allies to gain complete possession of the Italian mainland.

CHAPTER FOUR

NOW THAT THE protracted excitement over the Italian Armistice had subsided, I was able to devote more time to the new departmental problems which the changing course of the war raised continuously. The most urgent issue was the fate of our amendment to the proposal of the American Combined Chiefs of Staff that control of propaganda policy for all theatres of war should be concentrated in Washington. I had put forward an alternative scheme for Emergency Committees for each theatre of war, the European Committee to sit in London. Mr. Eden had raised the matter at Quebec. The Combined Chiefs of Staff had agreed to the amendment which had been submitted to the President and the Prime Minister.

I had some confidence that neither the President nor the Prime Minister would ever agree to any encroachment by the Combined Chiefs of Staff on policy matters, but they were very busy men to whom propaganda was a minor issue in the vast problems with which they had to deal, and until the matter was settled I felt uneasy. Fortunately, the Foreign Office, who had given full support to the amended proposals, received a telegram from Washington a few days before Mr. Churchill's return to England. The President and the Prime Minister had approved the setting up of the London Propaganda Committee to deal with emergency policy problems of propaganda for Europe. In his comment to the President, the Prime Minister had added characteristically: "The Committee will not interfere with you and me taking decisions."

In point of fact, the Committee met only two or three times in all until the end of the war. But it served its purpose in scotching a dangerous Washington proposal. Propaganda cannot be conducted by committees for the simple reason that, before a committee can be assembled, action has to be taken. On almost all occasions when policy guidance was needed urgently, it was quicker and more practical to get it direct from Mr. Eden. In the last resort it was the President and the Prime Minister, and not the soldiers, who decided high policy. A committee, operating in Europe from Washington, would merely have been another spanner in an already over-clumsy piece of machinery.

Meanwhile, we had already begun to plan for the Second Front. Brooks and I had paid several visits to General "Freddie" Morgan, who was in charge of the planning operations, and we were in the closest contact with Mr. Charles Peake, his Foreign Office adviser. As far as our part was concerned, everything was still very vague. It was to remain vague for a considerable time. Indeed, when I reported the gist of our talks to Mr. Eden, he told me not to go too fast. The Second Front was still some way off. I foresaw trouble with the Russians.

Indeed, the trouble had already come, for, although the Russians were doing well and during the summer had been conducting an offensive instead of repelling a German one, it was from now onwards that Stalin began to exert his strongest pressure for the Second Front in Europe. In that September of 1943 M. Shvernik, a member of the Politbureau and today President of the U.S.S.R., had come to England as the head of a Russian Trade Union Delegation and at the Southport Conference had made a strong and not too friendly demand for the Second Front. He gave an unmistakable indication that, in the opinion of the Russians, the British and the Americans were pulling their war punches. Sir Walter Citrine had replied vigorously in defence of Britain, but the sting of the Russian demand remained and it made some impression on the pro-Russian elements in the British public.

There were other pointers to Russian impatience in the stream of stories, typically Russian in their humour, which flowed from the fountain-head of Russian propaganda. The best of these was of a Russian beggar who for weeks took his place daily in the Kremlin Square and, with a little bowl in front of him, prayed from dawn till sun-down. At last he attracted Stalin's attention. The Generalissimo sent for him and questioned him:

"Why do you pray so earnestly and so long?"

"I am praying for the Second Front."

"How much money do your prayers bring you?"

"About eleven roubles a week."

"Eleven roubles a week! That is too little."

"Yes, comrade, but you see it's a permanent job."

These stories were, I think, more effective than the open outbursts of Russian politicians like M. Shvernik. There was only one way to counter this propaganda—by putting all our cards on the table and being absolutely frank. There was in Britain one man who was capable of doing it—Mr. Eden. But the Anglo-American conduct of the war, including of course policy, was dominated by President Roosevelt and Mr. Churchill, and both by temperament and by his past Mr. Churchill was handicapped in his relations with the Russians.

On September 23 I had an opportunity of meeting M. Shvernik when Mr. Eden invited me to a luncheon party in his tiny flat at the top of the Foreign Office. In addition to myself there were only six guests: M. Shvernik, M. Borisenko, the head of the Russian Trade Delegation in Britain, M. Sobolev, the Russian Charge d'Affaires, Lord Cranborne, Lord Leathers and Mr. Herbert Morrison. I found, somewhat to my horror, that M. Shvernik spoke no English and that I was expected to interpret.

Over cocktails—and I took a couple to loosen my tongue—I asked M. Shvernik what impressions he had formed during his first visit to England. He was gracious and gave me a long and factual eulogy of our production. Obviously he had formed a very favourable opinion of our war factories. Mr. Eden then asked him how long he proposed to stay in England. Mr. Shvernik at once replied: "That depends on you. We need transport and haven't got it yet." Mr. Eden then brought forward Lord Leathers and introduced him as the King of Transport, whereupon M. Shvernik reminded Mr. Eden that he had met him in Moscow in December, 1941.

"I remember very well," said Mr. Eden, "I am going to Moscow again quite soon."

"I know," replied M. Shvernik, "and I want to be there to welcome you."

He got his transport then and there. I saw at once that there were no flies on this Russian. Short, plump and square-shouldered, with iron-grey hair, small moustache and tiny imperial, he had both dignity and a sense of humour and, although outwardly stolid, was obviously capable of holding his own in any company. He was dressed in a dark grey suit of excellent cloth and very passable cut.

M. Sobolev, whom I already knew, wore the short black coat and striped trousers of official diplomacy and was a striking example of the new type of professional Russian diplomat. Highly intelligent and full of self-confidence, he had been trained for diplomacy in a technical factory where he had qualified as an expert in steam-engines. With his dark countenance, twinkling eyes, and quick-witted mind, M. Borisenko was the least Russian-looking of the three.

When we went into luncheon, Mr. Eden asked me to explain to M. Shvernik that Mr. Morrison was not only our Home Secretary, but also our Minister of Home Security. Not wishing to make a dangerous comparison, I translated Minister of Security as "head of our Okhrana"—Okhrana being the word for the old Tsarist Security Organisation.

M. Shvernik smiled broadly. "Ah, I see," he said, "the head of your Ogpu."

Not having spoken any Russian during the war, I had a rough quarter of an hour in translating a highly technical discussion between M. Shvernik and Mr. Morrison on unemployment benefit, social insurance, piece work and other sociological matters. Fortunately, the talk switched to the theatre and, in particular, to Korney-chuk's *Front* which, M. Shvernik said, had enjoyed an immense success all over Russia. As a play, it was a formidable indictment of bone-headed generals and out-of-date methods of warfare. He added that Russia had produced some very fine war-songs. Mr. Eden asked why they had not been sent to England and, when M. Shvernik said that the Russians were afraid that we would regard them as propaganda, at once retorted: "Nonsense, there is no propaganda between Allies."

M. Shvernik went on to say that the most popular play in Russia at that moment was *The School for Scandal*, adding, incidentally, that Stalin was very fond of Shakespeare. Mr. Eden, who knows his Shakespeare better than most Englishmen, pointed out that Shakespeare's characters were much more like modern Englishmen than Sheridan's. Here M. Sobolev took up the propaganda point. It was, he said, very difficult to put on Russian war-plays in England. The London theatres would have nothing to do with war-plays. Up came Mr. Morrison to the patriotic rescue. The Russians, he said bluntly, went to the theatre to have their feelings harrowed. The British public had had too much real harrowing; it wanted relaxation. He then told a story of an old labour woman in Cardiff who, when the sirens sounded, used to drink a glass of whisky and read a chapter of the Bible. The chapter finished, she had another glass. Then she undressed, got into bed, made two into a better three, and, pulling the bed clothes right over her head, ejaculated: "Now, Mr. Hitler, you can bloody well go to Hell."

At last the conversation turned to drink, and I felt that the luncheon was going well. Mr. Eden gave high praise to Russian hospitality and said that, while he himself had got through his dinner with Stalin safely enough, there were others who hadn't. At first M. Shvernik did not know quite how to take this remark, and started a long dissertation on the Russian laws of hospitality. It was a tradition, he said, to give everything one had to the guest. The rest depended on the restraint of the guest himself. In Georgia, Stalin's country, hospitality reached its zenith. He then went on to tell a story of Sir Walter Citrine whom he once took to inspect a large war-factory near Moscow. After a long tour M. Shvernik had invited his English guest to have a cup of tea.

At this point Mr. Morrison laughed loudly. M. Shvernik was taken aback and, thinking that he had made a mistake, looked confused. I reassured him hastily and told him that his listeners merely wished to know what had happened to Citrine who was almost a teetotaller. M. Shvernik saw the point at once. Then he went on:

"I took him into the buffet prepared by the factory manager. There was everything imaginable in the way of food and drink—except tea."

"What did Citrine do?" asked Mr. Morrison with almost indecent haste.

"Took everything that was given to him," replied M. Shvernik without even a twinkle in his eye.

This time the whole table laughed.

Having created the right atmosphere with his story, M. Shvernik now risked what he thought was a delicate question. Where was Hess and what were we doing with him? His visit to England, M. Shvernik said frankly, had aroused many suspicions in Russia.

Mr. Eden replied at once: "Would you like to have the documents?"

M. Sobolev looked at M. Shvernik as if to ask his approval. M. Shvernik nodded, and M. Sobolev asked: "Do you mean the British statement or the *procès-verbal*?"

"Of course, the *procès-verbal* if you want it and provided that you keep it secret," said Mr. Eden. And on that condition the documents were promised and given.

It was easy to see that the Russians were surprised and delighted by Mr. Eden's frankness and, following up his advantage, he twitted them good-humouredly about being altogether too suspicious.

M. Shvernik came back at him: "Perhaps we have long-standing reasons for our suspicions."

Obviously he was harking back to our intervention in 1918 and to the aid which we had given to the Whites in the early days of the Soviet Republic. As I translated M. Shvernik's remark, I told Mr. Eden what was in the Russian's mind. Mr. Eden laughed and pointed to me:

"Bruce here", he said, "was the cause of the intervention."

Fearful lest the Russians might misunderstand this banter, I said to M. Shvernik: "I was the victim, not the cause of the intervention."

To my surprise M. Shvernik took my remark seriously and said: "I was in Moscow at the time; I remember you well. I think that today we would agree that you were the centre of events which are still very difficult to unravel."

Mr. Eden, talking now very seriously, rubbed in his point. There was only one way to be rid of the suspicions in both countries. Both sides must speak their minds more frankly and openly than they had done hitherto. There should be no secrets between Allies.

M. Shvernik agreed warmly and said that he knew that Stalin would approve.

The luncheon ended with a discussion on the Nazi leaders, and somewhat to my surprise there was general agreement that Ribbentrop was the most untrustworthy and the most unpleasant. The meeting had been a great success. I have taken part in many talks with the Russians and on various occasions have interpreted for leading British politicians. I have seen no one handle Russians so tactfully and so successfully as Mr. Eden. Perhaps it is because he has a dash of Slav blood in his veins. At any rate he has always believed in the necessity of an understanding with Russia. This does not mean that he underestimates the difficulties. Few men realise better the impossibility of persuading Russia to abandon one jot of her national sovereignty. He shares none of the illusions of the pro-Russian sentimentalists who believe that the Russian and British peoples have only to get together and all will be plain sailing. It is within the limits of the inhibitions which exist and which will continue to exist indefinitely in a country which has always been ruled by a dictatorship that he seeks an understanding and believes that it can be achieved. In negotiation he makes a deep impression of sincerity, because as a politician his integrity is great. I am confident while the Russians recognise and welcome this integrity, they neither regard him as a pro-Russian on whose support they can always count nor underestimate his ability to defend British interests.

After the guests had left, Mr. Eden kept me back and told me that he was leaving for Moscow on October 4 for the meeting of the Foreign Ministers. (In point of fact, he did not leave until ten days later owing to a hitch in Mr. Hull's arrangements.) All attempts to hold the Conference of the Foreign Secretaries in London had failed, Stalin having insisted that he could not spare M. Molotov at so critical a moment in the war. A full agenda, supported by draft memoranda, had been sent to the Russians who had also sent us their agenda. It contained only one item: the Second Front.

Obviously Mr. Eden was in for a difficult time. Personally I had always held the view that our post-war problems with Russia should be settled during the war, preferably while Russia still desired and needed our help, and that every postponement increased the danger of a post-war conflict between East and West. The timing was the all-important factor. However difficult a hard and fast understanding might be, every month's delay made it more difficult. Unfortunately and perhaps inevitably, both President Roosevelt and Mr. Churchill were so absorbed in the strategical problems of a war that was not yet won that post-war problems tended to be relegated to a background of vague and indeterminate discussion. The inclination to burke difficulties was strengthened by President Roosevelt's increasing preoccupation with the campaign for his fourth term, a period in which American politics are always characterised by caution and deferred decisions.

Two days after Mr. Eden's Russian luncheon I went to spend the week-end at Cherkley. The other guests included Sir John and Lady Anderson. When I arrived, the changes in Mr. Churchill's Government had just been announced. Sir John had been appointed Chancellor of the Exchequer. Lord Cranborne had become Secretary of State for the Dominions; and Mr. Richard Law, Minister of State in the Foreign Office. Lord Beaverbrook had rejoined the Government as Lord Privy Seal. The new appointments caused the usual speculation in Whitehall with the chief interest and much guessing concentrated on the new Lord Privy Seal. Many people thought and feared that he would take over Sir John Anderson's previous job as Chairman of all kinds of Committees for settling problems which the Prime Minister had no time to handle. Others again were convinced that he was to wield a super Geddes Axe on the swollen bureaucracy. Personally I doubted the Committee story. Lord Beaverbrook possesses many qualities. Some verge on genius; one or two are bad. But no one could accuse him of liking or believing in committees. The success of the Anderson Committees came from Sir John's remarkable knowledge of government machinery and from his ability to listen to and sift evidence. Lord Beaverbrook's mind would be made up before the committee started. I inclined to the Geddes Axe theory, mainly because I hoped it was true. I suspected that he was back because the Prime Minister wanted his whetstone.

On my arrival I was shown into his library. The strain of the past two months had taken its toll on me. My skin trouble had started again in aggravated form, and 1 felt wretchedly ill. Nevertheless, I enjoyed the scene that met my eyes. His Lordship was seated in a deep chair beside his dictaphone and his telephone. His valet, his secretary and his agent were by his side. A pile of letters and papers lay on the floor. He waved me to a chair, and I waited while he answered calls of congratulation on the telephone, dictated half a dozen letters, engaged farmers, ordered stock to be sent to his new farm in Somerset, and discussed a new asthma cure. Everything was settled in ten minutes, and the cavalcade withdrew. Then he turned to me and said: "What is Whitehall saying about my appointment?" I told him, emphasising the fears of the officials of a new Geddes Axe. He roared with laughter and said that the only pleasure that his appointment had given him was the knowledge that most of his colleagues would be fuming. He was in a puckish and most jovial mood, but like most of his jokes this one contained a strong element of truth.

On the Sunday evening we had some serious talk on Russia. General Fuller had written a powerful article on Russia in the *Sunday Pictorial* suggesting that the German retreat in Russia was a well-planned strategic withdrawal which was intended to be the prelude to a separate peace between Germany and Russia. The idea had some support in certain circles in Whitehall. I was therefore delighted to hear Sir John Anderson dismiss it as ridiculous. I was glad, too, that Lord Beaverbrook had returned to the Government. As a determined Second Fronter he had been, in his private capacity, a source of disunity, for Stalin was always quoting him to our Ambassador in Moscow. It was better for Britain that Lord Beaverbrook should state his views on the Second Front as a member of the Government, than that Stalin should quote them for him when he was outside it.

Always preoccupied with the Russian problem, I was becoming increasingly perturbed by the contrast between the speed of events and our slowness in tackling with the Russians the whole post-war settlement of Europe. Russia was the key to nearly all the problems of my own department.

To clear my mind, I again went to see President Beneš whom I regarded as an excellent barometer of Central European opinion. I found him in one of his rare pessimistic moods. Perturbed by our lethargy and lack of a clear-cut policy for Europe, he had long wanted to go to Moscow to make his own terms with the Russians. His whole policy was based on an understanding between the Anglo-Americans and the Russians. Without it there was no future for Czechoslovak democracy and perhaps none for an independent Czechoslovakia. He was irritated because we were putting obstacles in the way of his Moscow visit. He was confident that Russia would never make a separate peace with Germany, although it was possible and even probable that Germany might offer one. His main apprehension was that the Russian advance would be so rapid that the Russians would settle the German, Polish and Balkan problems by occupation before we were ready even to discuss them. There would then be no peace except a Russian peace in Central and South-Eastern Europe. And there would be no Poland. In somewhat gloomy terms he emphasised the urgency of a full settlement. Soon, he said, it would be too late.

I was perturbed by this talk. President Beneš was not given to pessimism, and today he had been more than pessimistic; he had been alarmed. His reasoning seemed to me to be sound. Unless we went more than halfway to bring the Russians to a European settlement, they would pursue evasive and delaying tactics until they had occupied all the points of vantage. A common danger had kept the Allies together. Even in Britain, national unity was merely a suspension by national danger of long-standing political differences. Now that the danger was receding, the national differences were beginning to reveal themselves. They were already manifest and, indeed, becoming a nuisance in a temporary department like P.W.E., which was vastly more political-minded than the permanent departments. Was it not then certain that these differences would develop a thousand times more quickly and more dangerously between Allies whose standards of conduct, of civilisation, and of life itself were so different? What I feared most was the traditional tendency of British foreign policy never to enter into future commitments. And Mr. Churchill, who towered over his colleagues and dominated their counsels, was by temperament and by training a traditionalist.

The day after my meeting with Dr. Beneš I went to luncheon with M. Mikolajczyk in a private room at the Dorchester. The only other guests were M. Retinger and M. Stefan Litauer. I had always admired M. Mikolajczyk whom I had found the most reasonable and broad-minded of the Polish Ministers in London. He had the courage common to all Poles. What I think he lacked in his difficult London surroundings was self-confidence. In Poland he had been a fairly prominent member of the Polish Peasant Party, but he had never been more than a local official. His colleagues in the London Polish Government were either generals or ex-ministers of pre-war Polish Governments. All were men of the world. They overshadowed the modest and unassuming Mikolajczyk, who had all the right ideas, was pro-Czech when most of his colleagues regarded the Czecho-slovaks as an inferior race, and favoured an understanding with Russia. Since General Sikorski's lamented death he had gradually won the confidence of the British Government.

M. Retinger, able, courageous, and far-seeing, had been the man of confidence of General Sikorski, but was mistrusted by many mem-bers of the London Government, partly because of his influence with the British which was considerable and partly because he him-self was not a pure Pole. M. Litauer had been for many years a Polish correspondent in London and as President of the Foreign Press Association had established a considerable position for himself. He knew British politics and British politicians thoroughly. But he, too, was mistrusted by many Poles because of his Jewish ancestry and of his pro-Russian attitude.

Although September was not yet ended, the day was raw and damp with the early chill of winter. The weather seemed to conform with the dejected spirits of my hosts who were frank, but gloomy. They gave me a candid account of the splits and factions in the Polish Government in London and of the wide gulf between the Polish military and the Polish politicians. All three men saw the terrible tragedy that already overshadowed their country. Poland would be occupied by the Russians and, they said without reservation, many Poles in Poland would support them. All three were in favour of immediate negotiations with the Russians. M. Retinger and M. Litauer wanted M. Mikolajczyk to break with the London Govern-ment or at least to force them to break with him by going resolutely to Moscow. M. Mikolajczyk undoubtedly wanted to go to Moscow, but it was obvious that he dreaded the risk of being accused of betraying not only his colleagues in exile but also the Polish army which had fought so gallantly for the Allied cause. In the end all three men turned to me. What were the British and American Governments going to do? They made it clear that they expected little. I could not enlighten them. I did not know.

I went away sorrowfully, because I felt and had always felt that the Polish Government in London was doomed unless it could come to terms with Russia. There were no more gallant fighters than the

Poles, but their attitude towards other peoples and, especially, towards the other Slav nations had always been highly unreal. No other nation, not even Nazi Germany, had so obstinately under-estimated the military strength of the Soviet Union. Many of the Polish politicians in London had based their calculations on the defeat of both Russia and Germany and on an Anglo-American victory. Unfortunately, too, there were certain elements in the Polish Government in London who, like many *émigrés,* were never able to admit even for a second that possibly Poland did not pine for them as much as they pined for Poland.

Looking back today when M. Mikolajczyk is risking his life daily in Poland in a valiant effort to retain for his country some of the Western ideals for which it has always stood, I find it unduly hard to criticise his tactics during that autumn of 1943. It is, however, just possible that had he taken his Moscow plunge without so much initial hesitation he might have gained more both for Poland and for those Poles who were of his way of thinking.

Although I did not realise it when I said goodbye, this was the last time that I was to see M. Mikolajczyk. I was now seriously ill with my skin trouble. My legs and arms were badly swollen, and my face was disfigured. I went to bed for four days, but there was no improvement. Dejected and full of misgivings, I went to see a well-known specialist who had cured one of my best Foreign Office friends of the same complaint. He gave me a bad report and expressed surprise that I was still able to go about. I must have two months in bed with skilled nursing. It would be three months before I could think of work again. There were no proper facilities in London. The best thing I could do was to go back to Percival in Edinburgh. I had been foolish to neglect my condition for so long. It was, he said, more important for officials to have leave in war-time than in peace.

Finding no comfort in the reflection that I had not spared myself, I went to the Foreign Office to report. Sargent was away on sick-leave, and I saw William Strang. When I told him that I should have to go away indefinitely, he put down his pen with a rattle. "There," he said, "I knew this would happen. Have you seen Findlater Stewart's paper on the health of senior civil servants in the fifth year of the war? It is based on calculations of the last war and it shows that a high percentage will break down or be useless on sheer physical grounds."

"There's Moley Sargent," he went on. "He had to go away at a most inconvenient moment. He's been feeling like death for some time and had to tell the Secretary of State that if he did not rest now he would fall down. Now there's you, and there will be many more."

I found some confirmation of his fears when I went to my own office to make the necessary arrangements for my absence. There was a telegram from Algiers. Our key man in General Eisenhower's psychological warfare unit had developed thrombosis and would have to come home for treatment. He was only thirty-six. Then Ivone Kirkpatrick came in to my room, told me that he had been run down for many months, and said that he was doubtful how long he could carry on. This accumulation of trouble was grim. Fortunately Dallas Brooks, who possessed a magnificent physique and a most equable temperament, made light of all the difficulties, and together we sat down to work out a new scheme of organisation and to provide substitutes for the sick men. He was always at his best in a crisis, and his optimism was worth more than a car-load of doctors.

I spent the next two days in completing our arrangements. Mr. Bracken, himself far from fit, insisted that this time there was to be no question of coming back half-cured. I also saw Mr. Eden, then on the eve of his departure for Moscow, and reported to him my talks with Dr. Beneš and M. Mikolajczyk. He had the interests of the Poles very much at heart and was eager for M. Mikolajczyk to go to Moscow as soon as possible. That same night I left for Edinburgh, saw my doctor and was sent to a nursing-home in Great King Street. I was immediately swathed from head to foot in bandages. I felt miserable, but the news was good. My first day in the home was the anniversary of Hitler's boast in October, 1941, that the war in the East was over and that the Russian armies had been annihilated. Now the Russians were advancing rapidly, had taken Reval, and might, indeed, be in Poland even before the Moscow meeting of the Foreign Secretaries. Once again our propagandists rubbed in the contrast between the boasts of 1941 and the unconvincing excuses of 1943 in what I think was a successful effort to undermine Hitler's infallibility as a prophet and a strategist.

The next morning I was gratified to receive a very kind letter from Mr. Eden and a reassuring and friendly telegram from Mr. Bracken. Their treatment of me throughout the war was generous and long-suffering. On this occasion I needed their encouragement, for my cure was to be both long and painful.

CHAPTER FIVE

THROUGHOUT THE WAR I had buoyed myself with thoughts of returning to Scotland. To me it was the desert island that was the popular
dream of escapism; and in my worst moments it sustained such
courage and perseverance as I possessed. But when it took place, it
was not what I had expected. Certainly it was good to be back in the
city where I had spent my schooldays, good to be treated by Scottish
doctors whom as a Scot I regarded as the best in the world, and best
of all to be looked after by Scottish nurses. Certainly, too, I was surrounded by every kindness. Friends sent me fresh eggs and honey
and books. Alistair Fraser Lee, my Edinburgh doctor and one of my
oldest friends, came to see me every day and cheered me with all the
local gossip. Dr. Percival, too, who was again handling my case,
visited me regularly, sometimes twice a day, inspected every inch of
my wretched body, superintended my dressings, and rang the
changes on my treatment. Everything that Scottish efficiency could
do to make me well was done. But I made no progress or, to be
accurate, I made the most depressing kind of progress. For three or
four days there would be a marked change for the better. Dr. Percival
would express mild optimism; the nurses smiled, and my own hopes
would soar. Then on the fifth day there would be a severe relapse;
my bandages would burn until I could not resist tearing them off,
and my condition was worse than ever.

Throughout the last fortnight of October the sun shone uninterruptedly, but when November came with a long succession of fog
and rain and sullen skies, the darkness entered into my soul. There
was little or nothing that I could do. My arms were too swollen to
enable me to write or even to hold a book. Most of my head was
shaved and my face and neck enveloped in bags of cold starch. When
I looked in the mirror, I fancied myself as an Arctic explorer setting
out on a long sledge trip, but my secretary said I was the exact image
of the man in the pre-war advertisement for Michelin tyres.

My windows on the first floor looked out on the grey stone houses
across the street. My only view was of a black baby—a living testi-
mony to the cosmopolitan life of war-time Edinburgh—that several
times a day was helped up by its white mother at the window
opposite to see the doctors' cars arriving at the home. Dr. Percival,
who wanted me to have complete rest, put a severe limitation on my

visitors. Above all, he did not wish me to think or talk of the war. He was, of course, asking the impossible.

Fortunately, I had an excellent radio set and for the first time in the war I was able to listen-in uninterruptedly not only to the home news but also to the foreign language broadcasts, including our own. It was a valuable experience, for listening to the live voice is a much better test of the effect of propaganda than studying the monitoring reports. In my office I had, of course, no time for listening-in except on very special occasions.

Soon after I entered the home, I heard the announcement of Admiral Sir Dudley Pound's death. Before I left London, I knew that he was dangerously ill, but now the news came as a great shock. I did not know him very well. I had seen him when I had gone before the Chiefs of Staff. I had met him with Mr. A. V. Alexander and more than once had run into him in the long corridor of the Admiralty stumping along with his game leg and tap-tap-tapping on the stone with his stick, for all the world like Pew, the blind pirate in *Treasure Island*. He had always stopped, asked how our propaganda was progressing, and given me a few words of encouragement. Not that I think that he was interested in propaganda. That was merely his way. His whole being was centred in the Navy. During the four years that he had been First Sea Lord he had scarcely spent a night away from the Admiralty. He had held his post during the most critical period of our existence when the Navy had to carry the chief burden of the war. He had been criticised, and the criticism left him unruffled. He always knew what ought to be done and did it with the quietest efficiency. During the evacuation of Dunkirk, and indeed many times since, I heard Mr. Alexander say with forthright British fervour: "Thank God for Dudley Pound." In the end he killed himself with overwork. He was a great man.

Two days after Sir Dudley Pound's death I met Munro Kerr, a brother of Admiral Munro Kerr. He told me a curious story about a previous illness of Sir Dudley Pound. Not long before the war, when he was Commander-in-Chief, Mediterranean, Sir Dudley had to have an infected tooth out. After the extraction the tooth fell down his throat and lodged in a place where an operation would have been dangerous. For some hours there were grave fears for the Commander-in-Chief's life. In this event Admiral Munro Kerr would almost certainly have succeeded him and become First Sea Lord in the war. During the night Sir Dudley coughed the tooth up.

Almost at the same time I received the alarming news that our chief political warfare expert with General Eisenhower was on the danger list in a London nursing-home. The thrombosis which had necessitated his return from Algiers had produced a clot of blood on the lung, and for ten days his life hung in the balance. Fortunately, his own robust physique and the co-operation of Mr. Bracken and of General Brooks, who spared no trouble to obtain for him the best medical attention, pulled him through, and within four months he was able to return to work and to play a leading part in the integrated Anglo-American Psychological Warfare Unit under General Eisenhower.

Occasionally a member of my department would visit me and keep me informed of the course of events, and Brooks wrote regularly. Mr. Eden had done well in Moscow. The ground had been cleared for the United Nations organisation and a European Advisory Committee had been appointed with headquarters in London in order to deal with the problems which would arise after victory. The Big Three were to meet at Teheran at the beginning of December. In Algiers General de Gaulle had at last established his position as head of the Provisional Government of France, and Giraud had retired into the obscurity to which he belonged. In spite of Italy's declaration of war on Germany, military progress in Italy was slow. On the whole, the news was satisfactory.

There were also various departmental problems, mostly concerned with replacements for members of the staff who had broken down in health. But as it was hopeless for me and, indeed, for any sick man who was miles away from the centre of events, to interfere or even make recommendations, I told Brooks that he had my full confidence and a completely free hand.

Towards the end of November I had made sufficient progress to be allowed to go for an occasional drive with Fraser Lee when he was doing his rounds. The result was unfortunate, for I developed a mild attack of influenza. A rise of my temperature restarted my skin trouble in the worst form that I had yet experienced, and Dr. Percival decided to move me to the skin ward in the Royal Infirmary.

I moved on December 8 and felt thoroughly dejected by the reflection that after nearly two months in Great King Street, where I had been very well treated, I should have to come to the famous infirmary which Henley had described as "half-workhouse and half-jail". At first I shared his view, although his sonnet had been written of the old infirmary and not of the magnificent new buildings in Lauriston Place. Obviously other people also regarded the infirmary as a workhouse, for on the day after my move my nurse brought in a card bearing the name of Mr. A. C. Trotter, Editor of the *Scottish Express*. My first inclination was to say that I was too ill to see anyone. But, having been a journalist myself, I relented. I would see him and tell him gently that, as a member of a secret or semi-secret department, I could not be interviewed.

His first words took my breath away. He had come from Glasgow not to interview me, but in response to a telephone call from Lord Beaverbrook who had heard of my change of address from Mr. Bracken. Mr. Trotter's orders were (1) to remove me at once to the best nursing-home in Scotland; (2) to arrange for a consultation of the best doctors; (3) to say that Lord Beaverbrook would be responsible for all expenses; and (4) to report to his Lordship as soon as his instructions had been carried out. Tears of weakness, some of vexation and some of emotional gratitude, came into my eyes. I guessed at once that Lord Beaverbrook had assumed that my change of sickbeds had been dictated by the exiguousness of my financial resources.

I made up my mind at once. My room—in reality a tiny cubicle—was uncomfortable. There was no means of regulating the central heating. When it was turned on, the heat was unbearable. When it was shut off, I froze. But to move again would be cowardice. The infirmary was a great Scottish institution. I was determined to give it a full trial. I therefore told Mr. Trotter that the Infirmary Skin Ward was the only efficient department of its kind in the British Isles and that I was in the best possible hands. He was sympathetic and sensible and promised to send a favourable report to Lord Beaverbrook. The next day, and on all the succeeding days of my illness, presents of grapes and fruit arrived regularly at the infirmary. They came from Lord Beaverbrook who also wrote several times saying that his offer was always open and urging me to follow his advice if my progress was unsatisfactory. Then there was silence, and I guessed correctly from the announcement of Mr. Churchill's serious illness that Lord Beaverbrook had gone to join him at Marrakesh.

For some time I regretted my decision. The régime in the infirmary was much more severe than it had been in the nursing-home. My dressings were a strain on my temper and my patience. They took nearly two hours in the morning and as long again in the evening. My head was now completely shaved by an efficient nurse who wielded her cut-throat razor with a speed that terrified me. Still more was I afraid of Sister Toddie, the only woman in the infirmary who was in complete charge of a ward. She ran it with an iron discipline and stood for no nonsense either from patients or from her large staff of nurses. But her efficiency impressed me forcibly from the start. She had handled thousands of skin cases in her life, knew instinctively how to meet each sudden change, and, conscious of her knowledge, feared neither professor nor superintendent. Her sense of duty was supreme. She exacted hard work from everyone and the hardest of all from herself. I soon discovered that beneath the business-like exterior she had a heart of gold. She would have been a great woman in any walk of life. In the skin ward she was the genius of the place. We became great friends.

In the infirmary I had my only real Christmas of the war. It began at 6 a.m. when the nurses, about five hundred strong and very picturesque in their bright red capes, went round all the departments of the huge series of buildings and sang carols. I thought I had not slept all night, but when I looked around in the morning I found a large white stocking pinned to my bed. In it were presents from the infirmary Santa Claus: a wooden parrot that swung for minutes on end on his perch, a comic little man who turned somersaults by himself on parallel bars, and a poem in my honour beautifully illustrated and written by Miss Rae, the secretary of the ward, and entitled a Jaconet Lament (a gentle skit on my hatred of the jaconet substitute for oilskin which kept damp the painful silver nitrate "soaks" with which my skin was dressed), and various other knick-knacks. Nothing had been bought. Everything had been made in the infirmary. In the afternoon there were theatricals and a concert, and, although I was too ill to attend, my door was left open so that I could hear the singing of the Scottish songs.

It was a great day, but the morrow was even better. Kind Sister Toddie had taken pity on my misery. Without telling me, she had been working for days to get permission to move me. It was no easy matter, for the infirmary had only two tiny private rooms. But at the top of the building there was an empty ward which was being kept for eventual casualties from gas warfare. Attached to it was a large room which was intended for the head of the ward. And to this paradise I was moved on Boxing Day. It had a huge window-front with a superb view of the Pentlands. My bed was beside the window, and by stretching a little I could also see the Lammermoors. I felt as if I were on top of Edinburgh. And with this happiness came a new confidence. Two weeks in the infirmary had made a wonderful improvement in my condition. I had been given a thorough medical overhaul, and all the reports were favourable. I was now allowed to read and was given morphia which, if it did not make me sleep, banished all pain and irritation and left me with a feeling of nirvana which I found delightful.

The news was good. General Eisenhower had been appointed Supreme Allied Commander for the Second Front which was to be established not later than the early summer of 1944. We had sunk the *Scharnhorst*. The Russians had taken Zhitomir. The Old Year went out to a fierce Edinburgh gale which filled my lonely top floor with eerie melancholy noises so that sleep was impossible. After listening-in to Goebbels's hysterical boast that the German fortress of Europe was impregnable and that Germany had a secret weapon which would soon force the Allies to sue for peace, I read Gerrarte's *Medieval Moscow* all night. My mind was at rest. The gale blew from the West. It would carry us to victory.

My progress was not, of course, so rapid as I expected, for eczema in all its various forms is a puzzling affliction whose cause and cure have long baffled the medical profession. More working days were lost by it during the war than by any other illness, but, although it is so wide-spread, the means of dealing with it properly in our hospitals are hopelessly inadequate. Until 1946, when, thanks to the generosity of Sir Robert Grant, Edinburgh took the lead, there was no chair of dermatology in any university in the United Kingdom. It is a sad story of neglect of which the working man is the chief victim. I was more fortunate than many, and gradually after the New Year my zest for life returned. Throughout the war I had hardly moved out-side official circles. My own department was a microcosm of its own and lived solely for the war. In it was represented every shade of political opinion from the leftest of Socialists to the fiercest of Tories. I had enthusiasts who carried their belief in the freedom of the Press to such an extent that they wished to give the *Daily Worker* to the German prisoners of war. I had a hard-bitten Tory who was deter-mined to ban even the works of Thomas Mann. The main tendency, however, was to the Left, and eagerness to raise the banner of revolu-tion in Europe was widespread. Here in the infirmary I was in another world where people had little time to discuss strategy or even to think much about the war. The cases were their main concern and their main topic of conversation. Their chief interest in Mr. Churchill was his health. The pessimists among the nurses doubted whether even with M and B a man of his age could survive further attacks of pneumonia. The optimists, whose faith in their doctors was sublime, expressed complete confidence. All were strongly pro-Churchill for the war, although some questioned his ability to see the country through the changes which everyone assumed would come after victory.

The nurses came from all over Scotland and even England. One of my night nurses, an artist with the hypodermic needle, for I never felt even a twinge, came from Skye. Another was a farmer's daughter. Two of my day nurses were daughters of naval captains. With its world-wide reputation for efficiency the infirmary was a great magnet as a training establishment and, as soon as they had passed their examination, most of the younger girls left in order to join the hospital staffs of the fighting services.

Not all of them liked Edinburgh which, virtually untouched throughout the war, had become a leave city for American, Norwegian, Polish and Dominion troops. Drunkenness, rowdiness, and immorality were unbridled, and on Saturday nights an unescorted girl avoided Princes Street. In the infirmary itself I had a side-light of this aspect of Edinburgh life. From my window I could look down on the out-patients assembling for treatment in the venereal disease ward. Many of them looked like children. I asked the doctors if they were as young as they looked. The answer was yes. Many of the girls were under sixteen. Their fathers were away at the war; their mothers were in factories. The street had always been their playground. To girls who had never had a ten-shilling note in their hands the pounds which the American soldiers distributed freely were an irresistible magnet. Bare legs were now clad in silk stockings, and where one girl had found a new world of easy wealth hundreds followed. The process of demoralisation was rapid. I am not easily shocked, but I confess that, when I was able to go about, war-time Edinburgh opened even my eyes. The doctors—whether rightly or not I do not know—attributed much of the venereal disease to the Poles. But the Poles were not rowdy. They pursued women relentlessly but they treated them with the courtesy of old-world cavaliers, and their successes were many. I could see that when the Scottish men came back from the war there would be trouble. The real disturbers of a once staid Edinburgh were the Americans who made themselves unpopular. Loaded with money, they thought nothing of paying five and six pounds for a bottle of whisky, cleaned out the taverns of their scanty stocks, and left nothing for the unfortunate Scottish soldiers who could not compete financially. They drank by day and by night with apparently no other object than to get drunk as quickly as possible.

To do them justice it was not their fault. Mistakenly in my opinion, the American Red Cross had insisted from the beginning that they—and they only—must be responsible for the entertainment of the American soldiers on leave. A complete damper was therefore set on all Scottish efforts to look after them. On their arrival they dutifully spent two days in being piloted round the Castle, Holyrood, St. Giles and Roslin Chapel. Then, bored with too much culture, they sought their own entertainment in the only places that they could find it—in the streets and in the public-houses. The results were perhaps unfortunate for both Scots and Americans.

In the King Street nursing-home I had heard a good deal of this Saturday-night rowdiness. In my aerie in the baronial infirmary I was remote from all noise, and during my long rest my mind had undergone a complete spiritual regeneration. I was now able to read with enjoyment, and I read voraciously. Indeed, my reading list for the first six weeks of 1944 was the fullest that I could show for many years. It included three books of the *Odyssey,* the first six books of the *Aeneid,* part one of *Faust,* Krupskaia's *Memories of Lenin,* Macaulay's *History of England,* two volumes of Gibbon, Mackie's *History of Scotland,* Paleologue's *Les Précurseurs de Lenine,* and Padover's *Life of Jefferson.* Thinking that the war had destroyed my once good memory, I tested it by learning by heart reams of poetry including Russian and French and found that with practice I could memorise and retain what I had learnt as easily as ever.

To pass my time usefully, I engaged a Russian and a Czech to spend an hour in conversation with me on alternate days. Both were women. The Russian, a middle-aged Jewess, whose elder son was a naval constructor in the Royal Navy and the younger a scholar at a well-known English public school, slaved for her two boys. She was extremely intelligent, had been a Trotskist, but was now all or nearly all for Stalin whom, however, she criticised for his faking of history and his suppression of the great part that Trotsky had played in the creation of the Red Army. She was pro-British, was grateful for the shelter which she had received as an exile, but was—I think genuinely—shocked by the contrasts between poverty and wealth in Britain. She was obsessed by the belief that, whereas in Russia there was cruelty and suppression but no corruption, in Britain everything that was needed by the poor—a house, food, clothes, extra milk—could be obtained by bribery. My Czechoslovak lady—she was a Slovak—was more phlegmatic and less vehement, but she, too, regarded Britain as a country where the rich enjoyed privileges

K

unknown in any other European country and said that Masaryk's Czechoslovakia would have been ashamed of our slums.

I enjoyed these conversations. In Whitehall long hours and masses of paper shut me off to a large extent from normal intercourse. I wondered how much the senior officials in Whitehall knew what was being said and thought behind that stolid English exterior of national unity. Not very much I concluded, and the ministers perhaps knew even less.

In Edinburgh I felt the presence of a dying civilisation. In my lifetime it has never been a capital as Dublin is and always has been. The stones of a great city remained; the men who had raised it were gone. For some years now Princes Street had struck me as a kind of corridor-queue full of healthy young men with old-school-tie scarves round their necks and solid brogues on their feet and of even healthier women dressed in sturdier fashion, hurrying in the direction either of Waverley or of the Caledonian Station and bent with equal zest on business or on sport.

In forty years the street, which had once been the pride of Scotland and the envy of all foreigners, had vulgarised itself almost beyond recognition. Where once had stood solid Scottish shops were now glaring cinemas and the multiple stores of the foreign invaders—Woolworths, Boots, Montague Burton and The Fifty Shilling Tailor. Edinburgh and Scotland itself had become provincialised. A nation was losing its individuality and its virtues. If there were any possibility of a golden era of internationalism, of one race absorbing all races, it was perhaps a good thing that the Scots should be the first to sink their individuality, and lose their national virtues. But there was no sign of such a Utopia coming. Indeed, in a world from which all tenderness had departed there were fewer signs of idealism than after the first world war. What seemed to me obvious was that without a national revival Scotland was doomed beyond salvation.

By the end of January I had improved so much that Dr. Percival pronounced me convalescent. I could return to work in three weeks provided, as before, that I could stand the test of walking. On this occasion, however, he put a veto on any trip to the Highlands or, indeed, anywhere on my own. I was to spend my convalescence in the infirmary where I could be under constant inspection.

The three weeks were spent most pleasantly. The weather was reasonably clement and sunny for an Edinburgh February. I went out every day for a walk or a drive with my doctor, Fraser Lee. I saw my friends, bought books, visited the picture exhibitions and in a fit of extravagant exuberance bought the original of Russell Flint's famous water-colour of Saint Malo. On Sunday, February 6, I had a close-up view of General Montgomery whom I had never met or even seen. He was walking along Princes Street, his face blue with cold, for an icy wind was blowing, and a crowd was already gathering at his heels. It was his first visit to Edinburgh, and the manner of it was, as one might expect, highly dramatic. No one— except perhaps Sir William Darling, the Lord Provost, who may have been in the secret—had expected him. For all Edinburgh and the rest of the world knew, the General was on his way further North on a tour of inspection. He had stepped off at Waverley Station on the Sunday morning, and the first that Edinburgh folk saw of him was when, dressed in battle-dress, he walked into St. Giles in the middle of the service. Later in the day he made a little speech which gave him the headlines in Monday's *Scotsman*. It was a double-edged tribute to the Edinburgh weather. "In these parts", he said, "you either die early or live for ever." It hit exactly the right note with the people of Edinburgh.

Whatever his views of official propaganda were—and he had not been over-kind to our front-line propaganda unit in Italy, the General certainly understood the art. Like everything else connected even vaguely with soldiering, he had studied it. Indeed his brother, who was at one period a War Office liaison officer with P.W.E., once told me that "Monty" did not like making speeches or indulging in propaganda but that, remembering how generals had been rough-handled by the politicians in the first world war, he was determined to play the politicians at their own game and keep his own end up with the public. His speeches and his touches of personal propaganda were made for that purpose.

My outings were both a physical and a spiritual tonic. It was pleasant to walk up Castle Street and gaze at the window of No. 39 where the young night-bucks of Edinburgh had watched the moving hand of Sir Walter Scott as he wrote all night in order to pay his debts; very pleasant to pass by Fettes and Inverleith and to recall the days at the beginning of the century when Scotland led the world in Rugby football and my Fettes contemporaries contributed a third and more to the Cambridge and Scottish Fifteens; pleasanter still to drive out to the Forth Bridge, see the *Nelson* and other great battleships lying in the anchorage, and look across the Firth to the Highland hills clearly visible in the rarified atmosphere of a clear and cold February morning; pleasantest of all, perhaps, to ascend Arthur's Seat and look across the huddle of grey stone houses and church steeples that were the real Edinburgh until weaker men and acquisitive builders scattered, helter-skelter and haphazard as if in a drunken orgy, the ring of gaudy and offensive stucco and brick which has made an eyesore of a once beautiful city, and then, having looked, to turn to the glorious, broad estuary with the fair and fertile fields and woods of East Lothian stretching to Berwick and the Bass Rock, and to wonder wistfully how many thousands of Scots had been driven from this cold city by persecution and intolerance to give to the building of Canada and New Zealand the brains and energy which could have made a new Scotland.

In the years before the war, when I was living in Scotland, it had seemed to me that the old religious intolerance which had rent the country was gone and that Scotland had become a godless country. I was wrong.

There might be fewer people in the churches, but the old flames of religious intolerance were banked, not extinguished. They flared again during my illness, when the Lord Provost dared to attend officially the Pontifical Mass at St. Patrick's, Edinburgh, for the Allied forces. High representatives of the British fighting services attended this Mass as an official mark of respect for the Poles and other Catholic Allies who had fought so gallantly. Was the Lord Provost of Edinburgh to refuse to go? He went, but the Evangelicals did everything to make his life miserable. They protested, forced a motion in the Town Council and were heavily defeated. Still rampant they made a demonstration on the actual day, and they published in the *Scotsman* an advertisement, so violent in language, that I doubt if any London newspaper would have printed it.

It was an extraordinary manifestation, but it was supported, I think, by only a tiny minority. The bulk of the people seemed apathetic. Indeed, except among the big business and financial men whose interests were more and more tied to London, apathy seemed to have settled like a dry-rot on the masses who, worse housed than any people in Europe, seemed to have lost their former energy and pride of independence. It struck me more forcibly than ever that without a national revival Scotland was doomed beyond recovery. My conscience pricked me. For some years before the war I had always been planning to return to Scotland for good. But when the chances came I had always hesitated to take the risk and had said to myself that I must wait a little longer to ensure my financial independence. Doubtless, there were many voluntary Scottish exiles who used the same argument.

To seek consolation, I went to see Tom Johnston, then at the height of his glory as the most popular Secretary of State that Scotland had ever known. I had seen him from time to time during the war. Soon after I had become Director-General of P.W.E., he sent for me, and we had a long discussion. Later, he had invited me to come to Edinburgh to give to the Scottish editors and members of his department one of those off-the-record talks which he had instituted with great success. He was one of those rare men who by their complete integrity and natural charm of manner command respect and affection at the first contact. A life-long Socialist, he had held, in his early days as founder and editor of *Forward,* views which were then regarded as extreme. A keen student of history, he had written a classic on the working-classes of Scotland and an amusing and somewhat scurrilous account of the origins and back-slidings of the Scottish nobility. He had begun the war as Regional Commissioner for Scotland under an English Secretary of State! Then had come the change of Government, and Mr. Churchill had offered him the post of Secretary of State. Tom—for he is Tom to all Scotland—had refused, pleading that he was tired and wished to write history. Mr. Churchill had retorted: "Come to London and *make* history with me." And Tom had gone.

He had been a success from the word go. Experience of office and the distressful state of Scotland had matured his judgment. He was a Scot before he was a Socialist, and he had now reached the stage when a Scottish judge or industrialist who was interested in the future of Scotland meant more to him than a Labour colleague who wasn't. In Edinburgh he had assembled round him a Council of State of all the former Secretaries of State and a Council of Industry in which capital and labour sat side by side in an effort to work out their problems. He was determined to regenerate Scottish industry and to stop the trend to the South of England which between the wars had nearly ruined Scotland. He was, he told me, finished with Whitehall and the House of Commons. He was sick of Party politics. He would devote what remained of his life to the revival of Scotland. His vigour was amazing for a man who throughout the war had spent the middle of the week in London and the rest of it in St. Andrew's House in Edinburgh. Virtually a teetotaller and a non-smoker, he had no priggishness about him, and his conversation was embroidered with a rich and sometimes pungent Doric. He had a great admiration and emotional affection for Mr. Churchill and said bluntly that, as far as the war was concerned, he was worth the rest of the Cabinet put together. No other man could handle the House of Commons or, indeed, men generally with such superb craftsmanship as the Prime Minister.

He gave me a personal illustration of Mr. Churchill's handling of ministers. Tom had had a dispute with Mr. Herbert Morrison about the rights of the Minister of Home Security to interfere in Scottish matters without reference to the Secretary of State. They had been unable to agree and in the end had taken their problem to the Prime Minister who had listened in silence while each man made his case. Mr. Churchill had then delivered a judgment of Solomon and had given each man about fifty per cent. of what he wanted. He had then read them a gentle lecture, expressing the hope that they would be firm friends in future and that he would hear no more of this trouble. The Cabinet must row together. There must be no rocking of the boat. London must set the example to the rest of the country.

Mr. Morrison, who is a Cockney Scot, had then had a crack at Tom. "Do you know, Prime Minister, what building in London Tom likes best—Euston Station, because it takes him out of the place." Mr. Johnston, a tough fighter for all his gentle manner, had bristled. But Mr. Churchill at once poured balm in the wound. "I share Mr. Lloyd George's views about Scots," he said quickly. "They've only one fault, there are too few of them."

Tom was delighted. As he told me the story, his eyes glistened. "What other man", he said, "could have put Herbert in his place so beautifully and so tactfully?"

He confessed to me that at this moment he was having some difficulty with Mr. Churchill who could not understand why Tom wished to quit politics. There must be some political reason. Did he want a higher post? Recently Tom had received a hint that the higher post was in the offing. He had retired post-haste to Scotland. He went nominally on urgent business, but he confessed to me that his real reason was fear lest Mr. Churchill should exercise his powers of persuasion on him and that he himself would give in against his will. It was a remarkable tribute to Mr. Churchill's magnetism as a war leader.

Tom's admiration, however, did not bias his judgment of Mr. Churchill's future. He had seen, he told me, many signs that the Prime Minister intended to carry on after the war and to assemble some Labour men round him. Inevitably, Tom said, he would be beaten. If anything was certain as regards the future, it was that Labour would win the next election.

As we said goodbye, Tom said to me warmly and insistently: "Now, mind, you'll come back to Scotland after the war. There's a job for you to do here, and I'll find it for you."

I went away rather sadly like the rich young man in the Bible— not that I had wealth or possessions, but only debts and the necessity of earning my living after six years as a reluctant bureaucrat.

By the middle of February I was in good shape again, my skin having stood up well to more exercise than I had ever been able to take in London. Dr. Percival was pleased, and, subject to the usual precautions about regular hours and adequate rest, reported me fit for duty as from February 22. During the last six weeks my skin had been treated with applications of crude tar. It was the Percival cure. He told me that I had responded to it well. Solemnly I handed him a sheet of paper with a note which I had typed from Macaulay's *History*. It described how Burt, an early traveller to the Highlands had found that the local inhabitants smeared themselves with tar— presumably as a cure for the itch. There was also a verse from Cleland's *Highland Host* which ran:

"The reason is, they're smeared with tar,
    Which doth defend their head and neck,
    Just as it doth their sheep protect."

He read it and laughed. "Your cure is as old as the Highland hills," I said. "Obviously it suits the Macgregor blood in me."

I booked my sleeper, packed my books and belongings and announced my arrival in London for the morning of February 22. The next morning my forefinger was swollen. Sister Toddie diagnosed an incipient whitlow and said that I must postpone my departure for three or four days by which time it would subside or have to be lanced. Three days later Mr. Paterson Brown, one of the infirmary surgeons, lanced it, and I left for London the same evening.

I was met at King's Cross in the first light of a dark February morning by McCoy, my chauffeur—a confirmed pessimist whose face looked longer even than usual.

"My orders are to take you to the Savoy," he said gloomily.

"What on earth for?" I asked testily.

He shrugged his shoulders. "Jerry was over last night. Your room's been smashed to hell."

We drove round to see the damage. It was not quite so lurid as

McCoy had led me to expect but it was bad enough. The room was full of rubble. My books in the open bookcase had suffered, but the wardrobe was intact. There was a wide gap in the wall behind my bed. The mirror had been wrenched off the toilet table and the glass smashed to powder. Lying across the bed itself was the heavy door.

It is an ill whitlow that brings no benefit. Had I been able to travel on my original date, I might have been in another hospital.

CHAPTER SIX

FOR THE FIRST few days after my return to London I felt completely lost. Not only had I to pick up all the threads of my work after a long absence; I had also to settle the immediate problem of my own future. Dr. Percival, alarmed by my early breakdown after my first illness, had written a strong letter to Mr. Eden and Mr. Bracken and had warned them that, unless I led a regular life and had plenty of fresh air, I should break down again. The human and warm-hearted Mr. Bracken, whom I saw first, had taken this letter seriously and had a plan for me. It was that Mr. Eden should make me ambassador to one of the Allied Governments in London and that I should remain as policy adviser with P.W.E.

"I have discussed this proposal with Anthony," Mr. Bracken said, "and he is in favour of it. You can have Czechoslovakia if you like."

I thought the matter over for twenty-four hours. On various occasions Mr. Eden had told me that he would like me to stay on after the war and had asked me what I wanted. But I had never committed myself. In truth I had thought very little about my future. When I did think, my reactions were strongly against a bureaucratic existence. To succeed, the modern civil servant has to be not only civil but servile, and a masterly inactivity is a surer road to promotion and to a high pension than action. I did not even consider a return to the Czechoslovaks. Phil Nichols, who had been appointed Ambassador in 1941, was a much younger man. He was doing excellent work, and I knew that he had already won the confidence of both President Beneš and Jan Masaryk. It was infinitely better for the Czechoslovaks to have a career diplomatist as Ambassador than an outsider like myself who was probably regarded by most of the Foreign Office as a biased supporter. On one thing I was determined. Advisers were the dogs-bodies of everyone and the masters of none. I was grateful to Mr. Bracken, but rather than take on such a job I should go out altogether.

I then discussed the proposal with Mr. Eden. Certainly I could have an Embassy. I might have to wait a little. He did not like the idea of an adviser for P.W.E. and expressed concern about my successor if I were unable to carry on. We were approaching the critical stage of the war. He must have someone who knew the work and on whose judgment he could rely. Where at this stage of the war were we to find the man? I told him that I was fit enough to continue—at any rate until the Second Front had been established.

Back I went to Mr. Bracken who suggested that I should get a second medical opinion from a prominent physician. I saw Lord Moran, whom I had known off and on for many years. I told him that there was no use in my trying to row a half-stroke in a boat like P.W.E. He was kind and sensible. He held out no promises but said that, given reasonable regularity, I could take what was in war-time a legitimate risk. I therefore decided to carry on.

In the end I was given Mr. Kirkpatrick as an extra Deputy Director-General and was instructed to get myself a house in the country. The house was not easy to get, and four months passed before I found an old-world cottage near Radlett, exactly half-way between Bush House and our secret establishment at Woburn.

The acquisition of Mr. Kirkpatrick was an immense advantage. Quick, decisive, and thoroughly experienced, he had no fears of responsibility and he took many burdens off my shoulders. He was succeeded in the European Service of the B.B.C. by Mr. J. B. Clark who combined great knowledge of all broadcasting technicalities with high principles, a good mind, and a natural capacity for straight dealing which made him a most useful and pleasant colleague.

P.W.E. was now better staffed than at any previous period during the war. There were, however, many new problems which required solving. The most important were (1) our propaganda to the Balkans; (2) our co-operation in political warfare with the Russians, and (3) our preparations for the Second Front or D-day, as it was now called.

The fluctuating situation in the Balkans was a perpetual source of trouble to our propaganda on account of the conflicting policies or rather series of improvisations devised, not by the Foreign Office, but by the Prime Minister and the Chiefs of Staff who, at a time when Britain was being sorely pressed, decided to support and arm any group or groups in the Balkans which were prepared to fight the Germans. As a result of this policy British agents had supplied money, material and arms to both Mihailovic and Tito in Yugoslavia and to E.L.A.S. and to E.L.I.N. in Greece. In both countries the rival groups held widely divergent political views and contained all the elements which make for civil war. The policy could be justified, if at all, only by military necessity and by quick results. We had tried a similar policy in Russia in 1918 when we had a mission with all the rival groups in the civil war. Trotsky had described it as the throw of

a desperate gambler who by putting a chip on every number hopes to win. The results had been disastrous. We had lost all our friends.

At this moment the situation in Greece and Yugoslavia was entering into a similar phase. In each country two national groups were waging guerilla warfare against the Germans, and just how effective this resistance was has never been accurately established. Inevitably the British missions with the two groups supported their own man with enthusiastic zeal, for in troubled times every individual leader must possess personal magnetism. Otherwise, he would command no following. What is clear today, and should have been clear from the beginning, is that long before the war was over civil war was in progress in both Yugoslavia and Greece. And when civil war starts foreign enemies and, indeed, all other considerations are relegated to a secondary background.

In March of 1944 the Prime Minister had already decided that Tito was the stronger man, and was now trying to create Yugoslav unity by promising full recognition to a Tito Government provided that the Communist leader accepted King Peter. The clearest proof that Tito was already master of the situation was his refusal of the Prime Minister's offer. In Greece the situation was not so far advanced, but here we were already beginning to curtail support of the Communist-dominated E.L.A.S. and to attempt to create a democratic Central Government half-way between the Right and Left extremists.

Not unnaturally the propagandists in P.W.E. did not know where they were. The McLean Mission with Tito, of which Major Randolph Churchill was a member, criticised us constantly for our failure to supply more propaganda in favour of the Partisans. Mihailovic supporters in England accused us not only of supporting Communism but of being Communist-minded.

On the whole the rank and file in the Yugoslav and Greek sections of both P.W.E. and the European Service of the B.B.C. were Left in sympathy, and this was particularly true of the Greeks and Yugoslavs whom we employed. There was, too, a general tendency both in P.W.E. and in the European Service of the B.B.C. to believe that propaganda had an important contribution to make to victory by raising revolution in the occupied countries. The revolution which the British officials envisaged was a pale-pink affair of the British Socialist type. They did not realise or were unwilling to admit that, with the possible exception of Czechoslovakia, the prospects of establishing anything like a British Labour democracy in any of the

Central and South-Eastern European countries were so remote as to be hopeless. Their instinct told them that Europe was going Left. They saw no reason why it should not go the British way.

The Foreign Office took a more cautious view, and during this period Foreign Office policy guidance consisted mainly of a series of don'ts, and, until we intervened actively in Greece, our propaganda to the Balkans was confined almost entirely to straight news. It was a period of irritating frustration, for German propaganda to Britain was now taking the line that we were losing and had, indeed, already lost Europe to Russia.

Nor had we made any progress in our efforts to establish co-ordination with the Russians. Sir Archibald Clark Kerr had raised the matter several times in Moscow, but had received no answer. When it comes to "stalling", the Russian bureaucracy has no equal in any country. With the object of forcing a decision Sir Orme Sargent asked Mr. Phil Hamblet, the permanent London representative of O.W.I., and myself to luncheon in order to discuss the whole matter with M. Sobolev, the able Counsellor of the Russian Embassy. There had been, Sargent told me, a glimmer of hope from Moscow. M. Sobolev had been instructed by the Kremlin to supply further information about P.W.E. and O.W.I. We told him quite frankly how Anglo-American co-operation in propaganda worked, emphasised its smoothness, and offered him places for the Russians not only at our weekly Anglo-American policy meetings but also on the London Propaganda Committee. M. Sobolev seemed co-operative. My feeling was that, whether or not we ever had genuine co-operation, the Russians would take advantage of this opportunity to appoint officials to both Committees if only in order to act as observers and reporters to their own Government. My instinct was correct, but four months were to pass before the Russians took their decision.

We all liked M. Sobolev. He talked freely and was eloquent on the achievements of Russia during the last twenty-five years. In the first world war, he said, the Russians could not handle machinery. They were a race of peasants who were still using the most primitive forms of agricultural implements. Stalin had made them tractor-minded and the process from being tractor-minded to being tank-minded was quick and natural. The Russian successes, however, could never have been achieved without the parallel conversion of an illiterate people into a literate people during the same period. In 1911 seventy-seven per cent. of the Russians were illiterates. Today the

figures were exactly reversed, and for the first time the people were discovering Russia's past history and Russian traditions with the keenness and enthusiasm of discoverers. Moreover, they were reading with zest and appreciation all the Anglo-American classics. I asked him who were the most popular Anglo-American authors. Without hesitation he put Jack London a long way first, followed by Dickens and Mark Twain!

Franker and more direct in method than M. Maisky and more forthright than the silent and enigmatic M. Gusev, M. Sobolev struck me as the ablest Soviet diplomat that I had yet met. His knowledge of industrial matters was not just theoretical. M. Gusev had served his apprenticeship to diplomacy in the Ogpu. M. Sobolev was translated from the management of an industrial plant in Leningrad to a high position in the Russian Foreign Office. I was not surprised when at the end of the war he was elevated to the post of political adviser to General Zhukov and, later to that of Deputy Secretary-General of the United Nations organisation.

These Balkan and Slav problems, however, were of secondary importance compared with our tasks in connexion with the invasion of Europe. General Eisenhower had arrived in England in January, and his appointment as Supreme Commander of the Allied Expeditionary Force had been made public at once. On March 5, he had established his headquarters at Widewing, a well-camouflaged, walled-in camp near Kingston-on-Thames, with strongly built brick buildings inside and the outward appearance of a great green mound. Preparations for D-day, which was then fixed for the beginning of May, were already in active progress. In broad outline the preparations had to cover two separate stages: (1) continuous aerial bombardment of German transport and lines of communication in France which would soften the way for the invading Allied armies and (2) the actual invasion itself. P.W.E. had an important part to play in explaining the aerial bombardment to the French people as a whole and, more particularly, to the French inhabitants in the target area.

P.W.E's problems were now complicated by the fact that General Eisenhower's Psychological Warfare unit was in London. It had now changed its name from Psychological Warfare Branch to Psychological Warfare Division and was now known as P.W.D. When it was in Algiers, co-ordination with P.W.E. and O.W.I., London, which were the parent civil agencies, had worked comparatively smoothly. Algiers had accepted London's guidance in policy, but, within the framework of that policy, had inevitably and, indeed,

quite properly acquired a considerable degree of independence. Now that P.W.D. was temporarily established in London, a delicate situation had arisen regarding responsibility for the planning of the political warfare campaign. In addition to their undisputed right to control policy, P.W.E. and O.W.I. not only paid the salaries of their representatives in P.W.D., but were financially responsible for all equipment, printing, supplies and other expenses. Moreover, neither Mr. Churchill nor President Roosevelt ever tolerated any interference by the military in matters which in any way impinged on policy, and intervened forcibly whenever such attempts came to their notice.

The position of P.W.E. and O.W.I. was, therefore, strong. But in order to avoid any possibility of misunderstanding, Bob Sherwood and I went out to Widewing to see Bedell Smith who had invited us to luncheon. He did not look quite so fit as when I had first met him in the autumn of 1942, but he was as quick, as decisive and as pleasantly tough as ever. Like all great soldiers he was so completely master of his time that he always seemed to have minutes to spare for everyone. We were asked to luncheon at 1 p.m. and on the stroke of one we were at our seats in the senior officers' mess. To me it was a wonderful meal: with a juicy beefsteak of pre-war size and fried potatoes. Bedell Smith himself had a cup of soup and a sandwich. He was in very good form, told me that he had been in Scotland on an inspection, had stolen one day off in order to fish the late Ivan Cobbold's water on the Dee, and had caught his first salmon. Turning to more serious matters, he criticised with his usual frankness the scheme for a three or four zone occupation of Germany which was then being worked out by the European Advisory Committee. It would lead, he said, to certain trouble. Unless there were a joint Anglo-American zone the Russians would play the British off against the Americans and vice versa, and the Germans would play all three off against each other. Events were to justify nearly everything he said.

After our meal he took me into his office, a large well-lit room with a table, on which stood photographs of the chief Anglo-American commanders and Chiefs of Staff, and a big desk without a single paper on it. We had five or ten minutes of quick and decisive talk about our propaganda problems. Bedell Smith, as keen as General Eisenhower on Anglo-American integration and the complete submergence of separate nationalities, said that we must all work together. I told him briefly that such was my intention. While S.H.A.E.F. (Supreme Headquarters Allied Expeditionary Force)

remained in London, O.W.I., P.W.E. and P.W.D. should co-operate in all planning and preparations. When S.H.A.E.F. moved to France, P.W.E. and O.W.I. should be responsible for policy guidance and, as in North Africa, P.W.D. should conduct their propaganda in conformity with the policy guidance. Bedell Smith agreed at once. "That's right," he said. "This has my backing. If there is any difficulty, if there are any changes you want, come straight to me. The door is always open; you have only to walk in." I felt relieved. Bedell Smith was a man who never said anything that he did not mean.

In the end we established a reasonably satisfactory system of co-ordination by regular Tripartite meetings of P.W.D., O.W.I. and P.W.E. under my chairmanship. It was not perfect. Some of the American military had an inborn mistrust of the "politicos" and would have liked to militarise all propaganda. The civil agencies who, if things went wrong, received all the knocks from their respective Governments, resented any encroachment by the military on purely political matters. But General McClure, the military head of P.W.D., was a model of fairness and square dealing, and the propaganda experts who did the real work were so keen on their job that disagreements were almost invariably over technical and not personal matters.

I have already extolled the success of Anglo-American integration. Nevertheless, it might very easily have gone wrong. Indeed, it depended on a handful of senior officers on both sides, and the chief credit must go to General Eisenhower and the American officers closest to him. One of these U.S. officers was Bob McClure who, with several other senior officers of Eisenhower's staff, had been a cadet with him at West Point. As the military head of P.W.D. who had to deal with the civil agencies, he had a most difficult job. He handled it with rare tact and skill. A business-like professional soldier, he brought to his task not only a generous spirit of compromise but a truly remarkable impartiality. Intrigue was entirely foreign to his nature, and I soon found that I could discuss with him with complete frankness on both sides even the most delicate problems of Anglo-American difficulties. Had we had a different type of American or had McClure himself not been so indissolubly wedded to Eisenhower's policy of integration, serious friction would have been inevitable.

By the beginning of April the Anglo-American bombing of communications in France had reached a high pitch of intensity. It caused deep anxiety both to the Prime Minister and to Mr. Eden who feared that the inevitable loss of French lives would embitter Anglo-French relations for several generations. Their fears were not allayed by a report of the Ministry of Home Security who, basing their calculations on the German bombing of Britain, forecast a high figure for the probable French casualties. P.W.E. were given the two tasks that I have already indicated: (1) to warn the French population on the Western seaboard to evacuate their homes and (2) to explain to the French people generally the necessity for the bombing. In addition, we had to report daily to the Prime Minister and to General Ismay on the reactions of the French public. While, therefore, the senior members of P.W.E. were wrestling with the multifarious problems of preparation for D-day itself, the printing of proclamations and leaflets under Top Secret conditions, the launching of an airborne newspaper for the German troops, and the serious difficulty of procuring extra paper for our increased requirements, my own time was almost wholly taken up by the provision of material for the political aspects of the Anglo-American bombing strategy.

The crisis was acute. The politicians were very properly preoccupied by the long-term consequences of the bombing. The soldiers, intent on the success of the invasion, were insistent on the absolute necessity of what they called the softening process. Everyone knew that the decisive crisis of the war had arrived. No one doubted the outcome, but nerves were jumpy, and with the increasing tempo of the war, co-ordination between the various departments of Whitehall became more difficult. P.W.E's work was now under close scrutiny by the Prime Minister. At first he was not satisfied with our reports and wished to set up a ministerial Committee to deal with the whole problem of French reactions. He had never underrated the hazards of a landing on the open beaches of France, and his fears of the Anglo-American bombing strategy were aggravated by a combined protest of the French and Belgian Cardinals and Bishops. His suggestion of a ministerial Committee was resisted by Mr. Eden and Mr. Bracken who, however, increased their pressure on P.W.E. Moreover, Dr. Goebbels made full use of the opportunities offered to him by the crisis, and in his propaganda to France he concentrated all his efforts on emphasising the cynical indifference of the British Government to French lives. In his broadcasts to England he took the line that Germany welcomed the Allied invasion of Europe. It would give the German army the eagerly sought opportunity of bringing the war to a speedy end.

Subjected to constant cross-fire from high quarters I had a harassing time. Fortunately our task was eased by Air Marshal Tedder who as Deputy Supreme Commander was responsible for the strategic plan of the Allied Air Forces. On him therefore fell the whole burden of defending the bombing policy. Far more interested in propaganda than most commanders, he naturally followed very closely our work at this particular moment. I had never met him until one day I was pulled out of a conference to answer the telephone and heard a voice say: "Tedder speaking. I've wanted to see you for a long time." I replied that I had not liked to worry him, but that I had, in fact, arranged for Mr. Eden to ask him to luncheon.

"That's all right," said Tedder, "but let's start on a lower level and begin now." I was asked to meet him that day at the Athenaeum at 12.45 p.m.

I arrived five minutes before my time and sat down in the hall to watch the elderly bishops, scientists and retired civil servants creeping in for the early luncheon which in war-time brought the only good food. At the appointed minute a young, athletic figure burst through the door, threw off his heavy Air Force overcoat, and shook hands. It was a wonderful sight to see him arrive in the gloomy Athenaeum hall with its dark and rather dirty portraits of Huxley, Darwin and Matthew Arnold.

He kept me till 2.30, and we covered every aspect of the bombing crisis. He asked me what line we were taking in our next report to the Prime Minister. I told him that our line was that French reactions would not be bad provided that big casualties were avoided and that the time-lag until D-day, which had now been deferred until June, was not too long. He agreed, insisted that the bombing was essential to the success of the landings, and complained bitterly that no agreement had yet been reached and that even now plans might be altered by the politicians when no time was left. He made a vigorous criticism of the so-called experts who were advising the Prime Minister and who, he said, had no practical experience of bombing and did not understand the problem. He gave the highest praise to General Eisenhower who, he said, had done a wonderful job in establishing the most successful and harmonious integration of the Anglo-American forces. In North Africa they had been a very happy team. They were not so happy in London where they were too close to the politicians and to the bureaucracy. He had a poor opinion of Whitehall where the machine was far too big and encouraged the shelving of responsibility and the suppression of talent and wasted hours of time in over-planning and in the postponement of decisions. There were far too many old men in the service departments.

"I am fifty myself and I'm too old," he said. Then he added rather bitterly: "In the Mediterranean we had nothing and did everything; here we have everything and can get nothing done."

He asked me if I had any troubles, and I told him of the difficulties of triangular co-ordination with two civil propaganda agencies in London and a military propaganda organisation which would eventually be in France and which, although composed mainly of members of O.W.I. and P.W.E., was controlled by a S.H.A.E.F. general. He told me not to make heavy weather about P.W.D. but to come straight to him with my problems or suggestions.

"I can settle these matters easily," he said pleasantly. "After all, that is one of the very few advantages that I enjoy as Deputy Supreme Commander."

I went away greatly relieved. There was no nonsense and no narrowness about this lean spare vigorous man who for all his fifty years looked almost absurdly young for his job.

The next day, in the presence of Sir Orme Sargent, Mr. Oliver Harvey and Mr. Harold Mack of the Foreign Office, I had a useful talk with M. Louis Marin, the veteran French statesman and the Conservative member of the resistance Council, who had just been safely smuggled over to Britain for consultation. His news and views were encouraging. For the moment at least, the resistance groups were united, from the extreme Right to the Communists, in their determination to expel the Germans. All France listened to our broadcasts in French and to nothing else. Naturally the French people who were being bombed did not like our bombing, but the country as a whole understood and accepted it, regarding it as a prelude to invasion and to the liberation of France. Provided that this assumption was correct and that the invasion did not come too late, Frenchmen could and would "take it". He told a good story of the help given to the activists by the Vichy gendarmes who had facilitated his own escape. A gendarme would be sent to his own village to interrogate a suspected member of the resistance. He would say to him: "Well, my friend, what do you think of the Germans and our Laval?"

The suspect would reply cautiously: "Much the same as you do, I expect."

"H'm," the gendarme would say, "Then in that case I really ought to arrest you."

I embodied M. Marin's views in our next report on French

reactions to our bombing, and hoped for the best. It came quickly. President Roosevelt was a firm supporter of the bombing policy and gave his full backing to the soldiers. In the end the Prime Minister and Mr. Eden were satisfied. The bombing, which, in fact, had never stopped, continued with ever greater intensity. It was helped by the good weather which we enjoyed that spring. Its effect was prodigious. Its accuracy was such that the cost in French lives was infinitely less than the Home Security experts had predicted.

By the end of May, P.W.E. had finished its preparations. It had, indeed, over-planned, not entirely through its own fault, for the amendments and alterations by other departments had never ceased. Now all was ready, and I hoped for a quiet week before D-day which was now fixed for the early hours of June 5.

My hopes were illusory. On May 31, I was involved in a ministerial storm which would never have arisen but for the D-day tension which was now telling on everyone. P.W.D. had prepared a broadcast for General Eisenhower to deliver to Germany and had sent a copy to me. As it touched on political matters, I had no other course but to submit it to the Foreign Office who, in turn, put it up to the Cabinet. The Prime Minister had been annoyed and had written to General Bedell Smith to complain of interference by the military in political matters, and Bedell Smith had vented his wrath on General McClure, the head of P.W.D., for having provoked the Prime Minister "to put his thumb up my nose". Unfortunately, too, the proposed broadcast had been prepared by a British member of P.W.D., and the Foreign Office took this opportunity to submit a paper to the War Cabinet suggesting that special machinery should be set up to control S.H.A.E.F. broadcasts. In the stress of the moment Mr. Eden signed it. P.W.E., in whom this control was already vested, was not consulted. Worse still, Mr. Bracken, who was responsible to Parliament for all broadcasting problems, knew nothing about the paper until he saw it in the Cabinet. He was angry and was determined to submit a counter-paper. I spent the next four days in trying to heal the breach. Mr. Eden, whose department had sinned grievously, was ready to apologise, but Mr. Bracken was sore and, when I tried to make peace, denounced me as a door-mat and a lackey of the Foreign Office. It had treated me disgracefully. What was the use of my being a Deputy Under-Secretary if I were not consulted on a matter which was my direct concern?

I was miserable. All my sympathies were with Mr. Bracken. He had been treated badly, but Mr. Eden had admitted the blunder and had, in fact, already washed the heads of the offending Foreign Office officials, and I felt that with D-day at hand the dispute should be ended. On the Monday morning of June 5 it had not been ended.

Help came from an unexpected quarter and in a highly dramatic manner. The weather was stormy, and on the Sunday night General Eisenhower had postponed D-day for twenty-four hours. That day General de Gaulle had been flown to England from Algiers in a special aeroplane provided by the Prime Minister. His arrival was to provoke a storm to which the Eden-Bracken squabble was a tea-cup affair. He had gone down to the camouflaged train in Hampshire which was General Eisenhower's temporary headquarters. There he met the Prime Minister, had been taken into all the secrets of the invasion and had been shown the texts of the various proclamations. There was no mention of him in the American texts. He was furious.

The real excitement began on the Monday evening. On the Sunday I had taken a room at the Savoy Hotel for several days in order to be near Bush House. For rather far-fetched reasons of security, for the Savoy staff had known me for the best part of twenty years, Dallas Brooks had insisted on booking the room, not in my name but in that of our assistant administrative officer, Mrs. Deacon. I had had a last meeting at Bush House at 10 p.m. when I had taken all our Regional directors into full confidence.

As the release of the news and of the official proclamations was not to be made until 10 a.m. the next morning, I went back to the Savoy with Brooks and Jack Wheeler-Bennett, who was now our liaison officer with Charles Peake, the Foreign Office political adviser to S.H.A.E.F. I gave them a drink, sent them off home, and was just preparing to go to bed when I was called back to Bush House to sign some directives. All was well, except for the absence of any script from General de Gaulle whose broadcast we were supposed to release with the other Allied declarations the next morning. The P.W.E. official in charge, who had worked like a hero and, indeed, had done most of the planning, was worried. I telephoned to Mr. Eden. He had no news for me. De Gaulle was being difficult. He would let me know more in half an hour or so. He told me that all was well now between Mr. Bracken and himself. As he sounded quite cheerful, I was not unduly worried. There was, however, no question now of going to bed, so with my colleague I walked down to Inveresk House, almost next door to us, to see our O.W.I. friends, telling our telephone operators to put me through on the direct line if there were any messages. We found Phil Hamblet, George Backer and

Bob Sherwood seated in Sherwood's office. It was their first experience of handling the propaganda side of a big operation, and they were determined not to miss one minute of it. As Hamblet said, Bob's play *And There Shall be No Night* was running only a few doors up the street. We might as well take the sign down and put it up over Inveresk House. It was now 12.30 a.m. There was no message from Mr. Eden.

At last at three in the morning I was called to the telephone. It was Mr. Eden.

"Where on earth have you been?" he said. "We've been trying to get you for ages? Have you been on a binge?"

I felt righteously indignant. "No, Sir. I am at my office. Where else should I be on the eve of D-day?"

"Oh," he replied, "Charles Peake swore you were staying at the Savoy, but they insisted that you were not, until Peake asked for the manager and was at last told that you must be the gentleman registered as Mrs. Deacon!"

Then he got down to business. There had been a great rumpus between de Gaulle and the Prime Minister. Matters had nearly reached breaking point. At last the General had agreed to broadcast. It was now too late for him to speak at the same time as the other Allied leaders. He had better speak during the day. Charles Peake was with him at the Connaught Hotel. I had better ring him up there and arrange the final details.

"Is that all clear now?" Mr. Eden asked.

I replied: "Shall we take the risk of announcing at 10 a.m., when approximately the other official releases will be made, that de Gaulle will speak during the day. If we don't, the omission may cause some stir in France."

"How big is the risk?"

"You know better than I do, Sir," I said. "You have been with him."

"Well," said Mr. Eden, "we've had a crazy night, but you had better go ahead."

I rang up Charles Peake and asked him to arrange a time for the General's broadcast. The General was in the room and finally agreed to record at Bush House at 12.30 p.m. the next day.

Back we went to Bush House, collected our French team, and prepared a statement about de Gaulle's broadcast. I also rang up General McClure and told him that de Gaulle had at last consented to speak on the air. Bob McClure, who had gone to bed, was not amused.

"I never want to hear his name again," he said wearily and turned over to sleep again.

I was just about to follow his example when suddenly I realised that I had made a gaffe. Surely, after all that had happened, the script would have to be approved. I had forgotten to ask Mr. Eden by whom.

I rang up the Foreign Office. There was no answer from Mr. Eden's flat. I rang up No. 10 Downing Street. Mr. Eden was not there. In despair I rang up the Resident Clerk at the Foreign Office who woke up Mrs. Eden who, in turn, roused her husband.

I told him my trouble and said that the Americans would be satisfied if either Mr. Churchill or he himself approved the script. I apologised for pulling him out of bed.

"You did rightly," he said. "Of course the script must be vetted. The Foreign Office must do it. I'll arrange for it first thing in the morning."

Although it was now after 4 in the morning, there was not a trace of irritation in his voice.

We had some tea in the office and shortly before 5 a.m. I was ready to go to bed. Rain was falling, and dead-beat we sat in silence waiting for it to stop. Soon we heard the massed droning of aeroplanes. We removed the black-out. The rain had stopped. The sky was a delicate sheen of the faintest blue, and high up the cohorts of 'planes pursued their course to France in relentless rows. They looked like silver fish in a tropical sea.

I walked back alone to the Savoy along the empty Strand and, going up to my room on the top floor, I pulled up the blinds and looked out at a dawn which had now become rosy-fingered. The view down the river was superb. Moreover, the waters of the Thames were unruffled. The wind, which had caused one postponement and very nearly a second, had dropped. All, I prayed, would now be well.

I was in bed by 6 a.m. and went to sleep at once. At 7 I was awakened by the telephone ringing in my ear. It was my colleague at Bush House. The Germans were already announcing on the wireless that the Allies had landed in France and the B.B.C. were quoting the German statements in the Home News; that is, forestalling the official releases of the Allies. Could I do anything to stop this? I could not and said so, I fear, rather testily.

I laid my head on my pillow again. But sleep was gone for good. I felt no tiredness. The operation was "on". The greatest invasion that the world had ever seen had begun.

I dressed and went over to Bush House. The releases went out without a hitch. At 11 a.m. we received a message from S.H.A.E.F. that the landings had been exceptionally successful. Frayed nerves were marvellously restored, and everyone from the Prime Minister downwards was in the best of spirits. But I felt uneasy. General de Gaulle had still to broadcast. The morning meeting at the Foreign Office had been a failure. General de Gaulle's script was not ready, and it was left to Ivone Kirkpatrick and myself to "vet" it while the General was recording it.

At 11.30 Mr. Bracken telephoned to me to say that the Prime Minister wished me to pay every deference to General de Gaulle when he came to Bush House. I guessed that Mr. Churchill's irritation had subsided. In point of fact, Mr. Eden and Mr. Bracken had been working on him to this end. Kirkpatrick and I therefore went down to the Aldwych entrance to await the great man. To my surprise I found General McClure and two of his colleagues already there. We had not invited them. But the Americans were hypersensitive on the subject of de Gaulle, and I expect that McClure was acting on instructions.

Five minutes before his appointed time the giant figure of the General blocked the entrance door. His face was set. One glance told me that he was in his grimmest mood. His greeting to Kirkpatrick and me was restrained but friendly. I introduced him to the three Americans. He stiffened into complete frigidity, made three half-turns as he gave the limpest of hands to each, then, drawing himself to the full stretch of his immense height, strode forward along the stone corridor.

We went down into the bowels of the earth to the studios, and the B.B.C. staff, Gaullist almost to a man, turned out to welcome the General who, alone of all the Allied leaders, had taken lessons in order to make himself a broadcaster. He relaxed a little at the demonstration and greeted the French B.B.C. team with some show of warmth. Then there was a terrifying hitch. He had, he said, no script. He had had no time to prepare more than a few notes. Moreover, he had received reliable news that the Germans were going to cut off the electricity in the Paris area. He wished to broadcast live—that is, without recording—at one o'clock. I thought that we were lost. If we said that the script must be "vetted", he would refuse to broadcast.

Then Ivone Kirkpatrick had a flash of genius. "General," he said with eloquent conviction, "your broadcast today is the most momentous that you have ever made, perhaps that you ever will make. Its effect will reach far beyond the limits of France. All the oppressed countries are waiting for your lead. We have made arrangements to put your talk out in twenty-four languages. We must have a record for our translations."

The General gave way, and in deathly silence we grouped ourselves round the glass walls of the recording room. Without a trace of nervousness he delivered a superb broadcast. He began with a reference to this England which, when all seemed lost, had stood alone against the greatest military machine the world had ever seen. "Today", he said, "it was right and fitting that this old bastion of freedom should be the base from which the armies of liberation were going on their errand of mercy and justice to free France and all Europe." His voice, solemn, slow and well modulated, carried the conviction of sincerity in every word. Tears came into my eyes and, self-conscious in my lack of control, I looked at my neighbours and found comfort. They, too, were deeply moved.

The General made no mention of the Americans. It was the riposte in kind and it was fair. They had not mentioned him.

But he had committed one sin. He had talked of his own Government as "le gouvernement français"; he had left out the unwelcome stigma of "provisoire". In a recorded broadcast it is possible to remove a word; it is technically impossible to insert one. It was a venial sin. Surely, I thought, it would not hold up our approval. I still felt uneasy.

I waited while the written text was prepared. Then I rushed down to the Foreign Office to seek Mr. Eden's approval. He was engaged when I arrived, and Mr. Duff Cooper was waiting in the Private Secretaries' room. But today I had priority, and Mr. Eden saw me almost at once. I gave him the text and drew his attention to the omission of "Provisional". He read it through. He pointed to the omission. "I'll have trouble with the Prime Minister about this," he said, "but we'll let it go." He was smiling. He thanked me for the help he said I had given him. De Gaulle had been very obstinate and had annoyed the Prime Minister. Mr. Bracken had been very helpful.

I went to see Mr. Bracken who had asked me to drink a cup of tea with him. Celtic sensitiveness had yielded to Celtic generosity and Celtic warm-heartedness, and he was in his most endearing mood. He chaffed me unmercifully about being registered at the Savoy as Mrs. Deacon. Then, turning serious for a moment, he said to me, "You realise why I made this row with the Foreign Office. It was not because of any trouble with Anthony; we've always been friends and always worked together. It was solely to improve your position."

"As a matter of fact," he went on, "Anthony and I are hunting together now. Yesterday we put in a joint paper to the Cabinet on de Gaulle and French affairs."

He paused for a second, and his face lit up with a smile of almost impish satisfaction.

"Last night", he said, "the P.M. called me a lackey of the Foreign Office."

CHAPTER SEVEN

THE ALLIED INVASION of Europe fired the imagination of the whole world and in the oppressed countries stirred the flickering embers of long-deferred hopes into a flame of optimism. From Stalin it drew the most laudatory public statement that he had ever made on the war effort of his Allies. "The history of war", he said, "knows no other similar undertaking as regards breadth of design, vastness of scale and high skill of execution." And this time his statement was given, not to the correspondent of some foreign newspaper, but to the representative of his own *Pravda*. Nor was the Russian delight mere propaganda, for Sir Archibald Clark Kerr telegraphed a graphic report of the elation of Moscow and of the congratulations which he had received from high Soviet officials many of whom had greeted him with unfeigned enthusiasm and such expressions as: "Now we know you are our friends."

In Britain excitement ran so high that nearly everyone assumed that the war was as good as over, and even General Ismay, who was steeled by long experience against wishful thinking, committed himself to the prophesy that hostilities would end on the hundredth day after D-day. In Italy the usually silent General Alexander, who had just taken Rome, was infected by the prevalent spirit of optimism and expressed a cautious hope that he would soon be able to push the Germans back to the Alps, and, nine months previously, General Eisenhower had bet Field-Marshal Montgomery five pounds that the victorious end would come before December 31 of 1944.

Our propagandists shared the general enthusiasm and, not unreasonably, felt that this time they had made a direct, if secondary contribution to the success of the landings. Certainly their effort had been considerable. It included several new features. In preparation for D-day, P.W.E. had initiated a new series of broadcasts entitled "The Voice of S.H.A.E.F." Their object was to provide General Eisenhower with a channel for direct instructions to the civilian populations everywhere on the Western seaboard. The project was approved by General Bedell Smith. The "master voice" was that of the mysterious "Colonel Britton" who had been the spokesman of the V-campaign and who, after a temporary death, had been resuscitated for the D-day preparations. In order to fit in with the deception plan the broadcasts went out in five languages: English, Danish, Dutch, French and Flemish.

The preparation of the actual D-day broadcasts involved elaborate security arrangements. For a week before the actual invasion translators were kept in "purdah" in Woburn while they translated the proclamations of General Eisenhower and of the national leaders into all the languages of Western Europe. These language broadcasts were done by members of the European Service of the B.B.C.

The leaflet operations were on a vast scale. Four days before D-day two printing presses were put under security control in order to print the invasion leaflets. They included General Eisenhower's statement supported in the Norwegian, Belgian and Dutch leaflets by the proclamations of the national leaders. Special leaflets were also prepared for the French and Belgian transport workers, for the German troops in the actual landing zone, for the German reserves who were moving up, and for the Polish soldiers in the German armies. In addition, a special last-minute warning leaflet was produced for the French population in the zone of operations and, by arrangement with the Allied Air Forces, was dropped on D-day one hour before the intensive bombing began. Perhaps the most remarkable leaflet effort was made two days after D-day, when we received a demand from the Divisional Commanders in the front line for leaflets which would induce Germans to surrender. We had anticipated this request and were able to provide the Tactical Air Forces with supplies and to arrange simultaneously for dissemination by Bomber Command. One million and a half of these leaflets were dropped on front-line targets three days after D-day. We were told that they had produced a good effect. Altogether approximately thirty-four million leaflets were dropped during the immediate invasion period.

Finally D-day marked the culmination of our most ambitious achievement of the war. This was the production of a daily airborne newspaper which would give the German troops the plain truth about every aspect of the war on all fronts. The idea came from the fertile mind of a famous British correspondent whose knowledge of Germany is unrivalled. Preparation of the project began in March of 1944, and after many experiments the first issue appeared on April 25. On D-day we printed a million copies. The newspaper, called *Nachrichten für die Truppe,* carried war pictures and maps in addition to text and was in the fullest sense a wonderful production. The chief credit belongs to the British correspondent who personally superintended the editorial matter for every number, wrote much of it himself and inspired all his staff with his own enthusiasm, to our production manager, a genius at his job, and to the two private provincial printing firms who worked for us and who never once let us down either by delay or by any breach of security.

The planning of the propaganda campaign for D-day was a combined effort of P.W.E., O.W.I., P.W.D., and the European Service of the B.B.C., but our American friends would be the first to admit that the main burden fell on P.W.E. Once again the propaganda experts did the work, the main task of Brooks and myself being confined to giving guidance, smoothing the way with ministers, the Foreign Office and the Chiefs of Staff, and ensuring the necessary conditions of security.

Concurrently with our preparations for D-day the ordinary work of P.W.E. had been carried on without relaxation, and the demands on my time had been more than usually heavy. In May, Fitzroy McLean, the head of the British Mission to Tito, had visited London and had brought with him General Velebit, the personal aide-de-camp of the Yugoslav leader. I saw the General both with my colleagues and alone. Dark, clean-shaven and heavily built, with smooth and glossy black hair and pince-nez, he looked more like an intellectual than a soldier. He was, in fact, a Zagreb lawyer who had become a war-time general. He spoke English fluently. He made a good impression on my colleagues mainly because he emphasised with considerable skill the democratic nature of Tito's army which, he said, was composed of sixty per cent. Serbs, thirty per cent. Croats, and ten per cent. Slovenes. The percentages corresponded roughly to the racial divisions in Yugoslavia. Only five per cent. of the army were Communists. He gave an impressive list of the professional officers and prominent non-Communists who were serving under Tito's banner. He also made great play with the importance of British propaganda to Yugoslavia, complained of its meagreness, and put in a strong claim for increased activity. Alone with me, he went much further. He admitted with a great show of frankness that the partisan leadership was Communist, but assured me that Tito stood four-square for independence and understood very well that, if he relied solely on the Russians, he might one day be the slave of Moscow. He, therefore, wished to build a bridge between East and West. In this manner he could strengthen his own position.

Obviously he was trying to sell Tito to us as a kind of Beneš. Nor was he wholly unsuccessful in his effort. His suavity of manner and his interest in propaganda flattered my experts. By saying what we wished to believe he made a strong, if only temporary, impression in higher circles. In particular, he emphasised Tito's desire for a federal Yugoslavia, and this gambit, I believe, was the shrewdest of all Tito's moves, for it appealed to all Yugoslavs and gave him a formidable advantage over the Pan-Serb entourage of Mihailovic.

Velebit himself was no mean propagandist and in different circumstances would, I felt, have made a good head of P.W.E. His story, however, was too plausible. Even accepting his figure of only five per cent. Communists in Tito's army, I felt that a small band of resolute people who already controlled the machine and who knew exactly what they wanted were far stronger than the other ninety-five per cent. who didn't. If the Russian advance continued more or less in pace with our own, the Russians would be in Yugoslavia first. The Communists would be the masters, and, whatever we might or could do, Yugoslavia, with a great show of unity, would enter the Russian orbit. As President Beneš had always said, the peace of Europe would depend on the extent to which the Anglo-Americans would be prepared to recognise an entirely new situation in Eastern and South-Eastern Europe.

President Beneš himself had occupied some of my time during this exciting period. Nine days before D-day he had celebrated his six-tieth birthday. Almost at the last minute I was asked by the B.B.C. to give a talk on him in the postscript to the Home News. The pressure of events forced me to refuse, but I made a broadcast in Czech and I also undertook to write an article on my memories of him for the birthday book which his American and English friends were presenting to him. The broadcast went well enough. At any rate I received a charming message from the President saying that Madame Beneš and he had listened-in and had understood almost every word! But the article was hard going. It was the first writing that I had done since 1939, but once a journalist always a journalist, and in a spirit of duty I wrote my article in the sweat and agony of a hot, sleepless night. Great was my revulsion when the book was not published until two years later!

There was, too, a difficult problem in the Mediterranean. During the operations in North Africa, P.W.E. had had its own mission in Cairo, and in addition, had supplied some of its best experts to General Eisenhower's Psychological Warfare Branch in Algiers. On his transfer to Western Europe General Eisenhower had taken with him the cream of the talent in P.W.B., Mediterranean. It was now necessary to strengthen P.W.B., to find a new head for it, and to bring our Cairo Mission under its control. The obvious choice was Paul Vellacott, the former headmaster of Harrow and present Master of Peterhouse, who in the first world war had won a D.S.O. and risen to the rank of Brigadier. As head of the Cairo Mission he had done a first-class job in bringing order into the legacy of an unsavoury mess.

Unfortunately, after General Eisenhower's departure the situation in Algiers had changed for the worse. General Eisenhower had been succeeded by a British general in the person of Sir Henry Maitland Wilson. His deputy was the American General Devers, who had been switched to Algiers from London where he had been co-operating with General Morgan in the planning for D-day. Doubtless, he had expected to take a prominent part in the invasion of Europe and can hardly fail to have been a little disappointed. Moreover, as General Alexander was commanding the armies in Italy, where the fighting was being done, much of the glory had departed from Allied Force Headquarters, Algiers. Inevitably Anglo-American integration did not work so smoothly as under General Eisenhower. Unfortunately, too, Vellacott, who had been badly wounded in the first world war, had been ill during this period of transition. General Wilson had given high praise to his work in Cairo and had approved his transfer to Algiers. But when, in April, Vellacott was well enough to take up his new post, the British Commander hesitated to upset the delicate balance of Anglo-American co-operation which, after some initial difficulties, he had succeeded in establishing.

The truth was that new gods had arisen in Algiers. The genial General McClure, whose scrupulous fairness had been an invaluable asset to a mixed Anglo-American team like P.W.B., had departed with General Eisenhower, and his successor lacked both his tact and his experience. When Vellacott arrived in Algiers, he was given no authority and was, in fact, relegated to the unenviable position of an adviser, and the top positions in P.W.B. were left to the Americans.

In this unhappy situation Vellacott's health broke down once more, and after six weeks he was forced to come home. He was a great loss, for in mental capacity and in organising ability he was head and shoulders above anyone in P.W.B. Like all strong men he was a little difficult, but I felt then, and feel even more strongly today, that he would have been a dominant factor in achieving Anglo-American co-operation and that he would have commanded the respect of the soldiers as no one else available would have been able to do. His withdrawal did not improve relations and was regarded by the British and, indeed, by Mr. Eden and Mr. Bracken as an act of weakness on the part of General Wilson and Mr. Harold Macmillan. Fortunately, Mr. Barnes, the senior O.W.I. representative of P.W.B., had the tact of a born diplomat, and, thanks to him, good relations were re-established and P.W.B. operated harmoniously as an integrated Anglo-American unit until the end of the war.

When part of General Alexander's forces were withdrawn to reinforce the Allied landings in the South of France on August 15, the chances of a quick and decisive success in Italy were removed. Mr. Churchill, who favoured a rapid advance through Italy into Austria, had been opposed to the landing in the South of France but had had to give way to President Roosevelt. General Marshall had never taken kindly to the Mediterranean strategy. From the political point of view quick successes in Western Europe were essential to Mr. Roosevelt's victory in the presidential election in which he was standing for his fourth term of office. And no one wanted his election more than we. Inevitably the main interest of the public was now concentrated on the battle in France. Inevitably, too, it became the main target for our propaganda.

Our task was not so easy as it seemed, for the bad weather, which had so nearly wrecked the landings, continued and interfered seriously with the support which the Allied Air Forces could give to the troops. A fortnight after D-day the Anglo-American operations were behind schedule. S.H.A.E.F. remained calm and confident, but, during the fierce battle of the hinge, public morale at home swayed irritatingly between extremes of optimism and pessimism. P.W.E. had therefore to steer a middle course. Our task and duty was to maintain the confidence of the French and of the oppressed peoples in the occupied countries. At the same time we had to be careful not to annoy the British public and, above all, the Allied fighting forces by excessive optimism and by any suggestion that Germany was at her last gasp.

The treatment of General de Gaulle also required delicate handling. His D-day broadcast still rankled with the Americans, and even Bob Sherwood, acting presumably on higher instructions, had complained to me officially that the B.B.C's treatment of the broadcast had been anti-American. I went through the B.B.C. comment with him word for word and I hope satisfied him. On the other hand, the British public, not to mention the French resistance groups, was painfully surprised when soon after D-day the Prime Minister and

Field-Marshal Smuts visited France without General de Gaulle. A newspaper cartoon showing the two statesmen on their way to France, with General de Gaulle stranded on the English coast, and bearing the caption, "One of our Liberators is Missing," accurately reflected the uneasiness of the public. Presumably it had some effect, for a few days later General de Gaulle was given permission to visit France where he received a jubilant welcome. These differences with General de Gaulle and, above all, the antipathy of President Roosevelt to the French leader were unfortunate, for, in General Eisenhower's words, the French resistance groups were rendering assistance " above his expectations", and at that moment de Gaulle was the acknowledged hero of metropolitan France. Unfortunately, too, further painful incidents occurred, notably in August when the General refused to meet Mr. Churchill and, later, President Roosevelt.

Meanwhile, the Germans, sorely harassed by the simultaneous Allied offensives from the East and from the West, had found comfort and consolation in the launching of the first of their long-promised new weapons. On the night of June 12 the first "doodle-bugs", officially christened later by the Prime Minister as flying-bombs, crossed the Channel. Only four landed in the London area. At first they were greeted with official silence and the public, still ignorant of the extent of the danger, showed no outward uneasiness. Six days later the Guards' Chapel was hit during the Sunday service. The heavy casualties could not be concealed and came as a shock to a startled public. General Bedell Smith had a narrow escape. A great friend of Ivan Cobbold, himself a victim of the tragedy, "Beedle" had been invited to attend the service. His car was at the door of Widewing, and he was on the point of leaving for the Chapel when a top-secret and most urgent telegram from Washington, demanding his immediate attention, was handed to him.

Within less than a month the new weapon had claimed 2752 fatal casualties or, as the Prime Minister announced, one death for every bomb launched. The figures were strictly accurate, but slightly misleading, for a considerable percentage of the bombs fell harmlessly. The effect on morale was not good, and the public, which had stood the early Blitz with immense courage, had hoped and believed that its worst trials were past. The South London areas suffered heavily, and in the fifth year of the war the unfortunate Londoners found the day and night incursions of the bombs hard to stand. In Bush House we were neighbours of the Air Ministry whose spotters gave us the over-head danger signal. At first we paid no attention to either the alerts or the signals. The latter were not pleasant. From my room on the second-top floor I could see the spotters on the roof and each time that they would suddenly run to the exit from the roof and a chorus of bells would ring violently I had an empty feeling in my stomach.

On June 30, a bomb landed in the Aldwych between the Air Ministry building and Bush House. Casualties in the street were heavy. P.W.E. itself was lucky, for, although considerable damage was done, the bomb fell at 2 p.m. when many people were at luncheon. Some forty members of the staff received treatment for cuts and minor injuries. There were only three serious casualties and, fortunately, all recovered. Morale, however, was visibly, but not seriously affected, and afterwards, when the overhead danger signal sounded we came away from the glass with which we were surrounded and congregated in the centre of the building. Interference with work, however, was negligible.

I had one curious personal experience. During the period of the flying-bombs Mr. Eden kindly asked me to spend the week-end with him at Binderton, his attractive country house in the heart of the Sussex Downs, in order to get a good night's sleep. Mr. Winant was the only other guest. Mr. Eden is at his best in the country. His energy is amazing. Every minute of his week-end is put to good use, and I discovered the secret of his remarkable capacity for dealing with official papers. He brings home with him a vast pile of official reading-matter and long before his guests are down he has read and carefully minuted those that require his attention. In the atmosphere of Binderton even the attractive but usually silent Mr. Winant—a frequent visitor and a great admirer of Mr. Eden—became eloquent and revealed an unsuspected sense of humour. On this occasion he told a good story of Mr. Bevin. He had been at some big war-charity show at which there had been dancing. Mr. Bevin had taken the floor, and Mr. Winant, who was standing next the Prime Minister, was puzzled by the somewhat elaborate and cumbersome foot-work of Mr. Bevin. Thinking this must be some old English country dance, he turned to his neighbour: "What do you call that dance?"

Mr. Churchill watched the gyrations on the floor.

"Ah," he said, benevolently, "that's what we call the Labour movement."

Mr. Winant left Binderton on the Sunday evening, and I went to bed in the happiest frame of mind, fully prepared to benefit by the quiet night's sleep which Mr. Eden had promised. Scarcely had I turned in, when there was a loud explosion followed by a crash of broken glass. My door blew open, and for a moment I felt as if I were being lifted out of bed. An anti-aircraft battery had brought down a flying-bomb in a field in front of Binderton.

There was another curious incident during that week-end. On the Saturday afternoon Mr. Eden was called to the telephone. The voice at the other end was that of Sir Alexander Cadogan. M. Gusev, the Russian Ambassador, had made a scene at the Foreign Office because Sir Alexander would not and, indeed, could not attach immediately three coaches to a train to evacuate the women personnel of the Russian Embassy to Blackpool!

In their propaganda to their own people the German propagandists gave fantastic accounts of the flying-bomb which they called the "reprisal-weapon", and in his broadcasts in English Lord Haw-Haw excelled himself in blood-curdling stories of new weapons and further horrors to come. He also developed the theme that victory was useless to Britain because Russia would dominate Europe, and the United States would take over the British Empire. For P.W.E's benefit he added a special rider, declaring that a Germany, steeled against Bolshevism in the East and against Jewish power-politics in the West, was impervious to propaganda, and that in broadcasting to Germany we were wasting our time and the taxpayers' money. We countered mildly by asking why, if no Germans wanted to hear our foreign broadcasts, the German Government had recently increased the penalties for listening-in.

We had a harder task when on July 20, Count Stauffenberg placed his time-bomb in the room in which Hitler was holding a conference with his military advisers, and, although the attempt failed, the conspiracy of a group of high German officers was revealed to the world. The excitement in Britain was intense, and in ministerial circles opinions varied widely, some ministers holding that the whole story was a propaganda trick to increase Hitler's popularity and others insisting that it was the beginning of the German revolution. It goes without saying that our propagandists were eager to exploit and to exaggerate the situation, but Mr. Eden gave a safe and, as events proved, a sound ruling.

We should ignore any idea that the attempt was a propaganda "stunt". On the other hand, we should be careful not to credit without a thorough sifting the wild rumours of civil war and open revolt which were then circulating. We gave a full and dramatic reconstruction of the attempted assassination. The Germans helped us by producing Hitler at the microphone. His voice—and we were certain that it was his voice—showed that he had been badly shaken. After the first excitement had passed, it became clear that the attempted assassination had produced no major change in the internal situation of Germany. Failures rarely do anywhere.

Of far more consequence to our propaganda was the news from the military fronts. By the beginning of August the hard and relentless fighting in Normandy was beginning to bear fruit, and the Germans were wilting under the hammer-blows of the Anglo-American armies. During July the Russians had made great advances and had taken Lvov and Brest-Litovsk and, even if their progress had now slowed down, the two-front war was obviously telling on the German war-machine.

On August 2, Brooks and I went before the Chiefs of Staff to report on our propaganda. We had an easy time. Whatever we did, propaganda was rarely criticised when the military position was favourable. We gave an account of the changed tactics of Dr. Goebbels. He had now made a complete *volte-face,* had dropped all boasting and was telling his people frankly of the "mortal danger" which threatened Germany. He went so far as to call on them to imitate the admirable phlegm and confidence of the British in the grim years of 1940 and 1941.

In our own propaganda we took care to remind the Germans of Hitler's numerous boasts in the days when a German victory seemed a foregone conclusion to all Germans. The wheel of fortune had now swung full-turn against Germany, but Goebbels had still one asset: the Allied policy of unconditional surrender which, in spite of all we could say by way of explanation, he was able to exploit to his own people as the official avowal of the Allied intention to destroy Germany. It was to remain an asset until the end of the war.

There was, indeed, only one dark spot on the war-horizon. Anticipating a speedy advance by the Russians, the Poles in Warsaw had risen against their oppressors. The expected aid from the Russians had not come, and in its absence the Polish insurgents were fighting a heroic and hopeless battle. The Russian army of General Rokossovsky had, in fact, been repulsed with heavy losses by the Germans East of Warsaw, but the subsequent attacks by the Moscow radio on the Warsaw Poles, whose leader, General Bor-Komorovski, was a supporter of the Polish Government in London, seemed merely to confirm a widely held opinion that the Russians were deliberately withholding their aid.

Apart from this tragedy which boded ill for the peace, the Chiefs of Staff had no criticisms to make. Although always business-like and never given to emotional enthusiasms, they were obviously in a cheerful mood, and Brooks and I went out well satisfied. The same day we met Major-General John Kennedy, the A.C.I.G.S. (Operations) and a shrewd calculator who rarely indulged in speculations about the future. He informed us that he had just made a modest bet that the Anglo-Americans would be in Paris before the Russians took Warsaw. At the moment it seemed a risky wager.

But still better news was to come. On August 14, Field-Marshal Montgomery had sent a most optimistic telegram to the Prime Minister who was in Italy. The Field-Marshal was not afraid to prophesy. He had, in fact, made many predictions. But—until then at any rate—he had never been wrong. On the same day General Eisenhower, who rarely boasted, issued a proclamation calling for a special effort from his armies to exploit "a fleeting, but definite chance of a smashing victory". Six days later came the news that the German resistance in Western France had collapsed. In the highest circles in Whitehall there was the greatest optimism, and the prevalent view was that the Germans would be out of the Pas de Calais and most of Belgium in a fortnight and would withdraw to the line of the Meuse. The same evening there were rumours in London, started perhaps by the official announcement of General de Gaulle's arrival in Cherbourg, that Paris had fallen.

The rumours had merely anticipated events. On Wednesday, August 23, J. B. Clark, the Controller of the European Service of the B.B.C., "buzzed" me on our inside telephone. He had just received an official communiqué from General Koenig stating that the French Forces of the Interior had liberated Paris. I asked him if the news had been confirmed by S.H.A.E.F. Clark replied that the communiqué had been received in the ordinary way, that Koenig's communiqués were released automatically by the B.B.C. and that the French General was a member of Eisenhower's staff. I felt a little suspicious and told Clark to publish the news as from General Koenig but not to exult until I had checked it. I telephoned at once to Mr. Eden and Mr. Bracken. Both were surprised and sceptical, but, before I had finished telephoning, the news had gone out on the twelve-thirty French bulletin.

Then followed the most bewildering forty-eight hours in the

history of P.W.E. We rang up S.H.A.E.F. who had no news to give. They told us to stand by for a communiqué which would shortly be issued. It never came. More suspicious than ever, I went to see General Ismay. He did not believe the French communiqué. He thought it possible that the French had taken action on their own initiative. If they had, it was a serious matter, for their action would probably force us to detach forces from the pursuit of the retreating German armies. He was annoyed. The Foreign Office, which I visited in order to ask Mr. Eden to broadcast in French, shared Ismay's views, and Sargent, fearing lest Paris should prove a second Warsaw, was even more apprehensive.

By evening there was still no news from S.H.A.E.F., but in spite of their silence we put on an extra French programme in the European Service of the B.B.C. The French members of the B.B.C., who, like most people, believed the communiqués of their own countrymen more implicitly than those of others, were delirious with delight, and Jacques Duchesne, their admirable leader, who came to see me to discuss the recording of Mr. Eden's broadcast, could hardly speak for tears. My own feelings were constrained by the agony of uncertainty.

The morning brought no relief. S.H.A.E.F. was still silent. I spent a harassed forenoon trying to arrange a time for Mr. Eden to be recorded at the Foreign Office. There was a long hitch, because the French team of the B.B.C., who had been celebrating all night, were late in coming to Bush House. Finally we arranged for Duchesne to make the recording at 4.30 p.m. An hour later we received the long-expected message from S.H.A.E.F. It was alarming in its curtness. Paris was not liberated. In any event liberation of the capital was not important in comparison with the main task of defeating the retreating German armies. I telephoned to Mr. Eden who by now had gone to a special Cabinet meeting on Poland. But I got the message to him. At 6.15 p.m. Sargent came out of the meeting to give me Mr. Eden's reply. He had received a communication from General Bedell Smith. The French were not masters of the situation. The very thing that S.H.A.E.F. had wished to avoid had happened. General Eisenhower would now have to divert troops from the main battle in order to support Paris. Mr. Eden's broadcast would have to be postponed. I guessed—I think rightly—that the Americans were sore and that they blamed de Gaulle.

The sky was now inky black. The storm burst with a fury of lightning, thunder and heavy rain. A long alert was in process. The

Germans were releasing a last spate of "doodle-bugs" before abandoning the Pas de Calais sites, and in the hurtling confusion it was
difficult to distinguish the peals of thunder from the crash of bombs.
My heart sank. Dejectedly I told J. B. Clark that the broadcast would
have to be postponed. Fortunately I had already taken the precaution
to inform him not to make any previous announcement of the
broadcast. Within five minutes of my speaking to Clark, he was on
the telephone again. He had startling news. Broadcast messages from
President Roosevelt and Mr. Stimson on the liberation of Paris had
just gone out to the world. I sent a message through to Mr. Eden.
Presently he came on the telephone himself, and I read him the
eloquent words of President Roosevelt.

"This is a bit hot," he said. "What do we do now?"

"Put your broadcast out," I replied.

"Very good, you can let it go."

I pressed my "buzzer" to Clark. "J. B.," I said, "full steam ahead!"

Mr. Eden went on the air at 9.30 p.m. He spoke in French. His
broadcast was first-class both in delivery and in content. I telephoned
to him and told him so, adding that we had put him on before Mr.
Stimson and the President. He seemed pleased, and I took advantage
of the moment to suggest that we should give a dinner to the French
and that he should come. He asked me to arrange an evening when
he was free.

I now felt tolerably sure that Paris was now French again. But my
suspense was not ended. After the storm the Friday of August 25 was
one of the few perfect days of a wretched summer. There was still
little or no news from Paris, and the pessimists were sceptical
throughout the day. In the evening I dined with Sargent and
Wheeler-Bennett. Sargent was not yet satisfied. He had been present
at all the Cabinet meetings. The situation was grave. Fighting had
been going on all Thursday. There were 8,000 German troops in
Paris, who after a preliminary surrender had withdrawn it. He feared
the worst. It might take weeks to capture the city street by street,
and then it would be a ruin. He was still harping on a second Warsaw. It was significant, he said, that the Russians had not mentioned
the fall of Paris.

At dinner I drank to drown my depression. Then Sargent turned
on the wireless. All was well. This time the German commander in
Paris had finally surrendered with all his forces. De Gaulle was in
Paris. He had spoken, and his words had released the pent-up emotions of his long-suffering countrymen. This unaccommodating

Norman, whom M. Massigli once described to me as rigid but in-fallible in his long-term judgment of events, had chanced his hand and had succeeded. Whatever the future might be, he had received a fitting reward for a courage which had never failed and for a faith which never doubted the greatness of France or her right to be treated as an equal by every Great Power.

As I listened, I was hard put to it to suppress the tears which clouded my eyes. The relief from a long drawn-out suspense had released my emotions. But even stronger was the joy and gratitude that France, who, whatever her weaknesses may have been, had suffered grievously from our unpreparedness, should have freed her capital by her own efforts. It was a triumph which, if it owed almost everything to the Anglo-American armies, no Englishman and no American could begrudge.

I was so delighted that I forgot to tease Sargent for his pessimism. Yet P.W.E. had made its greatest and—who knows—perhaps its most successful mistake of the war. It had liberated Paris twenty-four hours before a French or other Allied soldier had entered the pre-cincts of the city.

The dinner to the French was a great success. We held it on September 5, because it was the first night which Mr. Eden had free. We had also asked M. Delfosse, the Belgian Minister of Information with whom we had co-operated very closely in stimulating and feeding the Belgian resistance movement. As Brussels had been liberated that very afternoon, we could not have been more fortunate in our choice of date. We sat down twelve, including Moley Sargent and Oliver Harvey from the Foreign Office, J. B. Clark, and Jacques Duchesne. Both Delfosse and Duchesne, each in his own style a superb orator, paid eloquent and deeply moving tributes to the British. Both took the line that out of evil would come good, for the Belgians and French who had lived in England through the long, testing years of war had learnt to know us and appreciate us as never before. Mr. Eden, who had not been told that he would be expected to speak, made the best speech that I have ever heard him deliver. He spoke a little more haltingly than usual, but was extraordinarily sin-cere and effective. He struck exactly the right note with our guests when he said that only by the West holding together could we hope to establish a settled Europe.

During the evening there was one untoward incident. Just before coming to the dinner Sargent had received a telegram from Clark Kerr in Moscow saying that the Russians had declared war on Bulgaria without giving previous notice to the British and Americans. As we were negotiating an armistice with Bulgaria at that moment, the news was disturbing, if indeed, not sinister.

The war against our enemies was going well; the peace for which we were fighting was already being threatened by divisions among the Allies.

BOOK V

RELUCTANT BUREAUCRAT

"HE IS NO wise man who will quit a certainty for an uncertainty."

SAMUEL JOHNSON

"THE ROMAN EMPIRE fell at last, sick unto death, and beyond recovery, as we now see, from over-administration."

T. R. GLOVER

CHAPTER ONE

THE LIBERATION OF France and Belgium marked the peak of P.W.E's activities as the central British organisation for political warfare. These activities were not to diminish. Indeed, with the increased tempo of the war greater demands than ever were to be made on the department, but the character of its work was to undergo a change. P.W.D., S.H.A.E.F. had now moved to France. Propaganda was becoming more and more closely linked to military operations, and inevitably the forward propaganda units were to acquire greater independence and greater authority. P.W.E. would remain as the main vehicle for official guidance on propaganda policy, but it was to become more and more a rear echelon agency for supplying personnel and material for the forward units on the Continent. The change came gradually and was not easily accepted by the experts who remained in London and who, indeed, had devised the whole technique of modern propaganda.

Moreover, the Allied Governments with whom we had worked so closely were eager to return home as soon as their countries were liberated, and they, too, found it easier to co-operate with the propagandists on the spot than with London. Inevitably, P.W.D. made continuous demands for additional staff which had to be supplied from rapidly diminishing sources and with no possibility of replacement.

The Foreign Office, too, was now faced with the task of re-establishing embassies in the liberated countries and, itself woefully short of staff, began to draw on P.W.E. Ivone Kirkpatrick had already been recalled in August. His withdrawal had been a severe loss, and with the liberation of Brussels it was followed by an urgent request for Peter Scarlett, my Foreign Office assistant, and for the Director of my Belgian Region. My Director of Plans had collapsed in July with an arachnoid haemorrhage and, although he had made an amazing recovery, was not yet fit for work. The Admiralty, I knew, wanted Brooks, and I was merely waiting for the blow to fall. P.W.E. was a temporary department which would not continue after the war. It was, therefore, a fair preserve for everyone to raid.

On the other hand, suggestions to wind up P.W.E. as soon as possible were frowned on by the traditional departments who found it useful for the various extraneous and temporary commitments which they themselves were not yet ready to undertake and which, in fact, were beyond the scope of P.W.E's charter. But from talks with the Treasury I knew that we were already condemned although we were to be an unconscionable time in dying and were to have many unexpected adventures before the death rattle. It was a situation that I was compelled to accept.

To my great grief one commitment which I had ardently desired was removed from us with dramatic and disturbing suddenness. The long efforts of Sherwood and myself to associate the Russians with our political warfare had at last been crowned with success, and early in August the Kremlin appointed M. Saksin and General Vassiliev to attend the Anglo-American weekly policy meeting and to co-operate with us generally in propaganda to Germany. We took them completely into our confidence and gave them not only our policy directive, but also the analysis of German propaganda which served as a background to our own propagandists and to the European Service of the B.B.C.

The meetings were rather difficult because the Russians spoke no English, and I had to act not only as chairman but also as interpreter. In every other respect relations seemed to be excellent. M. Saksin, a shy and timid professional diplomat, said little, but was friendly. General Vassiliev, a cheerful, frank and bluff soldier, was an acquisition, for he talked freely and well on military subjects and gave us valuable information.

For a month all went smoothly, and on September 1, Sherwood and two of his O.W.I. colleagues and J. B. Clark and myself were invited to luncheon at the Russian Embassy. We were given a sumptuous meal beginning with vodka, caviare and smoked salmon. I tossed down my first glass of vodka in the approved Russian manner, was not allowed to stop at one, but had to have three more: one for victory, one for the good news, and one for good luck. After these libations conversation became pleasantly free.

General Vassiliev told me that the Russians were launching a new attack in the North and that soon we should have good news. The Germans, he said, had now only two hopes: their secret weapons and their conviction that the Allies would quarrel before the war was over. Both contingencies, especially the second, were, he insisted warmly, vain hopes. The atmosphere was most cordial. Even the stolid M. Gusev thawed, and we all took our leave, confident that at last the ice was broken and that we could now make real progress. The Russians came to our next meeting. Nothing untoward happened. True, M. Saksin pointed out that we had made a mistake the previous week in stating that the armistice terms for Bulgaria had been drafted in consultation with Russia. He also criticised the title, "Guidance for Output," of our analysis of German propaganda as misleading and suggested that it should be altered. We at once agreed. He seemed well-satisfied, and both Russians readily accepted an invitation from Mr. J. B. Clark to visit the various establishments of the B.B.C. a few days later. At our next meeting the Russians failed to appear, nor did they keep their appointment with Clark. Eventually we discovered that both men had been recalled to Moscow.

We telegraphed to Sir Archibald Clark Kerr to ask him what had happened. After some delay came a blast from M. Lozovsky, the head of the Russian propaganda services. Our analysis of German propaganda had contained a statement that Himmler was now advocating a separate peace with Russia. This was an insult to Russia. M. Lozovsky professed to believe and continued to assert that this statement was part of our directive. Long and tedious explanations produced no result. The Russians never declared that they refused co-operation in propaganda. They merely made no attempt to renew it, and this inactive persistence was maintained until the end of the war.

Doubtless, the Russians had now made up their minds to go their own way. They had already taken their own line in Roumania and in Bulgaria and, although M. Mikolajczyk had at last made the journey to Moscow, a Russian-sponsored Polish Government was already in being in the Russian capital. In the absence of any agreed post-war plans for Europe it was clear that the new frontiers would be established, not by treaty, but by the limits of the line of advance of the Allied armies.

The fall of Warsaw on October 2, after sixty-three days of heroic fighting by the Polish insurgents, intensified the Polish-Russian crisis. Feeling in Britain ran high, and there were bitter recriminations between the pro-Poles and the pro-Russians. If you were pro-Polish, you said bluntly that Poland had been crucified. If you were pro-Russian, you shrugged your shoulders and maintained that the Poles had committed suicide.

The truth lay somewhere between the two extremes. There was the security problem. Most people admitted willingly that Russia had a right to insist on a friendly Poland. Yet many elements in the Polish Government in London were bitterly anti-Russian. There was, too, the long historical past replete with tragic examples of Polish-

Russian antagonism. Bearing a more direct influence on the immediate crisis was the background of the years immediately following the first world war when Poland, profiting by Russia's weakness and not content with the extensive frontiers which had already been given to her, marched on Kiev with the intention of adding further territory to her already swollen domains. Later, she had driven a hard bargain with a Bolshevik Government still engaged in fighting a civil war in which its opponents were supported by the British Government. Yet there were at most 25,000,000 Poles against the 150,000,000 Russians. The hyper-sensitive Russians remembered these tragic days. Nor did they forget that the chief supporter of the anti-Bolshevik crusade had been Mr. Churchill. It was inevitable that in their new strength the Russians would have nothing to do with those Poles who retained the spirit of 1920, and there were several in the Polish Government in London.

The impasse in which the Polish Government now found itself imposed a difficult task on our propaganda. During the battle of Warsaw the Polish Region of P.W.E. had given full support to the insurgents, and in their free time on the air the London Poles had been allowed to say what they liked, short of direct attacks on the Russians. This limited freedom of action satisfied neither the London Poles nor the pro-Polish elements in the British House of Commons, by whom P.W.E. was severely criticised.

On October 8, Mr. Churchill and Mr. Eden left for Moscow. As far as military matters were concerned, the visit was a success, with Stalin taking a sober view of the duration of the war and giving the first of June, 1945 as his date-line for the end. But as far as the Polish problem was concerned, little progress was made, mainly on account of the hesitations of M. Mikolajczyk. Stalin said he was prepared to guarantee the frontiers of Poland on the basis of the Curzon Line and to accept M. Mikolajczyk as Prime Minister of the new Russian-sponsored Polish Government. But he insisted on the cession of Lvov. In spite of British recommendations to accept this compromise as his last chance, M. Mikolajczyk was unwilling to agree until he had consulted his colleagues in London. His position was unenviable. Probably he felt that, whatever he did, the end would be the same. But the delay hastened the process of disintegration. Two months later Mr. Churchill, in repudiating the Polish Government in London, was clearly preparing the way for recognition of the Russian-sponsored Polish Government in Lublin. The propaganda task of P.W.E's Polish Region had become impossible.

While Mr. Churchill and Mr. Eden were away in Moscow, I was forced to consider the problem of my own future which had now become acute. For some considerable time past Mr. Eden had asked me what I proposed to do after the war. He hoped, he said, that I would remain in the Foreign Office. A definite scheme had now been put forward. If I would stay on for a year or so to organise the new information services of the Foreign Office, I could have an embassy afterwards as an end to my career. My lost pension rights would be restored. Many of my friends urged me to accept this offer both for the job itself and for my personal security. I was getting on for sixty. In the new post-war England, should I be able to live as a writer? The bureaucratic state would be all-powerful. To serve it would be both interesting and safe.

For the last five years I had had little time to think about my future. Occasionally it had forced itself on my mind, but with my fatal facility for avoiding unpleasant thoughts I had always dismissed it. Now I hesitated and spent much time in discussing the problem with my friends, especially Moley Sargent and Jack Wheeler-Bennett. Sargent favoured acceptance. Wheeler-Bennett was against it and saw me wrestling till the end of my days in a fog of frustration. Under the Foreign Office the information service would never be more than a lame dog, for fundamentally all Foreign Offices disliked publicity. After the war the Treasury would cut down expenses. There would be no money to attract the talent which was necessary to create an efficient service.

His advice seemed good to me, but, irresolute before a decision which could no longer be avoided, I went for a long week-end to Sedbergh to consult my brother. He, too, advised acceptance, and, although given kindly, this irritated me. I spent my last day alone by the banks of the Lune. The autumn weather was superb. Against a blue sky the fells stood out in the clearest outline, and the broad dale, watered by four rivers, looked as warm and inviting as a Tyrolean valley in midsummer. Gloomily I reflected that were I twenty years younger I should not hesitate to leave Whitehall at the earliest moment. I had been a reluctant, not to say an unorthodox, bureaucrat. I had begun my career as an official but had resigned in 1922. Now for the first time war-weariness was making me think of personal security. My thoughts went back to the river. An old salmon, urged by the spawning instinct, was trying to climb the fall below Killington. The water was low, and his task seemed impossible. Nine times he leapt and fell back, but still he persevered. Then with a great spring he landed near the top, hung slithering for a moment on the slippery rock, and wriggled over on the right side. My heart leapt with him. Back to London I went with my mind made up. Security could go to hell. On October 28, I broadcast in Czech to the Czechs for their Independence Day and, in spite of Foreign Office admonitions of caution, told them that before the next anniversary we should meet in a free Prague. Two days later I received a new contract from my publishers and signed it at once.

When Mr. Eden returned from Moscow, he sent for me. I saw him in bed in his flat in the Foreign Office. For once he was in a slightly peevish mood. He was leaving for Paris that afternoon with Mr. Churchill and had been kept up very late at the Cabinet the previous night by a long discussion on the inadvisability of the Prime Minister's risking a visit to the still disturbed French capital. He made me a formal offer, and I refused it as gracefully as I could.

He seemed a little surprised. "I thought this was what you wanted," he said. I went back to my office and wrote him a letter thanking him for his trust in me and saying that there was no other Minister whom I would serve so willingly, but that, if the Foreign Office intended to establish a really efficient information service, several Goliaths would have to be slain and I was too old to be a David. He took it very well. Our personal relations suffered in no way, and, now that I could not be accused of angling for a job, I could talk to him more freely than ever before.

Indirectly the visit of Mr. Churchill and Mr. Eden to Moscow was responsible for one of those tragi-comic situations which relieve temporarily the gloom and horror of war. On November 7, the anniversary of the Bolshevik revolution, but now called Russia's National Day, I went to the reception at the Russian Embassy. The crowd was enormous, and even in the spacious rooms of Harrington House movement was almost impossible. In his anniversary speech Stalin had made pleasant references to Mr. Churchill and Mr. Eden, had emphasised Allied unity, and had announced that "in the none too distant future" the Red Army would hoist the flag of victory over Berlin. Ignorant of all the diplomatic difficulties, half London had flocked to congratulate the official representative of Russia. With some difficulty I made my way to the crowded buffet. To my surprise there was no vodka, no caviare.

It was at this moment that I noticed the genial figure of General Vassiliev, who had by now returned to London in a purely military capacity. He greeted me warmly and, drawing me into a corner, gave me a glass of vodka and a caviare sandwich. "On our national holiday," he said, "to drink is permissible." He handed me a box of cigarettes and pointed to the lettering on the lid. "Gvardejski" (Guards cigarettes), he said proudly. Then he told me that there was a room upstairs reserved for senior officials where I could get all I wanted. I went there and enjoyed myself. Here there was vodka in plenty. If this was a Communist celebration, the drinking was not communal. Had Russia changed or had something gone wrong?

Presently I ran into Jo Hollis, and he explained the mystery. When Mr. Churchill and Mr. Eden left Moscow, Stalin presented them with a great case of Russian delicacies. On arriving at the aeroplane which was to take them home, they found a second case which, as no one seemed to know anything about it, they assumed was a further mark of Stalin's hospitality. When they reached England, the goods were shared out among all the members of the Churchill-Eden mission.

On November 5, M. Gusev came to the Foreign Office in a state of agitation. The case from Moscow with his vodka and other good things for the celebration of November 7 had not arrived. He had been informed by Moscow that the case had been put on Mr. Churchill's aeroplane.

Realising the gravity of the situation, the Foreign Office sent out an urgent request for the return of the missing articles. Alas! only thirty per cent. was recovered. Fresh caviare does not improve by keeping. In Whitehall's opinion vodka was too good to keep anyway.

Meanwhile, after the great successes of August and September the advance of the Allied armies in Western Europe had slowed down. Bad weather had turned the heroic venture of Arnhem into a failure, and, although General Montgomery had announced publicly to his troops on September 20 that "We should finish the war this year," he had subsequently corrected his one mistaken prophecy. Opinion in high quarters now inclined to a date as remote as July 1, 1945. The flying-bomb had ceased to be a danger, but had been immediately followed by the V2, potentially much more dangerous because there was no defence against it, but less terrifying in its anticipatory effect because no one knew when it was coming. The public, however, were angry with Mr. Duncan Sandys who, on September 7, had declared over-jubilantly that "the battle of London was over". The first V2 fell the very next day.

Events had sobered public optimism, but there was no lack of confidence in the outcome. I was therefore surprised when on November 21 General Eisenhower sent a long telegram saying that German resistance was very tough and that, unless the phrase "unconditional surrender" could be modified, he saw no end to the war except a long and bitter process of fighting. If "unconditional surrender" must be adhered to, then everything possible should be done by propaganda and subversive means to "soften" German morale. He asked London to go into these matters which could not be dealt with by S.H.A.E.F. The message caused some commotion in high places, and telegrams flew between Mr. Churchill and President Roosevelt. Their decision was that it was too late now to go back on "unconditional surrender". At this stage any alteration would be regarded inevitably as a sign of weakness.

As propaganda was mentioned in the Eisenhower telegram, I was consulted both by Mr. Eden and General Ismay. Although both agreed that there was no short-cut to victory by propaganda, General Ismay held the view that everything possible should be done to meet General Eisenhower's wishes and recommended the setting up of a Committee to examine all the possibilities. His proposal was approved. A Committee was at once established under the control of the Chiefs of Staff organisation, and I was appointed chairman. I do not think that we accomplished very much more than the various propaganda agencies were already doing. At best the Committee helped to keep deception, subversion and propaganda on an even keel and to let the various experts feel that their views were being given consideration.

December, the month which I dislike most, brought a long series of set-backs and personal unpleasantness. It began with the departure of Brooks who had been connected with the organisation of our propaganda services since before the war. The Admiralty wanted him back. They had made their request in the nicest possible manner. The First Lord had asked me to luncheon. I had been told to come at one o'clock and, as luncheon was at one-thirty, I guessed at once what trouble was afoot. Admiral Sir Andrew (now Lord) Cunningham was there when I arrived.

Mr. Alexander went straight to the point. "We want Brooks," he said. "We've been good to you and let you keep him for longer than we ought. Now what about it?" I asked him what the Admiralty were prepared to do for him. Brooks, I said, had made a name for himself in Whitehall.

Sir Andrew Cunningham put the matter very succinctly. "Brooks," he said, "is one of our very best Marine officers. For your private information I can tell you that he is in the running for the post of Commandant-General of the Corps. If he comes back now, his chances are good. If he does not come back, he is out altogether."

I made up my mind at once. Even with ministerial backing there was little prospect of winning by fighting.

"If Brooks wants to go," I said, "I shall make no attempt to stand in his way."

They were pleased, and I took the opportunity of asking Admiral Cunningham to give me a good man in his place. He gave his promise and, what is rarer on such occasions, he kept it. He did not give me a Brooks. Indeed, I did not ask for one. But he released to me a first-class German expert who proved himself one of the best men we ever had. Brooks was a heavy loss both to the department and to me personally. We had been through most of the war together and we had never exchanged a cross word. Within fifteen months of leaving P.W.E. he became Commandant-General of the Royal Marine Corps.

Brooks's departure was followed by the resignation of the head of our Balkan Region, a remarkable young woman who knew her job thoroughly, handled the somewhat unruly Balkan members of the B.B.C. with tact and skill, and was *persona grata* with the Foreign Office. J. B. Clark had offered her a high post in the B.B.C. after the war. It meant security and a pension. But she had refused it. She wanted adventure. She wished to go to the Balkans. I told her that she was crazy. She looked at me for a moment and said quietly: "I have read your books. What would you have done at my age?"

And that was that.

The next set-back came through my own fault. I had been worried for a long time about the propaganda services to the Far East. When Japan had entered the war, the propaganda to that country and to the territories occupied by the Japanese should have become automatically the function of P.W.E. But we had no Far Eastern experts; the Ministry of Information had. I therefore made an arrangement with Sir Cyril Radcliffe whereby the Ministry of Information would continue to conduct all propaganda to the Far East. To give the requisite policy guidance, a Political Warfare Japan Committee had been set up, under the aegis of the Foreign Office, with Brooks as Chairman. Now that Brooks was leaving, I wanted the position regularised. I therefore submitted a paper to Mr. Eden recommending that the control of all propaganda to the Far East should formally be confirmed as the function of the Ministry of Information. Sir Cyril

Radcliffe, whom of course I had consulted, was in full agreement. I anticipated no objection from Mr. Bracken. When therefore Mr. Eden called a meeting to settle the matter, I went with a light heart. The discussion was opened by Mr. Sterndale Bennett, the head of the Far Eastern Department of the Foreign Office. A tiger for work and completely fearless, he came out flatly against my proposal. Propaganda to the Far East was now closely linked with operations, and operational secrets could not be divulged to the Ministry of Information. It must, he said, come under P.W.E. I fully expected Mr. Bracken to rise in his wrath, but to my surprise he not only made no protest but agreed at once. At that moment he was intent on closing his Ministry as soon as possible and feared that the Far Eastern commitment would prolong its existence. I was thus landed with a job for which I had neither staff nor accommodation.

In a somewhat similar fashion we had also been made officially responsible for the re-education of German prisoners of war, partly because no other department was willing to undertake the task. As ministers were divided in their opinions of its value and as Sir James Grigg, the Secretary of State for War, was strongly opposed to the whole scheme, we met with nothing but obstruction, and months were to pass before we made any real progress.

But by far the greatest unpleasantness was over Greece. We had landed troops there early in October in order to help an Allied people whom the German forces of occupation had left half-famished and bereft of all means of helping themselves. Our troops had been welcomed, but the civil war, which had already begun during the German occupation, had not subsided. The attempts of British diplomacy to establish a popular democratic government had met with little success, and early in December violent fighting took place in Athens itself. British troops were used to assist the Greek Government and to put down the Communist insurgents. At once public opinion in Britain was sharply divided, and with the war entering its final phase two forces, latent from the beginning, now revealed themselves: the one content merely to conserve what it had and the other eager for change. Both sides simplified a foreign crisis which bore no resemblance to any possible situation in Britain. The Conservatives, acutely conscious of the Russian menace to the British life-line in the Mediterranean, approved Mr. Churchill's policy of intervention. With self-generated illusion, Liberal and Labour opinion deplored it as an attack on the best democratic elements in

Greece, and many Labour leaders outside the Coalition boasted openly that Mr. Churchill's action would lose him the election. Feelings ran high. Public opinion in the United States was excited, and even Mr. Roosevelt was perturbed. At home it seemed for a moment as if the Coalition might be shattered, and on December 8 the Labour back-benchers in the House of Commons moved an amendment to the Address. It was, in fact, a challenge to the Prime Minister's policy in Greece. Mr. Churchill accepted it as such and demanded a vote of confidence. Although he had an easy triumph in the division, public opinion was far from satisfied.

Monday of December 11 was a day of wrath and trouble for me. The trouble began early with Mr. Eden ringing me on the telephone to complain of the B.B.C's summary of the Press comments on Greece. Worse was to come. In the afternoon Mr. Eden's private secretary telephoned to me. Mr. Leeper, the British Ambassador in Athens, had complained that in its account of the Greek debate in the House of Commons the Greek section of the B.B.C. had added the statement: "The vote of confidence is not the end for Greece. The people of England will express their real will at the next election."

I knew that both in P.W.E. and in the European Service of the B.B.C. there were sympathisers with the insurgents. But this was akin to mutiny. I guessed that some Greek had defeated the vigilance of the microphone controllers and had slipped in the offending sentences at the last second.

The same evening I was summoned to the War Cabinet. It was a bitterly cold day, and I wore my Russian fur coat. When I entered the ante-room at No. 10 Downing Street, several ministers were waiting, and Oliver Lyttelton greeted me loudly with: "Well, I must say, this is one of the finest entries into the Cabinet that I have ever seen."

I was soon to be deflated. It was a big meeting with a full agenda. I expected to be kept waiting a long time, but was summoned almost at once. Feeling like a worm, I crawled in and after a moment of bewilderment found an empty chair beside Mr. Ernest Bevin. I had a bad quarter of an hour. I had to read out the full text of the Greek script including the two inserted sentences. Mr. Churchill was most polite. He spoke more in sorrow than in anger. I made no excuses. I might have said that I had no administrative control over the European Service of the B.B.C., but the moment, I felt, was not propitious. Involuntarily I stared at the serried rows of faces round me and found no comfort. Then I heard Mr. Churchill thanking me for my courtesy "in finding time to come here today". Feeling like a guilty schoolboy who had had a painful interview with his headmaster and had escaped with a "pi-jaw" instead of a beating, I slunk from the room. As I went out, Lord Beaverbrook gave me a friendly wink.

Fortunately Mr. Bracken, who had been away ill, returned the next day and at once came to the rescue. In the end the "incident" was settled by changes in the Greek Section of the B.B.C.

Five days later I opened my Sunday newspapers and read optimistic headlines of "Germans Fleeing in the Rhineland". The truth however was that on the previous day Rundstedt had launched a fierce offensive in the Ardennes. It had had a considerable initial success, and German propaganda screamed that this was Germany's greatest hour. For several days the Germans continued to make headway, and, although the Chiefs of Staff remained confident, there was considerable anxiety both among the public and in ministerial circles. It was not fully allayed by December 25, and I spent a sober and rather gloomy Christmas at my house with Sargent and Wheeler-Bennett who was recovering from jaundice. I felt a little yellow myself. The war, far from ending in 1944, had taken a bad turn. Britain itself was clearly dividing into two camps, and in Greece we already seemed to be fighting our own election. Public disillusionment about the peace was manifest in a ditty which had appeared recently in the *Sunday Express*:

> "How can we build a better world,
> Where lovely peace shall reign,
> When so-called liberated folk
> Are falling out again?"

As for my own department, the gloom surrounding it seemed impenetrable. In the Far East and in the re-education of German prisoners of war I had been given two heavy new commitments. The cream of my senior staff had been taken away from me, and I was supposed, for the good of my health, to be taking things easily.

As usual, I was allowed little time for dismal reflections. On Christmas night Mr. Bracken telephoned to me. As he was speaking on an open line, he had to talk in a mumbo-jumbo language. The gist of the message was that I must immediately warn the European Service of the B.B.C. not to make any announcement on Greek matters without consulting me. He himself would speak to the Home Service and tell them to ring me. I spent some time in conveying rather cryptic instructions to the two departments of the B.B.C. Shortly before midnight, Mr. Ryan, the head of the News Department of the Home Service, telephoned to ask a conundrum: what was he to do if a reputable news agency announced that Mr. X and Mr. Y had arrived in a certain capital? I said: "Release it." He then told me that a Reuter's flash had announced the arrival of the Prime Minister and Mr. Eden in Athens.

I woke up Sargent who had gone to bed. He was surprised but was able to piece together the facts. Mr. Leeper had a new solution to the troubles of Greece. He wished to make Bishop Damaskinos Regent of the country. The Prime Minister must have made up his mind to go to see the new strong man for himself and had taken Mr. Eden with him.

It was true. The amazing Mr. Churchill, who since August had been to Italy, to Quebec and to Moscow, was off on his travels again. This time both Whitehall and the public were shocked by the spectacle of the Prime Minister of Britain setting out in bad weather, and without adequate arrangements for his security, to a capital where machine-gun and rifle shots were still regular accompaniments of the city's daily life. Fortunately Mr. Churchill was a convinced fatalist. Otherwise he would never have travelled at all in war-time.

New Year's Eve brought its comfort of good news, for General Ismay, whose judgment was rarely at fault, told me that not only was Rundstedt's advance stopped, but his armies were in difficulties. In his opinion, he added, the failure of this last desperate German attempt would shorten the war by several months.

On the strength of this I spent a mildly alcoholic Hogmanay with Wheeler-Bennett and my secretary.

CHAPTER TWO

FOG AND BITTER cold heralded the opening of the last year of the war and a pall of uncertainty shrouded the hopes that were in men's hearts. Although victory was now only a question of months, victory itself settled nothing. What mattered was the new world that would emerge from it. So far the statesmen had devised no clear pattern, but certain things to come had already begun to take their shape. The picture was not bright. True, nearly all occupied Europe had been freed, and in Germany the certainty of victory had now given way to scarcely concealed feelings of despair. But in the liberated countries the Germans had left behind them a legacy of famine and distress, and in the economic chaos new forces had arisen which threatened to turn the international war into a social war. To the countries of South-Eastern and Central Europe the Russians, both by the magnitude of their war effort and by their geographical proximity, had appeared not only as liberators but as the architects of their destiny. And in the small nations the feeling that their security depended on an alliance with Russia was stronger than their fear of Communism.

It was abundantly manifest that without a clear-cut understanding with Russia on the future shape of Europe there could be no peace. Yet in the way of such an understanding there were immense difficulties. The Russians wanted many changes in Eastern Europe. Their national security, they felt, entitled them to these changes. Inevitably they would demand a free hand, and a free hand meant a closed door, for no sensible person could believe that a régime, which after twenty-eight years of absolute power still banned foreigners from its soil, would not extend the iron curtain to the territories which came into its orbit. If we divided Europe into spheres of influence, I had little doubt that an understanding would be possible. But on these terms it would be unpalatable to the Western democracies on both sides of the Atlantic and to the vast mass of men and women who believed that in some form of world government and in some voluntary surrender of national sovereignty lay the only hope of a genuine peace.

How to reconcile these conflicting points of view was perhaps a superhuman task. Yet to Britain as a European Power the understanding with Russia was vital. Unfortunately, her position had weakened. After the first world war there had been three great victors: Great Britain, the United States and France. And because she had been the most exhausted and because she had borne the brunt of the early fighting, France was the weakest of the three. Now Britain, for much the same reasons, was in the position of France, and by the sheer weight of their war potential the United States and Russia stood together as the greatest military Powers of the world. Of the Big Triumvirate it was hard to decide at this stage whether Roosevelt or Stalin was Octavius. But, however great his personal stature, Mr. Churchill was indisputably Lepidus.

I spent the first week-end of the New Year at Mr. Eden's country house. Once again the only other guest was Mr. Winant. There was much talk on Russia. Mr. Eden was eager to have another meeting of the Foreign Secretaries in order to prepare a proper agenda and to clarify many outstanding problems before the next meeting of the Big Three. As the Yalta Conference was already as good as fixed for the beginning of February, I guessed that the preliminary meeting would not take place. Mr. Winant, although he agreed fully with the obvious advantages of such a meeting, was of the opinion that President Roosevelt would say "No". My sympathies were with Mr. Eden. Although I did not say so, I knew that few officials, either British or American, either civilian or soldier, ever came back from a meeting of the Big Three without an uneasy feeling that the immediate gains had always gone to Russia; the vague promises about the future to the United States and Britain. The reasons for this justifiable uneasiness were not far to seek. Temperamentally Mr. Churchill was an improviser. President Roosevelt believed that Stalin could be coaxed and that the way to do it was to prove to him that the tie between Britain and the United States was not so close as the Russians seemed to think. It was a policy of appeasement to which, willingly or unwillingly, Mr. Churchill had to subscribe. Moreover, both men always disliked prepared agenda which are the flesh and bones of every successful conference. They preferred to feel their way. Stalin got his way without the feeling.

The conferences were, doubtless, necessary and useful, but they never realised the expectations which the publicity given to them aroused in the hearts of the people. They took place in an atmosphere of unreality with no sense of time and no fixed programme except the continuous physical performance of feasting and toast-drinking. They took the form of talks at which no proper minutes were kept. Only the military decisions had any clarity, and such political decisions as were made usually kept the harassed officials busy for weeks in trying to unravel the skein of what had actually happened. For these shortcomings Stalin's persistent refusal to leave Russia and the peculiar methods of the Russians were largely responsible, but the final effect on the British and American publics was nearly always the same. Preliminary enthusiasm ended in disillusionment.

In this respect the Yalta Conference which took place in the first days of February differed only from previous meetings of the Big Three in the fact that President Roosevelt was visibly a sick man. An important decision was taken to "speed up" the Anglo-American offensive in the West. The determination to enforce terms of unconditional surrender on Germany was reaffirmed and measures were agreed to make it impossible for Germany ever to wage war again. The general conclusions, including the announcement of a Conference of the United Nations to be held at San Francisco in April, were impeccable, but the tentative solution of the particular and delicate problem of Poland was not so satisfactory. Stalin undertook to reorganise his Lublin Government on a broader democratic basis, with the inclusion of democratic leaders from Poland itself and from the Poles abroad and with a guarantee of free elections. On these conditions President Roosevelt and Mr. Churchill more or less committed themselves to recognition of the new Polish Government. It was perhaps the best that could be done at this late stage, but the loose definition which the word democracy had now acquired left the advantage with Stalin. It also meant the end of the Polish Government in London, and as such it was interpreted by the Poles abroad. The reaction of General Anders, who was commanding the large Polish army in Italy, was sharp and immediate. "We do not recognise," he announced, "and shall never recognise unilateral decisions." He made it clear that his Poles would not return to a Poland dominated by a Russian-sponsored Communist Government. To his great credit he ordered his Poles "to maintain discipline and dignity" and to continue the battle. Once again the unfortunate Poles were to learn that it was easier to die for Poland than to live in it.

For P.W.E. the period from the beginning of the year until the end of the war was one of frustration combined with feverish and rapidly improvised activity in which the gradual process towards final closing down was retarded by new commitments. Early in February General McClure raised the question of financial responsibility for the military information services in Germany after the war was over. P.W.D. had no funds. It was financed by O.W.I. and

P.W.E., the civil agencies. If they were to cease functioning immediately after the war, who was to provide the money? In default of the existence of any other organisation the civil agencies were instructed to continue their functions for as long as military government of Germany lasted. To meet both present and future needs we were asked to organise immediately a daily Press service in Morse to P.W.D. It was a big job. It was done efficiently.

We had, too, to do our best to organise a Far Eastern Department, and this was a thankless task. At this late stage the few existing experts had long been commandeered by other departments, and the War Office, faced with a man-power problem, refused to release any military staff. By patching here and borrowing there we gradually built a section, but it was a slow process and it was perhaps as well for us that the war in the East was to end suddenly without too severe a strain being put on our resources.

I was still woefully short of senior assistants and I owe very much to the noble conduct of two university dons, who, with priority releases and urgent demands to return to their colleges on pain of dismissal, sacrificed their future in order to help P.W.E. out of a murky hole. Fortunately one was rewarded later with a better post. The other has brains to make his name in almost any walk of life. On the other hand, many of the P.W.E. regional sections for the occupied countries were closing down.

I had therefore two main preoccupations: to find a suitable replacement for Brooks and an eventual successor to myself and to do the best I could for my large staff who with the red light of departmental extinction before them were becoming increasingly anxious about their future. As regards the staff, I had hoped to transfer many to the new information services which were being organised under the Foreign Office. Unfortunately, there was a long interim period during which the Foreign Office was not ready to assume control and the Ministry of Information continued to be responsible for the nomination of Press attachés and for foreign publicity generally. The Ministry held that propagandists were unsuited by temperament and training to the more sober activities of post-war publicity. Admittedly the argument had its points, but I thought it was wrong. P.W.E. possessed great talent, and I was sad that it should be lost. But when I studied the scale of salaries that were likely to be offered to possible P.W.E. candidates I changed my mind. We had men who in peace time had been earning large incomes, and these I advised strongly to abandon all thought of a bureaucratic career. The intermediate staff were easier to place. Some were absorbed by other Government departments. Others found jobs with commercial firms.

Finding a successor to Brooks was a more complicated business. I wanted a soldier, partly because our work was now largely with the armies in the field and partly because our relations with the War Office had never been good. Brooks was a marine; his military deputy was an air commodore. Every Service Department preferred dealing with an officer of its own service. I thought that a soldier would smoothe our relations with the War Office, particularly in regard to the re-education of German prisoners of war. Mr. Bracken recommended Major General Alec Bishop. General Ismay and General Hollis whom I consulted praised him highly, and I begged Mr. Bracken to write to Sir James Grigg. There was some fierce correspondence between the two Ministers both of whom are masters of a trenchant pen. In the end Mr. Bracken won, but two months passed before the transfer was agreed, and it was another month before General Bishop could join us.

Altogether it was a period of hail and farewell; of saying goodbye to departing colleagues and of adapting myself to newcomers. There was one farewell which affected me more than any other. President Beneš was going home. After more than six years of the bitterness of war, time, as the Czech proverb says, had brought him roses.

On the 17th of February I went to Aston Abbotts to spend the day with him and to say goodbye. After weeks of sharp cold and snow the day was damp and muggy. The house was already being dismantled; the atmosphere, one of pending departure. I nearly always lunched alone with the President, but today Madame Beneš was present. She was very emotional. She was glad, she said, to be going home, but she was leaving a large part of her heart in England. She reminded me of her first arrival soon after Munich when she was too shattered to see anyone for months. Her English friends had understood as no other people could have understood. She would never forget. She spoke very simply and quietly. I knew that every word came from her heart. She was distressed, too, because, five days before, the last male descendant of the great Masaryk, except Jan, had died. There had been two grandsons of the old President. The elder had been killed flying for Britain in the war; the younger, a promising violinist, had now died in Edinburgh. Madame Beneš was worried about Jan who had been ill himself and who, she knew, would be shattered by this new tragedy.

After luncheon I had a long talk with the President alone in his study. For the nth time he went over the political situation in full detail, expounding his ardent desire for an understanding between Russia and Britain and reiterating his belief in its feasibility. We must, he said, speak to the Russians plainly and honestly. That was what they wanted and understood. What they resented was flattery from the big politicians and criticism in the Anglo-American Press. That aroused their deepest suspicions.

I found it hard to concentrate on politics. My mind and heart were heavy with memories of the past, of my long association with the President extending over a quarter of a century, and of the many hours that I had spent with him during the war. I had been attached to him in September, 1939, when he had no standing and very little backing in Britain. Then in the middle of 1941 I had been pushed against my will into this political warfare job. But our association had continued, and I had spent two hours alone with him almost every week. He had given me his full confidence. I had found him an excellent barometer of the fluctuating situation in Europe; a barometer that was never allowed to fall and if sometimes set too high was always supported by sound reasoning. Above all, he had helped to strengthen my conviction of the virtues of the Anglo-Russian Treaty and of the imperative necessity of an Anglo-Russian understanding.

Involuntarily my eyes wandered round the room, to the overloaded book shelves, to the rows of maps in the corner, and to the ancient and, doubtless valuable Russian ikon presented to him by Litvinov. Finally, my gaze came to rest on Panuška's painting of the countryside near Asch where thirty years ago the young Eduard Beneš had slipped through the Austrian frontier guards to carry on from Paris the struggle for the first liberation. It was as fair a landscape as is to be found in Europe. I knew it well. Down below in the valley was a trout stream where I had spent many happy hours. Tomorrow the picture would be gone.

I thought of the curious nature of this unemotional little man who knew everybody and who had so little time for real friendships, of the languages which he had mastered not for pleasure but because they were necessary for his work, of his quaint gallicisms in English. I remembered the various people that I had brought to luncheon so that they could learn to know him better: Moley Sargent who had seen him in optimistic mood and whom the President had delighted by announcing with a smile: "The news is good; today

I am making my luggages." I remembered, too, the impression that he made on my son to whom he had given admirable advice on the virtues of action. The effect had nearly been spoilt by the solemn admonition: "In life you must take the bull by the corns." Now he was going home for good, and I should hear no more gallicisms.

At four o'clock Madame Beneš came in to say goodbye. I signed her autograph book. She thanked me for what she said I had done for her country, talked of my son to whom she had taken a great liking, and said that I must bring him with me on my first visit to Prague. There were tears in her eyes.

The President came out with me to the front door. For once he seemed embarrassed, and his face looked drawn. He thanked me more than generously. "You will come of course," he said quietly. "I know you understand that I may have difficulties." He paused and then continued firmly: "But I shall settle them."

We shook hands, and I climbed into my car while he stood in the doorway looking rather sadly towards the paddock. The sun had just come out from behind a watery cloud, and the delicate pattern of the Chilterns had begun to unfold itself. There was an awkward moment while my chauffeur struggled with the car. Then we started. I raised my hat, and the President waved his arm. Then slowly we proceeded down the drive past the sentries. I looked back once. The President was still standing in the doorway. I felt miserable and prayed that all would be well with this remarkable little man for whom I had a deep affection. To him it had been given twice in a lifetime to save his country. He deserved the distinction. He possessed all the qualities of greatness and the greatest of all qualities: courage in adversity.

A few days later I received a letter from him. It was warmly worded. It contained the sentence: "Your name will remain indelibly written in the annals of our second victorious struggle for national liberation."

I prize this letter, not for the praise, but for the feeling that my war-work for the Czechs was in a small sense a requital for the years of my youth that I had squandered in Prague.

In other circumstances these partings, coupled with my own problems, might have depressed me unduly, but in the sunshine of the best English spring that I can remember, all pessimism vanished. The war was going well, better perhaps than even the optimists hoped and believed. Since Brooks's departure I had been seeing much more of

General Ismay and, in particular, of General Hollis. He was small in stature, terribly overworked, and afflicted at times with asthma, but always spruce, always good-tempered and never showing a sign that he had a care in the world. He gave his opinion concisely. He permitted himself no enthusiasms. Neither bad news nor good news affected the tone of his voice. His long-term views on the course of the war had been consistently accurate. When most people were profoundly pessimistic of Russia's ability to resist the German attacks, he had remained confident. Now in February, 1945, both Ismay and he were sure that the end was near.

He came to spend a night with me at my country house and gave me a fuller account of the war than he had ever had time for when in his office. The picture he drew was more than reassuring. The weight of the Allied armament in the West was now colossal. March would see a series of hammer-blows which the Germans could hardly resist. Although our propaganda must keep pace with events, the end could not be far off.

There was better and most unexpected news to come. The Americans were doing remarkably well in the Pacific. The war with Japan, Hollis said confidently, would finish much sooner than most people expected. I asked how soon. "Possibly and even probably this year," he said. This was a remarkable forecast, for at that time and even as late as Potsdam many military experts were talking in terms of two years.

Hollis also gave me a wonderful word-portrait of Mr. Churchill, of whom he was a devoted admirer, and told me a personal story which illustrates the human side of a man who is commonly and quite erroneously supposed to be ruthless towards his subordinates. When the Prime Minister was dangerously ill at Marrakesh in December, 1942, Hollis was the only member of his staff who was with him. Mr. Churchill was a difficult patient. He could not stand being cut off from the inside news of the war and was irritated because he could not receive his telegrams. He was even more worried when Hollis proposed to fly to England to arrange for their despatch. After some argument, however, Hollis went, made the necessary arrangements, and was back within thirty hours. Mr. Churchill was pleased. Hollis must be rewarded for his devotion. In spite of his illness the Prime Minister took immense pains to conceal his intentions and for some days he carried on a secret communication with London. Then, when Hollis came down to breakfast one morning, he found a letter and a little packet on his plate. The letter contained his promotion to Major-General; the packet, the rank badges for his shoulder straps.

We had an exhilarating evening, and I went to bed happier than I had been for five and a half years. Many people still regarded victory as a close race with Germany's secret weapons, but, after hearing Hollis's carefully reasoned optimism, I felt confident that all would be well. P.W.E's problems now seemed much less difficult.

Everything that Hollis predicted came true. On March 2 German resistance on the front of the American Ninth Army crumbled, and on March 5 American tanks entered Cologne. These successes coincided with Mr. Churchill's visit to General Eisenhower's and Field-Marshal Montgomery's headquarters. He also drove through the Ninth Army's sector, chalked a huge shell with the words "Hitler—personally", fired the gun which sent the shell on the Germans escaping across the Rhine, and received a tumultuous welcome from the American troops. He was the first British statesman to set foot on German soil since Mr. Chamberlain went to Munich. The contrast between the two visits must have warmed his heart. The battle of the Rhine, which was to seal the doom of Germany, had begun.

At this moment—two days, in fact, before the 1st of March—I was completely immobilised by a violent attack of sciatica, and General Bishop, who had just joined us, had to take over the department single-handed and with no assistance from me apart from an occasional bedside consultation. Fortunately, he was a man of the highest ideals, absolutely selfless in his devotion to duty and tireless in his capacity for hard work. A civilian department like P.W.E., which I had found expedient to guide with a loose rein, must have come as a shock to him, for its ideas of discipline were very different from those of a military organisation. But he took the hurdle in his stride and tackled our problems with zeal and patience.

I spent my time listening-in to the news of the rapid Allied advances, of our successful crossing of the Rhine, and of General Patton's magnificent tank thrusts. As a self-imposed task I concentrated on the German broadcasts in Russian. They were curious in their appeal. The speakers were Russians and obviously Trotskists. The best was a woman who with great eloquence and vigour denounced Stalin as a tyrant who had destroyed the revolution. She gave lurid details of the purges of anti-Stalin Bolsheviks. Using Lenin's phrase, she called on all the Bolsheviks to rise against the oppressors and turn "the imperialist war into a civil war". As the Germans had destroyed every chance of creating civil disturbance in

Russia by their brutal treatment of every section of the population, the propaganda was a remarkable example of Nazi cynicism. I wrote a memorandum on my conclusions and sent it to Sargent.

By the beginning of April, I was able to hobble, but on the doctor's advice Mr. Bracken packed me off to Edinburgh again to have deep-ray treatment which, owing to its interference with radar operations, was unobtainable in London.

During my first night in the Royal Infirmary my nurses, despairing of getting me off to sleep anyway, gave me the news of President Roosevelt's death at Warm Springs. The nurses, who took little interest in politics and who see death every day, were distressed and asked me whether Mr. Roosevelt's demise was not a greater blow to Britain than a lost battle. Their instinct was sound. As far as the war was concerned, the President had completed his task. But to the cause of peace his death was a disaster. To Stalin and to the Kremlin he had meant much as an American who, among a large number of anti-Russians, stood for good relations and a square deal with the Soviet Union. In his own country the fierce hatred which he roused in the hearts of his opponents was in itself a tribute to his greatness. The United States, I felt, was unlikely to find another President of his calibre for many years to come. To Britain he had been a friend in her greatest need. Indeed we owed him almost as much as we owed to Mr. Churchill, for he had taken great risks to help us.

I remembered Bob Sherwood's tribute to Mr. Bracken who, at a dinner given to him by a group of American newspaper publishers in New York at the time of the second Quebec Conference, had been put on the spot by an awkward question: were the British Government supporting Franklin Roosevelt for his election as President for the fourth term? Mr. Bracken had replied at once. Neither the British Government nor the British people, he declared, were taking sides in the presidential election. It would be most improper of them to interfere in the internal affairs of the United States. But if Americans expected either the British Government or the British people to forget what Franklin Roosevelt had done to help the cause of Freedom before the United States came into the war, they were asking the impossible, for if the British people ever did forget, they would be unworthy of the name of human beings.

Bob Sherwood always declared that this was the best answer to an embarrassing question that any Englishman had ever made in the United States. Britain, I felt, would always remember F. D. R. The United States, I was sure, would soon have reason to regret his passing.

M

My treatment at the infirmary soon put me right, and I wrote another paper on Russia for Sargent, emphasising Russia's desire for security and the necessity of our recognising a new situation in Eastern and South-Eastern Europe and of deciding what we must concede and what we must resist. My recommendations were that, while maintaining the friendliest attitude and doing everything possible to remove Russian suspicions, we should assess all the points of difference, face them fearlessly and have them out frankly round the table while the Americans and we were still strong. This paper, with virtually no alterations, was printed as a memorandum for the Potsdam Conference three months later.

Tempted by the long spell of good weather, I went to Tomintoul for a week's convalescence before returning to London. It was a risky experiment at this time of the year and in one sense it failed, for scarcely had I passed the Drumochter water-shed than the snow began to fall. It never ceased for seven days. Huddled round the fire in the same room in which I had heard Mr. Chamberlain's tired voice announce the beginning of the war on September, 1939, I kept my ears glued to the radio.

The news was stupendous. The Russians were in Berlin. The German armies opposite Montgomery were surrendering. Hitler and Goebbels had committed suicide. Mussolini had been killed by his own people. It was the end; all, at least, except the official end.

My feelings were more of heartfelt relief than of violent enthusiasm. Was it, I wondered, because I was older or because the end was different from 1918. I recalled my talks with the young men of the village when they were going off to fight in those first days of September, 1939: their reasoning, their doubts, their hopes. How many would come back and in what mood? What peace would they find? Would there be a new world? Forebodingly I recalled a passage from Amiel's *Journal Intime* which I had been re-reading in the infirmary: "What terrible masters the Russians would be if ever they should spread the weight of their rule over the countries of the South! They would bring us a polar despotism such as the world has never known, silent as darkness, rigid as ice, insensible as bronze. Slavery without compensation or relief." It was written of the Russia of the Tsars in 1856. Today there was a new Russia, different from Amiel's picture but similar enough to cause anxiety and suspicion in the minds of many Anglo-Americans.

The little hotel at Tomintoul was not empty. There were several officers on leave including a squadron-leader. They showed no "mafficking spirit", only a profound gratitude that thousands of young lives would now be spared. Their thoughts were already busy with the future, and they were anxious thoughts. The squadron-leader, an airman of the first world war, had been a solicitor and, in order to fly again, had given up a good practice. He doubted if he could rebuild it, and wondered what the chances were at his age of finding an open-air job. The others talked in the same sober manner.

I was glad that I had heard the end in Tomintoul. But now I was restlessly eager to return to London. Three roads were blocked by snow, and I had to make a long circuitous drive to Aviemore. While I waited at the station, a train came in loaded with German prisoners. They had no overcoats. They were mostly young boys. They appeared dejected and miserable, but not under-fed. I turned away from them to the Cairngorms. They looked extraordinarily peaceful and innocent in their mantle of virgin snow—a symbol of the fresh opportunity that was being given to a war-mad world.

I arrived in London in the early morning of Saturday, May 5, and bought a *Daily Express*. It had a leader with the caption: "This is It." It quoted Walter Winchell's remark on the suicides of Hitler and Goebbels: "Well, they've killed the right people this time." But there was serious news from Moscow. After weeks of delay the Russians had admitted that they had arrested the Poles who had come from Poland to negotiate about the promised democratic expansion of the Lublin Government. Was this the shape of the peace to come? The day was horribly cold with dull, grey skies and sleet-like rain.

I went at once to my office and got into touch with Whitehall about the announcement of Victory Day. It was expected at any moment. We should be given sufficient advance notice. The time of the official announcement had to be synchronised with Moscow and Washington.

I spent the Monday morning of May 6 in writing a message of ministerial thanks to the members of P.W.E. with a special commendation of the women, who had been splendid. I was told privately that the Germans had surrendered officially at Rheims at 2.41 a.m. that morning. At 3 p.m. we were informed that the official announcement of V.E. Day would be made at 6 p.m. on the B.B.C. Meanwhile, we were to maintain complete secrecy. The suppressed excitement was intense, but was broken by a message which came an hour later. To please Stalin, who wanted the news suppressed until he could hold his big day in Berlin, our announcement was to be delayed until 3 p.m. the next day. We all felt dejected and irritated by the postponement. Fortunately, at 6 p.m. the B.B.C. gave the whole story. An American correspondent at S.H.A.E.F. had broken the secrecy code and had revealed the news of the surrender to the world. Rightly the British and American public, weary of delay, began to celebrate.

On Tuesday, May 7, I was at my office by nine o'clock. It was still officially a working day, but the streets had been crowded all night. I spent a busy morning and at one o'clock went to Claridge's for the farewell luncheon to General Fred Anderson, deputy to General Spaatz and in the opinion of his friends the coming man in the defence system of the United States. Throughout the war he had been most helpful to P.W.E. in providing aeroplanes for leaflets, and in experimenting with the leaflet bomb which, by its accuracy in dropping leaflets over a fixed target, was of immense value to our work. There was a brave show of generals and air-marshals, including Doolittle, Harris, Bottomley and Ismay.

Fred Anderson, who, having finished his job in Europe, was leaving immediately for Washington in order to play his part in the Pacific War, made a remarkable speech in which he gave most generous credit to the R.A.F. who, he said, "taught us everything." "Our Fortresses", he went on, "had received great publicity, but it was right that the public should know that they carried only the same bomb-weight as a Mosquito." Then, with some emotion, he drew a happy picture of Anglo-American co-operation, which, he said, not only had won the war but was the sole hope for the future. Rarely, if ever, have I heard a soldier speak so simply and so well.

Air-Marshal Bottomley replied for the R.A.F. and received an immense ovation. My luncheon neighbour was General Curtis, Spaatz's Chief of Staff, who had flown over from France for the occasion after being present at Rheims. He told me that Bottomley was the most popular of our own air-marshals with the Americans. "We have", he said, "immense respect for Portal who is a great man, but we *love* Bottomley."

The efficient Americans having provided a radio set, we remained at the table to hear Mr. Churchill's victory announcement at 3 p.m. A few minutes late the B.B.C. band struck the first bars of the National Anthem. As one man the Americans rose, made a half-turn left, and stood stiffly to attention. It was a solemn moment. Then came the voice of Mr. Churchill who had given so much to the war and who had borne so many of its burdens. He told us what everyone knew, but all wished to hear him say. The war in Europe was over. Hostilities would end officially at one minute past midnight. "Advance Britannia! Long live the cause of Freedom! God save The King!"

I wished god-speed to Fred Anderson, and set out for Bush House. On my way I heard the carillon, for the first time since 1939, playing "O God our Help in Ages Past". In offices people were tearing up paper and throwing it out of windows. Vast crowds, admirable in their restraint and patience, but with the joy of relief on every face, were surging towards Whitehall. Traffic was already congested, and I had some difficulty in reaching my office. All the staff were still there, but only General Bishop was working. I sent them home or out into the streets as they wished.

At about a quarter to six, Mr. Churchill appeared on the balcony of the Ministry of Health accompanied by the Chiefs of Staff. A roar like a long sustained roll of thunder greeted him. With tears in his eyes he tried to speak, but in the cheering even his great voice was hardly heard beyond the first rows of the serried mass of people. He had given his countrymen their finest hour. Now they were giving him his.

CHAPTER THREE

ALTHOUGH THE VICTORY celebrations continued for several days, the speed with which the atmosphere of the whole country changed from war to peace was startling. Public interest centred itself almost at once on the election which all felt was coming, and party divisions, long latent, now revealed themselves nakedly. The two great political Parties were jockeying for position and each was eager to foist on the other the responsibility for breaking the Coalition before the end of the war with Japan. Between May 20 and May 22 an exchange of letters took place between Mr. Churchill and Mr. Attlee. Mr. Churchill offered a continuation of the Coalition until the end of the war or for eighteen months, whichever date was shorter. If the offer were not accepted, then the election would be held in July. Several of the Labour leaders, including Mr. Attlee himself, were willing enough to continue the Coalition, but their followers, led by the redoubtable Mr. Aneurin Bevan, were determined on an immediate break with the Tories. Mr. Attlee, therefore, rejected Mr. Churchill's proposal and offered an election in the autumn. It was immediately clear that the election would be held in July. The Coalition, which had held office since May, 1940, and had carried the country to victory, resigned at once, and on May 25 the names of the "caretaker" Conservative Government were announced. The new Government had a luke-warm reception, and some of the appointments seemed to confirm the impression that in home affairs Mr. Churchill was opposed to the changes which many people desired and which the younger generation regarded as inevitable.

The altered sentiment of the country was, I think, accurately reflected in P.W.E., whose Socialist members not only outnumbered the Conservatives and Liberals but were much more active politically. Although they never refused to accept and to carry out the policy of the Government, they frequently disliked it. Perhaps the strongest feeling in P.W.E.—and it was not confined entirely to the Socialists —was against the privileged classes from which, irrespective of their talent, Mr. Churchill was accused of making all the important war appointments. The same feeling provoked much of P.W.E's hostility towards the Foreign Office. The talent of its individual members was respected, but the department as a whole was dismissed much too sweepingly as an antiquated institution which was out of touch with the realities of the new world.

The attitude of P.W.E. and the impressions which had been forced on me by my interpretation of all reports on home morale, left me with the conviction that, not only was Europe going Left, but that in her own way England was going with it, and, although in the London clubs nearly everyone assumed that Mr. Churchill would win the election off his own bat, I had for some time been picking up some minor but profitable bets on a Labour victory.

Inevitably the end of the war in Europe and the change of Government affected the status of P.W.E. Mr. Bracken had been transferred to the Admiralty, but before he went he had agreed to a reform which I had always wanted. P.W.E. was at last to come under one Minister, and Mr. Eden consented nobly, if a little reluctantly, to add this new responsibility to his many burdens. Although I had never liked dual control, I deeply regretted Mr. Bracken's departure. To me personally he had shown a kindness and consideration which I shall never forget. He had done much more than this. He had been at all times a doughty champion of the department's interests. He was at his best when things were going badly, for a crisis seemed to direct his superabundant and many-sided energy to the one point where it was most needed. In a high degree he commanded the affection of a remarkable variety of people from lame dogs who relied on his protection to brilliant intellectuals and men of high principle like Cyril Radcliffe. The reason was simple. One had only to know him to realise that the real Bracken was a very kind man and that his sometimes caustic tongue belied the warmest of hearts and a deep and genuine sympathy with all human suffering. We gave him a farewell dinner, and he delighted us by a typically racy speech, rich in wit and indiscretions, in which he praised the temporary civil servants at the expense of the permanent officials and the Service Departments.

There were other changes which caused an infinity of trouble. Now that the war in Europe was over, political warfare was a misnomer, and there was a considerable exodus from the department. Some members resigned in order to take part in the election. Others left in order to safeguard their future. Others again were taken away by commercial firms who, eager to restart their businesses, could not be refused. In this manner I lost my brilliant director of production. Yet our work, if now restricted to Germany and the Far East, had not decreased. With the division of Germany into zones, P.W.D.,

S.H.A.E.F. was breaking up, and with the cessation of Anglo-American integration each national army now had to have its own information service.

The Americans, already strongly represented in P.W.D., had a machine ready to hand and were moving into their zone with a numerous and well-equipped team of broadcasting and journalistic experts. The British army had to start from scratch. Moreover, its planning, based presumably on the British Government's policy of non-fraternisation, had been quite inadequate. As P.W.E. was still responsible for supplying material and personnel to the British Information Service in Germany, the chaotic conditions which at first prevailed, involved the frequent sending of our best experts on visits to Germany. Inevitably they made recommendations which were not always acceptable to the soldiers. Moreover, members of my senior staff were always being called away for special urgent jobs like the interrogation of important German prisoners like Ribbentrop and Goering. In a sense it was a compliment to our individual talent. But to the department as a whole it was unsettling, and I found it difficult to maintain even the essential services. Luckily Jack Wheeler-Bennett, who shared my house with me and who had been away ill for three months, came back, and his tact and his expert knowledge of Germany were of great advantage.

Early in June I received a knock-out blow when William Strang, who had been appointed Political Adviser to Field-Marshal Montgomery, asked if he could see me. I guessed that, as he was coming to me and wished to come at once, he wanted some favour. He began tactfully with a long account of the inadequacy of the information services in Germany. It was brilliantly done. At the end he turned to me. "I have a request to make to you," he said. "We've got to get the information service right. General Weeks (Montgomery's deputy in Berlin) wants Bishop to reorganise it. I must give him your answer tonight."

I took Wheeler-Bennett out of the room and asked his advice. He pointed out at once that, if I let Bishop go, I should inevitably have to remain longer in Government service. The argument was all too cogent. I had intended to leave on July 1. Although my skin had stood up fairly well to the strain of the last year, the doctors had told me that I was courting daily disaster. Without a deputy and a successor I could not leave. The prospects of getting one were small. On the other hand, there was an obvious advantage in having a P.W.E. man as head of the Information Services in Germany.

I went back to Strang in ten minutes and told him he could have Bishop. Twenty-four hours later I saw General Weeks, a most impressive man who combined the quick and orderly mind of a great business executive with a thorough knowledge of military matters. He thanked me for letting Bishop go. I told him that he must give me a first-class man to take his place.

"What about General Strong?" he asked. I did not know General Strong, but I knew that General Bedell Smith had the highest opinion of him. He had been General Eisenhower's director of Intelligence both in North Africa and in S.H.A.E.F. He was a great expert on Germany and had acted as interpreter at the Rheims surrender. Even with Mr. Eden's backing I was unlikely to get anyone a quarter as good from the War Office. The whole negotiation was finished in ten minutes. Through no fault of General Weeks it was August 2 before Strong was able to join us.

While the Allied armies were trying to evolve some order out of the state of chaos in which the Nazis had left Germany, political divisions between the Anglo-Americans and the Russians were becoming daily more accentuated. In Germany the Russians were already encouraging the formation of German political parties. The British were still bound by the policy of non-fraternisation, and Field-Marshal Montgomery was explaining that the reason why British soldiers "did not even speak to children was the necessity of proving to the German people the full extent of their guilt for the war". The Americans were pursuing a middle course with the G.I's determined to fraternise whatever the policy of their Government might be. In other parts of Europe there were similar danger points, and Tito's refusal to loosen his stranglehold on Trieste was, doubtless, backed by tacit Russian support. While Labour was still fooling itself with the delusion that, if a Labour Government were returned to power, relations with Moscow would improve, suspicions of Russia in Tory circles were now nearly as strong as Russian suspicions of Britain and of the United States.

One story, invented by some wag, but valuable as a symptom of the prevailing atmosphere, was current in Whitehall at this time. The Chiefs of Staff, it ran, were with Mr. Churchill one evening and, bewildered by the vagaries of Russian policy, had asked him: "What do you think the Russians really want?"

Mr. Churchill had replied gruffly: "Want? What they want is a good lesson."

As for Russian suspicions, they had already exceeded the limits of absurdity, for early in April Stalin had sent a telegram saying that he had been reliably informed that we had made an arrangement with the Germans behind his back whereby the German army was to surrender to the Anglo-Americans but was to continue fighting against the Russians. He had been given a very stiff answer by President Roosevelt whose telegram, conveying his indignation, was the last that he ever signed.

During May I had been seeing more than usual of the Russian representatives in this country. On May 16 I had attended the victory celebrations at the Russian Embassy and had had a surprisingly free talk with a high Russian officer who spoke no English. He told me that the Russian officers were not like the old Bolsheviks that I had known. They were, however, very conscious of Russia's contribution to the defeat of Germany and were not, he said, in the least afraid of the British and Americans. We should get nowhere by trying to brow-beat Russia as in the past. He was quite confident that there would be no trouble between Britain and Russia. The British working-man, he said, would never stand for any quarrel.

A week later I had also had a long talk with a member of the Russian Trade Delegation. He had been an officer, but was now a civilian. His confidence in Russia's future was complete. Russia, he said, would be glad of Anglo-American help in the early stages of her reconstruction, but it was not vital. In the last war the Russians knew nothing about machinery. Now they knew, and they no longer needed foreign engineers. Reconstruction had already started, and in Stalingrad, where not a building had been left undamaged, tractors were being manufactured again. He gave me a glowing account of the immense wealth of Siberia and of its development which he said would amaze the world by its rapidity. I was impressed by the picture which he drew, for he was a cultured man and, I guessed, not a Communist, and he spoke without boastfulness.

I had also been present at Mr. Eden's small luncheon-party on May 31 for the anniversary of the Anglo-Russian Treaty and sat between Marshal of the Royal Air Force Sir Charles Portal and General Sharapov, the new head of the Russian Military Mission. He was, I think, the third head, for our P.W.E. friend, General Vassiliev, had preceded him and in between there had been another General Vassiliev. Now as M. Sobolev had said, both V1 and V2 had gone. The luncheon was a heavy affair, although Mr. Eden struggled manfully with M. Gusev who, as usual, was almost painfully silent in every language including Russian. I had to interpret between

Portal and General Sharapov who spoke no English. The talk was mostly about the Russian army. General Sharapov, a pleasant, well-mannered man, who had been a lieutenant in the first world war, answered all questions quite freely. He explained that an officer's son who wished to be an officer could begin his career at nine. After that, provided that he passed his examinations, the State looked after him for the rest of his life. I asked if these schools were called cadet schools. "No," he replied gravely. "Cadet is a Tsarist term. The schools are called by various names: for instance, Suvorov School."

"Suvorov," I said, "is a great hero today."

"Yes," he replied, "but he has always been a hero to the Russian army."

I could see that the General, like so many of the new officers, had a great respect for the traditions of the Russian Army. Nevertheless, he was a modernist, and in no sense more so than in his tribute to the Russian women who, he said, had made an immense contribution to Russia's victory. Not only had they performed all the vast tasks of agriculture and heavy industry but also had worked right up to and in the front line and had driven tanks. They were, he said, far quicker in the uptake than the men.

I was deeply impressed by these Russian officers. They never discussed or criticised the internal politics of their own country. Indeed, it would have been foolish to ask them an indiscreet question, for it would at once have reduced them to a dogged silence. But their quick self-assurance was new to me and therefore doubly impressive. Certainly I had met no Russian officer who was not sincerely convinced that Russia had defeated Germany almost single-handed and that therefore Russia was the greatest military power in the world.

I thought of the Russia immediately after the first world war. It had been a period of great decadence marked by a dejected pacifism. It was symbolised in my mind by the songs of Vertinsky who had written:

> "I do not know why
> Or for what purpose
> Who sent them to death
> With relentless, untrembling hand.
> Only it was all so useless,
> So pitiless...."

How different was this barrenness from the war-poems of the new Russia, from Simonov's:

"Do you remember the roads around Smolensk, Alyosha,
How unceasingly the bitter rain fell from the sky,
How the tired women brought us milk in their pitchers,
Hugging them like children at their breasts to keep them dry;
How they murmured after us: 'May the Lord bless and save you,'
As in secret from their eyes they wiped away the tears,
And how once again they called themselves 'wives of soldiers',
As in the mighty Russia of bygone years?"

In this new Russia there was no questioning of the goal and purpose of the road which was being trod. There was not only a new Russia; there was a new Russian people, still in process of their awakening, but deeply conscious of the greatness of their future. One day they would be stronger than the Kremlin which had roused them from their slumber. There was no room for decadence in this self-reliant and over-confident new Russia. Were there signs of decadence in Britain? I had heard the Vertinsky note of pessimism in the war poems of our own young men. If the new Britain were to lack self-reliance, then the over-confidence of a still experimental and semi-ignorant Russia would be the greatest danger to Anglo-Russian understanding.

I had an appointment with Mr. Eden that afternoon, but after luncheon he drew me aside and said that he would have to put me off. He was going to see his doctor. He had been having internal pains for some time.

Two days later, on the Sunday night of June 3, I turned on my radio set for the 9 p.m. news. Mr. Eden's illness was announced. He was suffering from duodenal trouble and would require at least a fortnight's rest. Sargent was with me, and, regarding the "fortnight's rest" as a euphemism, we both took a gloomy view of the bulletin. We saw the future darkly: no Foreign Secretary and no Eden for the next meeting of the Big Three which had now been fixed for Potsdam on July 15. Even if we underestimated the recuperative powers of his wonderful constitution, it was clear that he could take no active part in the election campaign.

The next day the campaign started in real earnest with the first of the series of election broadcasts inaugurated by the B.B.C. with the agreement of the three political parties. It was delivered by Mr. Churchill and, brilliant broadcaster as he is, it was emphatically the worst broadcast that he had ever made. I listened-in and, like most people, was antagonised. His voice sounded unconvincing. The violence of his language contrasted strangely with the majestic sweep of his war-speeches in which he had always paid a deserved tribute to the unity of the country. The more thoughtful Conservatives were gloomy and felt that the broadcast would lose them many votes. The Socialists in P.W.E. were jubilant. They had never feared the Conservatives. They had been afraid of the political wizardry and immense popularity of Mr. Churchill. Now they felt that he had delivered himself into their hands. He was followed by Mr. Attlee who, quick to seize his advantage, delivered the dignified national broadcast which nearly everyone felt the Prime Minister should have made.

To the misfortune of the Tories, Mr. Churchill's broadcast set the tone of the other Conservative broadcasts which, with the exception of Sir John Anderson's (and he was a non-Party man!), were uniformly bad. It was not until June 27 that Mr. Eden spoke from his sick-bed at Binderton. Not usually a convincing broadcaster, he excelled himself on this occasion, and the B.B.C. experts were impressed by the improvement in his delivery. His voice was more natural. The matter of his speech, too, was excellent and quite free from abuse and extravagant promises. Above all, he succeeded for the first time in giving to each individual listener that impression of intimacy which is the secret of all successful broadcasting. As a matter of fact, he had picked up some useful hints on broadcasting during his last visit to the United States in April and on the advice of Bob Dixon, his principal Private Secretary, had addressed this particular talk to an imaginary listener. The man he chose was his sergeant in the first world war. This broadcast won him an overwhelming majority in his own constituency, but it came too late to have any influence on the Conservative campaign.

A week later I went down to Binderton to spend the day and stay the night with him. Mrs. Eden was away at Leamington fighting his election for him, and he was alone. He looked better than I had expected, his face being already brown from the fresh air of the country. I helped him to go through the huge pile of letters that he had received after his broadcast. They came from well-known and unknown people and from followers of all three political parties. The letters were of one pattern. They welcomed the contrast of his serious and sober talk with the blatancy of the other Tory broadcasts.

I told him that I did not like the manner in which the Conservatives had run their election campaign and that I thought they would be defeated. I do not know if he agreed, but he described the election as the cheapest and dirtiest that he could remember in his twenty-one years of Parliamentary life. I regretted his illness and wondered to myself whether, if he had been fit, he could have exercised some restraint on the Tory band-waggon. More likely his presence in London would have made no difference. The Prime Minister regarded him as an expert on foreign affairs. He had other advisers for the home front. Moreover, Mr. Churchill was an eighteenth-century figure who liked the rough-and-tumble and hard "scrapping" of an election dog-fight. Yet I felt that among the youth of the country Mr. Eden had the largest following of any Conservative.

Mr. Eden then told me about his son Simon, a corporal in a bomber squadron in Burma. He had been missing for over a week, and Mr. Eden had received the first news as he was about to make his broadcast. The boy, who had been trained in Canada, had been on what would have been his last operational flight before being transferred to Kandy. Mr. Eden showed me the various telegrams which Air-Marshal Park had sent him. To my mind they held out no hope. Although I said nothing, I realised that he knew that it was the end. I did not need to surmise what he felt. I had seen him together with his boys. He was a truly admirable father. He begged me earnestly not to mention his loss to anyone. He did not wish the news to be published until after the election.

We spent a very quiet evening until ten o'clock, when the Prime Minister telephoned. The news startled me. Mr. Churchill was leaving in a few days for the South-West of France. He wished Mr. Eden to return to London at once and take over. Otherwise, he would not see him until they met at Potsdam on July 15. I felt a great sympathy with Mr. Eden whose doctor was strongly opposed to a premature return. I was perturbed by the thought that the British preparations for the Potsdam Conference must suffer inevitably from this geographical separation.

When I returned to London, I found that in Tory circles betting on a Conservative victory had hardened. The Conservative Press, too, expressed great confidence. I found this difficult to understand, for a leading journalist, himself a Tory in close touch with all the special Press reports from the constituencies, told me that, in his opinion, the Conservatives would be well beaten. The Tories, he said, were concentrating on Mr. Churchill and the war against

Japan. The people were interested in housing, food, employment and social security.

I think that this opinion was correct. Whitehall was fully occupied by the war against Japan. The public, which had been shocked by the revelations of the horrors of the German concentration camps, was now passing through an intermediary stage in which the effect of Belsen and Dachau had declined and the nervous dread of a peace which was no peace had not yet affected the masses. National interest was now concentrated on the election and, in the election, on home affairs.

Polling day passed quietly. All that one knew was that the voting had been heavy. As the results were not to be declared until July 26, Mr. Churchill and Mr. Eden, accompanied by Mr. Attlee, set out for Potsdam on July 14. I saw General Ismay just before he was leaving. He looked unhappy and said: "I'd give a lot not to be going."

"I suppose the novelty of these meetings has worn off," I replied.

"That's true enough," he said, "but it's more than that. At the previous conference we had a big contribution to make—in the politico-strategic field the biggest of any country. With the Prime Minister, the Chiefs of Staff were the prima donnas. Now we're all entangled in a mess with the politicians."

He was right. At Potsdam the military problems went well enough. It was at this conference that the news of the successful test of the atom bomb was received—actually at the moment when the American Chiefs of Staff were emphasising the likelihood of the war lasting two more years. It was at Potsdam, too, that the decision was taken to use the bomb and that President Truman informed Stalin of our intention. But politically the Conference was no love-feast. Stalin was critical of our policy in Greece, in Italy, and, particularly, with regard to Trieste. The Russians were also blunt about Roumania, Bulgaria and Yugoslavia. We had no business to interfere, nor was there any need of foreign journalists in those countries. Only on one political issue was there general agreement. Germany would not be allowed to have a central government.

The Prime Minister and Mr. Eden came back from Potsdam for the announcement of the election results. The day was dull and cool after a short spell of humid tropical weather. It was to strike a numb chill into the hearts of the Tories. The big swing to Labour was clear from the first results and by luncheon time the Conservative Whips had conceded the victory to the Socialists. The smiling young faces in Bush House confirmed my impression that the prevailing sentiment in P.W.E. and in the European Service of the B.B.C. had been Left. By nightfall Britain had had her revolution in her own orderly way. For it to remain a peaceful revolution and for the changes which were bound to be made, it was, I felt, just as well that a Labour Government would now be in power.

Among the Tories there were many recriminations, and Lord Beaverbrook and Mr. Bracken were heavily blamed. Yet I doubt if their influence on Mr. Churchill was even a tenth part of what it was commonly supposed to be. That they had been responsible for Mr. Churchill's first broadcast was untrue. Unlike many ministers, Mr. Churchill allowed no one to write his speeches or his broadcasts for him. Fear of responsibility was never one of his weaknesses. On his own judgment, and often to the alarm of his colleagues and leading officials, he had taken many daring and wise decisions. If he had a fault as a war-leader, it was that, when he made a bad decision, no one could persuade him to alter it. By the unique services which he had rendered to his country he had made himself the undisputed master of the Tory Party which, indeed, placed all their hopes of victory on his war-record and on his personal popularity. He dictated the course which the Conservative campaign should take. Doubtless, the Socialists would have won whatever had happened. Between the two wars the Conservatives had had a long reign and, as Lenin said, even the best Government had only to remain in power long enough for everyone to desire its end. But in spite of this compelling factor the size of Labour's victory was largely determined by the faulty tactics of the Tories who turned what the vast majority of the public, especially the large class of new young voters, regarded as a most serious matter affecting their whole future, into a slanging match in which abuse of the Socialists took the place of a constructive programme. The fact that in Mr. Churchill's constituency a freak candidate threw his hat into the ring at the last moment and was able to poll 10,000 votes was the measure of the public's disapproval of Mr. Churchill's methods.

The Tory failure was, therefore, in the fullest sense his personal tragedy. And in its suddenness it was more poignant, more numbing than the tragedy of Clemenceau. Like the man who had saved France, the man who had saved Britain had been rejected, and the rejection seemed to reek of the same ingratitude. Yet I do not believe that the country was ungrateful. During his strenuous election tour it had given him a triumph such as no other Englishman had ever received. But the Tories and perhaps Mr. Churchill himself misread the signs. The cheers were given for his imperishable record as a war-leader. The votes were for the future. They were refused to Mr. Churchill because the country wanted a new England and felt rightly or wrongly that the only change which Mr. Churchill desired was to a past which, however glorious, was irrevocable.

Many people were profoundly moved by his defeat. Indeed, its magnitude came as a shock to the whole country, and there was widespread and sincere sympathy with the man whom all recognised as the greatest Englishman of his time. Personally I never recalled what he had done for Britain from 1933 to 1945 without the constantly recurring feeling that but for Mr. Churchill I should not be alive today. Nevertheless, many of his warmest admirers deplored his descent into the arena of party politics and his bandying of rude words with men who had recently been his colleagues, and regretted that he had not declared his intention to resign at the end of the war with Japan. His dignity and his unique position in the country would have been maintained. If he had been defeated, he could have spoken as an elder statesman with an authority which would have commanded the respect of all, and a younger man would have had the opportunity of reorganising and rejuvenating the Conservative Party. It was not his qualities as a war-leader which caused his fall and undermined his popularity. His weakness was the weakness of all great men who, having achieved power, cannot abandon it. I remember very vividly a brilliant analysis by Mr. Churchill on Lloyd George's failure to resign in 1918. The burden of it was that if, instead of clinging to power and fighting a Khaki election, L. G. had said to Parliament: "We have won the war, let others make the peace," all England and, indeed, all Europe would have begged him to come back two years later.

Lloyd George was 57 in 1918; in 1945 Mr. Churchill was 71. Power had come to him too late in life, and the legend, which is built around all great men and which inevitably extols their virtues at the expense of their faults, had perhaps given him a false sense of over-confidence. That was his tragedy. An indispensable war-leader, he felt himself indispensable for subsequent tasks for which both by temperament and by age he was probably unfitted. In the war he had said: "Give us the tools, and we will finish the job." He had finished it to the immense satisfaction of his grateful country and with imperishable fame to himself. Yet when it was done, he was unable to lay down the tools.

CHAPTER FOUR

THE PRINCIPAL RESULT of the election was to destroy the unity which had held the nation together during the war. The country was now divided into two camps, and the manner in which the election had been fought was a clear indication that with time the cleavage would become deeper. The real effects, however, were not immediately visible. The first reaction of the public was one of relief and rejoicing. The Labour victory was the common man's triumph, and to him it meant a new holiday spirit, better times, and relaxation from the monotonous years of factory-work in the black-out. Interest in the war against Japan, never strong in the rank and file of Socialist supporters, quickly evaporated.

In Whitehall, however, there was little change, and the permanent officials were busier than ever. In the afternoon of July 27, I went to the Ambassadors' Waiting-Room in the Foreign Office for the official leave-taking with Mr. Eden. All the senior officials were present except Sir Alexander Cadogan and the various experts who had remained at Potsdam. Everyone looked gloomy and depressed—everyone, that is, except Mr. Eden whose restraint and self-command were admirable. He made no speech, but with all of us he had a short private talk and a kind word for everyone. I wondered what he was feeling. If anything had happened to Mr. Churchill during the war, Mr. Eden would have been Prime Minister. A Tory victory in the election would have left him the most likely candidate for the succession. He had done a tremendous job in the war, most of it behind the scenes. He had been the most loyal of Mr. Churchill's colleagues. Abroad his integrity had counted for very much in Britain's reputation. I remembered that, when there had been some talk of Mr. Eden's leaving the Foreign Office and devoting himself solely to his duties as Leader of the House of Commons, Bob Sherwood had come to me in a state of mental agitation.

"What is this", he said, "about Anthony Eden's leaving the Foreign Office? Are you all mad? Do you realise what the effect will be on the United States and on Franklin Roosevelt? Eden is the one Englishman who is completely trusted by the United States."

Wallace Carroll, the former London representative of O.W.I. and an intimate friend of Mr. Winant, had told me that the American Ambassador felt exactly the same about Mr. Eden.

Now his whole future was uncertain. Yet he showed no trace of disappointment. I consoled myself with the reflection that now he had an opportunity of getting really well and that this he never could have done in the turmoil of his ministerial life.

In the few words that I had with him, he joked about our going out of Whitehall together, said that I must not neglect him and asked me to come to stay with him whenever I liked. I felt numb with sadness. He, I was confident, would come back. But I knew that I should never serve him again as an official.

Another parting which affected me deeply was with Cyril Radcliffe, the Director-General of the Ministry of Information who left the Ministry at this time. I owed him much. In the early days of P.W.E. our relations with the Ministry of Information had been strained. When Radcliffe became Director-General, the whole atmosphere changed. Both in character and in mental calibre he was perhaps the ablest man that I met during the war. Calm in temperament, resolute in decision, and firm as steel on fundamental principles, he had a brilliant and incisive mind which could reduce the most intricate problems to simple terms. His greatest virtue as an official was his dispassionate judgment. When he thought that the interests of his Ministry were being disregarded, he defended them with inflexible determination. But he never sought an unfair advantage, and intrigue of any kind disgusted him.

We had no secrets, and I frequently sought his advice on my own problems and regretted only those occasions when I failed to act on it. He never thought of himself; he never spared himself.

In Cyril Radcliffe and Walter Monckton the Bar gave two eminent K.C's to the Ministry of Information. Close friends, they were utterly different in character. Monckton, a first-class contact man with a host of friends, had a curious passion for official life and, doubtless, would have liked to remain in Whitehall. Yet he was, I think, too affable to make a good high official or even a Minister, and he was altogether too kind-hearted to take unpleasant decisions. Radcliffe, who had all the attributes of the very highest type of official, had only one ambition as far as Whitehall was concerned: to get out of it as soon as the war was over.

Away from his office he was a totally different person, and my most pleasant evenings of the war were spent at his house in Hampstead. Supremely happy in his marriage and an admirable host, he had a natural genius for organising charades for children. Everyone was made to enter into the spirit of the acting, and I shall always remember a brilliant performance by Julian Huxley as Hyde. Doubtless his impersonation of Stevenson's beast-man benefited from his long experience of animals. Certainly the growls which he emitted were as realistic as they were terrifying.

Radcliffe's departure made me all the more eager to get out of government service too as quickly as possible.

There were other more compelling reasons. All Dr. Percival's warnings had come true. In July my skin affliction had returned in a violent and painful form. Unluckily the arrangements which I had made with Mr. Eden had been oral and had been suspended by his illness and by the election. Now they would have to be put on paper and approved by the new Foreign Secretary. More by luck than by design P.W.E's affairs were now in better shape. Early in July Field-Marshal Montgomery had visited England. He had brought with him a letter for Mr. Eden. It contained several recommendations which implied a complete reversal of the British policy of non-fraternisation. In advocating this change the Field-Marshal emphasised the importance of an efficient information service. He wanted more newspapers and, above all, films. He wished to open the cinema theatres at once. He was prepared to make immediate use of re-educated German prisoners of war. What he asked for was "action now", and vigorous action at that.

This was great news, especially for our Prisoners of War Department which in spite of endless frustration had succeeded in segregating and re-educating several thousand German prisoners. I was particularly glad for the sake of the Air Commodore who was head of this department and who, indeed, had created it. There are only two methods of getting your own way in Whitehall. One is by a combination of diplomacy and persistent suavity; the other by sheer dogged determination. The first method rarely achieves more than half-measures. The second involves the risk of one's career. Our Air Commodore practised the second technique. Convinced that the policy of re-education was the right one, he fought for it with a single-minded perseverance, never despairing of success and always countering constant rebuffs with fresh attacks. At one time the opposition of the War Office was so strong that everyone except the Air Commodore had abandoned hope. Now with Field-Marshal Montgomery's backing, the Air Commodore was to receive, if not the full reward, at least some satisfaction for four years of persistent struggle.

I had to brief Mr. Eden on the Montgomery letter. I made certain recommendations which, if not implemented, would make vigorous action nugatory. They included the provision of proper accommodation and of transport in Germany for information officers and the sending of instructions by Field-Marshal Montgomery himself to his various army commanders, who had not always been helpful, on the importance of the information service. Mr. Eden embodied the recommendations in his reply.

The reasons for the Field-Marshal's sudden *volte face* were said in Whitehall to have been Marshal Zhukov's statement to him, when they met in Berlin, that "he who controls the Press and the radio is the master of Berlin". Be this as it may, I was delighted by Montgomery's typical decisiveness. He had made up his mind what was the right thing to do. He had challenged the Government and, having won his point, he proceeded to carry out the changes with a vigour and energy which overrode all obstacles.

As General Strong had now joined us and as I was immediately impressed by his ability, I saw no reason for outstaying my physical power, and on August 4 I submitted a memorandum setting out the functions that remained to P.W.E. and strongly recommending General Strong as my successor. It was accompanied by my resignation and a request for my release as from the first of September. I made this request with an easy conscience. P.W.E's main work was now confined to Germany and was concerned entirely with post-war problems. True, we still had our Far Eastern section, but luckily the war in the East was to end with startling suddenness.

Although I had to wait some time for an answer to my memorandum, I began to make spasmodic preparations for my departure and to take my leave of those who had helped me in my work. I had had to give up my country house in July and, London being full, had gone to stay at the Ritz with Jack Wheeler-Bennett who was returning to the United States in the middle of August. Obviously I could not afford to remain there for long.

The week-end of Bank Holiday I spent at Cherkley with Lord Beaverbrook. I had some serious conversation with him. He was subdued and predicted a difficult post-war period. The Potsdam Conference had been a Russian victory. Russia would be master of most of Europe. The war had lasted too long for a Britain which was now tired. The road to recovery would be long and arduous.

I said to him: "Then it is very important that the war against Japan should end quickly?"

He looked at me for a moment and then remarked cryptically:

"Bruce, you will see that the war with Japan will end *very* quickly."

Two days later the Americans dropped the first atom bomb on Hiroshima. The same evening I sat next to General Ismay at a farewell dinner given by Jack Wheeler-Bennett. All the guests were excited and depressed by the immensity of the destructive powers of the new bomb. Some believed that it would end the Japanese war and make all other wars impossible; others feared the end of civilisation. All were agreed that a new era had opened. General Ismay thought that the Americans were right in dropping the bomb. Other countries, including Germany, had been working on atomic weapons. Sooner or later, some nation would have used them in order to see if they produced the effect which the scientists claimed for them. If one or two bombs sufficed to end the war with Japan, they would serve the double purpose of saving hundreds of thousands of lives and of frightening the world into sanity.

I asked him what he implied by "ending the war". Did he mean before the end of the year?

"No," he replied, "before the end of August—perhaps in a few days."

Ismay was right. On August 10, J. B. Clark "buzzed" me on our inside telephone. The B.B.C. had picked up a message put out by the Domei Agency that Japan had accepted unconditional surrender and had sent a note to this effect to the Allies. The news was not official and so far lacked confirmation. I went to lunch at the Hungaria Restaurant with one of Mr. Arthur Rank's directors in order to discuss the possibility of enlisting the aid of the Rank organisation for Field-Marshal Montgomery who was clamouring for British films for Germany. Presently in came Mr. A. V. Alexander with two Labour colleagues. The First Lord's face was beaming. Attended by M. Vecchi, the restaurant manager, he stopped at a table near mine. Then Vecchi drew himself to his full height and clapped his hands for silence.

"Ladies and Gentlemen," he announced, "you will be glad to hear that the war is over—officially over. Japan 'az accepted the Potsdam terms." All stood up and cheered. The First Lord ordered a bottle of champagne and my film magnate ordered a half-bottle for me. I was still sceptical about the official nature of the news.

Presently Mr. Alexander came over to our table and shook hands. I asked him if Vecchi's statement was correct. "Yes," he said, "I've just told him."

The news spread rapidly. When I came out after luncheon, Lower

Regent Street was already strewn with paper, and a huge toilet-roll landed at the feet of my chauffeur as I was getting into my car. I had to go to Richmond Terrace where I had an appointment with Admiral Mountbatten who wished to see Mr. Arthur Rank and myself about films for the Far East. The streets were congested and a large crowd had gathered at the entrance to Downing Street. I found Mr. Rank already at Richmond Terrace and thought that I had been late for our appointment. But we had to wait for some minutes, during which we could feel the atmosphere of suppressed excitement. Staff officers kept coming in and out of Lord Louis' room. Although I know that of all the Allied war-leaders he laid most store by political warfare and throughout the war had given us more than one proof of his interest in our work, I was almost sure he would put us off. But I had underrated his immense energy, his capacity for detachment even in moments of the highest pressure, and his remarkable faculty of concentrating his mind on the smallest detail that required his attention. Presently he saw us and without a trace of excitement in his manner or voice talked films very seriously for about ten minutes. Then he excused himself. He had to go to the Cabinet at once. Everything was uncertain, but for the moment he was acting on the assumption that Japan was on the eve of surrender. If the news were correct, then his attack on Malaya, fixed for September, was off. In the prevailing uncertainty our meeting was in a sense a failure. But at any rate we were giving Mr. Rank plenty of excitement.

For five days there was no official news, and officials like Sargent who never counted their chickens in the egg were full of suspicion. The public, however, began to celebrate at once. It was perhaps just as well that they did, for in this way the effervescence of final victory was worked off in relayed releases. With Jack Wheeler-Bennett I sat up late every night looking at the crowds in Piccadilly from the narrow balcony of his sitting-room on the top floor of the Ritz and telephoning to my office for news. At last shortly after midnight of August 14, I heard much louder shouting than usual from the streets. For the nth time I rang Bush House. Was there any confirmation? Back came the duty officer's reply: "Yes, Sir, Mr. Attlee has just broadcast the official announcement of Japan's surrender."

We returned to the balcony. The news was already public property, and men and women were pouring out of houses, side-streets and alley-ways into Piccadilly. Seen from the top of the Ritz in the chiaroscuro effect of the arc lights, they looked tiny and reminded me of the line in Baudelaire's *Le Soir*: "Comme une fourmilière, elle ouvre ses issues."

Now that the official confirmation had been announced, the crowd was much larger than on previous nights. Its abandon and gaiety were infectious, and I laughed as we watched two naval commanders start a bonfire round a lamp-stand in the middle of the street below us. Soon they were joined by a band of American soldiers who danced an Indian war-dance round the flames. Rows of girls, their arms linked tightly together, swept up and down the centre of the street, swaying to one side or the other, as the soldiers tried to break their chain. Some girls wore witch hats with "Kiss Me Quick" chalked on them, and kissed they were with much shrieking and laughter. There was plenty of noise but no drunkenness. Young men jumped on the back of moving cars and enjoyed a precarious ride. What impressed me most was the restraint and amazing good temper of everyone. Yet the crowd was in complete command of the West End, and I felt a glow of pride in the thought that only the English could behave so well without police control and, to do full justice to the tact of the London police, without police interference. The scene recalled vague memories of Moscow during the March Revolution of 1917 when the crowds had been equally good-tempered. Yet eight months later the March Revolution had been followed by the bloody revolution of November, mainly because the democratic Government of Kerensky had been unable to cope with the hopeless economic situation created by the first world war.

We stayed on the balcony till 3 a.m., and the following afternoon I drove through the crowded streets to Airways House to see Jack Wheeler-Bennett off to America. Then I went back to the Ritz. It was the first of the two official V-J days, and I felt strangely alone and forlorn. Then my secretary arrived with a sheaf of messages. There was to be a meeting of the Foreign Office Under-Secretaries the next day to consider the future of P.W.E. and to settle the date of my release. There was also a message from Montgomery's headquarters. The Field-Marshal would like to see Mr. Rank and myself on August 23. He wanted his films and wanted them quickly.

I attended the meeting at the Foreign Office the next day. It went well. No difficulties were raised, but my paper on the future functions of P.W.E. and on my own release had to be formally approved by Mr. Bevin. The weather was dull, damp and depressing. At the end of the day I felt that nothing would ever be settled. I wanted to steal away like a thief in the night.

The next day there was little time for introspection. I had to arrange our flight to Field-Marshal Montgomery's headquarters. Having spent most of my life abroad, I found that I had lost my passport. I was given a new one at once, but telephoning to Germany was an ordeal, and it was not until the morning of August 22 that the final details of our programme were settled. It was a strenuous one. We were to be at Northolt Aerodrome at 5.30 a.m. on the morning of Thursday, August 23 and see the Field-Marshal that evening. On the Friday I was to go to Berlin to stay with William Strang and be back in London on Saturday afternoon. My secretary packed a small suitcase for me. It contained mostly bandages. She was dead against my journey and had a fixed premonition that I would not go.

At 5 p.m. on the Wednesday afternoon I received a telephone message from Bad Oynhausen. Field-Marshal Montgomery had made a forced landing in his aeroplane which had come down on a tree. He was not badly hurt and still hoped to see us. We were not to postpone our journey.

At 8 p.m. I received a second message. The Field-Marshal had been ordered complete rest. He would arrange to see us at a later date. I spent an hour trying to get Mr. Rank on the telephone. He was at Reigate celebrating the marriage of his daughter, and the telephone was engaged incessantly. When I got through to him, he was delighted not to have to go. My own feelings were mixed. In one sense I was relieved, because I was hardly fit to crawl, much less travel. On the other hand, I was bitterly disappointed not to see the Field-Marshal whom I had never met. One thought consoled me. The war had begun with a "phoney" period. Taking the king of Britain's Hollywood to visit Field-Marshal Montgomery would have been a "phoney" end for me.

Instead, I went to Binderton for the week-end. On the Saturday Senator Pepper and Mr. Winant came to luncheon, and the Senator, serious, squat and stockily built, told us how he had conceived and carried through the project of lend-lease. In spite of his even, unemotional and rather high-pitched voice, he told his story with dramatic precision. He had introduced the project into the Senate without a single supporter. When he continued to persevere, he met with fierce opposition. In particular, Senator Johnson had insisted that the resolution must be withdrawn as evil and immoral. Senator Pepper was determined not to abandon his project, but did not wish to embarrass President Roosevelt. He had consulted the President who had said at once: "Go ahead; it will be fine if we can get something like this." The Senator had gone ahead. His progress was slow. His support came, not from the Senate, but from the American people to whom he directed a stream of propaganda. He persuaded them to write to their Congressmen. The letters which began with a trickle became an avalanche, and in the end the battle was won. Lend-lease had triumphed on a correspondence course.

The Senator returned to his knife and fork, and Mr. Eden broke a slightly awkward silence by asking: "Senator Johnson is dead, is he not?"

"Yes, Sir," replied the Senator, "he has gone to his long isolationist rest."

I was about to laugh when suddenly I realised that there was neither humour nor the intention of it in the Senator's face and voice.

On my return to London I found good news. Mr. Bevin had initialled my paper which had been sent back to me. My appointment would terminate on September 30, but I could leave on the first of the month.

I made a list of the essential visits that I ought to make and then cut it down by half. My first call was on Phil Hamblet, the European head of O.W.I. which was also winding up its activities. He was almost embarrassing in his friendliness. Britain, he said, was not only his second home; it was going to be his permanent home. He told me with great satisfaction that forty per cent. of the American G.I's mail from France had been addressed to Britain. He praised the co-operation between O.W.I. and P.W.E. which he said had been far closer and smoother than that between any two American depart-ments. He spoke no more than the truth. Our relations with O.W.I. had been wonderfully harmonious, and in my own mind I had no doubt that the chief credit belonged to the Americans, to Bob Sher-wood, to Wallace Carroll, to George Backer and to Phil Hamblet himself.

Then I went to the Foreign Office to take my leave of the officials who had worked most closely with P.W.E. I had hoped to see Mr. Bevin, but a time was difficult to arrange, and Mr. Hector McNeil deputised for him. I had met him years before, when he had been a Beaverbrook journalist. We talked of journalism and of Scotland. He told me that when he had been made a junior minister, he had been warned to terminate his relations with Lord Beaverbrook. He had gone straight to Mr. Bevin and had told him that he would not stand for any interference with his private relationships. Lord Beaverbrook had been good to him. He proposed to continue seeing

him whenever he felt inclined. Mr. Bevin had approved. I liked
McNeil and thought that he would go far. Transparently honest and
straightforward, he had both tact and abundant common sense.

From the officials I heard warm eulogies of Mr. Bevin. He had
done remarkably well at Potsdam. He was quick to see a point.
Above all, he stood up fearlessly for his staff. His view of the Foreign
Office clerks was that there were too few of them—and that they
were too badly paid. Obviously, as far as the staff were concerned,
Mr. Bevin had made good in one short month.

As I walked along the stone corridors for the last time as an official,
I felt a momentary pang of sadness. Thirty-four years before, I had
entered the gloomy grey building for my first interview with the
Selection Committee. My knees had trembled, and the high rooms
had made me feel very small. My awe and respect had been overwhelming. The senior officials had seemed, and indeed were, very
fierce. Now I called nearly everybody by their Christian names.
The awe was gone. The building was antiquated, too small, and
quite inadequate for its swollen tasks. But I had made new friends:
men like Moley Sargent, wise in counsel, yet ready to take risks,
Oliver Harvey, who had always supported P.W.E., and Bob Dixon
and, indeed, all the private secretaries who arranged the ministerial
meetings and who, with their finger on the temperamental pulse of
ministers, told me when the moment was ripe to urge a forward
policy or to tread warily. I was sorry that in future I should drift inevitably out of their lives.

But I did not regret my decision to resign. I was not made for
bureaucratic life, and it was too late to begin now. I had made a rule
for myself: once out, stay out. In the past I had seen too many retired
ambassadors hanging round the Foreign Office and seeking to give
advice until the senior officials were too busy to see them and the
juniors groaned: "Gosh, here is that old bore X again." There was a
time to keep and a time to go.

Before I went, I had one more rite to perform. I knew that I was
to be given a farewell dinner by my senior colleagues. But at the last
minute they sprang a surprise on me. At the instigation of the telephone girls, who must have been sorely tried by my impatience, the
whole London staff wished to take leave of me, and on the afternoon
of August 31, they entertained me to tea in the restaurant of Bush
House. They came in their hundreds including many from Woburn.
I was deeply moved and wished I could have done more for the
women who formed by far the larger part of our staff and who had

worked long hours with unflagging zeal and without a single complaint.

The dinner, held the same evening, was admirably organised. As is usual on such occasions kind words were said which are perhaps remembered only by the recipient, and I found it hard to control my emotion. I owed a great debt of gratitude to my colleagues and collaborators both of P.W.E. and of the European Service of the B.B.C. We had had our troubles. There had been a few intrigues; there had been one or two ambitious careerists who had been difficult to handle, but, taken by and large, it was as pleasant and loyal a staff as anyone could wish to serve. During the four years that I had been with them I had made friends whom I should never forget. Some had confided in me their private troubles. Nearly all had consulted me about their future. They had been, too, almost fanatically zealous in their work, believing passionately in its value and chafing frequently under the official caution which too often wrecked their best-laid plans.

During those four years we had sent out over two million words weekly on the air from our open and secret radios; we had disseminated in countless millions of copies a vast collection of printed material in the form of special newspapers, magazines, leaflets and miniature books which to-day are treasured in an honoured place in the war museums of the liberated countries. What this immense effort had produced is difficult to estimate. In high quarters opinion was divided. Personally, in a world in which truth has been strangled as never before, I regard political warfare and propaganda as the most noxious influence. But in war it is a necessary evil. By holding closely to the truth, the British propaganda effort did more to sustain British influence in Europe than any other single factor. For five years it brought to the occupied countries of Europe the only news from the outside world. It kept alive the spark of hope in victory and was the backbone of the resistance movement in every country. In the occupied countries of Western Europe its successes were maintained until the victorious end. In Poland and in the Balkans much good work was nullified when these areas passed into the Russian orbit.

Of the enemy countries Italy was a fruitful field, and both Field-Marshal Alexander and Mr. Harold Macmillan gave high praise to the good work that was done by the propagandists behind the German lines. Germany was the big question-mark, and, although more newsprint and more time on the air were given to propaganda to

Germany, the results are more difficult to analyse. The Allied soldiers maintain that German morale was not affected by propaganda, and there is no denying that the German armies fought desperately until the end. But in total warfare, propaganda results are not to be gauged merely by their effect on front-line troops. Evidence received since the war shows that the Germans listened-in regularly to our German broadcasts and in order to do so were prepared to risk severe penalties. I am also satisfied that our secret propaganda had a very considerable effect in sapping and undermining the efficiency of the Nazi war-machine. Time and the future behaviour of the German people will determine how far our propaganda had any permanent effect on their minds. But when the Germans surrendered, the collapse was devastating in its completeness, and, in spite of the permanent handicap of unconditional surrender, it would be difficult to deny to British leaflets and to British radio some share in the demoralisation of the German people.

Taken by and large our propaganda suffered from two defects: premature and exaggerated claims of what it could achieve, and the slow reluctance of officialdom generally, and of certain ministers in particular, to realise its importance.

I left my dinner reasonably early because I was dead-beat, and, although my legs and arms were now raw and swollen, I slept peacefully. I awoke the next day a free man. The sky was leaden and rain was falling with the first chill of autumn. I had no feeling of rejoicing, no other sentiment than an immense relief that I had not to drag myself to Bush House for another day. Eighteen years of my life had been spent in the service of the Foreign Office, eleven of them war-years in which every year was equal to two. Now my official career was over—this time for ever, and in three days I was going back to the Royal Infirmary in Edinburgh.

September 2 was my fifty-eighth birthday, and while my friends packed for me I lay back and gave my thoughts free rein. I felt no pessimism. I had no anxiety about the new Government. Whitehall might be, and, indeed, was tired, but there were young men who were alive with zeal and abundant energy. Recovery might be slow, but the British genius, which had supplied the inventive power of the Allies, which had devised radar, the mulberries, and the best aeroplane engine, which had fought with unremitting courage in every part of the world, and performed marvels of production in the factories, and which had preserved an unbroken unity in the face of danger, would find a way out of all difficulties.

It would be a new England, and it was necessary that it should be. I saw the future in Europe, not as a battle for frontiers and strategic vantage points, but as a political contest between two ways of life. The Russians had their system. In no sense could it serve as a pattern for the British except by an unscrupulous propaganda and by a rigorous exclusion of any foreigner who wished to assess the merits of the system for himself. It behoved Britain to devise a way of life that would combine the virtue of economic democracy with political freedom.

If we were strong in self-reliance, we could do it. Nor did I doubt what the effect would be on other countries and, eventually, on Russia herself. She was a country of extremes, and for three centuries her history had been a series of cycles of extreme materialism and extreme idealism. Ruthless materialism had already had a long run, and the men who had enforced it were already old. During the period of transition an understanding might be difficult and certainly would not be facilitated by British sentimentalists who assumed that it was the easiest thing in the world. In both countries the future would be shaped by the young men who had fought the war. If the youth of Britain were sound—and I did not doubt that it was—Britain herself would be sound.

When my friends had left me, I took down from the mantelpiece my copy of Gissing's *The Private Papers of Henry Ryecroft*, which accompanied me on all my travels. It was a gift from Moir Mackenzie, an old school friend and a former famous Scottish "rugger" international. Turning over the pages, I came across the epitaph which Gissing had devised for himself: "He was ever hopeful and deemed it a crime to despair of his country."

It was a fine creed for all men and for all times, for the young men in whose hands lay the destiny of Britain, and, above all, for the old men who ought now to make way and give youth its chance. I was determined that it should be my creed. The knowledge that to-morrow I should be crossing the Tweed was in itself a comfort and a hope.

INDEX

INDEX

INTERNATIONAL PROPAGANDA AND COMMUNICATIONS

An Arno Press Collection

Bruntz, George G. **Allied Propaganda and the Collapse of the German Empire in 1918.** 1938

Childs, Harwood Lawrence, editor. **Propaganda and Dictatorship: A Collection of Papers.** 1936

Childs, Harwood L[awrence] and John B[oardman] Whitton, editors. **Propaganda By Short Wave** including C[harles] A. Rigby's **The War on the Short Waves.** 1942/1944

Codding, George Arthur, Jr. **The International Telecommunication Union: An Experiment in International Cooperation.** 1952

Creel, George. **How We Advertised America.** 1920

Desmond, Robert W. **The Press and World Affairs.** 1937

Farago, Ladislas, editor. **German Psychological Warfare.** 1942

Hadamovsky, Eugen. **Propaganda and National Power.** 1954

Huth, Arno. **La Radiodiffusion Puissance Mondiale.** 1937

International Propaganda/Communications: Selections from The Public Opinion Quarterly, **1943/1952/1956.** 1972

International Press Institute Surveys, Nos. 1-6. 1952-1962

International Press Institute. **The Flow of News.** 1953

Lavine, Harold and James Wechsler. **War Propaganda and the United States.** 1940

Lerner, Daniel, editor. **Propaganda in War and Crisis.** 1951

Linebarger, Paul M. A. **Psychological Warfare.** 1954

Lockhart, Sir R[obert] H. Bruce. **Comes the Reckoning.** 1947

Macmahon, Arthur W. **Memorandum on the Postwar International Information Program of the United States.** 1945

de Mendelssohn, Peter. **Japan's Political Warfare.** 1944

Nafziger, Ralph O., compiler. **International News and the Press: An Annotated Bibliography.** 1940

Read, James Morgan. **Atrocity Propaganda, 1914-1919.** 1941

Riegel, O[scar] W. **Mobilizing for Chaos: The Story of the New Propaganda.** 1934

Rogerson, Sidney. **Propaganda in the Next War.** 1938

Summers, Robert E., editor. **America's Weapons of Psychological Warfare.** 1951

Terrou, Fernand and Lucien Solal. **Legislation for Press, Film and Radio:** Comparative Study of the Main Types of Regulations Governing the Information Media. 1951

Thomson, Charles A. H. **Overseas Information Service of the United States Government.** 1948

Tribolet, Leslie Bennett. **The International Aspects of Electrical Communications in the Pacific Area.** 1929

Unesco. **Press Film Radio,** Volumes I-V *including* Supplements. 1947-1951. 3 volumes.

Unesco. **Television:** A World Survey *including* Supplement. 1953/1955

White, Llewellyn and Robert D. Leigh. **Peoples Speaking to Peoples:** A Report on International Mass Communication from The Commission on Freedom of the Press. 1946

Williams, Francis. **Transmitting World News.** 1953

Wright, Quincy, editor. **Public Opinion and World-Politics.** 1933